SAGE was founded in 1965 by Sara Miller McCune to support the dissemination of usable knowledge by publishing innovative and high-quality research and teaching content. Today, we publish more than 850 journals, including those of more than 300 learned societies, more than 800 new books per year, and a growing range of library products including archives, data, case studies, reports, conference highlights, and video. SAGE remains majority-owned by our founder, and after Sara's lifetime will become owned by a charitable trust that secures our continued independence.

Los Angeles | London | New Delhi | Singapore | Washington DC

CASTE, DISCRIMINATION, AND EXCLUSION IN MODERN INDIA

CASTE, DISCRIMINATION, AND EXCLUSION IN MODERN INDIA

Vani Kant Borooah • Nidhi Sadana Sabharwal
Dilip G. Diwakar • Vinod Kumar Mishra
Ajaya Kumar Naik

www.sagepublications.com
Los Angeles • London • New Delhi • Singapore • Washington DC

First published in 2015 by

 SAGE Publications India Pvt Ltd
B1/I-1 Mohan Cooperative Industrial Area
Mathura Road, New Delhi 110 044, India
www.sagepub.in

SAGE Publications Inc
2455 Teller Road
Thousand Oaks, California 91320, USA

SAGE Publications Ltd
1 Oliver's Yard
55 City Road
London EC1Y 1SP, United Kingdom

SAGE Publications Asia-Pacific Pte Ltd
3 Church Street
#10-04 Samsung Hub
Singapore 049483

Published by Vivek Mehra for SAGE Publications India Pvt Ltd, typeset in 10/13 pts Times by PrePSol Enterprises Private Limited. and printed at Chaman Enterprises, New Delhi.

Library of Congress Cataloging-in-Publication Data

Borooah, Vani Kant.
  Caste, discrimination, and exclusion in modern India / Vani Kant Borooah, Nidhi Sadana Sabharwal, Dilip G. Diwakar, Vinod Kumar Mishra, and Ajaya Kumar Naik.
      pages cm
  Includes bibliographical references and index.
    1. Caste–India.   2. Social stratification–India.   3. Equality–India.   4. Political planning–India.   5. Reverse discrimination–India.   I. Sabharwal, Nidhi Sadana.   II. Diwakar, Dilip G. III. Title.
HT720.B597   305.5'1220954—dc23   2015   2015019631

ISBN: 978-93-515-0267-8 (HB)

The SAGE Team: N. Unni Nair, Sanghamitra Patowary, Anju Saxena, and Rajinder Kaur

This book is dedicated to the memory of two great Indians, Jyotiba Phule (1827–90) and Babasaheb Ambedkar (1891–1956), who dedicated their lives to the cause of equality and justice for India's downtrodden.

Thank you for choosing a SAGE product!
If you have any comment, observation or feedback,
I would like to personally hear from you.
Please write to me at **contactceo@sagepub.in**

Vivek Mehra, Managing Director and CEO,
SAGE Publications India Pvt Ltd, New Delhi

Bulk Sales

SAGE India offers special discounts
for purchase of books in bulk.
We also make available special imprints
and excerpts from our books on demand.

For orders and enquiries, write to us at

Marketing Department
SAGE Publications India Pvt Ltd
B1/I-1, Mohan Cooperative Industrial Area
Mathura Road, Post Bag 7
New Delhi 110044, India

E-mail us at **marketing@sagepub.in**

Get to know more about SAGE

Be invited to SAGE events, get on our mailing list.
Write today to **marketing@sagepub.in**

This book is also available as an e-book.

I am a Jew. Hath not a Jew eyes? Hath not a Jew hands,
organs, dimensions, senses, affections, passions; fed with the same
food, hurt with the same weapons, subject to the same diseases,
heal'd by the same means, warm'd and cool'd by the same winter
and summer, as a Christian is? If you prick us, do we not bleed? If
you tickle us, do we not laugh? If you poison us, do we not die?

The Merchant of Venice, Act 3, Scene 1

Contents

List of Tables

List of Figures

List of Boxes

List of Abbreviations

A&S	Available and Seeking Work
AAY	Antyodaya Anna Yojana
APL	Above Poverty Line
ATE	Average Treatment Effect
AWC	Anganwadi Center
AWWs	Anganwadi Workers
B–O	Blinder–Oaxaca
BMI	Body Mass Index
BPL	Below Poverty Line
CVC	Central Vigilance Committee
CWE	Casual Wage Employment
EDE	Equally Distributed Equivalent
GDP	Gross Domestic Product
GER	Gross Enrollment Ratio
HCD	Head Count Ratio
HCH	High-caste Hindus
HCM	High-caste Muslims
HDI	Human Development Index
HE	Higher Education
HEI	Highest Education Index
HOBC	Hindus from the Other Backward Classes
ICDS	Integrated Child Development Scheme
IHDS	Indian Human Development Survey
IIDS	Indian Institute of Dalit Studies
INI	Income Index
INQ	Income Quintile
IPW	Inverse Probability Weighted
IQI	Income Quintile Index
JPI	*Jaan-pehchaan* Index
JSY	Janani Suraksha Yojana
LAD	Least Absolute Deviations

LCI	Living Condition Index
LEI	Life Expectancy Index
QR	Quantile Regression
M&HC	Morbidity and Health Care Survey
MDM	Midday Meal
MLM	Multinomial Logit Model
MOBC	Other Backward Class Muslims
MPCE	Monthly Per Capita Consumption Expenditure
MP	Madhya Pradesh
MP	Member of Parliament
MSGR	Mean Stunting Gap Ratio
NREG	National Rural Employment Guarantee
NREGA	National Rural Employment Guarantee Act
NSGR	Normalized Stunting Gap Ratio
NSS	National Sample Survey
NSSO	National Sample Survey Organisation
OAE	Own Account Employment
OAW	Own Account Worker
OBC	Other Backward Classes
OLS	Ordinary Least Squares
OTG	Other Groups
PDS	Public Distribution System
PIT	Poverty-inequality Trade-off
PSM	Propensity Score Matching
RSBY	Rashtriya Swasthya Bima Yojana
RSWE	Regular Salaried or Wage Employment
S&A	Seeking and/or Available for Work
SC	Scheduled Castes
SHfA	Standardized Height-for-age
SR	Stunting Rate
ST	Scheduled Tribes
ST(A)	Scheduled Tribe, *Adivasis*
ST(C)	Scheduled Tribe, Christian
TPA	Third Party Administrators
TPDS	Targeted Public Distribution System
UNDP	United Nations Development Program
UP	Uttar Pradesh
WHO	World Health Organization

Foreword

Social Exclusion and Group Inequalities

In 2012, the country's monthly per capita expenditure (MPCE), a close substitute of per capita income, was about 1646, with 2239 for higher castes, followed by 1518 for Other Backward Castes (OBCs), 1297 for Scheduled Castes (SCs), and 1123 for Scheduled Tribes (STs). The graded inequality which is a unique feature of the caste system still persists: income reduces as we go down in caste hierarchy from higher caste to OBC, to low-caste untouchables, and ultimately to become lowest for tribes. Graded inequality is reflected in poverty too: in 2011, 12.4 percent for higher caste, 25 percent for OBC, 30 percent for the SCs and 43 for tribal, the all-India average being about 23 percent. Similarly, the consumption expenditure on monthly basis is higher for majority Hindus, with 1642, as compared to two religious minorities, namely Muslims and Buddhists (the Christians and Sikhs do better than Hindus and Muslims). The Muslims and Buddhists tend to be poorer (about 25 percent) than the Hindus (23 percent). The Christians and Sikhs do better than Hindus and Muslims/Buddhists.

The issue of group inequalities on the line of caste, ethnicity, and religion is something which is a unique feature of the Indian society. This has induced discussions on policies to overcome group inequalities. While there is considerable agreement on the nature of group inequalities on the line of caste, ethnic, and religious identities, there are often differences on ways to deal with them. There is a view which believes that policies common to all poor are good enough to deal with the problem of the poverty of lower castes, tribals, religious minorities, such as Muslims and women. Others, on the other hand, argued that while the general pro-poor policies are necessary for all poor, there is also a need to supplement the general policies with group-specific policies with measures to ensure fair and non-discriminatory access to resources and opportunities to Dalits, *adivasi*s (original inhabitants), and religious minorities, such as Muslims and women, as these groups suffered from discriminatory access to the resources and opportunities which the rest of the population did not. Those who suggest common policies for all based their argument on the assumption that the markets and government institutions are governed by principles of merits and efficiency, and as such there is no need for specific policies for the excluded groups (Thorat and Newman, 2010).

To resolve the differences, what is required is the evidence through systematic empirical research on the nature of discrimination faced by discriminated groups in various market and nonmarket institutions, and the consequences of discrimination on income and poverty. Creditable research is also based on changes and persistence of discrimination and their causes. It is this evidence which will help us to form a specific view. The book *Caste, Discrimination, and Exclusion in Modern India* does precisely this. It provides empirical evidence of the group inequalities for caste, ethnic, and religious groups in as important indicators of human development, and estimates to what extent the group inequalities are due to social exclusion and discrimination. This is the central theme of this book. In the words of the authors:

> It is a book about the barriers that persons from the scheduled caste and the scheduled tribe, and Muslims, face in escaping poverty and social exclusion in India. The term "social exclusion"—meaning the process by which certain groups are unable to fully participate in the life of their communities—and the consequences thereof—in denial of sources of livelihood; secure, permanent employment; earnings; property; credit; land; housing; education, skills, and cultural capital; the welfare state. A major instrument of social exclusion is through discriminatory behavior when people are excluded from important activities by virtue of their belonging to certain groups which, for whatever reason, are viewed "unfavorably." Even when inclusion occurs it is on unequal terms and conditions which affect the ability of groups to interact freely and productively with others and to take full part in the economic, social, and political life of a community.

The strength of the empirical research is that it arrives at the conclusion using most recent statistical techniques of regression analysis to examine inter-group inequality. It also uses a modified audit method to capture the discrimination in government schemes related to food and health.

The book deals with the disadvantage and exclusion that people from India's marginalized groups face in a number of areas. First, it examines the relative achievements of social groups in India—high-caste Hindus, Muslims, the OBCs, SCs, and STs in respect of certain key indicators (education, life expectancy, and income) using the human development index (HDI) for these social groups. Going beyond the standard HDI, it also adds two new indicators not included in the HDI, the household living conditions and the extent and depth of household social networks. In the subsequent analysis, the authors examine patterns of inequality between households belonging to the different social groups with respect to their monthly per capita consumption expenditure, educational attainments of children, child malnutrition, status of adult health, age at death, the state of health of elderly persons, and the type and quality of pre and postnatal care received by pregnant mothers. In market analysis, it examines the labor market outcomes in employment and wage. This analysis is also extended to the SC women, since they suffer from the triple disadvantages of being poor, of belonging to the SC, and of being women. The book also examines two public policy programs of the Indian government—the Integrated Child Development Scheme and the Rashtriya Swasthya Bima Yojana health insurance program—and studies the social orientation of both schemes with a view to examining the extent to which they serve persons from marginal groups.

In these 10 areas of human development, inequality, poverty, educational attainments, child malnutrition, health, employment, wages, gender, and access to public goods, the authors observe significant intergroup disparities in achievement, and these disparities remain even after allowing for differences between the groups in their endowment of relevant attributes. In each of these areas, high-caste Hindu households performed the best, and the households from the SC and the ST as well as the Muslim households performed the worst, *even after controlling for the (non-group) factors that might have influenced the outcomes.*

Why Exclusion Persists? Insights from Theories

The studies in this volume attribute a part of group disparities to discrimination associated with caste, ethnic, and religious background in accessing employment and services from government programs related to education, nutrition, and health. The question is why does discrimination persist? The answer to this question is necessary to know the process of discrimination and to decide on the ways to deal with it. For seeking explanation, the authors looked for insights from theories. Few theoretical efforts that were encountered by economists and sociologists/psychologists will be discussed in brief. Way back in the mid 1950s, Baker argued that people discriminate because they have test for discrimination from which they derive utility and satisfaction. The test for discrimination emanates from prejudices that a group holds against the other group. In Baker's case, the other groups were Blacks and women (Becker, 1993). The other approach, known as belief-based theory, postulates that people discriminate not because of test for discrimination, but because they perceive that others, on average, have low skills. Due to imperfect information, the employer makes hiring and wage decisions based on the average productivity of the individual from a particular group, which may not be the case and, thus, may result in a discriminatory outcome. In this theory, the discrimination is based on a set of belief about others (Arrow, 1973). The third theoretical approach is the identity theory postulated by Akerlof and Kranton (2010). Akerlof and Kranton believe that while discrimination still persists, the test and belief-based theories cannot help us understand many patterns. In their opinion, the limitation of the test theory is that while it recognizes the role of a noneconomic motive, basic tests are assumed to be universal and any variation is attributed to idiosyncratic differences and personal experiences. By and large, tests are not assumed to vary with social context. The identity theory brings the influence of social context into economic decision by the individuals. The social categories and their norms constitute the identity. Individual pecuniary and non-pecuniary motivation, tests, and preferences are influenced by social context and norms. Insofar as identity theory brings the social context (that is who they are) and norms (and how should they behave or relate with others) in economic decision-making by individuals, this changed the old presumptions of economist old presumption that tests and preferences are individuals characteristics, independent of social context. The identity theory maintains that the social categories and their norms would decide how someone in those social categories would behave. According to the authors, this "socially framed conception of individual decision making should help economists working at various levels to construct sturdier account of the economy" (Akerlof and Kranton, 2010: 13–20). In its application to race and poverty, identity theory explains the racial discrimination in terms of what authors call "oppositional identity." The behavior of Whites toward Blacks is determined by different codes or norms, which perpetuate a distinction between "'us' and 'them'." Thus, white Americans think of Black Americans as "them" rather than include in "us all" (p. 100)." This division of "us and them" based on the norms, what authors call "oppositional identity" with expression of opposition and differences, results in discrimination that explain the high poverty of blacks.

Both in test and identity theory, the *prejudice* serve as the source of discrimination. Darity examined the source and role of prejudice drawing on two prominent writers on the subject of discrimination (Darity, 2014). One approach to the study of prejudice by Gordon Allport's *The Nature of Prejudice* (1954) treats prejudice primarily as a matter of *personal psychology*. A psychology of prejudice, in turn, produces stereotypical (false) beliefs about others, which translates into discriminatory behavior towards the subordinate *group*. It is this view of prejudice that is consistent with Gary Becker's (1993) taste-based approach to discrimination, observed Darity. However, Herbert Blumer (1958) questions Allport's construction of the theory of prejudice as a set of individual feelings. Blumer argued that "race prejudice exists in sense of group position rather than in a set of feelings which members of one racial group have toward members of another racial group" (Blumer, 1958: 3). Darity observed that Blumer shifts the locus of origin of prejudice from individual beliefs to attitudes of group about the *relative status and material benefits* associated with membership in the group harboring stereotypical beliefs toward the "other." Darity quotes Blumer (1958: 3–4):

> The body of feelings which scholars today are so inclined to regard as constituting the substance of race prejudice is actually a resultant of the way in which given racial groups conceive of themselves and of others. A basic under-standing of race prejudice must be sought in the processes

by which racial groups form images of themselves and of others. This process...is fundamentally a collective process.... To characterize another racial group is, by opposition, to define one's own group, or defining their positions vis-à-vis each other. It is the sense of social position emerging from this collective process of characterization which provides the basis of race prejudice.

According to Blumer, there are four basic types of *feelings or attitude* that seem to be always present in (race) prejudice in the dominant group: "(1) a feeling of superiority, (2) a feeling that the subordinate race is intrinsically different and alien, (3) a feeling of proprietary claim to certain areas of privilege and advantage, and (4) a fear and suspicion that the subordinate race harbors designs on the prerogatives of dominant race" (Blumer, 1958: 4). At the cost of space it is useful to reproduce the Blumer's elaboration on these four types of feelings that represent prejudice:

> In race prejudice there is self-assured feeling on the part of the dominant racial group of being naturally superior. This is commonly shown in a disparagement of qualities of the subordinate racial group.... The second feeling, that the subordinate race is an alien and fundamentally different stock—"they are not of our kind" is a common way in which this is likely to be expressed.... The combination of these two feeling of superiority and distinctiveness can easily give rise to feeling of aversion and even antipathy. The third feeling, the sense of propriety claim, is of crucial importance. It is the feeling on the part of the dominant group of being entitled to either exclusive or prior rights in many important area—such exclusive rights may be wide, covering the ownership of property such as choice lands and sites; the right to certain jobs, occupations, or professions; the claim to certain kinds of industry or lines of business; the claim to certain positions of control and decision-making as in government and law;.... Again, however this, feeling of superiority, feeling of distinctiveness and feeling of proprietary claims does not explain race prejudice.... The remaining feeling essential to race prejudice is a fear or apprehension that the subordinate racial group is threatening, or will threaten, the position of the dominant groups. Thus, acts or suspected acts that are interpreted as an attack on the natural superiority of dominant group, or an intrusion into their sphere of group exclusiveness, or enchainment on their property claims are crucial in arousing and fashioning race prejudice. (Blumer, 1958: 4)

Blumer shifts the axis of prejudice away from individual sentiments toward collective interests in maintaining a relative group position. Prejudice becomes an operative, mobilizing instrument for preserving the advantaged position of the dominant group. There are real (material) interests at stake in the efforts of the dominant group to preserve its privileged position, and also the more intangible and psychic benefit of a status advantage. According to Darity, these two types of benefits, material and psychic benefit of social status, need not be mutually exclusive and generally go hand in hand. Status advantage is performed by the display of the fruits of the proprietary claim; proprietary claim is conferred by the status advantage (Darity, 2014: 13).

Before we end Blumer's insightful contribution and switch over to Ambedkar's work, it is necessary to reiterate the most important shift that Blumer has brought in the notion of prejudice, that is, the crucial role of positional relation of dominant and subordinate groups in prejudice. The sense of group position (or consciousness) is at the very heart of the relation of dominant to the subordinate group. The source of prejudice lies in the challenges felt in this sense of group position of the dominant group for material and status advantages. In turn, the prejudice becomes a defensive reaction to such challenges of the sense of group position. In this sense, prejudice becomes a protective devise. Its function is to preserve the position of the dominant group. The group position needs to be seen as group-to-group relations, and not as individual to individual. Therefore, "proper and the fruitful area in which prejudice should be studied is the collective processes through which a sense of group position is formed.To seek, instead, to understand it or handle it in the area of individual feeling and of individual experience seems clearly misdirected" (Blumer, 1958: 7).

Ambedkar began where Blumer left. Blumer's articulation of prejudice is highly insightful and realistic, and helps to understand some of the contemporary patterns (as we will discuss the issue related to caste later). How the sense of group position, in the first place, is formed, is an issue where more clarity is required. In Blumer's view, the formation of group position is clearly a historical product. Although Blumer described the processes in some detail, it does not lead us to definite and final elements involved in the formation of four feelings which constitute prejudice. How does the norms that create, preserve, and galvanize the feelings that constitute prejudice are formed? It is here that we receive some insights from Ambedkar's perspective on the issue. Ambedkar's views on caste prejudice and discrimination are worth considering. Ambedkar delves into the processes that lead to the formation of dominant and subordinate groups, and prejudice. In the context of caste, Ambedkar emphasized the role of ideology—social and religious—in the formation of group position and prejudicial norms. Before we discuss this issue, it is useful to discuss Ambedkar's interpretation of caste system to understand his position on prejudice. Ambedkar recognized five main features of caste system. First, the caste system involves the division of Hindu people in to five groups called castes. These five castes are socially exclusive as endogamy (or marriage within each caste with restriction for inter-caste marriage) made it impossible for members of one caste to join another caste by marrying into it. The system then proceeded to assign rights and duties for each of the castes, but the rights and duties are assigned in an unequal manner across the five castes. The rights are also allocated in a graded manner such that as one goes down in the caste hierarchy, the entitlement to rights reduces. Graded inequality implies that every caste except brahmins, who are at the top of the caste hierarchy, suffer from the lack of rights to some degree. But the untouchables who are placed at the bottom of the caste ladder suffer the most, virtually without any rights—economic, civic, and religious. The principle of "graded inequality" became the bedrock of the caste system. The caste system in terms of status and rights is fixed and hereditary, without any possibility of change. In effect then, the caste system turns out to be an unfree social and economic order. In Ambedkar's view, these are the "essential feature of caste system" (Ambedkar, 1989b).

Ambedkar also refers to a "unique feature" of the caste system, which other scholars failed to recognize in clear terms (Ibid.). This unique feature of the caste system relates to the unlimited freedom and power to the dominant caste, the brahmins, who are placed at the top of the hierarchy. We have seen that various castes lack freedom in the choice of occupation or other economic and social rights, while castes other than brahmins do not enjoy freedom of occupations and other rights; an exception is made for brahmins. For instance, in the scheme of caste, in the case of occupation (or property rights), brahmins are assigned the occupation of teaching; kshatriya, the military; vaishya, the mercantile or trade; sudras, agriculture; and the untouchables, the service of the four castes above them. There is no freedom for castes other than brahmins to switch over to the occupation of other castes. Here too, an exception is made for brahmins; they can take the occupation of other castes, if they wish so. Ambedkar quotes *Manusmriti*:

Yet Brahmin, unable to subsist by his duties (which is teaching religion), may live by the duty of solider for that is the next rank. If unable to get subsistence by either of these employments (teaching and solider) the answer is, he may subsist as mercantile man, applying himself into tillage and attendance on cattle. (Ambedkar, 1989a: 60)

Thus, brahmins as the highest caste were given overwhelming power to take any occupation. Endogamy, that is, marriage within caste, is the core feature of the caste system which makes the caste exclusionary in nature. However, some exception was made for the brahmins. The justification is as Ambedkar quotes: "On account of his pre-eminence, on account of superiority of his origin, on account of his observance of (particular) rule and on account of his particular sanctification, the Brahmin are the lord of (all) Castes" (Ibid. 60).

Ambedkar further quotes, "Brahmin is (hereby) declared (to be) the creator (of the world), the punisher, the teachers (and lone) a benefactor (of all created being)" (Ibid. 62). Similar exception is made in civil, social, and legal rights. Ambedkar concludes: "The centre of the ideal [of Hinduism] is neither individual nor society. It is a class; it is a class of supermen called Brahmins. Anything which serves the interests of this class is, alone, entitled to be called good" (Ibid. 72). In serving this class of "Brahmins," the dominant group of Blumer is all over with massive power, superiority, and dominance, brilliantly articulated though religious doctrine and ideology.

Coming back to the essential feature of the caste system, the story does not end with the features mentioned earlier. There are two more features which make the system rigid, static, and less amenable to change. The idea of caste provides for a community-level mechanism in the form of social ostracism, with economic and social penalties for deviation from the prescribed norms and customary rules. Community-level action and the penalties for any deviation from the customary rules of caste act as restraints for change in the caste system. The high-caste community serves as police force to enforce laws related to caste. The last and equally important feature of the caste system is the philosophical support to the caste system by the Hindu religion. The caste system is a Hindu social organization with roots in the Hindu religious philosophy. After a careful analysis of the philosophy of Hinduism, Ambedkar observed:

> In Hinduism inequality is a religious doctrine, adopted and conscientiously preached as ascribed dogma. Inequality for Hindus is a divine prescribed way of life as religious doctrine.... It has become incarnate in Hindu society and is shaped and molded by its thoughts and its doing (Ambedkar, 1989a: 63).

Besides, the doctrines of karma (or deed or work), soul, and rebirth are developed in such a manner that they lend support and justification to the caste system. Thus, the mechanism of social ostracism (for any attempt to violate the rules and norms of caste) and philosophical support in religion provide enough solidity and strength to the caste system. Unlike other religions, inequality does not enter into caste system as an indirect consequence, or as a side effect; rather the principle of graded inequality is a constituent of its foundation on which the structure is erected, sanctified by Hindu religious moral, ethical, and legal philosophy, argued Ambedkar (Ibid.).

In the Ambedkar framework, Blumer's notion of four feelings which constitutes prejudice gets shaped by a religious and social ideology. Ideology serves as a source of group position and the prejudice articulated and codified as the social, moral, and legal framework for society to follow. In essence, therefore, the caste system, according to Ambedkar, in its outcome serves the economic and social ends of the dominant groups of high castes. And, in turn, it restricts occupational choice, education, and civil rights of the subordinate groups. In this context, Ambedkar observed: "The Hindus are the only people in the world whose economic order—the relation of workman to workman—is consecrated by religion and made sacred, eternal, and inviolate" (Ibid. 129).

It is quite clear how Blumer's four feelings—namely, the feeling of superiority, distinctiveness, proprietary rights, and the fear of other groups challenging the superior position of the dominant group—are met in their entirety in the scheme of caste system. Insofar as the higher caste considered themselves to be superior than lower castes to meet the condition of superiority, treated lower castes as distinct and inferior to meet the condition of distinctiveness, exclusive economic rights and high social status, at the same time denying the same to the lower castes to meet the condition of proprietary right, and finally used the mechanism of social ostracism and religious ideology against any deviation from the rules of caste, to provide complete protection from any kind of fear of encroachment on the rights of the dominant caste. The prejudice is ideologically grounded to serve the material interest and high social status for high castes. However, what Blumer possibly could not imagine and predict was that a dominant caste like the brahmins will have such a foresight or ingenuity to provide strong social safeguards in the form of social ostracism (involving economic, social, and violent penalties) and justification from the religious philosophy to avoid any possibility or fear of encroachment on their rights. Both social ostracism and religious sanctity would provide solidity to the caste system so that their superior position is not in jeopardy and that they continue to enjoy the position of privilege—economic and social. It seems possible to assume that Blumer's conceptualization of prejudice and its substantiation in Indian situation with Ambedkar's interpretation of caste provide a tool to comprehend contemporary responses with respect to the dominant groups of higher castes and the subordinate groups of lower castes in India.

Theories of Policies: Implications of Findings

The book revealed that in each of 10 areas of human development, high-caste Hindu households performed the best, and the households from the SC and ST, and the Muslim households performed the worst, *even after controlling for the (non-group) factors that might have influenced the outcomes.* The results point toward group-specific factors, particularly related to *exclusion.*

What insight do we receive from the theories on policies? The theoretical strands have their policy implications. The "test theory" predicts that in highly competitive markets, discrimination will prove to be a transitory phenomenon as there are costs associated with discrimination to the firms/employers that result in lowering of profits. Firms/employers who indulge in discrimination face the ultimate sanction imposed by the markets. This proposition sees the resulting erosion of profits as a self-correcting solution for eliminating discrimination. The test theory recommends the promotion of market competitiveness and belief-based perfect information theory to reduce market discrimination. However, it is argued that there are several reasons why economic discrimination might persist over longer periods.

First, even if the markets are sufficiently competitive, market discrimination will continue to persist if all firms discriminate, as all discriminatory firms would face identical cost, revenue, and profit frontiers. The persistence of decades of labor-market discrimination in high-income countries attests to the resilience of market discrimination. Second, in reality, not all markets are competitive. Indeed, in most of the economies, markets are imperfect and governed by oligopolistic and monopolistic market situations, which often empower the firms to discriminate at will. Similarly, belief-based or imperfect information theory argues for perfect information as a solution to the elimination of discrimination. Evidence from the Indian village studies indicates that the discriminators, due to the close proximity and long experience, know not only the productivity of the workers, but also their work ethics and behavior, and still the high-caste households prefer the worker of their own caste. Perfect knowledge does not deter the employer from discrimination in several works, if not all (Thorat and Newman, 2010).

The identity theory's position deviate from the test theory. Identity theory recognized that discrimination and occupational segregation persists in competitive market situation. In the context of gender discrimination, identity theory maintains that the real problem is *the norms that stipulate* that men and women should do particular jobs, irrespective of their individual tastes and abilities. Therefore, what is required is the social movement and government intervention rather than competitive market place to erode the discrimination against women (Akerlof and Krantom, 2010: 94). The government intervention necessarily is in the form of laws to prohibit discrimination and provide safeguards against it, program for change of norms, and positive government interventions for economic, educational and political empowerment of discriminated groups.

Put together, these theories have policy messages. We take caste as a typical case of prejudice for policy purposes (this framework may be extended to other categories, such as ethnic and religious). Blumer's perspective and its substantiation by Ambedkar in Indian situation become a useful example—a more systematic case of what may be called an "ideologically determined and shaped prejudice." In this perspective, the prejudicial feeling is articulated clearly by ideology—social and religious. Ideology defines the superior position of the dominant group, namely the higher caste with exclusive economic and social rights and privileges, and the denial of the same to the subordinate groups, namely the lower caste, due their inferior status. In this the prejudice is directly connected to the material interest and social status of the higher castes. The exclusionary and discriminatory practices become instrumental in preserving group advantage for those on the top of the caste hierarchy, but at the cost of the lower castes. Discrimination becomes a condition with a functional base for those who benefit from having a relative advantage (Darity, 2014).

Insofar as a caste assigns the economic and social rights unequally among castes, it becomes a direct cause of inter-caste inequality in access to resources and assets, education, and civic rights. Therefore, the task of policy is to eliminate the economic or material base of the prejudice. The first issue for policy purpose is to improve the ownership of resources, assets, education, and other opportunities to the lower castes, particularly the Dalits who were denied the right to property, agricultural land and private enterprise, and access to education. It calls for policy of redistribution of assets, agricultural land, and capital (improving for ownership of private enterprise and businesses). It also calls for a program of education advancement. This distributive strategy is justified as a compensation for the denial of equal economic rights in the past. The redistributive policy is necessarily an instrument to compensate for exclusion and discrimination in the past for a long period.

However, the discrimination also continues in the present in different spheres and forms, if not in their original forms, despite the provision of equal opportunity under the law. The discrimination serves as an instrument of the higher caste to protect their privileges in the ownership of assets, education, employment, and other. Caste discrimination, as Darity argued, serves as a functional base for the dominant caste to protect the wall of special rights and privileges. Therefore, the discriminated groups, particularly the Dalits, need protection from the discrimination in economic and social opportunities at present. Central to this view is the exposition that discriminated groups face discrimination in market and nonmarket channels, and in institutions of governance. Two measures are used, and need to be used where they are not. One is the legal safeguards against discrimination in the form ant-discrimination laws, such as the anti-untouchability Act of 1955 (renamed as Protection of civil Right Act) and Prevention of Atrocities Act of 1989, so that in the event of discrimination, the discriminated person can seek the protection of executive and judiciary.

Secondly, the persistence of discrimination demands a set of measures to ensure a fair share to the discriminated groups in various spheres, such as ownership of assets, education, employment, political participation, and governance. These measures are generally called affirmative action policies, but assume different names in different countries, for example, reservation policy in India. The affirmative action policy has both elements embedded in it. These measures by providing a fair share in the ownership of assets, education, and employment also empower the discriminated groups for economic enhancement in the future. The last points in this category of measures include the policy for fair share and participation in governance, which would include adequate representation in legislature, policy making, implementing and monitoring of policies and programs. Socially inclusive governance generally makes the implementation of legal measures and policies more effective.

These are some of the measures which are necessary for correcting the material consequences of caste prejudice and eliminate their material base. However, there is also a need to deal with the caste prejudice itself. Insofar as discrimination still continues in some forms, the unlearning of these ideas which are based on the notion of inequality and hierarchy is essential. And the learning of the alternative ideas of equality and justice among the people becomes necessary. Learning is a difficult process and never ends. This implies that the process of unlearning and learning is something which has to be carried out continuously without any gap. The fact that caste discrimination still persists in economic and social spheres is reflective of the fact that traditional principles and norms continue to govern the economic and social behavior of higher castes, despite the adoption of the idea of equality in economic, social, and political spheres. The ideas about caste discrimination and other forms of prejudices are developed among the children in family and society. Unlearning of the undemocratic ideas, norms, and customs which are picked by children early in life is a major challenge. Efforts are possibly needed on both fronts—education and civil society engagement and activism. Education, school, and higher education can play an important role in socialization of the children and adults, as most of the children and majority of the adults pass through education institutions at various stages in life. Education in schools and higher education can serve as an important channel and instrument where unlearning and learning can happen and which eventually can mold the thought and action of children and adults. This would necessarily mean education for citizenship learning. The civic learning in the education system would instill the values of nondiscrimination, equality, democracy, and justice among the children and adults in thought and action and make them better citizens.

In addition to the importance of education, the civil society can play an important role. There is a need for the engagement of the civil society to change the norms and prejudices that shape the undemocratic behavior of the people. Experience shows that it is the civil rights movement by people which has brought significant changes in curriculum, teaching, and policies for discriminated groups, such as women, Dalits, tribals, and so on.

Sukhadeo Thorat

Professor Emeritus,

Jawaharlal Nehru University, Delhi (India)

References

Allport, Gordon. (1954). *The nature of prejudice*. New York: Perseus Books.

Akerlof, George, & Kranton R.E. (2010). *Identity economics: How our identities shape our work, wage, and well-being*. Princeton University Press

Ambedkar, B. R. (1989a). Philosophy of Hinduism. In *Dr Babasheb Ambedkar writings and speeches* (vol. 3). Mumbai: Department of Education, Government of Maharashtra.

———(1989b). The essential features of Hindu social order. In *Dr Babasheb Ambedkar Writings and Speeches* (vol. 3), Mumbai: Department of Education, Government of Maharashtra.

———(1989c). The unique feature of Hindu social order. In *Dr Babasheb Ambedkar writings and speeches* (vol. 3), Mumbai: Department of Education, Government of Maharashtra.

Arrow, Keneth. (1973). The theory of discrimination. In Orley Albert Rees (Ed.), *Discrimination in labour market*. Princeton, NJ: Princeton University Press

Becker, Gary. (1993). *The economics of discrimination*. Chicago: University of Chicago Press.

Blumer, Herbert. (1958). Race prejudice as a sense of group position. *The Pacific Sociological Review*, *1*(1, Spring), 3–7.

Darity, William. (July–December, 2014). The economics of the dispossessed. *Journal of Social Inclusion Studies*, *1*(1), 7–15.

Thorat, Sukhadeo, & Newman, Katherine. (2010). *Blocked By caste: Economic discrimination in modern India*. New Delhi: Oxford.

Preface

This book provides an in-depth discussion and analysis of the broad issues that underpin social exclusion in India, particularly as it relates to caste and religion. Based on quantitative research using national surveys and surveys carried out by the Indian Institute of Dalit Studies (IIDS), New Delhi, *Caste, Discrimination, and Exclusion in Modern India* analyzes 10 areas where caste- and religion-based exclusion is most visible: human development, inequality, poverty, educational attainments, child malnutrition, health, employment, wages, gender, and access to public goods. In each of these areas, high-caste Hindu households performed the best, and households from the Scheduled Castes and the Scheduled Tribes—along with Muslim households—performed the worst, *even after controlling for the factors (non-group) that might have influenced the outcomes.*

Contained within the analysis of each of these areas is a discussion of the conceptual issues that underpin them, of the data on which the discussion is based, and of the methods of quantitative analysis used to interrogate the data. Each chapter, therefore, embeds social exclusion in a particular context within the general subject matter, theoretical and empirical, relating to that context.

In pedagogic terms, the book is appropriate for the general reader who is interested in issues of exclusion and deprivation in India as they pertain to issues of caste and religion. However, because this book has a strong analytical foundation, it inevitably contains technical matters. Such matters have been dealt with in three ways. First, several of the chapters contain boxes, which the more technical-minded reader may consult but which the general reader could skip without any loss of continuity. Second, the longer technical derivations are relegated to chapter appendices: Chapters 2, 3, 5, and 7 are suitably appended. Third, in Chapter 3, the section that deals with matters pertaining to economic theory has been marked with an asterisk (*) to indicate that it could be passed over by the reader uninterested in theoretical issues.

At the time of writing this book, all the authors were members of IIDS. The study of social exclusion among marginalized groups is the Institute's raison d'être and this book brings together, in a single volume, research conducted by some of its members. However, the contents of this book represent the personal views of the authors and should not be associated with those of the IIDS as an institutional entity.

Last, but not the least, we are grateful to our friends and colleagues, at IIDS and beyond, for their support and encouragement in the writing of this book and to the production team of SAGE for efficiently transforming our manuscript into the finished product.

New Delhi
June 2015

Vani Kant Borooah
Nidhi Sadana Sabharwal
Dilip G. Diwakar
Vinod Kumar Mishra
Ajaya Kumar Naik

1
Introduction

Millions of people in India are born with scars that will never fade over their lifetime. These are scars of social, rather than physical, blemish: they reduce the capacity of such persons to function in life, free of prejudice and untainted by stigma. This book details the many ways in which an accident of birth—being born to the *wrong* parents—affects a person's chances in India of achieving economic and social success. The two important instruments in India through which birth affects people's life chances are *caste* and *religion*. The contextual background to the book is, therefore, the division of Indian society into a number of social groups delineated by these two parameters.

There is, first, the caste system which stratifies Hindus, who constitute 80 percent of India's population into mutually exclusive caste groups, membership of which is determined entirely by birth. Very broadly, one can think of four subgroups: *brahmins, kshatriyas, vaisyas,* and *sudras*.[1] Brahmins, who were traditionally priests and teachers, represent the highest caste; kshatriyas (traditionally warriors and rulers) and vaisyas (traditionally, moneylenders and traders) are "high caste" (or equivalently, "forward" or "upper" caste or, as they are sometimes termed, "twice born") Hindus;[2] and the sudras (traditionally performing menial jobs) constitute the "other backward classes" (OBC).[3] Then, there are people (mostly Hindus, but some who have converted to Buddhism or Christianity) whom Hindus belonging to the four caste groups (listed earlier) regard as being outside the caste system because they are "untouchable" in the sense

---

[1] These four castes are said to have come from Brahma's mouth (*brahmin*), arms (*kshatriya*), highs (*vaisya*), and feet (*sudra*). This is termed as the *Purusasukta* legend, which appears in an appendix to the *Rig Veda*.

[2] However, confusingly, *vaisyas* are *forward* in some states (Uttar Pradesh) but *backward* in others (Bihar).

[3] The term "other" signifies in addition to those who are "outcastes." There is an important distinction within the OBC between those who are just "backward" (*Yadav*s, *Kurmi*s, *Lodhi*s) with many members of these sub-castes being traditional land owners, those who are "more backward" castes, and those who are "most backward" (*Saini, Prajapati, Pal*), whose degree of dispossession bears comparison to that of the "untouchable" group.

that physical contact with them—most usually the acceptance of food or water—is polluting or unclean.[4] They are referred to as the *ati-sudra*s or by their preferred name *Dalits* (meaning *broken* or *oppressed*).

Juxtaposed against the *caste system* (that is, the division of Hindu society into five "caste groups") are between 2,000 and 3,000 *jatis* or castes to which each Hindu *uniquely* belongs. These castes or jatis are the "primitives" of the caste system in the sense that they are the focus of a person's "caste loyalty." For example, Tamil Brahmins would divide themselves into the caste of *Aiyar* or *Aiyangar* brahmins—depending on whether they worshipped Shiva (*Aiyar*) or Vishnu (*Aiyangar*)—and inter-marry only within their caste. In a similar fashion, persons lying below the "pollution line" are themselves subdivided into many castes. The enumeration of these Dalit castes varies across different regions of India: for example, in Uttar Pradesh (UP)—the largest and most populous of the Indian states—there are 65 such Dalit castes (Verma, 2001).

There is—or supposed to be—a mapping of castes (or *jatis*) into the caste system (that is, the caste groups defined by the five varnas) and the caste group or varna with which a particular caste (or jati) is associ-ated *determines the social standing of that caste*. In many instances, the mapping of castes into caste groups is not contentious: brahmins of differ-ent jatis—be they *Aiyar*, *Maithili*, *Chitpavan*, etc.—are all placed in the brahmin varna; *Rajput*s and *Thakur*s are universally regarded as kshatriyas.

In other instances, a particular jati may claim a particular varna status, which may then be socially allowed. Even then, the social acceptance of this claim may vary by region. For example, the *kayasth*s (a caste whose hereditary occupation was that of clerks and accountants[5]) claim kshatriya status even though, overtly, they have little to do with either being warriors or rulers. In some parts of India (for example, Maharashtra and Kerala) this claim is accepted; in others (for example, Bengal) it is not. Yet again, it is possible for a jati to change its varna status: many members of the *kanbis*—a jati belonging to the sudra varna—migrated to East Africa and having accumulated wealth there, managed to gain acceptance as vaisyas under the new jati name of *patidar* (Chandra, 1997).

---

[4]   Stemming largely from the fact that, in occupational terms, they performed—and continue to perform—the dirtiest and lowliest of tasks, such as burials and disposal of carcasses, scavenging, and removal of excreta, etc.

[5]   For example, the Chandraseni Kayastha Prabhu of Maharashtra; the Nairs of Kerala; and the Kharwars of Bihar.

1.1. Birth and Rebirth

The cycle of birth and rebirth is central to the Hindu religion and a person's caste—and, therefore, his social status—depends upon how he conducted himself in his previous life (or lives). From this perspective, an upper-caste Hindu is simply reaping the reward of previous virtue while a Dalit, on the other hand, is paying the price for previous sins.

Also central to Hindu belief is the importance of accepting one's fate (*karma*) and doing what it is right for that person (*dharma*).[6] However, one person's *dharma* is different from another's: just as it is the *dharma* of a brahmin to devote his life to studying the sacred *Vedas*, so it is the *dharma* of a Dalit to perform menial jobs and to suffer, without complaint, the associated indignities. It is only by doing one's *dharma* that Dalits (and also brahmins) stand a chance of improving their lot in future lives[7]; conversely, it would be utterly wrong (*adharma*) for a Dalit to study the *Vedas* or for brahmins to do menial jobs: anyone who deviated from their *dharma*—be they Dalits who got above themselves, or brahmins who debased themselves by associating with Dalits—would jeopardize their chances of a favorable rebirth. However, as Gupta (2000) points out, this interpretation of Hinduism—under which the harshness of Dalit lives is viewed as the (deserved) punishment for misdemeanors committed in their previous lives—is not one to which Dalits subscribe. The caste hierarchy, which regards Dalits as an inferior group of people, to be accorded an inferior status, is accepted only by caste Hindus (that is, Hindus of the four varnas).[8]

In order to understand the Dalit perspective on caste hierarchy, first it is important to observe that each jati has its own theory for explaining its origin, in much the same way that brahmins explain their origin—and that of other varnas—by reference to the *Purusasukta* legend (see footnote 1).

[6]   For a fuller account of the role of *dharma* in Hindu living, see Smith (2009): xviii–xxi. As Smith points out, there is no term in English that entirely captures the essence of *dharma*: "law", "duty," and "virtue" all come close, but not close enough.
[7]   For a brahmin, *improvement* would take the form of liberation (*moksha*) from the cycle of birth and rebirth.
[8]   Even among caste Hindus, while there may be consensus that *Dalits* are at the bottom of the pile, there is no such consensus about the caste that is "most superior." For example, while both brahmins and kshatriyas agree about the hierarchical sequence, *bania, sudra,* and *dalit*, each would claim the top spot for themselves (Quigley, 1993).

In almost every case, jatis below the pollution line claim, in terms of their origin, parity with (if not superiority over) upper-caste Hindus, and they blame the upper castes for having duped them in the past and caused the wretchedness of their present circumstances.[9]

There are two important points about the reaction of Dalit jatis to their treatment at the hands of caste Hindus. First, many of them do not reject the caste system even though it treats them badly. Rather, they accept the caste system—and, by implication, the Hindu religion—but they do not accept the inferior position of their particular caste within that system; indeed, they affirm the superior position of their jati relative to other jatis.[10] Second, the different Dalit castes (jatis) are anxious to preserve their caste identity. Thus, *chamars* or *bhangis* (two important jatis among Dalits) would claim parity with brahmins but *without desiring to be brahmin*. So the question of caste assimilation through marriage—either from the upper caste or from Dalits—would never arise: each jati, no matter how lowly its position, ascribed its misfortune to being a "victim of circumstances"; it believed that it was the equal of, if not superior to, all other jatis and was, therefore, anxious to preserve its "purity."

1.2. Caste Associations

The formation of caste associations, which established horizontal solidarity between persons belonging to the same jati, but living in different parts of the country, had its origins in associations formed to petition the census commissioner for being assigned, by the census, to a varna consistent with the jati's status. From these origins, "caste associations" acquired a secular purpose and became associations for furthering the collective welfare of its members: in that sense they became interested and were intent on furthering the political and economic interests of the group (Rudolph and Rudolph, 1966).

---

[9] For example, Dalits of the chamar jati believe that their ancestor was the youngest of five brahmin brothers: when they found a cow struggling in the river, he (the youngest brother) was sent to rescue the cow but, before he could do so, the cow died; he was then compelled to dispose of the carcass and made *untouchable* because after performing this task, he had become unclean.

[10] The point has often been made that even Hindu converts to Christianity and Islam do not turn their back on their jati.

Nonetheless, the dilemma for caste associations was always whether to form associations with other jatis in a region—that is to seek vertical rather than horizontal solidarity—or to seek solidarity with the same jati in other regions. The latter route preserved the purity of the jati and assisted, through the process of "sanskritization," in acquiring a higher status within the Hindu Varna system.[11] The former path devalued the purity of a jati—and, thereby, undermined the Hindu caste system—but assisted the wider assemblage of castes in acquiring political and economic power. With the advent of elected representation to provincial legislatures, prior to Independence in 1947, caste associations in the south and in the west of India made very different decisions from caste associations elsewhere in the country.

In the west and in the south—due, in large part, to the inspired leadership of Jyotiba Phule in Maharashtra, and M.C. Rajah and Ramaswami Naicker in Madras—non-upper-caste Hindus portrayed themselves, collectively, as the original inhabitants of India and upper-caste Hindus as Aryan invaders from the north who conquered them by force of arms and then kept them subjugated by stigmatizing them as *unclean*. Consequently, in the west and in the south, caste was replaced by *ethnicity*: all persons who were not from the upper castes shared the common ethnicity of belonging to the original Dravidian civilization, a civilization which was displaced by the alien Aryan culture of upper-caste Hindus. This substitution of ethnic solidarity for caste fragmentation allowed *lower caste* Hindus to acquire and hold on to political power in both Maharashtra and Madras in the face of political opposition from upper-caste Hindus. In Maharashtra, non-upper-caste Hindus exercised power through the Congress Party, while, in Madras, they exercised power through the *Dravidar Kazhagam* and then the *Dravida Munnetra Kazhagam* party.

In the north, however, caste associations were more concerned with improving their status in the varna hierarchy than with establishing political alliances. The *Yadav* caste, which dominates the sudra varna in the north, was obsessed with the fact that, even though they claimed descent from the *Yadu* clan of the god Krishna, they were not regarded as kshatriyas by upper-caste Hindus. A great deal of *Yadav* energy was, in

---

[11] This process whereby castes lower down the hierarchy in the attempt to gain status by imitating the manners and mores of the upper castes has been termed "sanskritization" (Srinivas, 1962, 1996). It is the Hindu version of "keeping up with the Joneses."

consequence, poured into redressing this perceived injustice. In order to make their claim credible, they had to distance themselves from another, numerically strong, jati in the sudra varna, the *Kurmi*s. The upshot of this was that the *lower castes* in north India, in search of social status, rejected the *ethnic* mantle of being the original inhabitants of India—adopted by the *lower castes* in the south and in the west—and preferred instead to portray themselves as Aryans who were, in essence, no different from the upper-caste Hindus of the region. But, to do this, they had to distance themselves from other castes and, by corollary, to forgo the opportunity of establishing inter-caste solidarity.

1.3. Public Policy

In response to the burden of social stigma and economic backward-ness borne by persons belonging to India's "untouchable castes," the Constitution of India allows special provisions for their members. These are mainly in the form of reserved seats in the national parliament, state legislatures, municipality boards, and village councils (*panchayat*s); job reservations in the public sector; and reserved places in public higher educational institutions. Articles 341 and 342 include a list of castes entitled to such benefits, and all those groups included in this list—and subsequent modifications to this list—are referred to as, respectively, "Scheduled Castes (SC)." The term "Scheduled Castes" is, for all practi-cal purposes, synonymous with the former "untouchable" castes and that will be how they are referred to in this book. These collectively comprise about 180 million people. It is important to emphasize that the Constitution restricted SC status to *Hindu* groups in "unclean" occupations: their non-Hindu equivalents were not accorded this status and, therefore, could not benefit from reservation policies.[12]

Articles 341 and 342 also include a list of tribes entitled to similar benefits and all those groups included in this list—and subsequent modi-fications to this list—are referred to as the "Scheduled Tribes" (ST).

---

[12] For example, converts to Islam from Hindu *unclean occupations*: *Halalkhor*s, *Hela*s, *Lalbegi*s, *Dhobi*s, *Hajjam*s, *Chik*s, and *Faqir*s. However, subsequent extensions were made to this list for *Mazhabi Sikhs* (in 1956) and *neo-Buddhists* (in 1990).

Figure 1.1:
A diagrammatic representation of the caste system

The Four *Varna*s or Caste Groups

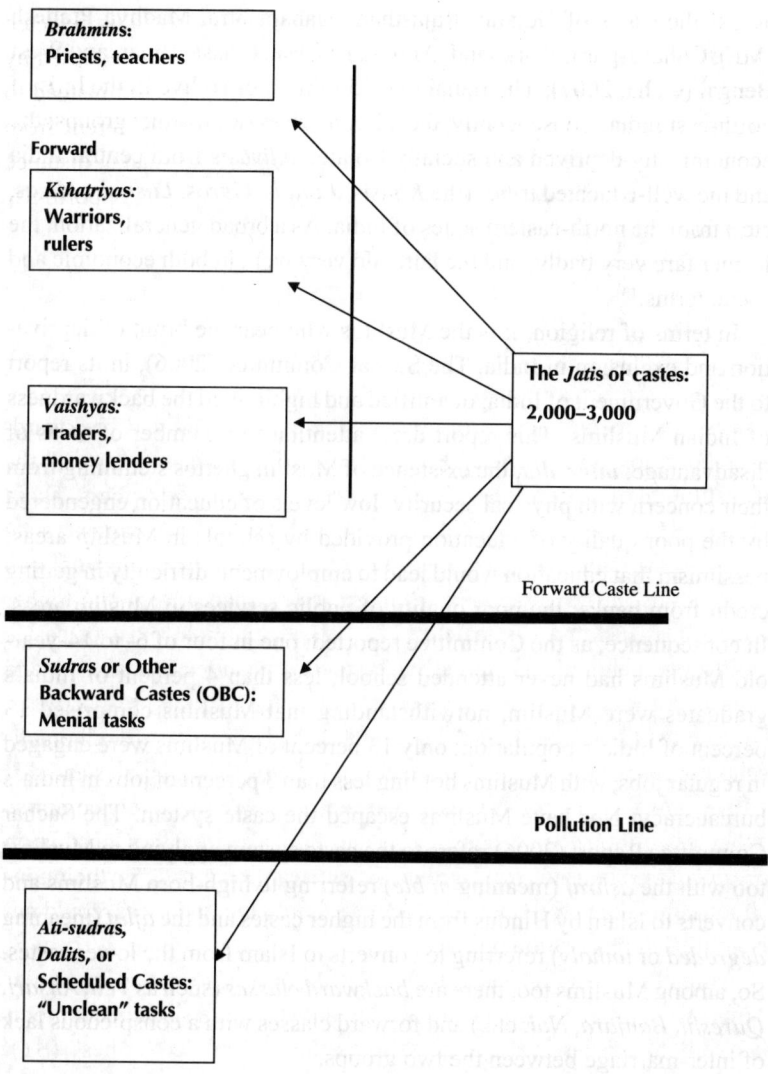

Source: Author.

There are about 85 million Indians classified as belonging to ST, Of these, *adivasi*s (meaning *original inhabitants*) refer to the 70 million who live in central India, in a relatively contiguous hill and forest belt extending across the states of Gujarat, Rajasthan, Maharashtra, Madhya Pradesh (MP), Chhattisgarh, Jharkhand, Andhra Pradesh, Orissa, Bihar, and West Bengal (Guha, 2007). The remaining 15 million or so live in the hills of north-east India. Consequently, the ST comprises two distinct groups: the economically deprived and socially isolated *adivasi*s from central India and the well-educated tribes (the *Khasi*s, *Jantia*s, *Garo*s, *Lushai*s, *Mizo*s, etc.) from the north-eastern states of India. As a broad generalization, the former fare very badly, and the latter do very well, in both economic and social terms.[13]

In terms of religion, it is the Muslims who bear the brunt of depriva-tion and exclusion in India. The Sachar Committee (2006), in its report to the Government of India, quantified and highlighted the backwardness of Indian Muslims. This report drew attention to a number of areas of disadvantage: *inter alia*, the existence of Muslim ghettos stemming from their concern with physical security; low levels of education engendered by the poor quality of education provided by schools in Muslim areas; pessimism that education would lead to employment; difficulty in getting credit from banks; the poor quality of public services in Muslim areas. In consequence, as the Committee reported: one in four of 6- to 14-year-old Muslims had never attended school; less than 4 percent of India's graduates were Muslim, notwithstanding that Muslims comprised 13 percent of India's population; only 13 percent of Muslims were engaged in regular jobs, with Muslims holding less than 3 percent of jobs in India's bureaucracy. Nor have Muslims escaped the caste system. The Sachar Committee Report (2006) refers to the caste system applying to Muslims too with the *ashraf* (meaning *noble*) referring to high-born Muslims and converts to Islam by Hindus from the higher castes and the *ajlaf* (meaning *degraded* or *unholy*) referring to converts to Islam from the lower castes. So, among Muslims too, there are *backward classes* (such as *Teli*, *Ansari*, *Qureshi*, *Banjara*, *Nai*, etc.) and forward classes with a conspicuous lack of inter-marriage between the two groups.

---

[13] It should be pointed out that many of the tribes from the *plains* of the north-eastern state of Assam, much as they might like to be, are not included in the list of STs.

1.4. What Is *Social Exclusion?*

This, then, is a book about the barriers that persons from the SC and the ST, and Muslims, face in escaping poverty and social exclusion in India. The term "social exclusion"—meaning the process by which certain groups are unable to fully participate in the life of their communities—and the consequences thereof—has, from its origins in the writings of Lenoir (1974), spawned a vast and eclectic literature as the list of things that people might be excluded from has grown. Silver (1995), for example, itemizes some of these: livelihood; secure, permanent employment; earnings; property; credit; land; housing; education, skills, and cultural capital; and the welfare state. The basis on which people are excluded also comprises a long list (see DFID, 2005): age, caste, gender, disability, ethnic background, HIV status, migrant status, religion, and sexual orientation. Such an uncontrolled proliferation of items has attracted criticism from some experts in poverty and development, epitomized by Oyen's (1997) dismissal of social integration/exclusion as "an umbrella concept for which there is limited theoretical underpinning."

More recently, Sen (2000) attempted to inject some rigor into the concept of social exclusion. He began by observing that, in the tradition initiated by Aristotle, and continued by Adam Smith (1776), poverty should properly be viewed in terms of "poor living" rather than simply "low income." From the former perspective, poverty is a multi-dimensional concept embracing low income; bad, or no, employment; illiteracy or, at best, low levels of education; poor health and access to health care, and most generally, difficulty experienced in taking part in the life of the community.[14]

Against this backdrop of a multi-dimensional view of poverty, Sen (2000) argued that the function of the concept of social exclusion was not to widen or otherwise alter our concept of poverty but, rather, to highlight the relational aspects and processes that underpin poverty. Thus, some of the critical issues that need to be addressed before judgment can be passed on the usefulness of social exclusion as a concept are the following: (i) Does it contribute to our understanding of the nature and causes

---

[14] As Adam Smith puts it, "an inability to appear in public without shame."

of poverty? (ii) Would our understanding be different if this concept did not exist? (iii) Does it enrich thinking about policies to alleviate poverty?

In answering these questions, Sen (2000) drew attention to two features of social exclusion. The first is that exclusion is a *relational* concept referring to the lack of affinity between an individual and the wider community. Second, in defining the relation between social exclusion and poverty, there is a fundamental distinction to be made between exclusion being *constitutively* a part of deprivation and being *instrumental* in causing deprivation. In the "constitutive" interpretation, exclusion from some (or all) aspects of social functioning in itself, and of itself, constitutes an important aspect of deprivation. In the "instrumental" interpretation, exclusion *per se* does not constitute deprivation; it is a cause of deprivation.

Some types of exclusion may be a constitutive part of deprivation, but not necessarily instrumental in causing deprivation. For example, denial of access to the village well to some families would not have consequences for them with respect to water supply if they had mains water supplied to their homes; however, being denied access might, *in itself*, constitute deprivation by robbing such families of a sense of "belonging" to the village.[15] Conversely, other types of exclusion may not be a constitutive part of deprivation but, nevertheless, might be instrumental in causing deprivation: a denial of credit might not be shameful *per se* but might lead to deprivation through an inability to pursue business opportunities. More generally, social exclusion might have both constitutive and instrumental importance for deprivation.

1.5. Sources of Discrimination

A major instrument of social exclusion is through discriminatory behavior when people are excluded from important activities by virtue of their belonging to certain groups which, for whatever reasons, are viewed "unfavorably." Even when inclusion occurs, it is on unequal terms

---

[15] In another example, with the social status attached to being an owner-occupier in the UK and the USA, a lack of access to the mortgage market might involve enforced living in rented accommodation, and thus a *feeling of shame*; however, if the quality of owned and rented accommodation was not very different, there would be no consequences for *housing hardship* emanating from this.

and conditions, which affect the ability of groups to interact freely and productively with others and to take full part in the economic, social, and political life of a community. Unequal terms affect the degree of exclusion and erode self-respect and dignity. In practical terms, discrimination may take place in many forms and encompass several areas of life, including the provision of public goods and services. In the Indian context, Thorat, Mahamallik, and Sadana (2010) detail many of the ways through which persons from marginalized groups are discriminated against.[16] All these observations beg the question of what the sources of discrimination might be. Whatever forms discrimination takes, it makes a distinction between persons *categorically* rather than *individually*. This means that any difference in treatment between persons is based on their group membership rather than on their relevant personal characteristics, and such difference in treatment constitutes discriminatory behavior.

However, in defining discrimination, economists follow the lead of Becker (1993: 18): "discrimination in the market place consists of voluntarily relinquishing profits in order to cater to prejudice." Defined in this sense, discrimination is the "price" of prejudice: it is the price paid by those who indulge their "taste for discrimination" in terms of foregone profits.[17] If we accept Becker's view of discrimination as forgone profits to satisfy a "taste for prejudice," then a consequence of discrimination is that a better qualified Black applicant is turned down in favor of a less qualified White applicant. So, *successful* Black applicants will, on average, be "better" than *successful* White applicants because they have had to meet a higher standard of compliance. If we do not observe these differences in outcome between the groups then there cannot be discrimination in that market: the decision-making agent is accepting the *same* standard of compliance (for example, in terms of qualifications, rent, credit risk) from members of both groups.

---

[16] For example, in the context of the rural labor market, discrimination takes the form of denial of work as agricultural workers (36 percent of villages practiced this), no touching while paying wages (37 percent of villages), lower wages for the same work (25 percent of villages), not employed in house building (29 percent of villages), denial of access to irrigation facilities (33 percent of villages), and denial of access to grazing/fishing grounds (21 percent of villages).

[17] For example, a less qualified White person is chosen for a job over a more qualified Black person so that the employer forgoes the higher profit from employing the more qualified person.

Another source of discrimination is statistical or belief-based. This form of discrimination arises when beliefs (or knowledge) about the characteristics of the group to which an individual belongs are used to make inferences about the individual's characteristics (Arrow, 1972a, 1972b, 1973; Lundberg and Startz, 2007; Phelps, 1972). Beliefs can also reflect prejudice through, for example, negative stereotypes of certain groups. Under a *negative stereotype*, a prior, negative belief about a group's average value of some relevant characteristic is used to assess the ability of all individuals from this group. So, the fact that, on average, a group scores poorly on a test is used to conclude that every member of that group would score poorly on that test; more accurately, the likelihood of a member of that group scoring poorly is greater than the corresponding likelihood for a person belonging to a group with a higher average score.

However, negative stereotypes about groups are a different type of prejudice from Becker's distaste for *all* individuals belonging to a certain group. Under a negative stereotype, assessment is only with respect to the relevant task and does not imply any further prejudice against the group. So, belief-based discrimination is a market-based explanation for discrimination which does not require a taste for discrimination. Also, unlike taste-based discrimination, it does not require a sacrifice of profits. Indeed, if the prior belief is true, *profits are expected to go up* as a result of discrimination.

Belief-based discrimination based on prior beliefs about the average performance of a group penalizes talented individuals from a group by ascribing to them the average quality of their group. Consequently, belief-based discrimination can change the behavior of a group. If the employer is going to judge by means of a negative group stereotype, there is no point in making human capital investments (education, study, diligence, work habits, attitudes to work) since such investments will carry low (if not zero) rates of return. As Elnslie and Sedo (1996: 474) observe in their development of this argument, "one initial bout of unemployment that is not productivity based can lay the foundation for continued future unemployment and persistently lower job status even if no future discrimination occurs."

More recently, social scientists have expressed interest in a phenomenon referred to as "stereotype threat." The persistent discrimination reduces the confidence of the victims and undermines their self-esteem as they begin to believe themselves to be of low worth. This is what Bertrand, Chugh, and Mullainathan (2005) call "implicit discrimination." In the context of experimental economics, Hoff and Pandey (2006) conducted an experiment in north India where children were asked to solve problems. When the children's castes were not revealed to the other participants, the performance of lower-caste children was not very different from that of the higher castes. Yet, when castes were publicly announced, performance by lower-caste children deteriorated significantly, suggesting that loss of self-confidence may have played a role in the performance decline.

The view that statistical discrimination based on negative stereotypes can discourage the motivation for equipping oneself for advancement is also consistent with evidence from India. For example, Jeffery and Jeffery (1997) in their study of Muslims in Bijnor argued that many Muslims regarded their relative economic weakness as stemming from them being excluded from jobs due to discriminatory practices in hiring. The belief that their sons would not get jobs then led Muslim parents to devalue the importance of education as an instrument of upward economic mobility. It was with such considerations in mind that Myrdal (1944) spoke of the "vicious circles of cumulative causation": the failure of discriminated groups to make progress justifies the prejudicial attitudes of dominant groups.

1.6. The Persistence of Discrimination

Market-based theories of explanation are not able to explain the *persistence* of discrimination. Taste-based discrimination cannot explain why arbitrage does not eliminate discrimination: employers without discriminatory tastes can earn higher profits than those with discriminatory tastes by simply hiring high productivity labor from the group that is discriminated against. Belief-based discrimination cannot explain why, through a Bayesian updating process, posterior experience does not erode prior beliefs and eliminate such discrimination. To explain persistence, it is necessary to turn to nonmarket reasons for discrimination. Market discrimination views discrimination as the result of an impersonal relation between market participants. Nonmarket discrimination, by contrast, emphasizes the social nature of transactions.

One form of nonmarket discrimination is the role of friends and acquaintances in securing a "favorable outcome": a job, a loan, a tenant, admission into an educational institution or hospital, etc. This is the network concept of allocation: it is who you know that determines the chance of a "favorable outcome" (see Granovetter, 1995: White, 1995). Applying this to discrimination, "who you know" (the density of one's network) depends critically on one's group identity. Strong group identity leads to social segregation and social segregation leads to segregation in economic outcomes. If the groups differ in social and economic strength, they will differ in terms of their network density and hence in terms of their chance of a "favorable outcome." The main point is that personal interactions occur throughout the search process and these are, if not more, important than impersonal market relationships. Discrimination offers social rewards to the discriminator, the returns on which can be realized in some later, reciprocal, transaction.

Another reason for the persistence of discriminatory behavior is that there is often stigma attached to the "victim" group. The key concept here is one of a *virtual social identity* based on easily identifiable markings (race, gender, caste). It is "virtual" because it can differ from a person's actual identity, and it is "social" because the imputation occurs within a social context. This virtual identity may differ from his *actual* identity, which is based on his personal characteristics. *Stigma* occurs when the imputed virtual identity is *dishonorable*: persons belonging to that group are seen as "flawed" or "damaged." Stigmatization is more than doubting a person's *productivity*; it doubts a person's *humanity* by regarding him or her as a lesser human being.

The origins of stigmatization often lie in a history of dishonor. So, the stigmatization of Blacks in the USA has its origins in slavery, which represented the violent domination of "natally inferior" persons (Loury, 2002; Patterson, 1982). Similarly, in the traditional scheme of the caste system, the untouchables in India, who are at the bottom of caste hierarchy, were denied rights—civil, social, cultural, religious, and economic—in a manner that was clearly specified in the customary laws of caste system. The *Manusmriti* (or the Laws of Manu) is the centerpiece of Hinduism's *varnasram-dharma* and determine the rights of obligations of all those born as Hindus (Doniger and Smith, 1992). Like the Black slaves on the plantations of the United States, who were punished for "getting above themselves," *Manusmriti* declares that "the king shall deprive of his property and banish a man of low caste who through covetousness lives by the occupations of a higher one," the reason for this occupational segregation being that "it is better (to discharge) one's own (appointed) duty incompletely than to perform completely that of another; for he who lives according to the law of another (caste) is instantly excluded from his own."[18]

The punishment for offending members of the lower castes was comparable in viciousness to that meted out to disobedient slaves in the USA's Antebellum South.[19] According to *Manusmriti*, "with whatever limb a man of a low caste does hurt to a man of the three highest castes, even that limb shall be cut off." Furthermore, "a low-caste man, who tries to place himself on the same seat with a man of a high caste, shall be branded on his hip and be banished, or (the king) shall cause his buttock to be gashed." And, if this was not enough, "a once-born man (a sudra), who insults a twice-born man with gross invective, shall have his tongue cut out; for he is of low origin" and "if he mentions the names and castes (jati) of the (twice-born) with contumely, an iron nail, ten fingers long, shall be thrust red-hot into his mouth."[20]

1.7. Ambedkar and Social Exclusion

No discussion of the persistence of social exclusion can be complete without reference to the views of one of India's towering intellects and greatest leaders, Bhim Rao (B.R.) Ambedkar (1891–1956). The 14th child of a family belonging to one of India's "untouchable" castes, Ambedkar was a brilliant student who overcame the social handicap of his caste to obtain a doctorate in economics from the USA's Columbia

---

[18] *Indian History Sourcebook: The Laws of Manu, c. 1500 BCE* translated by G. Buhler, New York: Fordham University (http://www.akademiktarih.com/ngilizce-belgeler/1026-lkca-tarih-metinleri-ve-kitabeleri-/27731-indian-history-sourcebook-the-laws-of-manu-c-1500-bce-translated-by-g-buhler.html, last accessed on July 15, 2014).

[19] As graphically depicted in the Oscar winning film: "*12 Years a Slave.*"

[20] *Indian History Sourcebook: The Laws of Manu, c. 1500 BCE* translated by G. Buhler, New York: Fordham University (http://www.akademiktarih.com/ngilizce-belgeler/1026-lkca-tarih-metinleri-ve-kitabeleri-/27731-indian-history-sourcebook-the-laws-of-manu-c-1500-bce-translated-by-g-buhler.html, last accessed on July 15, 2014).

University. In acknowledgment of his prodigious talent, he was given the key role, as the chairman of the Drafting Committee, in drafting India's post-independence Constitution in 1950—a role which he used to incorporate affirmative action for the SC, in education, employment, and electoral politics, into the constitutional document. As the architect of India's "reservation policy," his views on the social inclusion of the excluded deserve careful consideration. Ambedkar focused on two aspects of social exclusion. The first was the exclusionary nature of the caste system (underpinned by untouchability), which denied resources and opportunities to members of the lower castes. The second was a set of policy measures to ameliorate the effects of exclusion (Thorat and Kumar, 2008).

According to Ambedkar, the division of Hindu society by caste was a "closed" system because endogamy within each caste made it impossible for members of one caste to join another caste by marrying into it: no one could cease being an "untouchable" and, instead, became a brahmin. The caste system then proceeded to assign rights and duties across castes. The pernicious aspect of the system lay in two features. First, rights and duties were assigned according to caste hierarchy, with the upper castes claiming for themselves the largest number of rights and the most desirable duties, and the lower castes being assigned minimal rights and the most onerous of duties. Thus, the principle of "doing your duty"—which is the bedrock of Hindu religious belief—was very pleasant for a brahmin, devoting his life to prayer and reading, but not so pleasant for an "untouchable" having to do his duty by cleaning toilets. Second, the system was hereditary: once a brahmin or an "untouchable," always a brahmin or an "untouchable." Thus, Ambedkar viewed the logic of caste as imposing a *permanent* system of *graded inequality* on Hindu society, with rights diminishing and duties becoming more unpleasant as one moved down the caste hierarchy.

The denial of occupational choice and education to the lower castes lay at the heart of this graded inequality. The upper castes were free to choose their occupation, but the choices of the lower castes were confined to a small range of menial—and often dirty and unpleasant—jobs. In the absence of any government involvement in public education, the sole means of learning to read and write was through a study of the *Vedas*, which was permitted only to brahmins, kshatriyas, and vaisyas.[21] The laws of Manu (of which more in his chapter) ensured that lower case effrontery in attempting to study the *Veda*s would exact severe punishment. By virtue of doing their *dharma* (duty) by not studying, near universal illiteracy among the lower castes became part of their *karma* (fate). It was only in 1848 that Jyotiba Phule opened the first school for children of the "untouchable" castes.

In essence, therefore, the caste system, according to Ambedkar, was a system by which some groups of persons, *using the justification of religion practice and belief,* exploited for economic ends, other groups of persons. Religious sanctity was used to restrict occupational choice, access to learning, access to places of worship, access to public spaces and public goods, and to extract cheap labor to perform menial/dirty/dangerous jobs. In his own words: "The centre of the ideal [of Hinduism] is neither individual nor society. It is a class; it is a class of supermen called Brahmins. Anything which serves the interests of this class is alone, entitled to be called 'good'" (Ambedkar, 1987: 72). In serving this class of "supermen," he adds: "The Hindus are the only people in the world whose economic order—the relation of workman to workman—is consecrated by religion and made sacred, eternal, and inviolate" (Ambedkar, 1987: 129).

In taking the first step to breaking the brahmin stranglehold over the "untouchable" castes, Ambedkar took a leaf out of the Muslim book— the Government of India Act of 1909 (more commonly known as the Minto-Morley reforms) had conceded a separate electorate for Muslims on the grounds that they were a distinct community in terms of religion and history—by declaring, for the first time, before the Southborough Committee of 1919 (also known as the "Franchise Committee") that, contrary to the conventional belief that the "untouchables" were a part of the "Hindu community," they were a distinct and separate community from "caste Hindus." He then drew attention to the appalling denial of civil, social, and economic rights to untouchables and demanded "citizenship rights" for untouchables accompanied by legal safeguards against the violation of rights and policies for empowering untouchables by compensating them for the historical abuse of their rights (Thorat and Kumar, 2008). Today these views have resulted in, first, a substantial number of Dalits leaving Hinduism to become Buddhists, and second,

[21] Though only brahmins were allowed to teach the *Veda*s.

efforts by the Indian government to correct historical wrongs by a policy of reserving places in education, employment, and legislative bodies.

1.8. Detecting Discrimination: Regression Analysis

There are two main ways of detecting the existence of discrimination: *regression analysis* and *audit studies*. A great deal of the analysis contained in this book is based upon the regression method and, so, the essentials of this methodology are set out in this section. In regression analysis, the dependent variable is usually the outcome for persons and the regression equation is *controlled* by a number of personal characteristic variables, unrelated to group membership, *plus a group membership variable*. If the coefficient group on the group variable is significant, *after controlling for the other non-group variables*, discrimination is said to exist.

However, this method has pitfalls mainly connected with equation specification. If the equation is underspecified (relevant variables are omitted), the extent of discrimination will be overstated. On the other hand, if the equation is over-specified (irrelevant variables are included), the extent of discrimination will be overstated. So, it is only if one is certain that the equation is *exactly* specified (which one can never be) that one can be sure that discrimination has been correctly identified and measured.

In the previous method, a *single* regression was estimated over all persons regardless of the group to which they belonged. The implicit assumption was that all persons (say, Black or White) faced the *same* regression coefficients in the evaluation of their attributes and that the *only* coefficient that distinguished Blacks and Whites was the race variable. This assumption is relaxed by estimating separate equations between the two groups and allowing the coefficients to be different between them.

This raises the following question. When we observe a difference in mean achievement between Whites and Blacks, what is it due to? Is it the result of the superior attributes of Whites as manifest in relatively more favorable values of the explanatory variables for Whites compared to Blacks? Or is it due to the superior treatment of Whites as manifest in relatively more favorable coefficients for Whites compared to Blacks? Or is it due to some combination of superior attributes and favorable treatment and, if so, can we quantify how much is due to the former and how much to the latter? *Decomposition analysis* (which is frequently used in this book) allows us to answer these questions.

1.9. Detecting Discrimination: Audits

An audit is a matched-pair survey technique that allows researchers to observe how economic agents behave. In an audit study, two equally matched candidates from different groups are sent to accomplish a particular task with respect to a sample of agents whose behavior toward the candidates is then observed.

Audit studies avoid many of the pitfalls of regression analysis by equalizing many essential characteristics between candidates. But they pose their own problems (see Heckman, 1998; Yinger, 1998): first, there are challenges of both design and management—unobserved variables means all the relevant variables will not be matched (see Heckman and Siegelman, 1993); the audit refers to a particular stage of the transaction not to the entire transaction (Yinger, 1998); it refers to the sample of firms and not to the entire market (Heckman, 1998.). Second, there are problems in interpreting the results in the context of measuring discrimination. The majority of audit studies use one of the two measures (Wienk, Reid, Simouson, and Eggers, 1979):

1. The gross incidence of unfavorable treatment which is the share of audits in which the protected group is treated less favorably.
2. The net incidence of unfavorable treatment which is the share of audits in which the protected group is treated *less* favorably less the share of audits in which the protected group is treated *more* favorably.

The problem is that the gross and net measures can be far apart. Also, there are problems regarding the net measure as lower bound. Lastly, there is the problem of interpreting the net measure: the net measure shows that protected group members are more likely to encounter unfavorable treatment than members from the dominant group; however, that is not the same as discrimination (Yinger, 1998). In many cases, audit studies show symmetrical treatment: both were successful or both were unsuccessful. So, it is difficult to know how to interpret small differences in preferences.

1.10. Plan of the Book

Against this background, this book seeks to study the disadvantage and exclusion that people from India's marginalized groups face in a number of areas. In Chapter 2, we examine the relative achievements of social groups in India—high-caste Hindus (HCH), Muslims, the OBC, the SC, and the ST—with respect to certain key indicators (education, life expectancy, and income) that enter the United Nations Development Program's (UNDP) Human Development Index (HDI). Aggregating over these achievements yields the HDI values for these social groups. Following this, in this Chapter 2 we also examine new indicators not included in the UNDP index. These are household living conditions and the extent and depth of household social networks. We use these indicators to construct an extended, five-indicator, HDI for social groups. The calculation of these indices pays attention to the existence of inequality, both within and between social groups, in the distribution of achievements in order to compute "equity-sensitive" HDI values.

Chapter 3 examines patterns of inequality between households belonging to the different social groups with respect to their monthly per capita consumption expenditure (MPCE). The novelty of this chapter is that, compared to other studies, it links the MPCE of households more tightly to asset ownership, in particular to information on the ownership of tractors, threshers, tube wells, electric and diesel pumps, and draught and dairy livestock. Another feature of this chapter is that it analyses both inequality and poverty in India within the context of caste-based discrimination.

Chapter 4 analyses the educational attainments of children belonging to different social groups and identifies the household and environmental factors that influence these attainments. It shows that the social group to which the children belonged exerted a significant influence on their attainment, even after taking account of non-group factors like their parents' educational level and income.

Chapters 5 and 6 are concerned with the broad area of health, with child malnutrition analyzed in Chapter 5 and adult health in Chapter 6. In terms of the determinants of child malnutrition, our central finding is that a household's access to safe water and good sanitation are key determinants of the nutritional status of its children. Chapter 6 examines certain key aspects of adult health: age at death; the state of health of elderly persons; and the type and quality of pre- and post-natal care received by pregnant mothers. Both chapters find that, even after controlling for group-unrelated factors, the nutritional status of children and the health status of adults are significantly affected by the social groups to which they belong.

Chapter 7 examines labor market outcomes and, in particular, the areas of employment and wage disparities. This chapter addresses two vexed questions: first, the effectiveness of jobs reservation in India for the SC and the ST and, second, whether it should be extended to other groups. In this chapter, we also show that wage disparity is as much of an inter-group issue as disparity in employment outcomes. Chapter 8 examines the position of SC women since they suffer the triple disadvantage of being poor, of belonging to the SC, and of being women.

Chapters 9 and 10 examine two public policy programs of the Indian government—the Integrated Child Development Scheme (ICDS) and the Rashtriya Swasthya Bima Yojana (RSBY) health insurance program. We examine the social orientation of both these schemes with a view to examining the extent to which they serve persons from marginal groups.

This book is empirically driven and is based upon a statistical and econometric analysis of a large data set. An introduction would be incomplete without a few words on these data. The analyses of Chapters 2, 3, 4, 5, and 9 were based on data provided by the India Human Development Survey (IHDS). This survey was conducted in 2004–05 by the University of Maryland in collaboration with the National Council of Applied Economic Research, New Delhi, between November 2004 and October 2005. The nationally representative data cover 1,504 villages and 971 urban areas across 33 states and union territories of India. The survey covering 41,554 households, encompassing 215,754 persons, was carried out through face-to-face interviews by pairs of male and female enumerators in local languages. The respondents included a person who was knowledgeable about the household economic situation (usually the male head of the household) and an ever-married woman aged 15–49 years.

The detailed modules of the survey provide answers to a wide range of questions relating to *inter alia* economic activity, income and consumption expenditure, asset ownership, social capital, education, health, marriage, and fertility. The analyses of Chapters 6 and 7 were based on National Sample Survey (NSS) data, while the analysis of Chapter 10 was based on a survey conducted by the IIDS.

2

The Human Development Index

2.1. Introduction

There are murmurings of discontent—both from economists and non-economists—that, in identifying welfare exclusively with money income, the subject has missed a trick or two and, perhaps, even somewhat lost its way. Since this welfare-income identity is also subscribed to by many, if not most, people in public life, its concomitant is an undue concentration of both public and private resources on raising national income: "undue," because making people richer does not necessarily make them happier or, at any rate, not by enough to justify the outlay of resources in raising income. In other words, public policy, with its focus on raising national income, may not be giving people what they want and, for this reason, there is a growing restlessness among social scientists about the wisdom of harnessing economic policy to the yoke of economic performance (Frank, 1997, 1999; Layard, 2006).

The United Nations, too, has recognized that income is not an end in itself, but instead a means to achieving the much broader goal of "human development" and that toward achieving this goal, non-economic factors—such as levels of crime, the position of women, and respect for human rights—may, in addition to income, make an important contribution. In order to breathe life into this perspective, the UNDP regularly publishes, as part of its annual *Human Development Report*, a ranking of over 100 countries in terms of their values of the Human Development Index (HDI). This index, while having gross domestic product (GDP) performance as one of its components, also takes into account countries' "achievements" with regard to educational (for example, literacy rates) and health-related (for example, life expectancy) outcomes.[1] "Well-being," so conceived, may be related to poverty, but it is also quite distinct from it (Subramanian, 2004).

The term "human development" is widely used by the media, politicians, non-government organizations, and governments all over the world to mean the capacity of people to fulfill their potential in all the variety of domains in which they function—health, education, and income. This concept of development—based on an expansion of capabilities to function in life, in all its variety and richness—is arguably a more productive and more expressive view than the one based solely on economic growth. This is a concept that owes much to the work of, among others, Anand and Sen (1994, 1997), Haq (1994), and Sen (1992). The computation of the HDI, and the ranking of countries on the basis of their HDI values, has become a regular feature of public debate since the HDI was first published by the UNDP (UNDP, 1995). Another regular feature of HDI is its calculation on a national (and indeed, sub-national basis), in which different regions of a country are ranked on the basis of their human development (for example, for India, by Shariff, 1999).

Anand and Sen (1997), in a paper prepared for the *Human Development Report* (1995), pointed out that a country's non-economic achievements were unlikely to be equally distributed between subgroups of its population. For example, in terms of gender equality, which was the focus of their concern, the female literacy rate, or female life expectancy, was often lower than that for males. In the face of such inter-group inequality, they argued that a country's achievement with respect to a particular outcome should not be judged exclusively by its mean level of achievement (for example, by the average literacy rate for a country), but rather by the mean level *adjusted to take account of inter-group differences in achievements.* Anand and Sen (1997) proposed a method, based on Atkinson's (1970) seminal work on the relation between social welfare and inequality, for making such adjustments and they termed the resulting indicators *equity sensitive indicators.* They further suggested that assessment of country

---

[1] The rankings of the various countries in terms of their per capita GDP and their HDI index can often be very different. If one defines X as the *difference* between a country's GDP rank and its HDI rank, then as UNDP (2000) shows, X is significantly non-zero for several countries. For example, $X = 13$ for the UK (implying that the UK's HDI ranking was 13 places higher than its GDP ranking) while $X = -16$ for Luxembourg (implying that Luxembourg's HDI ranking was 16 places lower than its GDP ranking).

achievements should be made on the basis of such equity sensitive indicators rather than, as was often the case, on the basis of its *mean* level of achievement. This would then allow a comparison between two countries, one of which had a lower mean achievement level, but a more equitable distribution of achievement, than the other.[2]

Unfortunately, a neglected area in the study of human development has been differences in human development between *social groups* in a country. So, for example, we might know the value of the HDI for India in its entirety but fail to adjust this value for the fact that India's achievements with respect to the components of the HDI may be unequally distributed between its various social groups: an acceptable rate of national literacy may co-exist with high rates of literacy for upper-caste Hindus and low rates for the SCs and STs. A failure to take account of such inter-group inequalities might lead to India's developmental achievements being exaggerated. Conversely, one would get a more accurate picture of India's achievements with respect to human development only after one had taken account of the fact that the fruits of development were unequally distributed between its various communities.

There is, however, an additional issue. Not only are developmental fruits unequally distributed *between* groups—in the sense that, as observed above, inter-group average incomes may differ—but these fruits may be unequally distributed *within* the groups. The former type of inequality is the domain of *inter-group* inequality and the latter type of inequality is the domain of *within-group* inequality with *overall* inequality being a composite of "between"- and "within"-group inequality.[3] So, pursuing Anand and Sen's (1997) argument to its logical conclusion, a "proper" assessment of a country's achievement with respect to an indicator requires us to take account of not just inequality in the distribution of

---

[2] Anand and Sen (1997) compared Honduras (with an average literacy rate of 75 percent, distributed between men and women as 78 percent and 73 percent) and China (with an average literacy rate of 80 percent, distributed between men and women as 92 percent, and 68 percent) and asked which country should be regarded as having the "better" achievement with regard to literacy: China with a higher overall rate or the Honduras with greater gender equality?

[3] As we show in the Chapter 3, under certain specific conditions, overall inequality can be represented as the sum of between- and within-group inequality or, in the jargon of inequality analysis, inequality is additively decomposable.

that achievement between its social groups but also, *within each group*, inequality in the distribution of that achievement between its members.[4]

The details of the methodology that underpins this concept of "equity-adjusted achievement" adjustment are contained in an appendix to this chapter. Here, in the main text, we set out (Section 2.2) the broad thrust of the argument underlying this methodology. Then, in subsequent sections, we use this methodology to compute human development indices—and "extended" human development indices for a number of social groups in India. As is well known, conventional HDI embodies three elements: education (literacy rate), health (life expectancy), and income. To this list, we added two further components and, thereby, arrive at an "extended" HDI which includes living conditions and social networks as additional items. Living conditions are important because the vast majority of households in India lack, for example, even basic toilet facilities so that the majority of Indians defecate in the open. Social networks are important because there is a great volume of, admittedly anecdotal, evidence that it is difficult in India to have easy access to essential services unless one "knows someone" or, in the vernacular, has *jaan-pehchaan*.[5]

The empirical basis for the work in this chapter was provided by data from the IHDS. This survey was conducted in 2004–05 by the University of Maryland in collaboration with the National Council of Applied Economic Research, New Delhi between November 2004 and October 2005. The nationally representative data cover 1,504 villages and 971 urban areas across 33 states and union territories of India. The survey covering 41,554 households, encompassing 215,754 persons, was carried out through face-to-face interviews by pairs of male and female enumerators in local languages. The respondents included a person who was knowledgeable about the household economic situation (usually the male head of the household) and an ever-married woman aged 15–49 years. The detailed modules of the survey provide answers to a wide range of questions relating to *inter alia* economic activity, income and consumption expenditure, asset ownership, social capital, education, health, marriage, and fertility.

---

[4] These *members* could be households or persons.
[5] Indeed, in the words of a well-known Hindi song (now used to sell Heineken beer), *jaan-pehchaan hai, jeena asaan hai* (living is easy because I know people).

2.2. Equity Sensitive Achievements

We know that the average achievement of a country is not achieved by all its groups. Similarly, the average achievement of a group is not achieved by all its members. In other words, there is inequality in the distribution of achievements between groups and between individuals in groups. If, as is the convention in economics, we regard inequality as undesirable (*bad*) then, in assessing the achievement of a country or of a group, by how much should we reduce its average achievement to take account of inequality in achievements?

The answer to this question depends on how *averse we are to inequality*. In his seminal paper on income inequality, Atkinson (1970) argued that we (society) would be prepared to accept a reduction from a higher average income, which was *unequally* distributed to a lower average income that was *equally* distributed.[6] The size of this reduction would depend upon our degree of "inequality aversion," which Atkinson (1970) measured by the value of an "inequality aversion parameter," $\varepsilon \geq 0$. When $\varepsilon = 0$, we are *not at all* averse to inequality implying that we would not be prepared to accept even the smallest reduction in average income in order to secure an equitable distribution. The degree of inequality aversion increases with the value of ε: the higher the value of ε, the more *averse* we are to inequality and the *greater* the reduction in average income we would find acceptable to secure an equal distribution of income.

We can reduce the average "achievement, $\bar{X}$, of a country by the amount of inter-group inequality in achievements to arrive at X^e, an 'equity-sensitive' achievement for the country, $X^e \leq \bar{X}$." Similarly, we can reduce the average achievement of a group, $\bar{X}_k$, by the amount of intra-group inequality in achievements to arrive at X_k^e, a person/household "equity sensitive" achievement for the group, $X_k^e \leq \bar{X}_k$. We refer to X^e and X_k^e as *equally distributed equivalent* (EDE) achievements, X^e, when the achievement of each of the groups (equally distributed between the groups) is welfare equivalent to $\bar{X}$; and X_k^e, when the achievement of every member of group k (equally distributed between individuals in a group) is welfare equivalent to $\bar{X}_k$.

---

[6] In the language of economics, the two situations would yield the same level of social welfare, that is, be "welfare equivalent."

The size of these reductions (as given by the differences: $\bar{X} - X^e$ and $\bar{X}_k - X^e_k$) depends upon our aversion to inequality: the lower our aversion to inequality, the smaller will be the difference and, in the extreme case in which there is no aversion to inequality ($\varepsilon = 0$), there will be no difference between the average and the equity sensitive achievements.

Box 2.1:
Inequality aversion and the relationship between mean and EDE achievement

Three special cases, contingent upon the value assumed by ε, can be distinguished:

1. When $\varepsilon = 0$ (no inequality aversion), X^e and X^e_k are the *arithmetic means* of, respectively, the group achievements and of the achievements of persons in group k: $X^e = \bar{X}$ and $X^e_k = \bar{X}_k$.

2. When $\varepsilon = 1$, X^e and X^e_k are the *geometric means* of, respectively, the group achievements and of the achievements of persons in group k:

$$X^e = \left[\prod_{k=1}^{K} \left(X_k \right)^{N_k} \right]^{1/K} < \bar{X} \text{ and } X^e_k = \left[\prod_{i=1}^{N_k} X_{ik} \right]^{1/N_k} < \bar{X}_k.$$

3. When $\varepsilon = 2$, X^e and X^e_k are the *harmonic means* of, respectively, the group achievements and of achievements of persons in group k:

$$X^e = \left[\sum_{k=1}^{K} \frac{n_k}{X_k} \right]^{-1} < \bar{X} \text{ and } X^e_k = \left[\frac{1}{N_k} \sum_{i=1}^{N_k} \frac{1}{X_{ik}} \right]^{-1} < \bar{X}_k.$$

Source: Authors.

2.2.1. The Human Development Index (HDI)

The HDI has been formulated in terms of a country's shortfall with respect to three dimensions: life expectancy, education, and income. Suppose that *X*, *Y*, and *Z* are a country's "achievements" with respect to each of these three dimensions and suppose that Max(*X*), Max(*Y*), and Max(*Z*) are the maximum—and Min(*X*), Min(*Y*), and Min(*Z*) are the minimum—values of these achievements. For example, if, as a surrogate for the "education achievement," *X* is the literacy rate, Max(*X*) = 100 and Min(*X*) = 0. Table 2.1 shows the maximum and minimum values of the various achievements.

Table 2.1:
Maximum and minimum values of HDI achievements

	Minimum Value	Maximum Value
Life expectancy at birth	25 years	85 years
Adult literacy rate (age 15 years and above)	0%	100%
Combined gross enrollment ratio	0%	100%
GDP per capita (PPP US$)	$100	$40,000

Source: Author's own calculations.
Note: PPP, Purchasing power parity.

Following this, the index *for each achievement* is defined as:

$$\text{Index} = \frac{\text{Observed value} - \text{Minimum value}}{\text{Maximum value} - \text{Minimum value}} \times 100$$

and the HDI is defined as:

$$\text{HDI} = \frac{\text{Index}^x + \text{Index}^y + \text{Index}^z}{3}$$

Now suppose that there are five groups (explicitly defined in the next section). If we consider the income index (INI),[7] different households, within each group, will have different INI values and this will yield the group's average INI value: suppose $\bar{X}_1$ represents group 1's average INI value, $\bar{X}_2$ represents group 2's average INI value, and so on till $\bar{X}_5$, which represents group 5's average INI value.[8] The INI value for each group represents the distance between its *actual* achievement and its *potential* achievement, in this case with respect to income; so, for example, INI = 65 for a group means that it fulfils 65 percent of its income potential.

We can compute, *for each group*, its EDE achievement with respect to INI and these are denoted as $X_1^e,...,X_5^e$. In calculating these EDE income indices, we take account of the inequality between the households in each group. By definition:

$$X_1^e \leq \bar{X}_1, X_1^e \leq \bar{X}_2,..., X_5^e \leq \bar{X}_5$$

with equality holding if, and only if, there was no aversion to inequality in computing the EDE income indices.

[7] That is, $\text{Index}_{income} = \dfrac{\text{Observed Income} - \text{Minimum Income}}{\text{Maximum Income} - \text{Minimum Income}}$

[8] Unless explicitly stated otherwise, the average will always be taken to be the arithmetic mean.

Box 2.2:
The process of 1–ε averaging

For the more technically minded reader, the computation of the $X_1^e ... X_5^e$ is through a process of " $(1-\varepsilon)$ averaging," described in the appendix in equations (2.8) and (2.14). For the reader less interested in technical details, suffice it to say that along with X^e, we can also compute the EDE education indices for the five groups as, $Y_1^e ...Y_5^e$, and the EDE life-expectancy indices for the five groups as $Z_1^e ....Z_5^e$, and having done so, contrast them with their corresponding average values $\bar{Y}_1....\bar{Y}_5$ and $\bar{Z}_1....\bar{Z}_5$.

Following from this, we can compute the conventional and equity sensitive HDI for each group k $(k = 1...K)$—respectively, HDI_k^{avg} and HDI_k^{eqs} – as:

$$HDI_k^{avg} = \frac{\bar{X}_k + \bar{Y}_k + \bar{Z}_k}{3} \text{ and } HDI_k^{eqs} = \frac{X_k^e + Y_k^e + Z_k^e}{3}$$

This is equation (2.15) of the appendix.

Source: Authors.

We can then compute the EDE index values for the country, with respect to each of the three achievements by aggregating over the groups. In doing so, we take account of inequality in the distribution of the values of the INI over all the households in the country. That is, we take account of *both* inequality *between* groups and inequality *within* groups to compute the country's EDE achievement with respect to values of the INI. This is represented by X^e where $X^e \leq \bar{X}$ and the gap between the equity sensitive achievement, X^e and the average achivement, $\bar{X}$, depends upon our aversion to inequality: in the extreme case, when there is no aversion to inequality, $X^e = \bar{X}$. Similarly, we compute Y^e (EDE education index) and Z^e (EDE life-expectancy index).[9]

Following this, we can compute the *conventional* and the *equity sensitive* HDI for the country respectively, HDI^{avg} and HDI^{eqs} – as:[10]

$$HDI^{avg} = \frac{\bar{X} + \bar{Y} + \bar{Z}}{3} \text{ and } HDI^{eqs} = \frac{X^e + Y^e + Z^e}{3}$$

In the subsequent sections, we present calculations of the group-specific and the national HDI values for India: HDI_k^{avg}, HDI_k^{eqs}, HDI^{avg}, and HDI^{eqs}.

[9] As earlier, we use the technique of "1–ε averaging" as set out in equation (2.16).
[10] This is equation (2.17) of the appendix.

Box 2.3:
Only taking account of between-group inequality

We could have chosen to *ignore* within-group inequality by assuming that every household in a group earns that group's average income. On this assumption, we can compute the country's EDE achievement with respect to the income index as X_B^e where $X_B^e \leq \bar{X}$ and the gap between X_B^e and $\bar{X}$, the average achievement value, depends upon our aversion to inequality (in the extreme case, when there is no aversion to inequality, $X_B^e = \bar{X}$). Following from this, we can compute the conventional and equity sensitive HDI for the country respectively, HDI^{avg} and $\text{HDI}_B^{\text{eqs}}$ – *taking account only of between-group inequality*, as:

$$\text{HDI}^{\text{avg}} = \frac{\bar{X} + \bar{Y} + \bar{Z}}{3} \text{ and } \text{HDI}_B^{\text{eqs}} = \frac{X_B^e + Y_B^e + Z_B^e}{3}$$

This is equation (2.20) of the appendix.

Source: Authors.

2.3. Data and Analysis: The Component Indices

As mentioned earlier in the chapter, the data for the analysis were provided by the household file of the IHDS, which provided information, pertaining to 2004, on over 41,000 households spread over India. Using these data, the households were divided into the following mutually exclusive groups (with details in Table 2.2):

Table 2.2:
Caste and religion of households in the IHDS

	Upper-caste Hindus	OBC Hindus	Scheduled Castes*	Scheduled Tribes**	Muslims	All Groups***
Number of households (rural + urban)	9,540	13,875	8,333	3,439	4,708	39,885
Number of households (rural)	5,022	9,543	6,011	2,940	2,527	26,043
Number of households (urban)	4,518	4,332	2,322	499	2,181	13,852

Source: IHDS.

Notes: * Of the 8,333 SC households, 7,724 were Hindus and the rest were Buddhist, Christian, or Sikh.

** Of the 3,439 ST households, 2,488 were Hindus, 484 were Christians, and 412 were Tribals.

*** There were also 1,659 households (968 rural and 691 urban) who were Sikh/Jain/Christian. These were not analyzed.

1. HCH households comprising brahmin and other upper-caste Hindus
2. Hindus from the other backward classes (HOBC)
3. SCs
4. STs
5. Muslims

Subsequent chapters make a distinction between Muslims from the OBC and non-OBC Muslims. Here, however, for ease of analysis, we consider Muslims as a single group in this chapter. We began the exercise by computing each household's achievement with respect to: (i) education, (ii) life expectancy, and (iii) income. These outcomes are reported as follows.

2.3.1. *Education*

The indicator of a household's educational achievement was taken as the *highest* educational level of an adult in the household. The values of this variable, HEL_h, for household h, were coded as: 15 (highest value) for a graduate and 0 (lowest value) for "no education," and Table 2.3 shows its average value for different social groups in both rural and urban contexts. The average value of this variable was 7.7 for all households with the highest value of 10.2 being recorded for HCH households and lowest values being recorded for SC (6.1), ST (5.4), and Muslim (6.3) households.

Table 2.3:
The highest level of education of a household adult, by social group*

	All Households	High-caste Hindus	Scheduled Castes	Scheduled Tribes	OBC Hindus	Muslims
All-India						
Number of households	33,443	7,595	6,836	2,610	11,239	3,903
Education level	7.7	10.2	6.1	5.4	7.7	6.3
Rural						
Number of households	21,634	4,011	4,902	2,231	7,654	2,088
Education level	6.6	8.9	5.4	4.6	6.8	5.4
Urban						
Number of households	11.809	3,584	1,934	379	3,585	1,815
Education level	9.7	11.7	7.9	9.5	9.6	7.4

Source: IHDS.
Notes: *Defined as years of education: 0 (none), 1, 2, 3, 4, 5 (5th standard), 6, 7, 8, 9, 10 (matriculation), 11, 12 (higher secondary), 13, 14, 15 (graduate or above).

The household's "highest education" index, HEI_h, was defined (for minimum and maximum years of education of 0 and 15, respectively) as:

$$\text{HEI}_h = \frac{\text{HEI}_h - 0}{15 - 0} \times 100$$

This can be interpreted as its *achievement rate* with respect to education: it is the percentage distance, which a household has travelled in fulfilling its "educational potential." The values of this index are shown in Table 2.4 for different social groups, in both rural and urban contexts.

Table 2.4:
Highest education index values for India, by social group*

	All Households	High-caste Hindus	Scheduled Castes	Scheduled Tribes	OBC Hindus	Muslims
All-India						
Number of households	39,895	9,540	8,333	3,439	13,875	4,708
$\text{HEI}_{\varepsilon=0}$	49.7	67.5	39.5	34.8	49.9	41.6
$\text{HEI}_{\varepsilon=0.5}$	37.3	60.4	26.2	20.7	38.5	28.5
$\mu \times (1-\text{Gini})$	30.3	51.1	21.0	16.3	31.4	22.8
Rural						
Number of households	26,043	5,022	6,011	2,940	9,543	2,527
$\text{HEI}_{\varepsilon=0}$	41.9	57.2	34.5	30.1	43.8	35.3
$\text{HEI}_{\varepsilon=0.5}$	29.0	48.5	21.0	16.8	31.8	22.0
$\mu \times (1-\text{Gini})$	23.3	40.3	16.8	13.2	25.7	17.4
Urban						
Number of households	13,852	4,518	2,322	499	4,332	2,181
$\text{HEI}_{\varepsilon=0}$	64.3	78.9	52.7	62.2	63.2	48.9
$\text{HEI}_{\varepsilon=0.5}$	55.8	75.1	42.4	51.9	55.7	37.2
$\mu \times (1-\text{Gini})$	46.8	66.0	34.6	43.9	46.6	30.2

Source: IHDS.

Notes: *For *every household*, its HEI = [(Highest education level of adult–Minimum possible education level) / (Maximum possible education of household adult–Minimum possible education level)] × 100. The maximum and minimum possible education levels were, respectively, 15 and 0. Consequently, for every household, $0 \le \text{HEI} \le 100$.

ε is the degree of inequality aversion: $\varepsilon = 0$ implies no aversion to inequality; $\varepsilon > 0$ implies aversion to inequality.

μ is the mean level of attainment (HEI: $\varepsilon = 0$) and $\mu \times (1-\text{Gini})$ is Sen's measure of social welfare.

The row titled "$\text{HEI}_{\varepsilon=0}$," in Table 2.4, shows the mean value of the HEI. The values in this row show that households in India, *considered in their entirety*, realized 50 percent of their "educational potential." At the level of the groups, HCH households realized 68 percent of their potential compared to only 40 percent, 35 percent, and 42 percent for, respectively, SC, ST, and Muslim households.

The row titled "$HEI_{\varepsilon = 0.5}$" in Table 2.4 shows the *equity-sensitive* value of this index. The values of this index were obtained by adjusting the household HEI values for inequality with the value of the inequality aversion parameter, $\varepsilon = 0.5$. The values alongside this row are the EDE HEI values. For any group, $HEI_{\varepsilon = 0.5}$ takes account of inequality in the distribution of the HEI values between the households in that group. For India as a whole, $HEI_{\varepsilon = 0.5}$ takes account of the inequality in the distribution of the values of the HEI values over all the households in the country or, equivalently, *takes account of both inequality between groups and within groups.*

When inequality aversion is measured by $\varepsilon = 0.5$, we regard an achievement rate of 60 percent for HCH—*with every HCH household having this achievement rate*—as being "welfare equivalent" to (that is, yielding the same amount of social welfare as) a mean HCH rate of 68 percent with achievement rates varying across households in the HCH group. Similarly, we regard an SC achievement rate of 26 percent—*with every SC household having this achievement rate*—as being "welfare equivalent" to (that is, yielding the same amount of social welfare) a mean SC rate of 40 percent with achievement rates varying across households in the SC group. Compared to HCH households, the HEI values are more unequally distributed among the SC, ST, and Muslim households and, so, the fall from the mean index value ($HEI_{\varepsilon = 0}$) to the equity-sensitive value ($HEI_{\varepsilon = 0.5}$) is greatest for the SC (40 percent$\rightarrow$ 26 percent), ST (35 percent$\rightarrow$ 21 percent), and Muslim households (42 percent$\rightarrow$ 29 percent) and relatively small for HCH households (68 percent$\rightarrow$ 60 percent).

The row titled "$\mu \times (1-\text{Gini})$" in Table 2.3 is Sen's (1992) measure of social welfare. This measure says that the social welfare emanating from a given mean outcome (μ) should be adjusted downward by the amount of inequality in the distribution of outcomes between households to reflect the fact that inequality is welfare reducing. Sen's measure results from using the Gini coefficient as the inequality measure. Because the degree of inequality as measured by the Gini coefficient is greater than the degree of inequality as measured by Atkinson's index (with $\varepsilon = 0.5$), $\mu \times (1-\text{Gini})$ is smaller than $HEI_{\varepsilon = 0.5}$. In terms of "welfare equivalence," the mean achievement of 50 percent is worth an achievement rate of only 30 percent.

2.3.2. Life Expectancy

In order to determine life expectancy, we focused on the 1,603 households in which a death had occurred in the 12 months prior to the survey. Table 2.5 shows that the mean age at death, across all these 1,603 households in which a death had occurred in the past 12 months, was 52 years. The highest age at death was 56 years for HCH households, with SC, ST, and Muslim households recording the lowest ages at death of 49, 44, and 48 years, respectively.

Table 2.5:
Average age at death in India, by social group*

	All Households	High-caste Hindus	Scheduled Castes	Scheduled Tribes	OBC Hindus	Muslims
All-India						
Number of households	1,288	249	280	105	475	144
Age at death (years)	52	57	49	45	53	49
Rural						
Number of households	928	148	225	91	365	76
Age at death (years)	51	53	49	44	54	48
Urban						
Number of households	360	101	55	14	110	68
Age at death (years)	53	60	51	40	50	47

Source: IHDS.
Note: *For households in which a death had occurred in the past year.

The household's life expectancy index, LEI_h was defined as:

$$LEI_h = \frac{LEL_h - 0}{100 - 0} \times 100$$

and this can be interpreted as its *achievement rate* with respect to life expectancy: it is the percentage distance that a household has travelled in fulfilling its "life expectancy" potential. The values of this index (achievement rate) are shown in Table 2.6 for different social groups, in both rural and urban contexts.

As in Table 2.4, the row titled "LEI ($\varepsilon = 0$)," in Table 2.6, shows the mean value of the "life-expectancy" index. By construction, these values are equivalent to years of life and, in the discussion below, this is how they are referred to. The values in this row show that households in India, considered in their entirety, had a life expectancy (for their members) of 52 years, with a life expectancy of 57 years for HCH households and life expectancies of 50, 45, and 49 years, respectively, for SC, ST, and Muslim households.

The row titled "$LEI_{\varepsilon = 0.5}$" in Table 2.6 shows the *equity-sensitive* value of this index obtained by adjusting the household LEI values for inequality, with the value of the inequality aversion parameter, $\varepsilon = 0.5$.[11] A life expectancy of 52 years for HCH—*with every HCH household having this life expectancy*—is "welfare equivalent" to (that is, yields the same amount of social welfare) a mean HCH life expectancy of 57 years with this expectancy varying between households in the HCH group. Similarly, a life expectancy of 42 years for SC households—*with every SC household having this life expectancy*—is "welfare equivalent" to (that is, yields the same amount of social welfare as) a mean SC life expectancy of 50 years with this expectancy varying across households in the SC group.[12]

Table 2.6:
*Life-expectancy index values for India, by social group***

	All Households	High-caste Hindus	Scheduled Castes	Scheduled Tribes	OBC Hindus	Muslims
All-India						
Number of households	1,620	328	371	137	594	190
$LEI_{\varepsilon = 0}$	51.8	57.1	49.8	45.3	52.7	48.4
$LEI_{\varepsilon = 0.5}$	44.3	52.1	42.3	37.0	45.1	38.9
$\mu \times (1\text{–Gini})$	36.1	43.0	34.0	29.7	37.0	31.5

Table 2.6 continued

[11] For any group, $LEI_{\varepsilon = 0.5}$ takes account of inequality in the distribution of the LEI values between the households in that group. For India as a whole, $LEI_{\varepsilon = 0.5}$ takes account of inequality in the distribution of the values of the LEI values over all the households in the country or, equivalently, takes account of both inequality between groups and within groups.

[12] The row titled "$\mu \times (1\text{–Gini})$" in Table 2.6 is Sen's measure of social welfare. This measure says that the social welfare emanating from a given mean outcome (μ) should be adjusted downward by the amount of inequality (as measured by the Gini coefficient) in the distribution of outcomes between households to reflect the fact that inequality is welfare reducing.

Table 2.6 continued

	All Households	High-caste Hindus	Scheduled Castes	Scheduled Tribes	OBC Hindus	Muslims
Rural						
Number of households	*1,172*	*199*	*291*	*120*	*456*	*106*
$LEI_{\varepsilon=0}$	51.5	54.6	49.8	45.4	53.6	48.5
$LEI_{\varepsilon=0.5}$	43.8	48.9	42.1	37.0	45.9	38.7
$\mu \times (1-Gini)$	35.5	39.7	33.7	29.5	37.8	31.4
Urban						
Number of households	*448*	*129*	*80*	*17*	*138*	*84*
$LEI_{\varepsilon=0}$	52.6	60.7	49.8	45.1	50.1	48.3
$LEI_{\varepsilon=0.5}$	45.7	57.2	43.3	36.4	42.6	39.1
$\mu \times (1-Gini)$	37.7	48.4	35.1	32.0	34.8	31.8

Source: Author's own calculations from IHDS data.
Notes: * For each household, the LEI = [(Age at death–Minimum age of death)/(Maximum age at death–Minimum age of death)] × 100. The maximum age at death in the sample was 100 years. Consequently, 0 ≤ LEI ≤ 100.
ε is the degree of inequality aversion: $\varepsilon = 0$ implies no aversion to inequality; $\varepsilon > 0$ implies aversion to inequality.
μ is the mean level of attainment (LEI: $\varepsilon = 0$) and $\mu \times (1-Gini)$ is Sen's measure of social welfare.

2.3.3. *Income*

The IHDS reported the total income of each of the households in the survey with the mean and median monthly household incomes being, respectively, ₹52,369 and ₹30,790. From this income data, the IHDS constructed income quintiles (INQs) and reported each household according to the INQ to which it belonged: $INQ_h = 5$, if household h belonged to quintile 5 (richest), $INQ_h = 4$, if household h belonged to quintile 4, and so on till $INQ_h = 1$, if household h belonged to quintile 1 (poorest).[13] As Table 2.7 shows the mean value of INQ_h over all households was 3.1 with HCH and ST households having the highest and lowest INQ values: respectively, 3.7 and 2.6.

[13] Households reporting negative incomes were excluded.

Table 2.7:
Average quintile of total household income for India, by social group*

	All Households	High-caste Hindus	Scheduled Castes	Scheduled Tribes	OBC Hindus	Muslims
All-India						
Number of households	33,482	7,600	6,850	2,611	11,249	3,911
Income level	3.1	3.7	2.8	2.6	3.0	3.1
Rural						
Number of households	21,663	4,015	4,913	2,232	7,662	2,092
Income level	2.8	3.3	2.6	2.4	2.7	2.8
Urban						
Number of households	11.819	3,585	1,937	379	3,587	1,819
Income level	3.8	4.2	3.5	3.9	3.7	3.5

Source: Author's own calculations from IHDS data.
Note: *The income quintiles of household income were: 1st (poorest); 2nd and 3rd (middle); 4th and 5th (affluent).

The household's income quintile index, IQI_h was defined as:

$$IQI_h = \frac{INQ_h - 1}{5 - 1} \times 100$$

and this can be interpreted as its *achievement rate* with respect to income: it is the percentage distance that a household has travelled in fulfilling its *income* potential. The values of this index (achievement rate) are shown in Table 2.8 for different social groups, in both rural and urban contexts.

The row titled "$IQI_{\varepsilon = 0}$," in Table 2.8 shows the mean value of this index. On this calculation, households in India, considered in their entirety, realized 53 percent of their "income potential" in the context of which HCH households realized 69 percent of their potential while the SC, ST, and Muslim households were able to realize only 46 percent, 41 percent, and 54 percent, respectively, of their income potential. The row titled "$IQI_{\varepsilon = 0.5}$" in Table 2.8 shows the *equity-sensitive* value of this index: with the value of the inequality aversion parameter, ε, set to 0.5. The values alongside this row are the EDE INI values, taking into account inequality in the distribution of the *IQI* values between the relevant households. When inequality aversion is measured by ε = 0.5, we regard an index value of 41 percent—*with every household having this value*—as being "welfare equivalent" to a mean rate of 53 percent *with the IQI values being distributed unequally between the households.*

Table 2.8:
Income quintile index values for India, by social group *

	All Households	High-caste Hindus	Scheduled Castes	Scheduled Tribes	OBC Hindus	Muslims
All-India						
Number of households	39,895	9,540	8,333	3,439	13,875	4,708
$IQI_{\varepsilon=0}$	53.3	68.6	45.7	41.2	50.2	53.9
$IQI_{\varepsilon=0.5}$	41.4	59.3	34.0	27.9	37.8	43.6
μ × (1–Gini)	33.2	50.5	26.7	21.6	30.2	35.0
Rural						
Number of households	26,043	5,022	6,011	2,940	9,543	2,527
$IQI_{\varepsilon=0}$	44.2	57.8	38.8	35.8	42.5	46.2
$IQI_{\varepsilon=0.5}$	31.4	46.0	26.9	23.3	29.4	34.5
μ × (1–Gini)	24.6	37.7	21.0	17.9	23.1	27.2
Urban						
Number of households	13,852	4,518	2,322	499	4,332	2,181
$IQI_{\varepsilon=0}$	70.3	80.5	63.7	72.3	66.9	62.6
$IQI_{\varepsilon=0.5}$	63.4	75.8	55.9	63.8	59.4	55.3
μ × (1–Gini)	53.7	67.4	46.1	55.1	49.8	45.5

Source: Author's own calculations from IHDS data.
Notes: *For every household, its IQI = [(Household income quintile–Minimum possible income quintile)/(Maximum possible income quintile–Minimum possible income quintile)] × 100. The maximum and minimum possible income quintiles were, respectively, 5 and 1. Consequently, for every household, $0 \leq IQI \leq 100$.
ε is the degree of inequality aversion: ε = 0 implies no aversion to inequality; ε > 0 implies aversion to inequality.
μ is the mean level of attainment (*IQI*: ε = 0) and μ × (1–*Gini*) is Sen's measure of social welfare.

Because intra-group inequality in the distribution of the *IQI* values was not very different among the SC, ST, and Muslim households, compared to HCH households, the *reduction* from the mean achievement rate $(IQI_{\varepsilon=0})$[14]

[14] Note that the mean achievement rate is the EDE value for ε = 0, that is, when there is no aversion to inequality.

to the equity-sensitive rate ($IQI_{\varepsilon = 0.5}$) was not very different for the four household groups: SC households (46 percent→ 34 percent), ST households (41 percent→ 28 percent), Muslim households (54 percent→ 44 percent), and HCH households (69 percent→ 59 percent). Similarly, because the degree of inequality as measured by the Gini coefficient is greater than the degree of inequality as measured by Atkinson's index (with $\varepsilon = 0.5$), $\mu \times (1-Gini)$ is smaller than $IQI_{\varepsilon = 0.5}$. The mean achievement of 53 percent is, in terms of social welfare, worth an achievement rate of only 33 percent if inequality in the distribution of IQI between households is measured by the Gini coefficient.

2.3.4. Living Conditions Index

The IHDS reported on the living conditions of the households with respect to a number of indicators from which we chose three:

1. The proportion of households who defecated in the open.
2. The proportion of households who did not have piped water.
3. The proportion of households who did not have a vent in the cooking place.

As Table 2.9 shows, 54 percent of households defecated in the open on an all-India basis (70 percent in rural areas), 54 percent did not have piped water (68 percent in rural areas), and 31 percent of households did not have a vent in the cooking place (37 percent of households in rural areas).

Table 2.9:
Living conditions in India, by social group

	Proportion of households who defecate in the open					
	All Household	*High-caste Hindus*	*Scheduled Castes*	*Scheduled Tribes*	*OBC Hindus*	*Muslims*
All-India	53.7	38.2	69.6	74.1	58.9	37.6
Rural	69.8	59.8	80.4	81.4	74.3	49.5
Urban	24.0	13.9	42.2	31.3	25.7	23.9

Table 2.9 continued

Table 2.9 continued

	Proportion of households who do not have piped water					
	All Household	High-caste Hindus	Scheduled Castes	Scheduled Tribes	OBC Hindus	Muslims
All-India	53.9	42.4	57.2	68.0	54.3	59.2
Rural	68.0	59.1	69.1	75.7	66.1	78.6
Urban	27.9	23.7	27.0	22.7	29.1	36.9

	Proportion of households who do not have a vent in cooking place					
	All Household	High-caste Hindus	Scheduled Castes	Scheduled Tribes	OBC Hindus	Muslims
All-India	31.4	21.8	40.8	48.5	32.5	24.7
Rural	37.1	27.2	45.2	51.5	37.0	26.7
Urban	22.2	16.4	31.1	30.5	23.6	22.7

Source: Author's own calculations from IHDS data.

The "living condition" index (LCI) of a household was defined as:

$$LCI_h = \left(0.7 \times \text{Toilet} + 0.15 \times \text{Piped water} + 0.15 \times \text{Vent}\right) \times 100$$

where the relevant variable took the value 1 if the condition was present, 0 if it was not. Consequently, for every household, $0 \leq LCI_h \leq 100$. The values of the LCI are shown in Table 2.10.

Table 2.10:
Living condition index values for India, by social group*

	All Households	High-caste Hindus	Scheduled Castes	Scheduled Tribes	OBC Hindus	Muslims
All-India						
Number of households	30,663	7,442	5,959	2,866	11,030	3,366
LCI ($\varepsilon = 0$)	51.5	67.1	39.2	32.9	48.0	66.0
LCI ($\varepsilon = 0.5$)	38.5	57.2	26.8	18.8	35.1	56.5
$\mu \times (1\text{–Gini})$	29.4	47.3	19.0	13.3	26.2	47.0
Rural						
Number of households	19,382	3,712	4,140	2,445	7,383	1,702
LCI ($\varepsilon = 0$)	36.6	48.0	28.3	26.6	34.6	55.2
LCI ($\varepsilon = 0.5$)	24.1	36.4	17.4	13.9	22.6	44.0
$\mu \times (1\text{–Gini})$	17.1	27.0	12.0	9.7	15.8	35.0

Table 2.10 continued

Table 2.10 continued

Urban						
Number of households	*11,281*	*3,730*	*1,819*	*421*	*3,647*	*1,664*
LCI (ε = 0)	77.0	85.9	64.2	69.3	75.1	77.1
LCI (ε = 0.5)	70.8	82.5	55.5	61.1	68.5	71.0
μ × (1–Gini)	61.4	75.3	44.1	50.3	58.7	61.9

Source: Author's own calculations from IHDS data.

Notes: *For every household, its LCI = (0.7 × Use of toilet + 0.15 × Piped water × 0.15 × Vent in cooking place) × 100. The relevant variable takes the value 1 if the condition is present, 0 if it is not: consequently, for every household, $0 \leq LCI \leq 100$.

ε is the degree of inequality aversion: ε = 0 implies no aversion to inequality; ε > 0 implies aversion to inequality.

μ is the mean level of attainment (LCI: ε = 0) and μ × (1–Gini) is Sen's measure of social welfare.

The row titled "LCI (ε = 0)," in Table 2.10, shows the mean value of this index: on this calculation, households in India, considered in its entirety, realized 52 percent of their "living condition potential" in the context of which HCH households realized 67 percent of their potential, while the SC and ST households were able to realize only 39 percent and 33 percent, respectively, of their living condition potential.

The row titled "LCI (ε = 0.5)" in Table 2.10 shows the *equity-sensitive* value of this index with the value of the inequality aversion parameter, ε, set to 0.5. The values alongside this row are the EDELCI values taking into account inequality in the distribution of the LCI values between the relevant households. When inequality aversion is measured by ε = 0.5, we regard an achievement rate of 39 percent—*with every household having this achievement rate* as being "welfare equivalent" to a mean rate of 52 percent with the LCI values being distributed unequally between the households.[15]

Because intra-group inequality in the distribution of the LCI values was different among the HCH, SC, ST, and Muslim households, the *reduction* from the mean achievement rate ($LCI_{\varepsilon = 0}$) to the equity-sensitive rate ($LCI_{\varepsilon = 0.5}$) was different for the household groups: HCH households

---

[15] The row titled "μ × (1–Gini)" in Table 2.10 is Sen's measure of social welfare with respect to living conditions. This measure says that the social welfare emanating from a given mean outcome (μ) should be adjusted downward by the amount of inequality in the distribution of outcomes between households/individuals to reflect the fact that inequality is welfare reducing.

(67 percent → 57 percent), SC households (39 percent → 27 percent), ST households (33 percent → 19 percent), and Muslim households (66 percent → 57 percent). Similarly, because the degree of inequality as measured by the Gini coefficient was greater than the degree of inequality as measured by Atkinson's index (with $\varepsilon = 0.5$), $\mu \times (1-\text{Gini})$ was smaller than $\text{LCI}_{\varepsilon = 0.5}$. The mean achievement of 52 percent was, in terms of "welfare equivalence," worth an achievement rate of only 29 percent, if inequality in the distribution of LCI values between households was measured by the Gini coefficient.

2.3.5. Social Networks Index

The IHDS reported on the social networks of each household with respect to a number of indicators designed to measure the range, quality, and the closeness of social contacts:

1. Whether the household knew someone connected with medicine or education or government?
2. If so, was the person a doctor/teacher/officer?
3. If the household knew someone connected with the above areas, was he/she from the same or a different *jati* to the household?

As Table 2.11 shows, 33 percent of households knew someone associated with medicine, 41 percent knew someone connected with education, and 36 percent knew someone in government. Of those households who knew someone connected with medicine or education or government, 25 percent knew a doctor, 36 percent knew a teacher, and 16 percent knew an officer. Of those households who knew someone connected with medicine or education or government, the proportions of acquaintances from the same *jati* were: 12 percent for medicine, 20 percent for education, and 22 percent for government.

Table 2.11:
Social networks in India, by social group

	Proportion of households who know a person associated with medicine					
	All Households	*HCH Households*	*Scheduled Castes*	*Scheduled Tribes*	*OBC Hindus*	*Muslims*
All-India	32.7	41.6	27.6	22.6	32.6	26.9
Rural	30.8	40.9	26.3	19.5	31.6	26.2
Urban	36.2	42.3	30.9	40.7	34.7	27.7
If yes, from the same *jati*						
All-India	12.4	18.1	7.2	10.2	11.1	13.2
Rural	10.9	17.4	6.6	8.1	9.6	12.1
Urban	15.4	18.9	8.8	22.4	14.1	14.4
If yes, the person is a doctor						
All-India	24.7	32.5	20.9	14.9	24.7	20.4
Rural	23.2	32.0	19.9	12.7	23.9	20.0
Urban	27.6	33.2	23.3	27.4	26.2	20.9

	Proportion of households who know a person associated with education					
	All Households	*HCH Households*	*Scheduled Castes*	*Scheduled Tribes*	*OBC Hindus*	*Muslims*
All-India	41.3	52.7	34.1	32.6	41.9	33.0
Rural	40.5	53.8	33.9	29.8	42.1	34.2
Urban	42.6	51.4	34.8	48.8	41.5	31.5
If yes, from the same *jati*						
All-India	20.4	29.7	12.7	17.0	19.6	18.8
Rural	19.2	30.9	11.9	15.0	18.6	19.3
Urban	22.6	28.3	14.7	28.5	21.7	18.4
If yes, the person is a teacher						
All-India	36.0	45.9	29.8	28.6	36.7	28.3
Rural	35.8	48.2	30.0	26.7	37.0	29.4
Urban	36.4	43.4	29.3	39.8	36.1	26.9

	Proportion of households who know a person associated with government					
	All Households	*HCH Households*	*Scheduled Castes*	*Scheduled Tribes*	*OBC Hindus*	*Muslims*
All-India	35.6	49.3	30.5	23.8	33.6	28.4
Rural	30.6	44.6	26.7	19.1	29.4	24.9
Urban	44.8	54.6	40.0	51.2	42.6	32.5
If yes, from the same *jati*						
All-India	22.0	30.8	17.8	17.5	20.4	19.5
Rural	19.0	27.9	15.2	14.4	18.0	17.4
Urban	27.6	34.1	24.0	35.9	25.5	21.9

Table 2.11 continued

Table 2.11 continued

If yes, the person is an officer						
All-India	*15.9*	*26.2*	*12.0*	*10.7*	*13.6*	*10.3*
Rural	*13.1*	*23.4*	*10.6*	*8.2*	*10.9*	*10.0*
Urban	*21.1*	*29.3*	*15.5*	*25.6*	*19.2*	*10.4*

Source: Author's own calculations from IHDS data.

Using this information, we defined the *Jaan-pehchaan* index (JPI) with respect to the kth contact type (k = medicine, education, government) in terms of the three dimensions of existence, quality, and proximity as:

$$JPI_k = \left(0.5 \times Existence_k + 0.3 \times Quality_k + 0.2 \times Proximity_k\right) \times 100$$

The relevant variables in the above relation take the value 1 if the social network condition is present, namely has a contact; the contact is a high quality contact (doctor, teacher, officer); and the contact is of the same *jati*. It takes the value of 0 if it is not. Consequently, $0 \le JPI_k \le 100$. The overall index is:

$$JPI = \left(1/3\right)JPI_1 + \left(1/3\right)JPI_2 + \left(1/3\right)JPI_3$$

where, by construction, $0 \le JPI \le 100$.

Table 2.12 shows the values of this index for different groups on an all-India, rural India, and urban India basis. The row titled "$JPI_{\varepsilon=0}$" in Table 2.12 shows the mean value of this index: on this calculation, households in India, considered in their entirety, realized 29 percent of their "*Jaan-Pehchaan* potential" in the context of which HCH households realized 40 percent of their potential while the SC, ST, and Muslim households were able to realize only 24 percent, 22 percent, and 24 percent, respectively, of their *Jaan-pehchaan* potential.

The row titled "$JPI_{\varepsilon=0.5}$"in Table 2.12 shows the *equity-sensitive* value of this index with the value of the inequality aversion parameter, $\varepsilon = 0.5$. The values alongside this row are the EDE JPI values taking into account inequality in the distribution of the JPI values between the relevant households. When inequality aversion is measured by $\varepsilon = 0.5$, we regard a JPI value of 15 percent—*with every household having this value*—as being "welfare equivalent" to a mean rate of 29 percent ,with the JPI values being distributed unequally between the households.[16]

---

[16] The row titled "$\mu \times$ (1–Gini)" in Table 2.10 is Sen's measure of social welfare respect to living conditions. This measure says that the social welfare emanating from a given mean outcome (μ) should be adjusted downward by the amount of inequality in the distribution of outcomes between households/individuals to reflect the fact that inequality is welfare reducing.

Table 2.12:
Social network (Jaan-pehchaan) index values for India, by social group*

	All Households	HCH Households	Scheduled Castes	Scheduled Tribes	OBC Hindus	Muslims
All-India						
Number of households	*39,116*	*9,365*	*8,202*	*3,344*	*13,604*	*4,601*
$JPI_{\varepsilon=0}$	28.7	39.7	23.5	21.6	27.8	23.8
$JPI_{\varepsilon=0.5}$	14.9	25.8	10.7	8.7	14.4	10.7
$\mu \times (1–Gini)$	11.5	20.3	8.2	6.6	11.2	8.3
Rural						
Number of households	*25,508*	*4,945*	*5,919*	*2,849*	*9,344*	*2,451*
$JPI_{\varepsilon=0}$	26.4	38.2	22.0	18.5	26.1	23.0
$JPI_{\varepsilon=0.5}$	12.9	24.1	9.5	6.7	13.1	10.1
$\mu \times (1–Gini)$	10.0	19.0	7.4	5.1	10.2	7.8
Urban						
Number of households	*13,608*	*4,420*	*2,283*	*495*	*4,260*	*2,150*
$JPI_{\varepsilon=0}$	33.2	41.3	27.4	39.2	31.5	24.7
$JPI_{\varepsilon=0.5}$	19.1	27.9	14.1	24.3	17.5	11.5
$\mu \times (1–Gini)$	14.8	21.9	10.8	19.1	13.5	8.8

Source: Author's own calculations from IHDS data.
Notes: *Each household's $JPI_k = (0.5 \times$ Existence of contact $+ 0.20 \times$ Proximity of contact $+ 0.30 \times$ Quality of contact) $\times 100$ of the kth contact type. The relevant variables take the value 1 if the social network condition is present: knows a contact; the contact is of the same *jati*; is a high-quality contact and 0 if it is not. The JPI_k values were computed with respect to three different types of contacts: medical, educational, and government. The quality value of a contact was 1 if the contact was a doctor (medical), teacher (educational), or officer (government). Consequently, $0 \leq JPI_k \leq 100$. The overall index $JPI = (1/3)JPI_1 + (1/3)JPI_2 + (1/3)JPI_3$ where, by construction, $0 \leq JPI \leq 100$.
ε is the degree of inequality aversion: $\varepsilon = 0$ implies no aversion to inequality; $\varepsilon > 0$ implies aversion to inequality.
μ is the mean level of attainment (IQI: $\varepsilon = 0$) and $\mu \times (1–Gini)$ is Sen's measure of social welfare.

Because intra-group inequality in the distribution of the JPI values was different among the HCH, SC, ST, and Muslim households, the *reduction* from the mean achievement rate ($JPI_{\varepsilon=0}$) to the equity-sensitive rate ($JPI_{\varepsilon=0.5}$) was different for the household groups: HCH households (40 percent → 20 percent), SC households (24 percent → 8 percent), ST households (22 percent → 7 percent), and Muslim households (24 percent → 8 percent). Similarly, because the degree of inequality as measured by the Gini coefficient is greater than the degree of inequality as measured by Atkinson's index (with $\varepsilon = 0.5$), $\mu \times (1-\text{Gini})$ is smaller than $JPI_{\varepsilon = 0.5}$.

2.4. Data and Analysis: Aggregation over Social Groups

In order to obtain the group achievements with respect to the five components—education, life expectancy, income, living conditions, and social networks—we aggregated over *all* the households in *each* group to obtain the achievement rate of each group with respect to that component.[17] So, Tables 2.4, 2.6, and 2.8 showed the index values of each of the five social groups—HCH, SC, ST, HOBC, and Muslims—with respect to education (Table 2.4), life expectancy (Table 2.6), and INQ (Table 2.8). Tables 2.10 and 2.12 showed, respectively, the achievement rate of each of the five social groups with respect to living conditions (Table 2.10) and social networks (Table 2.12). Consequently, the HDI of *each* group (indexed, $k = 1 \ldots 5$), *with respect to a particular degree of inequality aversion*, for *three* household indicators (education, life expectancy, and income) is defined as the average over the relevant component indices. For three components, it is:

$$\text{HDI3}^k_{\varepsilon=0} = \frac{1}{3}\left(\text{HEI}^k_{\varepsilon=0} + \text{LEI}^k_{\varepsilon=0} + \text{IQI}^k_{\varepsilon=0}\right)$$

$$\text{HDI3}^k_{\varepsilon=0.5} = \frac{1}{3}\left(\text{HEI}^k_{\varepsilon=0.5} + \text{LEI}^k_{\varepsilon=0.5} + \text{IQI}^k_{\varepsilon=0.5}\right)$$

and for *five* household components (education, life expectancy, income, living conditions, and social networks), it is:

$$\text{HDI5}^k_{\varepsilon=0} = \frac{1}{5}\left(\text{HEI}^k_{\varepsilon=0} + \text{LEI}^k_{\varepsilon=0} + \text{IQI}^k_{\varepsilon=0} + \text{LCI}^k_{\varepsilon=0} + \text{JPI5}^k_{\varepsilon=0}\right)$$

$$\text{HDI5}^k_{\varepsilon=0.5} = \frac{1}{5}\left(\text{HEI}^k_{\varepsilon=0.5} + \text{LEI}^k_{\varepsilon=0.5} + \text{IQI}^k_{\varepsilon=0.5} + \text{LCI}^k_{\varepsilon=0.5} + \text{JPI5}^k_{\varepsilon=0.5}\right)$$

---

[17] Using the method of "1–ε averaging" discussed in Box 2.2.

The first panel of Table 2.13 shows the HDI values for each of the five groups taking account of *three* indicators (life expectancy, education, and income) while the second panel of Table 2.13 shows the HDI values for each of the five groups taking account of five indicators (life expectancy, education, income, living conditions, and social networks).

Table 2.13:
Human development index values for India, by social group*

	Panel 1: Three Components				
	HCH	SC	ST	HOBC	Muslims
			All-India		
$HDI_{\varepsilon=0}$	64.4	45.0	40.4	51.0	47.9
$HDI_{\varepsilon=0.5}$	57.3	34.2	28.5	40.5	37.0
			Rural		
$HDI_{\varepsilon=0}$	56.5	41.0	37.1	46.6	43.3
$HDI_{\varepsilon=0.5}$	47.8	30.0	25.7	35.7	31.7
			Urban		
$HDI_{\varepsilon=0}$	73.4	55.4	59.9	60.1	53.3
$HDI_{\varepsilon=0.5}$	69.4	47.2	50.7	52.6	43.9

	Panel 2: Five Components				
	HCH	SC	ST	HOBC	Muslims
			All-India		
$HDI_{\varepsilon=0}$	60.0	39.6	35.1	45.7	46.7
$HDI_{\varepsilon=0.5}$	51.0	28.0	22.6	34.2	35.7
			Rural		
$HDI_{\varepsilon=0}$	51.2	34.7	31.3	40.1	41.6
$HDI_{\varepsilon=0.5}$	40.8	23.4	19.6	28.6	29.9
			Urban		
$HDI_{\varepsilon=0}$	69.5	51.5	57.6	57.4	52.3
$HDI_{\varepsilon=0.5}$	63.7	42.2	47.5	48.7	42.8

Source: Author's own calculations from IHDS data.
Notes: *First panel has three indicators: life expectancy, education, income.
Each household's HDI = (1/3) × LEI + (1/3) × HEI + (1/3) × IQI.
Second panel has five indicators: life expectancy, education, income, living conditions, and social networks.
Each household's HDI = (1/5) × LEI + (1/5) × HEI + (1/5) × IQI + (1/5) × LCI + (1/5) × JPI.

If one interprets a group's HDI value as the percentage fulfillment of its "potential" then, on the basis of *three* indicators, HCH households fulfilled 64 percent of their potential when intra-HCH inequality was ignored

($HDI_{\varepsilon=0}$) and 57 percent of their potential when intra-HCH inequality was taken into account; on the basis of *five* indicators, HCH households fulfilled 60 percent of their potential when intra-HCH inequality was ignored ($HDI_{\varepsilon=0}$) and 51 percent of their potential when intra-HCH inequality was taken into account ($HDI_{\varepsilon=0.5}$).

At the other end of the HDI scale, on the basis of *three* indicators, SC and ST households fulfilled 45 percent and 40 percent, respectively, of their potential when intra-SC (or ST) inequality was ignored ($HDI_{\varepsilon=0}$) and 34 percent and 29 percent of their potential when intra-HCH inequality was taken into account ($HDI_{\varepsilon=0.5}$); on the basis of *five* indicators, SC and ST households fulfilled 40 percent and 35 percent of their potential when intra-SC (or ST) inequality was ignored ($HDI_{\varepsilon=0}$) and 28 percent and 23 percent of their potential when intra-SC (or ST) inequality was taken into account ($HDI_{\varepsilon=0.5}$).

The *all-India* index values for *each* of the five indicators were shown in Tables 2.4, 2.6, 2.8. 2.10, and 2.12, both when intra-household inequality (over *all* the households in India) was ignored ($\varepsilon = 0$) and when it was taken into account ($\varepsilon = 0.5$).[18] Using these values, the all-India HDI were defined, for three indicators, as:

$$HDI3_{\varepsilon=0} = \frac{1}{3}\left(HEI_{\varepsilon=0} + LEI_{\varepsilon=0} + IQI_{\varepsilon=0}\right) \text{ and}$$

$$HDI3_{\varepsilon=0.5} = \frac{1}{3}\left(HEI_{\varepsilon=0.5} + LEI_{\varepsilon=0.5} + IQI_{\varepsilon=0.5}\right)$$

And, for five indicators, as:

$$HDI5_{\varepsilon=0} = \frac{1}{3}\left(HEI_{\varepsilon=0} + LEI_{\varepsilon=0} + IQI_{\varepsilon=0} + LCI_{\varepsilon=0} + JPI5_{\varepsilon=0}\right)$$

$$HDI5_{\varepsilon=0.5} = \frac{1}{3}\left(HEI_{\varepsilon=0.5} + LEI_{\varepsilon=0.5} + IQI_{\varepsilon=0.5} + LCI_{\varepsilon=0.5} + JPI5_{\varepsilon=0.5}\right)$$

These values are shown in Figure 2.1.

---

[18] Note that strictly speaking, this is not the HDI for India since we have considered the social which, in their entirety, comprise most *but not all* of India's population. In particular, (non-SC/ST) Sikhs, Jains, and Christians have been omitted from the analysis.

Figure 2.1:
HDI values for India: Three and five indicators

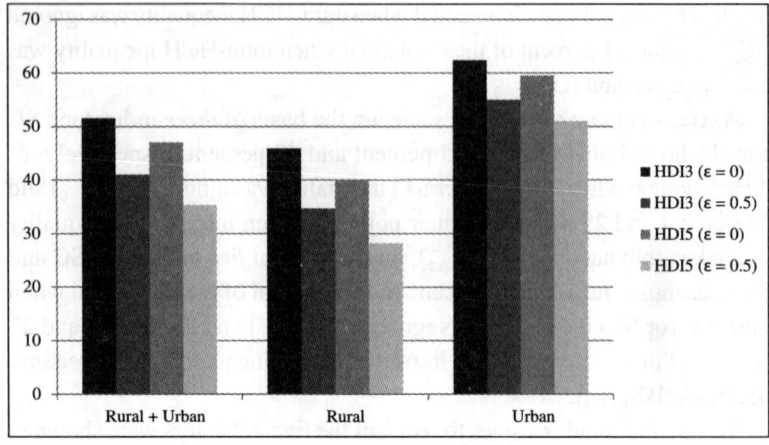

Source: Author's own calculations from IHDS data.

Households in India, considered in its entirety, fulfilled 52 percent of their potential, which could be broken down into: 52 percent for life expectancy, 50 percent for education, and 53 percent for income. When between-group inequality was taken into account, with Atkinson's measure of inequality ($\varepsilon = 0.5$), the overall level of achievement fell to 41 percent and the individual components fell from 52 percent→ 44 percent (life expectancy), 50 percent→ 37 percent (education), and 53 percent→ 41 percent (income).

When an additional two indicators—living conditions and social networks—were added to the three original indicators of life expectancy, education, and income (Table 2.12: second panel) households in India, considered in its entirety, fulfilled 47 percent of their potential, which could be broken down into: 52 percent for life expectancy, 50 percent for education; 53 percent for income; 52 percent for living conditions; and 29 percent for social networks. When between-group inequality was taken into account, with Atkinson's measure of inequality ($\varepsilon = 0.5$), the overall level of achievement fell to 35 percent and the individual components fell from 52 percent→ 38 percent (living conditions) and 29 percent→ 15 percent (social networks).

Box 2.4:
Decomposability

An issue that arises in the study of HDI by social is that of *decomposability*: can the overall HDI value for the country be expressed in terms of the HDI of the social groups that comprise that country's population? It is fairly obvious that when there is no aversion to inequality (that is, the inequality aversion parameter $\varepsilon = 0$), the HDI index can be expressed as a weighted average of the subgroup HDI indices, the weights being the population shares of the different groups. Consequently, the decomposability property is satisfied. However, when there is aversion to inequality ($\varepsilon > 0$), the decomposability property is *not* satisfied and the country HDI *cannot* be expressed as a function of the group HDI.

Source: Authors.

2.5. Conclusions

Although several studies of regional human development exist within the Indian context, the work reported in this chapter represents (to the best of our knowledge) the first systematic attempt to compute HDI values for India's social groups. The novelty of the results presented here is that, by accounting for inequality both within and between social groups, they extend the analysis of mean performance to encompass equity-sensitive human development indices. Another feature to note in our results is that they go beyond the conventional catalog of human development indicators—education, life expectancy, and income—to include living conditions and social networks.

A persistent, and worrying, feature of our analysis is that it shows greater intra-group inequality within marginalized and deprived groups—the SC, the ST, and Muslims—than among the "privileged" HCH. This raises issues of the existence of a "creamy layer" among the deprived groups—the relatively wealthy members of such groups whose existence only serves to highlight the abject poverty of those not in this prosperous category.[19] The existence of such a "creamy layer" implies that when allowance is made for intra-group inequality, the equally distributed index values for deprived groups are considerably lower than their corresponding mean values. Not only are the SC/ST/Muslims deprived, but their

[19] The term *creamy layer* is used here loosely to apply to SC/ST and Muslims. Strictly speaking, in the Indian legal context, it applies only to the OBC.

deprivation is compounded by the fact that such prosperity as might exist among them is captured by a privileged few.

The approach that policy makers in Indian have taken to overcome the economic and social "backwardness" of the SC and the ST has been two-pronged:

1. Specific measures to combat disparity, including legal safeguards against discrimination in education and employment and the practice of untouchability.
2. General measures for the economic and social development of all persons, including persons from the SC and ST.

These policies have, undeniably, brought about improvements but, as our analysis shows, there is considerable distance between the development levels of SC and ST households on the one hand, and HCH households on the other. This implies that in order to improve the performance of the disadvantaged groups on the human development front, it is imperative that measures are taken to improve access to assets like land, jobs, and education.

Like other economically and educationally backward sections from the higher castes, the SC and ST require education and skill development to improve their economic prospects. But, unlike other deprived persons, they face economic and social exclusion and, therefore, require additional protection in the form of anti-discriminatory measures. However, the existence of "exclusion-induced" deprivation means that addressing issues of economic and social exclusion is often more difficult than those of material poverty. Social and cultural sources of exclusion are rooted in "custom and practice," and include the practice of untouchability through caste stigmatization. In this context, efforts to effect the inclusion of groups, which are stigmatized takes on the special difficulty of combating actions sanctioned by religion, culture, custom, and practice. Achieving this is one of the more important challenges facing modern India.

Appendix: Equity Sensitive Indicators of Achievements

Suppose that there are N households in a country—with measured achievements, $X_1, X_2, ..., X_N$—which can be separated into K mutually exclusive social groups ($k = 1...K$) with N_k households ($i = 1...N_k$) in each group, each household with a achievement, X_{ik}, $i = 1...N_k$, $k = 1...K$. We can reduce the average achievement, $\bar{X} = \sum\limits_{i=1}^{N} X_i$, of a country by the amount of *inter-group* inequality in achievements to arrive at X^e, a "group-equity sensitive" achievement for the country, $X^e \leq \bar{X}$. Similarly, we can reduce the average achievement, $\bar{X}_k$, of a group by the amount of *intra-group* inequality in achievements to arrive at X_k^e, a "person-equity sensitive" achievement for the group, $X_k^e \leq \bar{X}_k$. We refer to X^e and X_k^e as *EDE achievements*: X^e, when it is the achievement of each of the groups (equally distributed between the groups), is *welfare equivalent* to $\bar{X}$; and X_k^e, when it is the achievement of every member of group k (equally distributed between individuals in a group), is *welfare equivalent* to $\bar{X}_k$.

The size of these reductions (as given by the differences: $\bar{X} - X^e$ and $\bar{X}_k - X_k^e$) depends upon our aversion to inequality: the lower our aversion to inequality, the smaller will be the difference; in the extreme case in which there is no aversion to inequality, there will be no difference between the average, and the equity sensitive, achievements.

More formally, social welfare, W, is defined as the sum of the concave group utility functions $F(\bar{X}_k)$ so that:

$$W = \sum_{k=1}^{K} N_k F(\bar{X}_k) \qquad (2.1)$$

The change in welfare following a change in the $\bar{X}_k$ is:

$$\Delta W = \sum_{k=1}^{K} a_k N_k \Delta X_k \qquad (2.2)$$

where $a_k = \dfrac{\partial F(\bar{X}_k)}{\partial \bar{X}_k} > 0$, is the marginal change in social welfare consequent upon changes in group achievements (ΔX_k) and also termed the "welfare weight" associated with group k. Since it is assumed that the functions $F(.)$ are strictly concave, marginal gain decreases with increasing achievements: consequently, social welfare is maximized when achievements equal across groups: $\bar{X}_1 = \bar{X}_2 = ... = \bar{X}_K$.

The social welfare function, W, in equation (2.1) has *constant elasticity* if, for $\varepsilon > 0$, $F(.)$ can be written as:

$$F(\bar{X}_k) = \frac{\bar{X}_k^{1-\varepsilon} - 1}{1-\varepsilon}, \quad \varepsilon \neq 1, \ \varepsilon > 0;$$

$$F(\bar{X}_k) = \alpha + \beta \log(\bar{X}_k), \quad \varepsilon = 1 \qquad (2.3)$$

since then: $a_k = \dfrac{\partial F(\bar{X}_k)}{\partial \bar{X}_k} = (\bar{X}_k)^{1-\varepsilon} \Rightarrow \dfrac{\partial a_k}{\partial \bar{X}_k} \dfrac{\bar{X}_k}{a_k} = -\varepsilon \bar{X}^{-(1+\varepsilon)} \dfrac{\bar{X}_k}{\bar{X}_k^{-\varepsilon}} = -\varepsilon.$

Consequently, the *percentage change* in the welfare weight associated with a group, a_k, following an increase in its achievement, $\bar{X}_k$ is *constant* and *negative*. The greater the value of the parameter $\varepsilon > 0$, the greater the fall in the welfare weight.

Similarly, the social welfare of a group $W_k, k = 1...K$ is defined as the sum of the concave utility functions of the group's members, $F(\bar{X}_k)$ so that:

$$W_k = \sum_{i=1}^{N_k} F(X_{ik}) \qquad (2.4)$$

Implying: $\Delta W_k = \sum_{i=1}^{N_k} a_{ik} \Delta X_{ik}$ where the welfare weights, a_{ik} are defined

as $a_{ik} = \dfrac{\partial F(X_{ik})}{\partial X_{ik}} > 0.$

The social welfare function, W_k, in equation (2.4) has *constant elasticity* if, for $\varepsilon > 0$, $F(.)$ can be written as:

$$F(X_{ik}) = \frac{X_{ik}^{1-\varepsilon} - 1}{1-\varepsilon}, \quad \varepsilon \neq 1, \ \varepsilon > 0;$$

$$F(X_{ik}) = \alpha + \beta \log(X_{ik}), \quad \varepsilon = 1 \qquad (2.5)$$

Since X^e is welfare equivalent to $\bar{X}$ and since X_k^e is welfare equivalent to $\bar{X}_k^e$, we have Atkinson's inequality index, I, derived as[20]:

---

[20] Since, by welfare equivalence of X^e and $\bar{X}$

$$NF(X^e) = \sum_{k=1}^{K} N_k F(X_k) \Rightarrow (X^e)^{1-\varepsilon} - 1 = \sum_{k=1}^{K} n_k (X_k^{1-\varepsilon} - 1) \Rightarrow (X^e)^{1-\varepsilon} = \sum_{k=1}^{K} n_k X_k^{1-\varepsilon}.$$

Dividing both sides by $\bar{X}^{1-\varepsilon}$,

$$\left(\frac{X^e}{\bar{X}}\right)^{1-\varepsilon} = \sum_{k=1}^{K} n_k \left(\frac{X_k}{\bar{X}}\right)^{1-\varepsilon} \Rightarrow 1 - \left(\frac{X^e}{\bar{X}}\right) = 1 - \left[\sum_{k=1}^{K} n_k \left(\frac{X_k}{\bar{X}}\right)^{1-\varepsilon}\right]^{1/1-\varepsilon}$$

$$I = 1 - \left(\frac{X^e}{\overline{X}} \right) = 1 - \left[\sum_{k=1}^{K} n_k \left(\frac{\overline{X}_k}{\overline{X}} \right)^{1-\varepsilon} \right]^{1/1-\varepsilon}$$

$$\text{and } I_k = 1 - \left(\frac{X_k^e}{\overline{X}_k} \right) = 1 - \left[\frac{1}{N_k} \sum_{i=1}^{N_k} \left(\frac{X_{ik}}{\overline{X}_k} \right)^{1-\varepsilon} \right]^{1/1-\varepsilon} \tag{2.6}$$

where, in equation (2.6), I represents the overall index and I_k represents the inequality index for group k.

From equation (2.6):

$$(X^e)^{1-\varepsilon} = \sum_{k=1}^{N_k} n_k (\overline{X}_k)^{1-\varepsilon} \text{ and } (X_k^e)^{1-\varepsilon} = \sum_{i=1}^{N_k} \frac{1}{N_k} X_{ik}^{\ 1-\varepsilon} \tag{2.7}$$

From equation (2.7):

$$(X^e)^{1-\varepsilon} = \sum_{i=1}^{N} \frac{1}{N} (X_{ik})^{1-\varepsilon}$$

$$= \frac{N_1}{N} \sum_{i=1}^{N_1} \frac{1}{N_1} (X_{i1})^{1-\varepsilon} + \frac{N_2}{N} \sum_{i=1}^{N_2} \frac{1}{N_2} (X_{i2})^{1-\varepsilon} + .. + \frac{N_K}{N} \sum_{i=1}^{N_K} \frac{1}{N_K} (X_{iK})^{1-\varepsilon}$$

$$= n_1 (X_1^e)^{1-\varepsilon} + n_2 (X_2^e)^{1-\varepsilon} + ... + n_K (X_K^e)^{1-\varepsilon} = \sum_{k=1}^{K} n_k (X_k^e)^{1-\varepsilon} \tag{2.8}$$

Equation (2.8) represents what Anand and Sen (1995) refer to as "$(1 - \varepsilon)$ averaging)": the overall EDE achievement, X^e is a weighted average, with exponent $1 - \varepsilon$, of the group EDE achievements, X_k^e ($k = 1...K$).

A special case occurs when $\varepsilon = 0$ (no inequality aversion). In that situation, X^e and X_k^e are the *arithmetic means* of, respectively, the group achievements and of the achievements of persons in group k: $X^e = \overline{X}$ and $X_k^e = \overline{X}_k$. When $\varepsilon > 0$ (there is positive inequality aversion), $X^e < \overline{X}$ and $X_k^e < \overline{X}_k$.

The Welfare Effects of Redistribution

To examine the welfare effects of an inter-group redistribution of achievements, consider two social groups—upper-caste Hindus *(k = C)* and "Dalits" (SC) *(k = D)* and suppose that, within the context of a fixed overall achievement $\bar{X}$, there is a redistribution of achievements (say, income) from upper-caste Hindus toward Dalits. Then this implies that

$$\Delta \bar{X} = n_C \Delta \bar{X}_C + n_D \Delta \bar{X}_D = 0 \Rightarrow -\Delta \bar{X}_C = (n_C / n_D)\bar{X}_D = \theta \Delta \bar{X}_D,$$

where $\Delta \bar{X}_C < 0, \Delta \bar{X}_D > 0$ \hfill (2.9)

The change in social welfare that results from this redistribution is:

$$\Delta W = \frac{\partial F(\bar{X}_C)}{\partial \bar{X}_C} N_C \Delta \bar{X}_C + \frac{\partial F(\bar{X}_D)}{\partial \bar{X}_D} N_D \Delta \bar{X}_D$$

$$= a_C N_C \Delta \bar{X}_C + a_D N_D \Delta \bar{X}_D = \bar{X}_C^{-\varepsilon} N_C \Delta \bar{X}_C + \bar{X}_L^{-\varepsilon} N_L \Delta \bar{X}_L \quad (2.10)$$

Setting $\Delta W = 0$ in equation (2.10) yields:

$$\left(\frac{\bar{X}_C}{\bar{X}_D}\right)^{-\varepsilon}\left(\frac{N_C}{N_D}\right)\Delta \bar{X}_C = \Delta \bar{X}_D \Rightarrow \Delta \bar{X}_C = \lambda^\varepsilon \theta \Delta \bar{X}_D \quad (2.11)$$

where $\lambda = \dfrac{\bar{X}_C}{\bar{X}_D} > 1$ and $\theta = \dfrac{N_D}{N_C}$.

Suppose that through appropriate redistribution policies, the achievement (income) is *increased* by one unit. From equation (2.10), in order to keep the *overall* achievement, $\bar{X}$, unchanged, the achievement (income) of upper-caste Hindus must fall by $\Delta \bar{X}_C = \theta$. From equation (2.11), if $\varepsilon = 0$, then the condition $\Delta \bar{X}_C = \theta \Rightarrow \Delta W = 0$ or that welfare will remain unchanged: a greater fall in the achievement of upper-caste Hindus would lower the overall achievement $\bar{X}$ and also overall welfare, W.

However, if $\varepsilon > 0$ the achievement of upper-caste Hindus can fall by more than θ ($\Delta \bar{X}_C = \lambda^\varepsilon \theta > \theta$)—the amount required to keep $\bar{X}$ unchanged—*and still keep welfare unchanged*. In other words, for $\varepsilon > 0$, society would be prepared to *tolerate a fall in the overall achievement* ($\Delta \bar{X} < 0$) in order to redistribute from upper-caste Hindus to Dalits, *leaving overall welfare unchanged*. The greater the value of ε, the greater will be this tolerance.

The Human Development Index

The HDI has been formulated in terms of a country's shortfall in respect of three dimensions: life expectancy, education, and income.

Thus, the attainment indicators are defined, in respect of each of the dimensions, as:

$$A_i = \frac{X_i - \text{Min}\{X_i\}}{\text{Max}\{X_i\} - \text{Min}\{X_i\}} \times 100 \qquad (2.12)$$

where A_i is the index of a country in respect of achievement i ($i = 1, 2, 3$), X_i is the value of indicator i and Max$\{X_i\}$ and Min$\{X_i\}$ are, respectively, the maximum and minimum values of the indicator (see Table 2.1 for the assigned maximum and minimum values).

Equation (2.12) implies that $0 \le A_i \le 100$, $i = 1, 2, 3$ such that A_{ij} represents the percentage achievement of country j with respect to the ith indicator. The overall attainment for the country is then its HDI value and it is defined as:

$$\text{HDI} = \frac{1}{3} \sum_{i=1}^{3} A_i \qquad (2.13)$$

In this chapter, we apply the idea of the HDI to a situation where the population of a country is subdivided into K mutually exclusive groups indexed $k = 1 \ldots K$. For every household in each group, we compute the value of its indicator in respect of three achievements: life expectancy, highest educational attainment, and income: A_{ikh}, $i = 1, 2, 3$; $k = 1 \ldots K$; and $h = 1 \ldots H_k$, where H_k is the number of households in group k. So, for any group k ($k = 1 \ldots K$) and achievement dimension i ($i = 1, 2, 3$), the components of the vector $A_{ij} = (A_{ij1}, A_{ij2}, \ldots A_{ijH_j})$ represents the distribution of achievements with respect to indicator i over the H_j household in social group j. We can then define by A_{ij}^e the EDE achievement of group k with respect to attainment i as the $(1 - \varepsilon)$ average—as defined in equation (2.8)—of the household attainments:

$$(A_{ik}^e)^{1-\varepsilon} = \frac{1}{H_k} \sum_{h=1}^{H_k} (A_{ikh})^{1-\varepsilon} \qquad (2.14)$$

When $\varepsilon = 0$, A_{ik}^e is the *arithmetic mean* of household achievements; when $\varepsilon > 0$ A_{ik}^e is less than the arithmetic mean of household achievements.

The *overall* EDE achievement index for group k, $k = 1 \ldots K$ is:

$$A_k^e = \frac{1}{3} A_{1k}^e + \frac{1}{3} A_{2k}^e + \frac{1}{3} A_{3k}^e \qquad (2.15)$$

The EDE achievement *aggregated over all the groups*, with respect to attainment i, and taking account of both within-group and between-group inequality, is denoted A_i^e where

$$\left(A_i^e\right)^{1-\varepsilon} = \frac{1}{H} \sum_{k=1}^{K} \sum_{h=1}^{H_k} \left(A_{ikh}^e\right)^{1-\varepsilon} \tag{2.16}$$

where $H = \sum_{k=1}^{K} H_k$ is the total number of households in the country.

The *overall* EDE achievement index over *all* the groups, *taking account of both inter- and intra-group inequality* is:

$$A^e = \frac{1}{3} A_1^e + \frac{1}{3} A_2^e + \frac{1}{3} A_3^e \tag{2.17}$$

Decomposition

Setting $\varepsilon = 0$ in equation (2.16) and using equation (2.14) yields:

$$A_i^e = \frac{1}{H} \sum_{k=1}^{K} \sum_{h=1}^{H_k} A_{ikh}^e = \frac{1}{H} \sum_{k=1}^{K} \frac{H_k}{H_k} \sum_{h=1}^{H_k} A_{ikh}^e$$

$$= \sum_{k=1}^{k} \frac{H_k}{H} \frac{1}{H_k} \sum_{h=1}^{H_k} A_{ikh}^e = \sum_{k=1}^{k} \frac{H_k}{H} A_{ik}^e \tag{2.18}$$

If within-group inequalities are ignored then, in each group, every household is assumed to have the mean achievement of that group: $A_{ihk} = \bar{A}_{ik}$, $h = 1 \dots H_k$, (for $i = 1 \dots 3$ and $k = 1, \dots K$). The only inequality is *between-group inequality* resulting from the fact that mean achievements of the groups are different: $\bar{A}_{i1} \neq \bar{A}_{i2} \neq \dots \neq \bar{A}_{iK}$. The EDE attainment, *aggregated over all the groups*, with respect to attainment i, *taking account of between-group inequalities only*, is denoted B_i^e where

$$\left(B_i^e\right)^{1-\varepsilon} = \sum_{k=1}^{K} n_k \left(\bar{A}_{ik}\right)^{1-\varepsilon} \tag{2.19}$$

where n_k is the proportion of households in group k, $k = 1 \dots K$. Then, the *overall* EDE achievement index over *all* the groups, *taking account of only inter-group inequality* is:

$$B^e = \frac{1}{3} B_1^e + \frac{1}{3} B_2^e + \frac{1}{3} B_3^e \tag{2.20}$$

3

Inequality and Poverty

3.1. Introduction

The measurement of disparity between households in the context of inequality and poverty raises the important issue of group bias. In the context of households being grouped according to some immutable characteristics—such as race in the USA and caste in India—the relevant question is whether households from some (racial or caste) groups *ceteris paribus* are more likely to find themselves at the bottom of the pile than households from other groups? Does the capacity to generate resources depend not just upon relevant attributes (like education and assets), but also upon irrelevant features like group identity?

Although in most developed countries, studies of well-being and poverty are based on income data which are available in many large national representative surveys, Meyer and Sullivan (2009, 2011) argue that analysis based on consumption, instead of income, provides more insight on well-being. The World Bank (Haughton and Khandker, 2009) echoes these feelings. Although income, defined in principle as *consumption + change in net worth*, is generally used as a measure of welfare in developed countries, it tends to be seriously understated in less developed countries. Consumption in developing countries is measured with greater accuracy and comes closer to measuring "permanent income." Following these observations, this chapter analyzes the *monthly per-capita consumption expenditure* (MPCE) of Indian households. The data for the analysis were obtained from the household file of the IHDS, discussed in previous chapters, which provided information, pertaining to the year 2004, on over 41,000 households spread over India.[1]

---

[1] Available from the Inter-University Consortium for Political and Social Research, http://www.icpsr.umich.edu (last accessed on April 20, 2011).

The richness of the information supplied by the IHDS allowed us to explore a number of areas neglected by other researchers. First, most economic studies of caste in India focus on the SC versus non-SC distinction. In other words, these studies lose sight of the considerable heterogeneity that exists within the non-SC category.[2] In particular, this latter category of non-SC persons comprises both HCH (brahmins, kshatriyas, vaisyas) as well as those belonging to the OBC (*sudras*). In addition, even within the group of persons who regard themselves as belonging to the OBC, there is a useful distinction to be made between Hindu OBCs and Muslim OBCs. For example, The Sachar Committee Report (2006) refers to the caste system applying also to Muslims with the *ashraf* (meaning "noble") referring to high-born Muslims and converts to Islam from higher castes and the *ajlaf* (meaning "degraded" or "unholy") referring to converts to Islam from lower castes. Following the Mandal Commission Report of 1990, adopted by the Government of India, reservation in jobs and education was extended to Hindus, but not to Muslims, from the OBC.[3]

In this chapter, we subdivide India's households into the following groups: HCH, OBC Hindus (HOBC), SC, ST, OBC Muslims (MOBC), high-caste Muslims (HCM). Those households, which were in none of these six groups were placed in a residual "other" group category (OTG): these were mostly (non-ST) Christian, Sikhs, and Jains. So, by distinguishing among three caste groups—HCH (brahmins, kshatriyas, and vaisyas); the HOBC (sudras); and the SC (outside the caste system), we employ a richer caste breakdown of Hindus compared to the usual SC/non-SC distinction adopted by other studies. Similarly, by distinguishing between MOBC and HCM, we depart from the usual stereotype of Muslims as a homogenous community.

Second, because of the richness of the data contained in the IHDS, compared to other studies, we could link the MPCE of households more

---

[2]   For example, the NSS defines four broad social groups: SCs, STs, OBCs, and "Others." "Others" is a reasonable approximation of the upper castes.

[3]   The 1980 report of the *Mandal* Commission recommended that, in addition to the 23 percent of government jobs reserved for the SC and ST, a *further* 27 percent be reserved for the OBC. In 1990, the V.P. Singh government announced plans to implement this recommendation triggering a wave of *anti-Mandal* rioting in India. In 1992, India's Supreme Court, in *Sawhney Vs. The Union of India*, upheld jobs reservation for the OBC but ruled that: (i) reservation was not to extend to more than 50 percent of the population and (ii) that groups within the OBC category who were manifestly not disadvantaged (the *creamy layer*) were to be excluded from reservation.

tightly to asset ownership. For example, the only physical asset considered by Gang, Sen, and Yun (2008) in explaining consumption expenditure for SC, ST, and non-SC/ST households was land ownership; the remaining variables were human capital variables relating to education and outcome variables relating to occupation. A similar point can be made about Kijima (2006). Likewise, Bhaumik and Chakrabarty (2010) did not use any information on physical assets in explaining the consumption expenditure of non-SC, SC, and Muslim households. In contrast, while explaining household MPCE, we are able to employ—in addition to information on land ownership—a set of information relating to information of ownership of tractors, threshers, tube wells, electric and diesel pumps, and draft and dairy livestock.

Third, in this chapter, we attempt to combine the two strands of research by analyzing inequality and poverty in India within the context of caste-based discrimination. An important policy issue in the developmental literature on inequality and poverty is the relation between the two with the general belief being that there is a trade-off between inequality and poverty: reducing poverty requires paying a price in terms of higher inequality and, conversely, wanting a more equal distribution of resources necessitates having to pay a price in terms of greater poverty. The next section of this chapter presents an analysis of this perceived trade-off in terms of choices dictated by considerations of political economy. We do so by first setting out a theoretical model of the poverty-inequality trade-off (PIT), which extends Basu's (2006) model, to understand why poverty and inequality outcomes might differ across the different Indian states. Readers with little appetite for economic theory might prefer to skip this section.

The empirical part of the chapter begins in Section 3.3, which first set outs the salient features of the households sampled in terms of their social, economic, and demographic characteristics. Section 3.4 then quantifies, using econometric estimation, the strength of the various factors that influence household MPCE. Section 3.5 uses the econometric results to decompose inter-group differences in mean MPCE into a term, which reflects inter-group differences in *attribute endowment* and another term, which reflects inter-group differences in *attribute return*.[4] The thinking

---

[4] Differences due to asset return can, in many instances, be plausibly attributed to discrimination between households in the different groups.

behind these decompositions is that the difference in mean MPCE, between households belonging to different groups, may be partly due to the fact that different groups have, on average, different endowments of consumption-enhancing attributes and, in part, due to households from different groups receiving, on average, unequal returns on their attributes.

After this analysis, we proceed to examine, in Section 3.6, the inequality between households in their consumption expenditure. The basic question that we ask is how much of overall inter-household inequality in consumption can be explained by the caste factor? How much can be explained by the regional factor? And how much can be explained by differences in education?

Lastly, we analyze, in Section 3.7 the probabilities of households of being "poor" (in the sense that their MPCE is below a critical threshold) and then, in Section 3.8, decompose their probabilities of being poor into: (a) a "discrimination effect", which stems from the fact that household MPCE depends upon group identity; and (b) an "attributes effect", which stems from the fact that there are systematic inter-group differences between households in their endowments of "poverty creating" factors.[5] In Section 3.8, we also examine the contribution that households from the different groups make to overall poverty and their risk of being poor. Section 3.9 concludes the chapter.

3.2. The Poverty-inequality Trade-off[6]

The concepts of inequality and poverty are conceptually distinct but, in practice, related. Reducing inequality is concerned with narrowing income or consumption differentials between households (or some suitably defined socio-economic unit). Reducing poverty is concerned with ensuring that the consumption or income levels of households are above some suitably defined threshold, usually termed the "poverty line." In practice, reducing inequality and poverty is related and, in the development literature, this relationship is often posited in the form of what Ravallion (2005)

---

[5]   Note that differences between groups in income-generating attributes can reflect historical discrimination. For example, a group is currently disadvantaged educationally because, in the past, it was denied access to education.

[6]   Readers impatient with the niceties of economic theory can skip this section.

terms the "poverty-inequality trade-off ": higher levels of inequality are associated with lower levels of poverty and, conversely, lower inequality with higher poverty. A PIT would occur if both poverty and inequality were related to growth, with higher growth leading to poverty reduction while at the same time, at least in the initial stages of development, being associated with rising inequality per Kuznet's (1955) "inverted U-curve hypothesis" (see Figure 3.1). Consequently, through their association with a third factor—growth—one could expect an inverse relationship between levels of inequality and poverty or, in other words, a PIT.

Figure 3.1:
The Kuznet's hypothesis and "Inverted U" curve

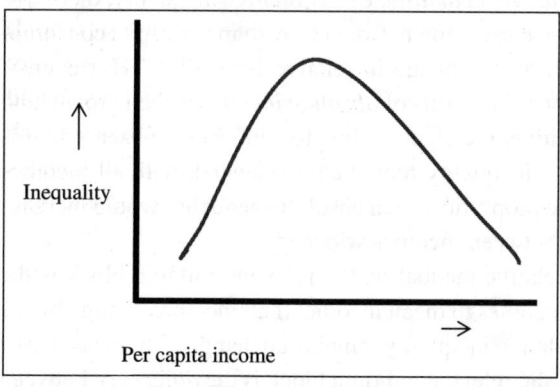

Source: Author.

A theoretical justification for Kuznet's (1955) inverted U relation between growth and inequality can be provided on the basis of the migration of workers from a low wage/low inequality rural sector to a high wage/ high inequality urban sector (Anand and Kanbur, 1993). Needless to say, rural-to-urban migration need not be the only source of the "inequality-increasing growth" story. Another possibility is that the removal of regulatory control of the economy—which artificially suppressed inequality—would have the effect of generating growth, increasing inequality, and reducing poverty and, thereby, leading to a PIT. Both India and China are cited as examples of PIT, generated through "freeing up" the economy. Over the last two decades of its economic freedom, the proportion of the Chinese population living under $1 per day fell by about two percentage points per year but the available evidence suggests that inequality has been rising sharply (OECD, 2004). The story that emerges from the nexus between growth, inequality, and poverty is that both inequality increases and poverty reductions are by-products of growth, the corollary being that attempts to dampen the magnitude of the inequality increased—by say, restricting rural/urban migration, or by lifting regulatory controls only partially—and that will reduce the growth rate below its optimal value.

Ravallion (2005) has examined the empirical validity of a PIT. His conclusion was that in cross-section studies of countries, there was evidence of a PIT: countries with higher mean incomes had higher levels of income inequality and lower levels of poverty. However, time series analysis of individual countries did not support a PIT provided inequality was measured by *relative inequality*. Under relative inequality, there was "only a weak positive correlation between growth in per capita consumption and the proportionate change in relative inequality." However, if inequality was measured in terms of *absolute inequality* then growth and inequality were positively related, leading to a PIT being observed. This is because if relative inequality remained unchanged, with all incomes growing by the same proportion, then absolute inequality would increase as the absolute gap between incomes widened.

In measures of relative inequality, the relevant building block is the *ratio* of individual incomes to mean income. If all incomes change by the same *proportion*, relative inequality remains unchanged.[7] In measures of absolute inequality, the relevant building block is the *difference* between individual incomes and mean income. If all incomes change by the same *amount*, absolute inequality remains unchanged. So, for example, in a two-household economy, if the rich household earns ₹100,000 and the poor household earns ₹10,000 and both incomes double, then relative inequality will remain unchanged since the rich household will continue to have an income 10 times that of the poor household. However, under this doubling, the *absolute* gap in incomes will increase from ₹90,000 to ₹180,000. So, absolute inequality will increase.

Ravallion and Chen (2004) question whether even China can be viewed as an example of a PIT. First, periods of rapid growth in China did not bring about sharp increases in inequality; indeed, periods of falling inequality were associated with the highest growth rates of household incomes.

[7] Inequality is usually measured in relative terms and the most popular measure for measuring (relative) inequality is the *Gini coefficient*.

Second, the provinces that experienced the sharpest rise in inequality saw smaller reductions in poverty compared to provinces in which inequality increases were smaller. Consequently, Ravallion's (2005) conclusion is that

> looking at the experience of 70 developing and transition economies in the 1990s, there is no sign of a systematic trade-off between absolute poverty incidence and relative inequality. Indeed lower (higher) poverty tends to come hand in hand with lower (higher) inequality. The main reason why the trade-off is not found in these data is that economic growth shows little correlation with changes in *relative* [emphasis added] inequality (p. 179).

However, when there is fixed amount of income there is scope, using an appropriate fiscal policy, for choosing between maximizing the income of the poor (doing one's best by poverty but leaving some, perhaps a significant amount of, inequality) or minimizing the gap between rich and poor (doing one's best by inequality but leaving more poverty than absolutely necessary). In Basu's (2006) model, in a population of N households, there are "productive" households (of which there are M) and "unproductive" households (of which there are L). The amount of work that a productive person does, represented by h where $h \in [0,1]$, is negatively associated with the tax rate (t): $h = (1 - t)$. With a 100 percent tax rate, $t = 1$, the productive household puts in $h = 0$ hours while in the complete absence of taxes, $t = 0$, the household puts in the maximum number of hours, $h = 1$. The pre-tax income of a household that puts in h hours of work is $Y = A \times h$. On the other hand, unproductive households generate income from the externalities generated by the work of productive households by producing goods and services for productive households. The income of unproductive households is $y = ah$ and depends on the hours worked by productive households.

The government taxes the income of productive households at a proportionate tax rate, t, and redistributes the tax collected to unproductive households thereby lowering the income of the former and raising the income of the latter. Consequently, the post-tax income of a productive household, and the post-distribution income of an unproductive household, is, respectively:

$$\bar{Y}(t) = (1-t)Y \text{ and } \bar{y} = y + \frac{M \times t \times Y}{L}$$

The government may choose to *maximize* the income of the poor with a tax rate of t^* or to *eliminate* inequality with a tax rate of t^{**}.

Box 3.1:
Computing the inequality eliminating and poverty minimizing tax rates

Substituting Ah for Y, ah for y, and $(1-t)$ for h, we have:

$$\bar{Y}(t) = (1-t)^2 A \text{ and } \bar{y}(t) = (1-t)\left[a + \frac{M \times A \times t}{L}\right]$$

If the policy of government is to maximize the incomes of the poor households, then it will choose t so as to maximize the income of the "poorest" households. If these are the unproductive households, then t will be chosen to maximize $\bar{y} = y + \frac{MtY}{L}$ implying $t^* = \frac{1}{2} - \frac{aL}{2AM}$. If the aim of the government is to eliminate inequality, then t will be chosen so that:

$$\bar{Y}(t) = \bar{y}(t) \Rightarrow (1-t)^2 A = (1-t)\left[a + \frac{M \times A \times t}{L}\right] \Rightarrow t^{**} = \frac{L(A-a)}{A(L+M)}$$

Source: Authors.

This is illustrated in Figure 3.2 in which the tax rate t^* maximizes the income of poor households (but does not eliminate inequality), the tax rate t^{**} eliminates inequality (but does not maximize poor incomes), and $t^* < t^{**}$. This figure draws attention to the fact that the space for fiscal policy lies with respect to a tax rate, t, such that $t^* \leq t \leq t^{**}$.

Figure 3.2:
The trade-off between inequality and poverty

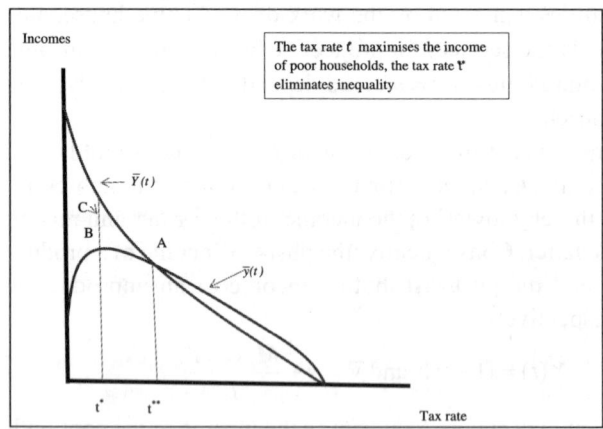

Source: Basu, 2006.

To see how this policy space is utilized by governments in different Indian states, one may think of the "Kerala model" in which low household incomes co-exist with little or no difference between the incomes of "productive" and "unproductive" households: this is represented by the point A in Figure 3.2. On the other hand, one may think of the "Gujarat model" in which higher incomes of "unproductive" households co-exist with considerable difference between the incomes of *"productive"* and "unproductive" households: this is represented by the points B (unproductive households) and C (productive households) in Figure 3.2. A major reason for this difference is, needless to say, the political complexion of the party in power: Kerala's "left-wing" government is more sympathetic to income equality and less to high income; conversely, Gujarat's "right-wing" government favors growth and high income and is less inclined to worry about income gaps. In turn, the complexion of a state government is determined by the preferences of its voters. In the context of India's political economy, Bhaumik and Chakrabarty (2010) make reference to the fact that "the emergence of caste- and religion-based politics can have a significant impact on inter-caste and inter-religion differences in earnings" (p. 237).

If the gap between the (post-tax) incomes of productive and unproductive households is denoted as $G(t) = \overline{Y}(t) - \overline{y}(t)$ and taken as proxy for "inequality," then voters' preferences can be assumed to be such that "voter satisfaction" is lowered when $G(t)$ increases, but is raised when the incomes of poor households, $\overline{y}(t)$, rises. Consequently, overall voter satisfaction in state j, with respect to a particular tax rate, $V_j(t)$ may be conceived of as a weighted average of the "income gap" and "poor incomes."

$$V_j(t) = \alpha_j \times G_j(t) + \beta_j \times \overline{y}_j(t)$$

where, in the above equation, α and β are weights.[8]

Box 3.2:
Derives the political support curves

The choice that different states make with respect to "inequality versus poverty reduction" is illustrated in Figure 3.3. The income gap $G(t)$ is measured along the X-axis of Figure 3.3. This is derived from Figure 3.2 as the gap between the $\overline{Y}(t)$ and the $\overline{y}(t)$ curves. The income of poor households, $\overline{y}(t)$ is measured along the Y-axis. When, at $t = t^{**}$, $G(t^{**}) = Y(t^*) - y(t^{**}) = 0$, the minimum value of poor households, $\overline{y}(t^{**})$ is obtained. This is the counterpart of point A in Figure 3.2. When, at $t = t^*$, $G(t^*) = Y(t^*) - y(t^{**})$, the maximum value of poor

[8] For the sake of simplicity, voter satisfaction is taken as a linear function of the income gap and poor incomes.

households, $\bar{y}(t^*)$ is obtained. This is the counterpart of point B in Figure 3.2 and $G(t^*)$ is the income gap BC in Figure 3.2. The curve ZZ joins the various combinations of $G(t)$ and $\bar{y}(t)$ obtained as t takes values between t^* and t^{**}.

Source: Authors.

The lines *KK* and *JJ* in Figure 3.3 show the voter satisfaction lines for Kerala and Gujarat: the higher the lines, the greater the level of voter satisfaction.[9] Each government chooses a tax rate, t (and therefore, an income gap $G(t) = \bar{Y}(t) - \bar{y}(t)$ and a level of poor income, $\bar{y}(t)$) to reach the highest level of voter satisfaction subject to the PIT constraint represented by the curve ZZ. In consequence, each state will establish an equilibrium tax rate t where its voter satisfaction line is tangential to ZZ. This is illustrated for Kerala and Gujarat in Figure 3.3: Kerala chooses lower inequality at the expense of lower "poor household" income; Gujarat is prepared to pay a price in terms of higher inequality in order to secure a higher "poor household" income.

Figure 3.3:
Policy choice between inequality and poverty reduction

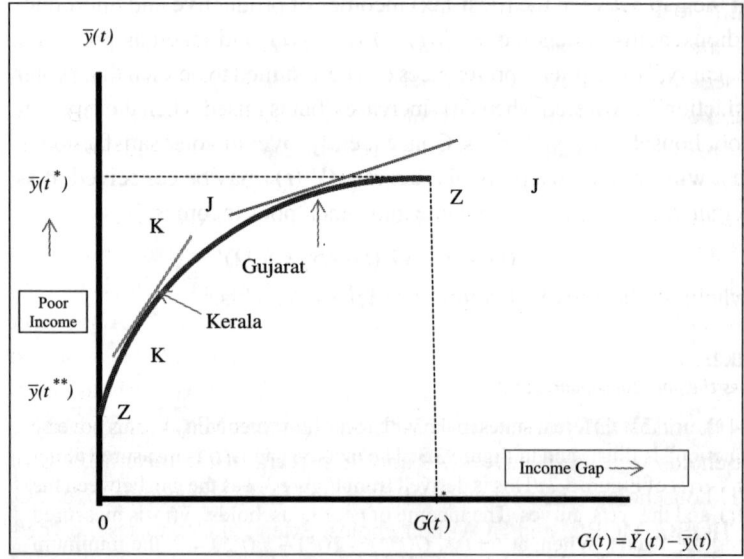

Source: Author.

[9] For a given G, a higher line will be associated with a higher $\bar{y}(t)$ and, therefore, with a higher level of voter satisfaction.

3.3. Inter-caste Disparities in Households' Monthly Per Capita Consumption Expenditure

Following the theoretical analysis of the previous section, this section describes the characteristics of households from the IHDS. This was conducted in 2004–05 by the University of Maryland in collaboration with the National Council of Applied Economic Research, New Delhi, between November 2004 and October 2005. The nationally representative data cover 1,504 villages and 971 urban areas across 33 states and union territories of India. The survey covering 41,554 households was carried out through face-to-face interviews by pairs of male and female enumerators in local languages. The respondents included a person who was knowledgeable about the household economic situation (usually the male head of the household) and an ever-married woman aged 15–49 years. The detailed modules of the survey provide answers to a wide range of questions relating to economic activity, income and consumption expenditure, asset ownership, social capital, education, health, marriage, and fertility, etc.

Figure 3.4 and Table 3.1 provide information on the caste and religion of households in the IHDS. Of the total 41,554 households, 23 percent (9,540 households) were HCH; 34 percent (13,875 households) were HOBC; 20 percent (8,333 households) were SC; 8 percent (3,439 households) were ST; 5 percent (2,014 households) were MOBC; 6 percent (2,694 households) were HCM; and 4 percent (1,659 households) were in the "Other" group.

Table 3.2 provides information on the income and assets of *rural* households in India, by social group. This shows that OTG households had the highest MPCE (₹1,356), followed by HCH households (₹1,037). At the other end of the scale, rural ST households had the lowest MPCE (₹511), followed by SC households (₹657), MOBC households (₹727), HCM households (₹743), and HOBC households (₹748). So, the mean MPCE of ST and SC households were, respectively, 49 and 63 percent of the mean MPCE of HCH households. The advantage of HCH and OTG households, over SC, ST, HOBC, MOBC, and HCM households, extended also to asset ownership. For example, 74 percent of HCH households owned land compared to only 65 percent of HOBC households, 44 percent of SC households, 62 percent of ST households, 44 percent of MOBC households, and 54 percent of HCM households.

Figure 3.4:
Percentage of households in the IHDS in various groups

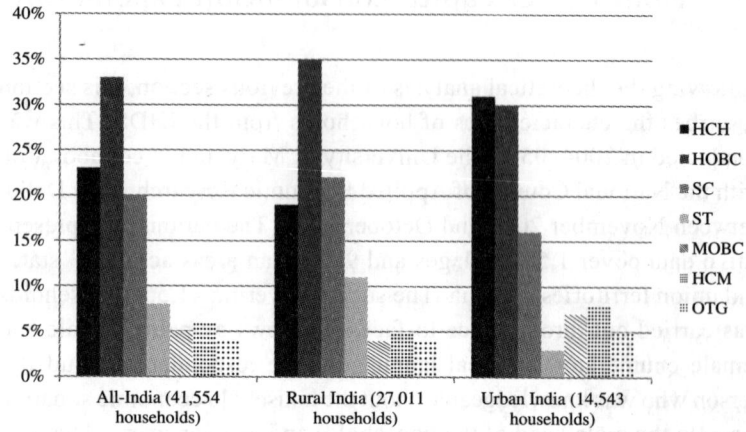

Source: IHDS.

Table 3.1:
Caste and religion of households in the IHDS

	Upper-caste Hindus	OBC Hindus	Scheduled castes*	Scheduled Tribes**	OBC Muslims	High-caste Muslims	Others	All Groups
Number of Households (Rural + Urban)	9,540	13,875	8,333	3,439	2,014	2,694	1,659	41,554
Number of Households (Rural)	5,022	9,543	6,011	2,940	1,055	1,472	968	27,011
Number of Households (Urban)	4,518	4,332	2,322	499	959	1,222	691	14,543

Source: IHDS.
Notes: * Of the 8,333 SC households, 7,724 were Hindus and the rest were Buddhists, Christians, or Sikhs.
** Of the 3,439 ST households, 2,488 were Hindus, 484 were Christians, and 412 were Tribals.

Although only 56 percent of OTG households owned land, their average land holding was considerably larger than for other households. Setting the land area owned by HCH households at 100, Table 3.2 shows that the average area owned by OTG households was 627, or in other words, 6.27 times that of HCH households. At the other end of the scale, the average land holding of SC and HCM households was only one-fourth that of HCH households; the average land holding of MOBC households was half that of HCH households; and the average land holding of HOBC and ST households was three-fourths that of HCH households. In terms of non-land assets as well, SC and ST households were the worst off compared to HCH households. For example, 96 percent of SC and 97 percent of ST households *did not* own a tube well compared to 86 percent of HCH households and 78 percent of OTG households; 52 percent of SC and 64 percent of ST households *did not* own a buffalo compared to 42 percent of HCH households and 37 percent of OTG households.

Table 3.3 shows the mean MPCE of urban households by caste and religion. This shows that HCH and OTG households had, on average, the highest MPCE at, respectively, ₹1,683 and ₹1,653; on the other hand, MOBC households had the lowest average MPCE (₹804), followed by SC households (₹981). An interesting feature of Table 3.3 is that while HCM households had a significantly higher MPCE than their MOBC counterparts (₹1,047 versus ₹804), their MPCE, on average was significantly lower than that of HCH households (₹1,047 versus ₹1,683). Table 3.3 also shows that average household MPCE was considerably higher in metro (Mumbai, Delhi, Kolkata, Chennai, Bangalore, and Hyderabad) compared to non-metro areas (₹1,526 versus ₹1,218) and considerably lower in slum areas compared to non-slum areas (₹1,306 versus ₹937). However, in all these various situations, HCH and OTG households were able to maintain considerable distance between their MPCE and the MPCE of households from the other social groups.

A comparison of Tables 3.2 and 3.3 reveals an interesting feature: ST households have the lowest MPCE in a rural setting, but one of the highest MPCEs in an urban setting. Indeed, in a rural context, the average MPCE of ST households was 77 percent of that of SC households (₹511 versus ₹657) but, in an urban context, the average MPCE of a ST household was 7 percent higher than that of a SC household (₹1,047 versus ₹981). This is because the ST comprises two distinct groups: the economically and socially deprived *adivasis* from the states of Jharkhand, MP, Chhattisgarh, and Orissa, characterized by high rates of illiteracy and ill-health, and the educated tribes from the north-eastern states of India (the Khasis, Garos, Mizos, etc.) who, more often than not, are relatively proficient in English. The former, living in rural areas, fare very badly, and the latter, living largely in urban areas, do very well, on India's economic ladder.

Figure 3.5 facilitates a comparison of average rural and urban MPCE for the seven groups distinguished in this chapter. This shows that in the urban–rural context, MOBC households benefit very little by living in urban, compared to rural areas. On the other hand, their HCM counterparts benefit considerably by being placed in an urban setting. Households who benefit the most from a rural to urban shift are, as noted above, ST households but, as Figure 3.5 shows, urbanization also raises the average MPCE of HCH, HOBC, and ST households.

Table 3.2:
Rural households' MPCE and assets, by caste and religion

	Upper-caste Hindus	Other Backward Classes	Scheduled Castes*	Scheduled Tribes	OBC Muslims	High-caste Muslims	Other Groups	All Groups
Number of Households	5,018	9,536	6,002	2,936	1,055	1,470	964	26,981
Mean number of persons in a household	5.39	5.34	5.25	5.09	6.15	5.89	5.21	5.36
Mean Household per capita consumption (₹)	1,037	748	657	511	727	743	1,356	776
Proportion of households owning or cultivating land	74	65	44	62	44	54	56	60
Average area owned (High caste = 100)	100	78	25	75	51	26	627	64
Percentage of owned area that is cultivated	84	87	84	89	85	90	85	86
Proportion of households not owning a tube well (%)	86	89	96	97	94	92	78	91
Proportion of households not owning an electric pump (%)	86	91	97	96	96	97	73	92

Table 3.2 continued

Table 3.2 continued

Proportion of households not owning a diesel pump (%)	93	94	97	97	97	93	83	95
Proportion of households not owning a bullock cart (%)	89	90	97	93	97	95	86	92
Proportion of households not owning a tractor (%)	95	97	99	99	98	98	87	97
Proportion of households not owning a thresher (%)	96	98	99	99	99	98	97	98
Proportion of households not owning a cow (%)	43	48	50	52	54	49	53	49
Proportion of households not owning a buffalo (%)	42	52	52	64	49	58	37	51

Source: IHDS.

Table 3.3:
Urban households' MPCE, by caste and religion

	Upper-caste Hindus	Other Backward Classes	Scheduled Castes*	Scheduled Tribes	OBC Muslims	High-caste Muslims	Other Groups	All Groups
Number of Households	4,498	4,327	2,320	497	957	1,222	689	14,510
Mean number of persons in a household	4.5	4.8	5.0	4.9	5.9	5.6	4.5	4.9
Mean household per capita consumption (₹)	1,683	1,176	981	1,124	804	1,047	1,653	1,288
Mean Household per capita consumption (₹): Metro	1,819	1,424	1,141	1,209	1,016	1,126	2,137	1,526

Table 3.3 continued

Table 3.3 continued

Mean household per capita consumption (₹): non-metro	1,627	1,119	930	1,120	783	1,019	1,514	1,218
Mean household per capita consumption (₹): Slum	1,500	951	860	681	628	1,080	1,280	937
Mean household per capita consumption (₹): Non-slum	1,685	1,188	993	1,170	820	1,044	1,664	1,306

Source: IHDS.

Figure 3.5:
Rural–urban comparison of mean MPCE, by social group (₹)

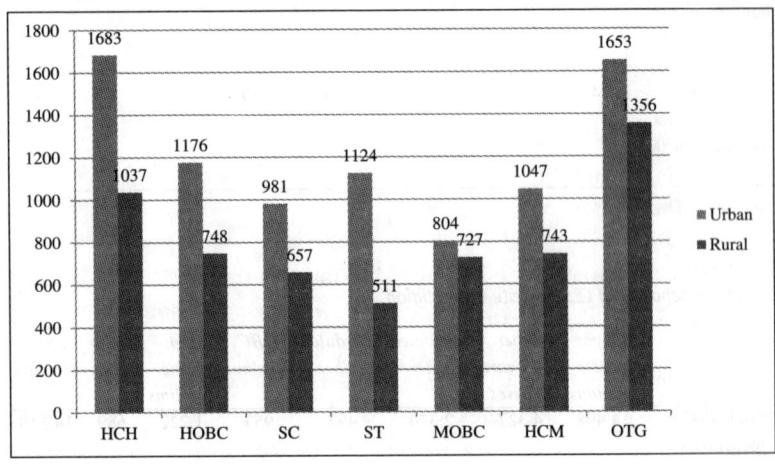

Source: IHDS.

3.4. Modeling Differences in Inter-group Differences in MPCE

The previous section set out the salient features of the households in the sample in terms of their social, demographic, and economic background.

This section draws these diverse threads together to estimate the relative strengths of the different factors affecting households' MPCE. This section estimates the relative strengths of the different factors affecting households' MPCE. To keep the analysis tractable, the analysis is confined to *rural Hindu* households, that is HCH, HOBC, or SC households.[10] It was hypothesized that a household's MPCE would *inter alia* depend upon the following factors:

1. The caste of the household: HCH, HOBC, or SC
2. Whether the household contained a literate person
3. The highest education level of an adult in the household:
   (i) low, if up to class 5;
   (ii) medium, if higher than class 5 but less than class 10 (Matric);
   (iii) high, if Matric or above.[11]
4. Whether the household owned any of the following assets:
   (i) Tube well
   (ii) Electric pump
   (iii) Diesel pump
   (iv) Bullock cart
   (v) Tractor
   (vi) Thresher
   (vii) Cows, including the number of cows
   (viii) Buffaloes, including the number of buffaloes
5. The region in which the household lived: central, south, west, east, and north.[12]

The coefficient on each of the variables listed under list items 2–5, above was allowed to vary according to the caste of the household (which is variable 1, above). Consequently, if X_i represents the value of an explanatory

---

[10] Of the 6,011 SC households in the rural sample, 5,498 households (91 percent) were Hindus, 78 households were Christians, 228 households were Sikhs, and 165 households were Buddhists.

[11] *Matric* is a term commonly used in India to refer to the final year of high school, which ends at 10th standard (10th grade); the qualification received after passing the *matriculation exams*, usually at the age of 15–16 years, is referred to as *matric (passed)*.

[12] The central region, comprising Bihar, Madhya Pradesh, Rajasthan, and Uttar Pradesh; the south, comprising Andhra Pradesh, Karnataka, Kerala, and Tamil Nadu; the west, comprising Maharashtra and Gujarat; the east, comprising Assam, Bengal, and Orissa; and the north, comprising Haryana, Himachal Pradesh, and Punjab.

variable for household i ($i = 1 \ldots N$), then the equations that were estimated took the form:

$$MCE_i = \alpha_1 \times HCH_i + \alpha_2 \times OBC_i + \alpha_3 \times SC_i$$
$$+ \beta_1 \times X_i + \beta_2 \times (X_i \times OBC_i) + \beta_3 \times (X_i \times SC_i) + \varepsilon_i$$

where there are N households, indexed $i = 1 \ldots N$ such that:

1. $MPCE_i$ is the monthly per capita consumption expenditure of household i
2. $HCH_i = 1$, the if household i is a HCH household, zero otherwise
3. $HOBC_i = 1$, if household i is a Hindu OBC household, zero otherwise
4. $SC_i = 1$, if household i is a SC household, zero otherwise
5. X_i is the value of the explanatory variable for household i
6. The α and β are coefficients

The interpretation of the coefficients in equation (3.1) is as follows:

1. The coefficients α_1, α_2, and α_3 are the intercept terms associated with HCH, HOBC, and SC households. The presence of these terms ensures that the equation passes through the mean. In other words, if all the explanatory variables took as values their sample means, the predicted value of income would be the mean consumption.
2. The coefficient β_1 is the effect associated with the explanatory variable *for all households.*
3. The coefficient β_2 is the *additional* effect associated with the explanatory variable for *HOBC households only.*

   If β_2 is significantly different from zero, then this means that the variable has a (statistically significant) different effect on HOBC households compared to its effect on HCH households. If β_2 is not significantly different from zero, then this means that there is no (statistically significant) difference in the variable's effect between HOBC and HCH households.
4. The coefficient β_3 is the *additional* effect associated with the explanatory variable for *SC households only.*

   If β_3 is significantly different from zero, then this means that the variable has a (statistically significant) different effect on SC households compared to its effect on HCH households. If β_3 is not significantly different from zero, then this means that there is no (statistically significant) difference in the variable's effect between SC and HCH households.

Table 3.4 shows the results of estimating the above equation using rural Hindu households' MPCE as the dependent variable. Using the results of Table 3.4, Table 3.5 shows that the monthly MPCE of a rural HCH household, living in the east, and without any assets (education, land, non-land productive assets) would be ₹664. Acquiring educational assets in the form of a literate person in the household would add ₹27 to this and acquiring educational assets in the form of an adult in the household educated to the level of Matric (or higher) would add ₹407.

Households that owned or cultivated land would add ₹91 to their MPCE and the further acquisition of complementary non-land productive assets would increase MPCE as shown below, the largest increase (₹264) going to households who acquired a tractor followed by an increase of ₹107 for households owning a diesel pump. Owning cows and buffaloes increased MPCE, with the increase per animal being considerably greater for buffaloes (₹38) compared to cows (₹5).

A household's MPCE also depended on the region in which it lived. With the east as the reference region, living in the north *added* ₹279, and living in the south *added* ₹194, to MPCE. On the other hand, compared to living in the east, living in the west and in the central *reduced* MPCE by, respectively, ₹187 and ₹218.

Table 3.4:
Regression estimates for the MPCE generating equation for rural households*

Household Type ↓	Coefficient Estimate	Standard Error	T Value
High-caste Hindu	663.63	35.52	18.68
HOBC	514.68	26.58	19.37
Scheduled Castes	583.27	25.79	22.62
Literate in household	27.42	13.50	2.03
Highest education level for adult in household is higher than Matric	407.29	24.31	16.76
Highest education level for adult in HOBC household is higher than Matric	−135.28	31.32	−4.32
Highest education level for adult in SC household is higher than Matric	−112.96	37.54	−3.01
Household owns land	91.00	29.01	3.14

Table 3.4 continued

Table 3.4 continued

HOBC household owns land	−50.01	34.00	−1.47
SC household owns land	−114.41	35.83	−3.19
Household owns a tube well	54.15	22.81	2.37
Household owns an electric pump	50.44	23.18	2.18
Household owns a diesel pump	107.39	28.46	3.77
Household owns a tractor	264.42	43.64	6.06
Household owns a thresher	54.29	45.65	1.19
Household owns cows	5.33	3.96	1.35
Household owns buffaloes	37.80	5.76	6.56
HOBC household owns buffaloes	−28.29	6.12	−4.62
SC household owns buffaloes	−41.67	6.35	−6.56
North	279.03	28.67	9.73
SC households in the north	−70.69	44.99	−1.57
South	193.72	23.19	8.35
SC households in the south	−178.89	37.53	−4.77
West	−187.32	34.09	−5.49
HOBC households in the west	278.05	39.51	7.04
SC households in the west	238.15	53.60	4.44
Central	−217.82	33.04	−6.59
HOBC households in the central	147.63	34.68	4.26
SC households in the central	111.06	43.32	2.56

Equation statistics	
Number of observations	17,829
Adjusted R^2	0.546
$F(14,16905)$	738.8
Root mean square error	742

Source: Author's own calculations from IHDS data.
Note: *Dependent variable is per capita monthly consumption (MPCE).

Table 3.5:
MPCE of HCH households

Source	Amount (₹)
Intercept	664
Literate in household adds	27
Matric or more of highest educated adult adds	407
Owning/cultivating land adds	91
Owning a tube well adds	54

Table 3.5 continued

Table 3.5 continued

Owning an electric pump adds	50
Owning a diesel pump adds	107
Owning a tractor adds	264
Owning a thresher adds	54
Owning 2.58 cows adds	₹5 × 2.58 = 13
Owning 2.66 buffaloes adds	₹37 × 2.66 = 98
Living in the north adds	279
Living in the south adds	194
Living in the west adds	−187
Living in the central adds	−218

Source: Author's own calculations from IHDS data.

These results pertain to a HCH household. They change with respect to HOBC and SC household in several respects:

1. Compared to HCH households, the return on Matric (or higher) level education is lower for HOBC and SC households: for HCH households, the presence of an adult educated to Matric (or higher) level added ₹407 to MPCE; for HOBC and SC households, this added only ₹272 and ₹294, respectively.[13]

2. Compared to HCH households, the return on owning/cultivating land is lower for HOBC and SC households: for HCH households, owning/cultivating land added ₹91 to MPCE; for HOBC households, owning/cultivating land increased MPCE by ₹40 while, for SC households, owning/cultivating land reduced MPCE by ₹23.

3. Compared to HCH households, the return on owning buffaloes is lower for HOBC and SC households: for HCH households, owning a buffalo added ₹38 to MPCE; for HOBC households, owning a buffalo increased MPCE just ₹10 while, for SC households, owning a buffalo reduced MPCE by ₹4.

4. Compared to living in the east, living in the north increased the MPCE of HCH households by ₹279 but it increased the income of SC households by only ₹208; again compared to living in the east, living in the south increased the MPCE of HCH households by ₹194 but it increased the MPCE of SC households by ₹15. In

[13] The null hypothesis that the coefficients on OBC × X and SC × X being equal could not be rejected with an $F(1,16907) = 0.56$, where X is the variable, "the highest level of education for an adult in the household is greater than Matric."

other words, the advantage of living in the more prosperous parts of India, in terms of higher MPCE, was significantly greater for HCH households than it was for SC households.

5. However, compared to HCH households in the east, the MPCE of HCH households in the west was ₹187 lower; the same comparison made for HOBC and SC households, with equivalent households in the east, shows, however, that MPCE was higher by, respectively, ₹278 and ₹238.

It is difficult to compare the results set out above with those from other studies because in explaining households' MPCE, the specification employed here (see Tables 3.4 and 3.5) contains many more asset variables than hitherto used by researchers. Unlike previous studies (Bhaumik and Chakrabarty, 2010; Gang, Sen, and Yun, 2008; Kijima, 2006) that focused on education, occupation, and land ownership, this chapter exploits—in addition to information on land ownership—a rich set of data relating to ownership of (non-land) physical assets: tractors, tube wells, electric and diesel pumps, and draft and dairy livestock. Using this information, this study presents a more nuanced explanation of inter-household variations in MPCE than hitherto attempted for India.

Table 3.5 makes clear that, in rural India, a household's MPCE is significantly and considerably increased when ownership of land is buttressed by ownership of cultivation-related, productivity-enhancing physical assets. For example, the expenditure-boosting effects of tractors and diesel pumps are greater than that of land ownership *per se* and tube wells, threshers, and electric pumps, by raising the productivity of agricultural land, substantially increase a rural Indian household's MPCE. So this chapter suggests that previous studies of consumption expenditure in India, which included land as an explanatory variable, but did not take account of ancillary, productivity-enhancing inputs to land, were misspecified in terms of omitting key variables.

The effects of *land* ownership on household consumption varied across the caste groups (see list item 2, above) but the effects of *non-land* asset ownership were *caste neutral* in that there was no evidence of significant inter-caste disparity in their consumption-enhancing effects. There was, however, an exception to his general finding and this related to the ownership of buffaloes: these milch animals offered HCH households a significantly higher return than they did to HOBC and SC households—the excess return quantified in point 3 of the earlier list. Thorat, Mahamallik, and Sadana (2010) point out that because of the perceived "impure status" of the lower castes, upper-caste Hindus avoided buying edible products—particularly milk and vegetables—from them. In a survey conducted by them, out of 16 HCH households who would not buy milk from SC households, 11 said it was because they considered the SC to be "unclean and polluting." A feature of our results is that it offers econometric corroboration, based on a large sample size, of such grassroots findings.

3.5. The Decomposition of Inter-caste Differences in Household MPCE

The preceding section showed that the attributes that resulted in a higher level of MPCE by households were not uniformly rewarded across the different caste groups. So, for example, a high level of education of adults in a household would result in a higher MPCE for *all* households but, compared to HCH households, this effect would be smaller for HOBC and SC households.[14] Or, in other words, the returns to education, in terms of higher MPCE, were significantly greater for HCH households compared to HOBC and SC households. So, one reason for inter-caste disparities in MPCE is differences in *rates of return on assets*: education, land, non-land productive assets, and region of residence. However, another reason for such inter-caste disparities might be that there are systematic differences in *asset endowments* between households in the different caste groups (as evidenced in Table 3.1) so that, for example, compared to HCH households, a smaller proportion of SC households contain an adult who is a Matric (or higher).

These observations require one to distinguish empirically between the contribution of inter-caste differences *in asset rates of return,* and inter-caste differences in *asset ownership,* to the overall difference between households,

---

[14] Similarly, in the context of physical assets, the returns to ownership/cultivation of land and the ownership of buffalos were significantly greater for HCH households compared to OBC and SC households. In terms of geography, the returns to living in the north and the south of India, in terms of higher MPCE, were significantly greater for HCH households compared to OBC and SC households.

belonging to the different caste groups, in their MPCE. The problem is that households from the HCH, HOBC, and the SC groups differ in terms of both attributes and coefficients. So the first step is to ask what the HCH/SC difference (and the HCH/HOBC difference) would have been if both sets of attributes were evaluated at a *common* coefficient vector. This difference could then be entirely ascribed to a difference in attributes since coefficient differences would have been neutralized. Call this the *difference due to asset ownership* or the *explained difference*. Then the *observed* difference less the *explained difference* (due to asset ownership) is the *residual* or *unexplained* difference. The mathematical details of the decomposition are contained in the appendix to this chapter (see Blinder, 1973; Jann, 2008; Oaxaca, 1973).

3.5.1. *Decomposition Results: Aggregate*

Tables 3.6 and 3.7 show the results from decomposing the difference in MPCE between HCH rural households and, respectively, SC and HOBC rural households (using the method detailed in equation (3.8) of the appendix). Both tables show two decompositions. The first decomposition

Table 3.6:

The decomposition of the difference in mean per-capita consumption expenditure between HCH and SC households

	Value	Standard Error	z Value	P > z
HCH: Mean household per capita expenditure	1,020.17	17.86	57.10	0
SC: Mean household per capita expenditure	644.94	7.85	82.12	0
Difference between HCH and SC households	375.23	19.52	19.23	0
Decomposition of the difference between HCH and SC households using HCH coefficient vector				
Explained	141.83	19.30	7.35	0
Unexplained	233.39	26.27	8.88	0
Decomposition of the difference between HCH and SC households using SC coefficient vector				
Explained	165.12	38.98	4.24	0
Unexplained	210.11	42.53	4.94	0

Source: Author's own calculations from IHDS data.
Note: Decomposition using equation (3.10) of the appendix, 9,561 observations.

relates to evaluating what the difference *would have been* if SC/HOBC assets had received HCH rates of return (equation 3.9).[15] The second decomposition relates to evaluating what the difference would have been if HCH assets had received SC/HOBC rates of return (equation 3.10).[16]

Table 3.7:
The decomposition of the difference in mean per-capita consumption expenditure between HCH and HOBC households

	Value	Standard Error	z Value	P > z
HCH: Mean household per capita expenditure	1,020.17	17.86	57.10	0
HOBC: Mean household per capita expenditure	726.70	7.18	101.20	0
Difference between HCH and HOBC households	293.47	19.25	15.24	0
Decomposition of the difference between HCH and SC households using HCH coefficient vector				
Explained	130.01	14.07	9.24	0
Unexplained	163.46	22.48	7.27	0
Decomposition of the difference between HCH and SC households using SC coefficient vector				
Explained	153.57	27.56	5.57	0
Unexplained	139.90	32.33	4.33	0

Source: Author's own calculations from IHDS data.
Note: Decomposition using equation (3.10) of the appendix: 12,361 observations.

Table 3.6 shows that when SC and HCH assets were evaluated using the HCH coefficient (asset returns) vector, of the total difference of ₹375.23 in MPCE between HCH and SC rural households, ₹141.83 (38 percent) could be explained by differences in asset endowments between the two groups of households. However, when SC and HCH assets were evaluated using the SC coefficient (asset returns) vector, ₹165.12 (44 percent) of the total difference of ₹375.23 could be explained by differences in asset endowments between the two groups of households.[17]

Table 3.7 shows that when HOBC and HCH assets were evaluated using the HCH coefficient (asset returns) vector, of the total difference of ₹293.47 in MPCE between HCH and HOBC rural households, ₹130.01

[15] This is the term U in equation (3.8) of the appendix with β^* replaced by β^{HCH}.
[16] This is the term U in equation (3.8) of the appendix with β^* replaced by β^{SC} (or β^{OBC}).
[17] The remaining difference of, respectively, 61 and 54 percent was the "unexplained difference" which is the term V in equation (3.8).

(44 percent) could be explained by differences in asset endowments between the two groups of households. However, when HOBC and HCH assets were evaluated using the HOBC coefficient (asset returns) vector, ₹153.57 (52 percent) of the total difference of ₹293.47 could be explained by differences in asset endowments between the two groups of households.[18] The outcomes are illustrated in Figures 3.6–3.9.

Figure 3.6:
The decomposition of mean difference between HCH and SC households, HCH evaluation

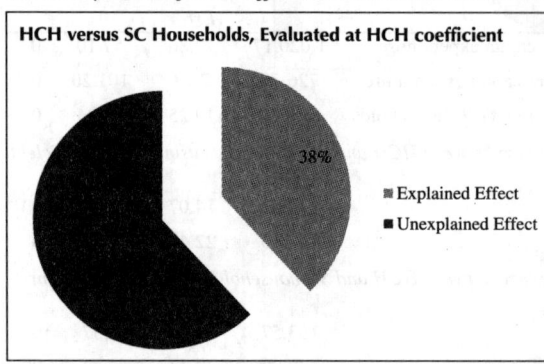

Source: Author's own calculations from IHDS data.

Figure 3.7:
The decomposition of mean difference between HCH and SC households, SC evaluation

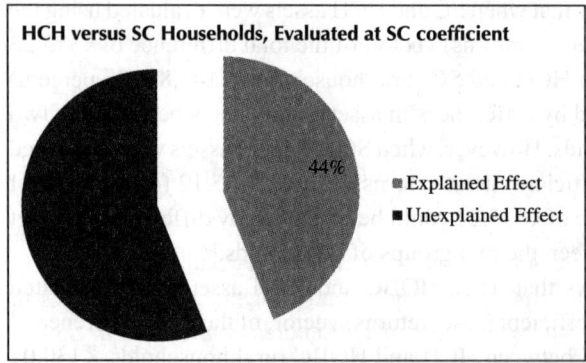

Source: Author's own calculations from IHDS data.

---

[18] The remaining difference of, respectively, 57 and 53 percent was the "unexplained difference," which is the term *V* in equation (3.8).

Figure 3.8:
The decomposition of mean difference between HCH and HOBC households, HCH evaluation

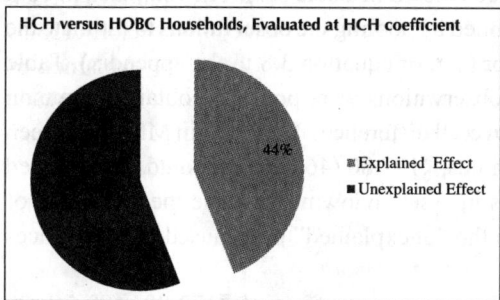

Source: Author's own calculations from IHDS data.

Figure 3.9:
The decomposition of mean difference between HCH and HOBC households, HOBC evaluation

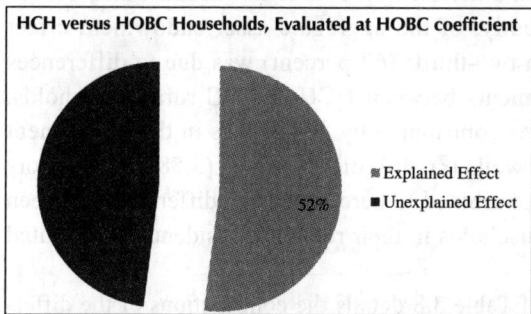

Source: Author's own calculations from IHDS data.

3.5.2. *Asset Endowment and Returns Breakdown: SC*

The results of Tables 3.6 and 3.7 show aggregate results: they quantify the extent to which differences in asset endowments and differences in asset returns between two groups of households *contributed in aggregate* to differences between them in their MPCE. However, this begs the question: which of the specific assets (and their returns) made the largest contribution to the aggregate picture?

Table 3.8 breaks down the aggregate results for the HCH and SC difference (shown in Table 3.6) into the contributions made by the individual variables while Table 3.9 does the same for the aggregate results for the HCH and HOBC difference (shown in Table 3.7). The estimates in both Tables 3.8 and 3.9 are obtained by pooling the observations to estimate the common coefficient vector ($\beta*$, of equation 3.8 in the appendix). Table 3.8 shows that when the observations were pooled to obtain a common coefficient vector, of the overall difference of ₹375.23 in MPCE between HCH and SC rural households, ₹172.80 (46 percent) could be explained by inter-group differences in asset endowments while the remainder of ₹198.41 (54 percent) was the "unexplained" part caused by differences in asset returns.

Of the aggregate asset endowment effect of ₹172.80, ₹99.56 (58 percent) was caused by differences between HCH and SC groups in the proportion of their respective households in which the highest level of education of an adult was Matric or higher. Differences in the proportion of households with a literate in the household contributed ₹15.44 (9 percent). Consequently, of the aggregate asset endowment effect of ₹164.26, more than two-thirds (67 percent) was due to differences in educational endowments between HCH and SC rural households. Another 13 percent was contributed by differences in the endowment of land (₹22.61); tube wells (₹6.46), diesel pumps (3.58), and tractors (₹12.39) collectively contributed 13 percent. Lastly, differences between HCH and SC rural households in their region of residence contributed ₹16.38 (9 percent).[19]

The second panel of Table 3.8 details the contributions of the different assets to the "unexplained" contribution of ₹202.42 to the overall difference between HCH and SC households in their MPCE. In terms of contribution to the "unexplained part" stemming from asset ownership, differences between HCH and SC groups, in which the highest level of education of an adult was Matric or higher, contributed ₹12.99 (6 percent); differences between HCH and SC groups in their ownership of land contributed ₹74.74 (37 percent); and differences between HCH and SC groups in their ownership of buffaloes contributed ₹94.18 (47 percent). Lastly, differences between HCH and SC rural households in their region of residence contributed ₹22.43 (10 percent). Figure 3.10 is a diagrammatic representation of these results.

[19] North: ₹17.69; south: ₹–4.18; west: ₹–7.60; and central: ₹10.47.

Table 3.8:

Individual contributions to the decomposition of the difference in mean per-capita consumption expenditure between HCH and SC households, pooled estimates

	Value	Standard Error	z Value	P > z
HCH: Mean household per capita expenditure	1,020.17	17.84	57.20	0
SC: Mean household per capita expenditure	644.94	7.84	82.22	0
Difference between HCH and SC households	375.23	19.48	19.26	0
Explained difference				
Literate in household	15.44	3.37	4.58	0.00
Highest education level of adult in household is ≥ Matric	99.56	7.63	13.04	0.00
Household owns land	22.61	6.41	3.53	0.00
Household owns tube well	6.46	8.22	0.79	0.43
Household owns electric pump	–0.93	4.76	–0.20	0.85
Household owns diesel pump	3.58	2.15	1.66	0.10
Household owns tractor	12.39	5.24	2.37	0.02
Household owns thresher	–0.44	1.61	–0.27	0.78
Household owns cows	–0.62	1.00	–0.62	0.53
Household owns buffalo	–1.62	1.04	–1.55	0.12
Household lives in north	17.69	2.99	5.92	0.00
Household lives in south	–4.18	2.43	–1.72	0.09
Household lives in west	–7.60	3.88	–1.96	0.05
Household lives in central	10.47	1.94	5.39	0.00
Total	172.80	10.91	15.83	0.00
Unexplained difference				
Literate in household	29.62	27.03	1.10	0.27
Highest education level of adult in household is ≥ Matric	12.99	12.32	1.05	0.29
Household owns land	74.74	35.80	2.09	0.04
Household owns tube well	2.03	7.60	0.27	0.79
Household owns electric pump	–10.49	5.01	–2.09	0.04
Household owns diesel pump	–3.29	3.64	–0.90	0.37
Household owns tractor	–1.01	2.00	–0.51	0.61

Table 3.8 continued

Table 3.8 continued

Household owns thresher	−2.22	1.64	−1.36	0.18
Household owns cows	−10.24	27.61	−0.37	0.71
Household owns buffalo	94.18	26.59	3.54	0.00
Household lives in north	−6.32	11.63	−0.54	0.59
Household lives in south	19.09	15.94	1.20	0.23
Household lives in west	−47.55	9.08	−5.23	0.00
Household lives in central	−44.03	12.92	−3.41	0.00
Intercept	94.92	73.68	1.29	0.20
Total	202.42	14.29	14.16	0.00

Source: Author's own calculations from IHDS data.

Figure 3.10:
Contributions of various assets to difference in mean MPCE between HCH and SC households

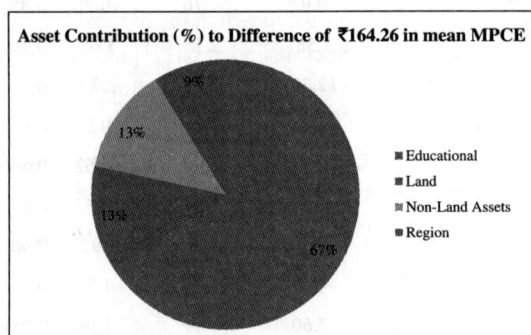

Source: Author's own calculations from IHDS data.

3.5.3. *Asset Endowment and Returns Breakdown: HOBC*

Table 3.9 shows that when the observations were pooled to obtain a common coefficient vector, of the overall difference of ₹293.47 in MPCE between HCH and HOBC rural households, ₹136.71 (47 percent) could be explained by inter-group differences in asset endowments while the remainder of ₹156.76 (53 percent) was the "unexplained" part caused by differences in asset returns.

Of the aggregate asset endowment effect of ₹136.71, ₹57.33 (42 percent) was caused by differences between HCH and HOBC groups in the proportion of their respective households in which the highest level of education of an adult was Matric or higher. Differences in the proportion of households with a literate in the household contributed ₹6.52 (5 percent). Consequently, of the aggregate asset endowment effect of ₹133.29 between HCH and HOBC households, nearly a half (47 percent) was due to differences in educational endowments between HCH and HOBC rural households. Another ₹5.17 (4 percent) was contributed by differences in the endowment of land; tractors (₹6.18), diesel pumps (₹1.15), and buffaloes (₹5.13) collectively contributed 9 percent. Lastly, differences between HCH and HOBC rural households in their region of residence contributed ₹50.15 (37 percent).[20]

The second panel of Table 3.9 details the contributions of the different assets to the "unexplained" contribution of ₹156.76 to the overall difference between HCH and HOBC households in their MPCE. In terms of contribution to the "unexplained part" stemming from asset ownership, differences between HCH and HOBC groups, in which the highest level of education of an adult was Matric or higher, contributed ₹42.71 (27 percent); differences between HCH and HOBC groups in their ownership of electric pumps contributed ₹–21.59 (–14 percent); and differences between HCH and HOBC groups in their ownership of buffaloes contributed ₹52.77 (34 percent). Lastly, differences between HCH and HOBC rural households in their region of residence contributed ₹36.29 (23 percent). Figure 3.11 is a diagrammatic representation of these results.

Table 3.9:

Individual contributions to the decomposition of the difference in mean per-capita consumption expenditure between HCH and HOBC households, pooled estimates

	Value	*Standard Error*	*z Value*	*P > z*
HCH: Mean household per capita expenditure	1,020.17	17.84	57.20	0.00
SC: Mean household per capita expenditure	726.70	7.17	101.28	0.00
Difference between HCH and SC households	293.47	19.22	15.27	0.00
Explained difference				
Literate in household	6.52	1.76	3.71	0.00

Table 3.9 continued

[20] North: ₹53.80; south: ₹–20.41; west: ₹1.36; and central: ₹18.12.

Table 3.9 continued

Highest education level of adult in household is ≥ Matric	57.33	4.67	12.29	0.00
Household owns land	5.17	1.62	3.20	0.00
Household owns tube well	2.23	1.75	1.27	0.20
Household owns electric pump	1.94	1.43	1.36	0.17
Household owns diesel pump	1.15	0.63	1.82	0.07
Household owns tractor	6.18	2.21	2.80	0.01
Household owns thresher	0.46	0.60	0.77	0.44
Household owns cows	0.45	0.76	0.59	0.55
Household owns buffalo	5.13	1.59	3.23	0.00
Household lives in north	53.80	5.60	9.61	0.00
Household lives in south	−20.41	3.79	−5.39	0.00
Household lives in west	−1.36	2.05	−0.66	0.51
Household lives in central	18.12	2.83	6.41	0.00
Total	136.71	7.95	17.20	0.00
Unexplained difference				
Literate in household	22.04	28.50	0.77	0.44
Highest education level of adult in household is ≥ Matric	42.71	13.66	3.13	0.00
Household owns land	64.63	39.51	1.64	0.10
Household owns tube well	−0.89	14.34	−0.06	0.95
Household owns electric pump	−21.59	8.72	−2.48	0.01
Household owns diesel pump	−4.71	5.23	−0.90	0.37
Household owns tractor	0.98	5.51	0.18	0.86
Household owns thresher	−4.74	3.00	−1.58	0.12
Household owns cows	2.13	23.67	0.09	0.93
Household owns buffalo	52.77	22.49	2.35	0.02
Household lives in north	−32.87	8.53	−3.85	0.00
Household lives in south	−30.09	16.78	−1.79	0.07
Household lives in west	−65.72	9.87	−6.66	0.00
Household lives in central	−69.49	14.11	−4.92	0.00
Intercept	201.59	75.43	2.67	0.01
Total	156.76	16.42	9.55	0.00

Source: Author's own calculations from IHDS data.

Figure 3.11:

Contributions of various assets to difference in mean MPCE between HCH and HOBC households

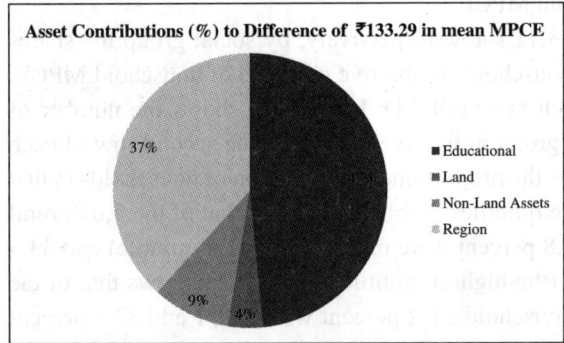

Source: Author's own calculations from IHDS data.

3.6. The Decomposition of Inequality in Household Monthly (per capita) Consumption Expenditure

The previous two sections examined the determinants of MPCE in terms of asset ownership and asset returns. A related issue is how asset ownership and asset returns coalesce to produce inequality between households in terms of their consumption expenditure. What are the determinants of inter-household inequality? Does it depend upon their social identity? Where do they live, and what is their level of education? And if it does depend, at least in part, on these items, how much do they contribute to overall inequality? These questions are answered in this section using the tool of inequality decomposition.

A summary measure of inequality is provided by Kuznet's (1955) ratio, which measures the ratio of income (or consumption) share accruing to the richest 20 percent, to the share accruing to the poorest 20 percent, of households. The mean MPCE of the richest and poorest 20 percent of the total of 26,981 *rural* households analyzed were, respectively, ₹1,795 and ₹265, yielding a Kuznet's ratio of 6.8. For urban India, the mean MPCE of the richest and poorest 20 percent of the total of 14,510 *urban* households analyzed were, respectively, ₹2,995 and ₹427, yielding a Kuznet's ratio of 7.0. The computation of Kuznet's ratio, with its focus on households in the top and bottom quintiles leads us to examine the proportionate presence of the three caste groups in the bottom (poorest) and the top (richest) quintiles of household MPCE.

Tables 3.10 and 3.11 show, respectively, by social group the shares of rural and urban households in the five quintiles of household MPCE. The first row of each table (HHLD: household) shows the number of households for that group in the five quintiles. The second row of each table (Row %) shows the proportionate distribution of households in that group across the five quintiles: Table 3.10 shows that of the 5,018 rural HCH households, 7.8 percent were in Q1 (the lowest quintile) and 33.3 percent were in Q5 (the highest quintile); Table 3.11 shows that of the 4,498 urban HCH households, 8.2 percent were in Q1 and 32.4 percent were in Q5. The third row of each table (Col%) shows for each quintile, the composition of each quintile in terms of the seven social groups: Table 3.10 shows that in the lowest quintile of rural MPCE, 7.2 percent of households were HCH, 33.9 percent of households were HOBC, 25.6 percent of households were SC and so on; Table 3.11 shows that in the lowest quintile of urban MPCE, 12.7 percent of households were HCH, 32.4 percent of households were HOBC, 24.4 percent of households were SC and so on.

Tables 3.10 and 3.11 also allow one to assess the extent of under-representation or over-representation of each social group in the different quintiles. For example, from Table 3.10, HCH households comprise 18.6 percent of the total number of rural households (5,018 out of 26,981 households) but they comprise only 7.2 percent of households in the lowest quintile of rural MPCE (390 out of 5,427) and 31 percent of households in the highest quintile of rural MPCE (1,673 out of 5,394). At the other end of the scale, from Table 3.10, ST households comprise 10.9 percent of the total number of rural households (2,936 out of 26,981 households) but they comprise 24.2 percent of households in the lowest quintile of rural MPCE (1,313 out of 5,427) and only 4.6 percent of households in the highest quintile of rural MPCE (246 out of 5,394).

A similar story can be told with respect to urban households. So, from Table 3.11, HCH households comprise 31 percent of the total number of urban households (4,498 out of 14,510 households) but they comprise only 12.7 percent of households in the lowest quintile of urban MPCE (369 out of 2,910) and over half of all households in the highest quintile

Table 3.10:
Shares of the social groups by quintile of MPCE, rural households

HCH	Q1	Q2	Q3	Q4	Q5	Total
HHLD	390	720	994	1,241	1,673	5,018
Row%	7.8	14.4	19.8	24.7	33.3	100
Col%	7.2	13.4	18.4	23.0	31.0	18.6
HOBC						
HHLD	1,840	1,993	1,969	1,976	1,758	9,536
Row%	19.3	20.9	20.7	20.7	18.4	100
Col%	33.9	37.0	36.5	36.7	32.6	35.3
SC						
HHLD	1,389	1,402	1,307	1,110	794	6,002
Row%	23.1	23.4	21.8	18.5	13.2	100
Col%	25.6	26.1	24.3	20.6	14.7	22.3
ST						
HHLD	1,313	581	445	351	246	2,936
Row%	44.7	19.8	15.2	12.0	8.4	100
Col%	24.2	10.8	8.3	6.5	4.6	10.9
MOBC						
HHLD	198	244	217	209	187	1,055
Row%	18.8	23.1	20.6	19.8	17.7	100
Col%	3.7	4.5	4.0	3.9	3.5	3.9
HCM						
HHLD	256	382	325	245	262	1,470
Row%	17.4	26.0	22.1	16.7	17.8	100
Col%	4.7	7.1	6.0	4.6	4.9	5.5
OTG						
HHLD	41	60	133	256	474	964
Row%	4.3	6.2	13.8	26.6	49.2	100
Col%	0.8	1.1	2.5	4.8	8.8	3.6
Total						
HHLD	5,427	5,382	5,390	5,388	5,394	26,981
Row%	20.1	20.0	20.0	20.0	20.0	100
Col%	100	100	100	100	100	100

Source: Author's own calculations from IHDS data.

Table 3.11:
Shares of the social groups by quintile of MPCE, urban households

HCH	Q1	Q2	Q3	Q4	Q5	Total
HHLD	369	653	869	1,151	1,456	4,498
Row%	8.2	14.5	19.3	25.6	32.4	100
Col%	12.7	22.5	30.0	39.7	50.2	31
HOBC						
HHLD	942	989	889	810	697	4,327
Row%	21.8	22.9	20.6	18.7	16.1	100
Col%	32.4	34.1	30.7	27.9	24.0	29.8
SC						
HHLD	710	543	458	376	233	2,320
Row%	30.6	23.4	19.7	16.2	10.0	100
Col%	24.4	18.7	15.8	13.0	8.0	16.0
ST						
HHLD	123	98	113	81	82	497
Row%	24.8	19.7	22.7	16.3	16.5	100
Col%	4.2	3.4	3.9	2.8	2.8	3.4
MOBC						
HHLD	391	229	175	107	55	957
Row%	40.9	23.9	18.3	11.2	5.8	100
Col%	13.4	7.9	6.1	3.7	1.9	6.6
HCM						
HHLD	321	286	262	203	150	1,222
Row%	26.3	23.4	21.4	16.6	12.3	100
Col%	11.0	9.9	9.1	7.0	5.2	8.4
OTG						
HHLD	54	104	128	174	229	689
Row%	7.8	15.1	18.6	25.3	33.2	100
Col%	1.9	3.6	4.4	6.0	7.9	4.8
Total						
HHLD	2,910	2,902	2,894	2,902	2,902	14,510
Row%	20.1	20.0	19.9	20.0	20.0	100
Col%	100	100	100	100	100	100

Source: Author's own calculations from IHDS data.

of rural MPCE (1,456 out of 2,902). At the other end of the scale, from Table 3.11, SC households comprise 16 percent of the total number of urban households (2,320 out of 14,510 households) but they comprise 24.4 percent of households in the lowest quintile of urban MPCE (710 out of 2,910) and only 8 percent of households in the highest quintile of urban MPCE (233 out of 2,902).

Even in the lowest quintile of MPCE, HCH households had a higher mean MPCE than SC, ST, or MOBC households: for rural areas, ₹285 for HCH households versus ₹273 for SC households, ₹238 for ST households, and ₹268 for MOBC households; for urban areas, ₹446 for HCH households versus ₹418 for SC households, ₹406 for ST households, and ₹414 for MOBC households. Equally, in the highest quintile of MPCE, HCH households had a higher mean MPCE than SC, ST, or MOBC households: for rural areas, ₹1,896 for HCH households versus ₹1,650 for SC households, ₹1,630 for ST households, and ₹1,686 for MOBC households; for urban areas, ₹3,103 for HCH households versus ₹2,829 for SC households, ₹2,684 for ST households, and ₹2,631 for MOBC households. These outcomes are illustrated in Figures 3.12 (rural households) and 3.13 (urban households).

Figure 3.12:
Mean MPCE (₹) of rural households, by social group, in top and bottom MPCE quintiles

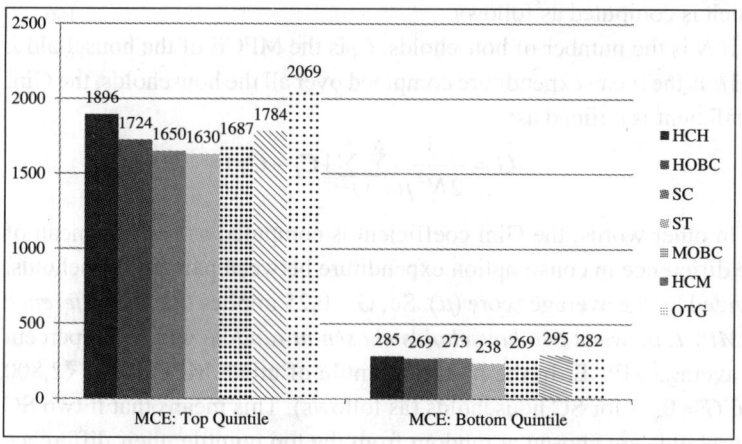

Source: Author's own calculations from IHDS data.

Figure 3.13:

Mean MPCE (₹) of urban households, by social group, in top and bottom MPCE quintiles

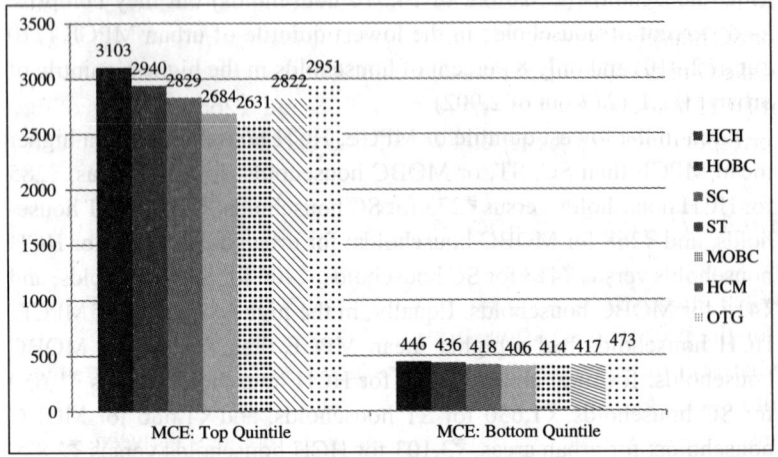

Source: Author's own calculations from IHDS data.

Although the mean incomes of households in the different groups were different in each quintile, the degree of inequality in a quintile, in the distribution of household MPCE, did not vary much by social group. The most usual way of measuring inequality is by the *Gini coefficient*, which is computed as follows.

If N is the number of households, C_i is the MPCE of the household i, and μ is the mean expenditure computed over all the households, the Gini coefficient is defined as:

$$G = \frac{1}{2N^2\mu} \sum_{i=1}^{N} \sum_{j=1}^{N} |C_i - C_j|$$

In other words, the Gini coefficient is computed as half the mean of the difference in consumption expenditure between pairs of households, divided by the average score (μ). So, $G = 0.25$ implies that the *difference in MPCE between two households chosen at random* will be 50 percent of average MPCE. In the highest quintile of urban MPCE, $\mu = ₹2,800$ and $G = 0.25$ for SC households (as follows). This means that if two SC households are chosen at random from the top quintile, their difference in consumption will be 50 percent of ₹2,800, that is, ₹1,400.

In the *lowest* quintile, the values of the Gini coefficients for the distribution of the rural and urban MPCE of HCH households were, respectively, 0.11 and 0.12; the values of the corresponding Gini coefficients for SC households were 0.12 and 0.13. In the *highest* quintile, the values of the Gini coefficients for the distribution of the rural and urban MPCE of HCH households were, respectively, 0.29 and 0.26; the values of the corresponding Gini coefficients for SC households were 0.24 and 0.25.[21]

3.6.1. *The Decomposition of Inequality*

When one observes a certain level of inequality between households (for the present discussion, in their MPCE), we would like to know what *explains* it. Is it due to the fact that households are segmented into social groups? In that case, we would expect that some of the observed inequality can be explained by differences *between* social groups because households from some groups have, on average, a lower MPCE compared to households from other groups. But not all of inequality can be explained by differences between groups—some of the observed overall inequality will be due to to the fact that there is inequality *within* household groups: for example, not all households *within* a particular group have the same MPCE. Of course, one need not subdivide households by caste—one could, equally well, have subdivided them by region (north, south, east, west, and central) or by education (literate or illiterate). Whenever, and however, one subdivides households there are two sources of inequality: *between-group* and *within-group*. The method of inequality decomposition attempts to separate (or decompose) overall inequality into its constituent parts: between-group and within-group. When the decomposition is *additive*, overall inequality can be written as the *sum* of within-group and between-group inequality:

$$I = A + B$$

Overall ineqality   Within group inequality   Between group inequality

---

[21] The exception to this general observation was ST households. There was much greater inequality for ST households, compared to other groups, in the lowest quintile and much less inequality in the highest quintile. The Gini values for ST households were, for the lowest quintile, 0.16 (rural) and 0.14 (urban) and, for the highest quintile, 0.21 (rural) and 0.19 (urban).

When inequality is additively decomposed, then one can say that the basis on which the households were subdivided (say, caste/religion) contributed [(B/I) × 100]% to overall inequality, the remaining inequality, [(A/I) × 100]%, being due to inequality *within* the caste/religion groups. If one subdivided the households by *caste/religion* and *region*, so that one had 35 categories, then by additively decomposing inequality, as above, one could say that caste/religion *and* region collectively accounted for [(B/I) × 100]% of overall inequality, the remaining inequality being due to inequality within the 35 categories.[22] So, inequality decomposition provides a way of analyzing the extent to which inter-household inequality is "explained" by a constellation of factors. For example, it allows one to answer how much of the observed inequality in household MPCE can be accounted for by differences—either singly or collectively—in caste, education, and region. The details of the methodology of "inequality decomposition" are contained in the appendix to this chapter. Suffice it to say here that in order to decompose inequality *additively*, inequality has to be measured in a very specific way.[23]

Table 3.12 shows the results from decomposing households' MPCE by subdividing the sample of *rural* and *urban* households along one of the following lines:

1. Caste/religion: HCH, HOBC, SC, ST, MOBC, HCH, and OTG
2. Region: Central, north, south, west, and east
3. Highest education of adult in household: Matric (or higher) or non-Matric

The first point that emerges from Table 3.12 is that the level of inequality was slightly, but consistently, higher for urban, compared to rural, households. The second point is that social division in the form of caste/religion played the same role in explaining urban and rural, inequality in household MPCE: 11 percent of total inequality in both rural and urban areas could be explained by social division. The third point is that the region of residence played a relatively major role in explaining rural, compared to urban, disparities in household MPCE: 10 percent compared

[22] Seven social (caste/religion) groups × five regions.
[23] This involves using an inequality index from the family of *Generalized Entropy Indices*.

to 3 percent. The fourth point is that a high level of education played a major role in explaining urban, compared to rural, inequality in household MPCE: 25 percent compared to 12 percent. The fifth, and final point, was that when all three factors—caste, region, and education—were considered collectively; they together explained 25 percent of rural, and 31 percent of urban, inequality between households in their MPCE.

Table 3.12:

Percentage within- and between-group contributions to inequality in per capita household MPCE

Decomposition by ↓	MLD Value (Gini Value)	Within-Group Contribution (%)	Between-Group Contribution (%)
Rural households			
Caste/religion: 26,981 households	0.251 (0.388)	89	11
Region: 25,534 households	0.248 (0.386)	90	10
High education level of adult in household: 23,880 households	0.252 (0.390)	88	12
All three combined: 22,728 households	0.252 (0.389)	75	25
Urban households			
Caste/religion: 14,510 households	0.256 (0.393)	89	11
Region: 13,578 households	0.261 (0.397)	97	3
High education level of adult in household: 12,338 households	0.268 (0.402)	75	25
All three combined: 11,582 households	0.271 (0.404)	69	31

Source: Author's own calculations from IHDS data.
Note: MLD, mean logarithmic deviation.

An interesting question is how much of overall inequality is due to the fact that the mean MPCE of the quintiles differ or, in other words, due to the fact that the mean MPCE of "rich" households in much more than that of "poor" households. This calculation would indicate the amount by which inequality would fall if mean MPCE between the quintiles were equalized by an *equi-proportionate* reduction in the MPCE of all rich and the (same) proportionate increase in the MPCE of all poor households. This would maintain inequality *within* quintiles but eliminate inequality *between* quintiles. On our calculation, overall inequality would fall by 86 percent in rural India and by 88 percent in urban India.

Earlier, we referred to the fact Kuznet's ratio (the ratio of mean MPCE of the highest quintile to mean MPCE of the lowest quintile) was 6.8 for rural India and 7.0 for urban India. Reducing this difference would go a long way to reducing inequality in India. For example, the Gini coefficient computed over all households' MPCE (that is, rural and urban) was 0.39, and Kuznet's ratio was 7.7 (₹2,297/₹297), and mean household MPCE was ₹955. If the MPCE of *all* households in the *top* quintile was reduced by 9 percent, and the MPCE of *all* households in the *bottom* quintile was increased by 25 percent, *household MPCE in the other quintiles unchanged*, mean household MPCE would remain at ₹955. However, because of the redistribution between the top and bottom quintiles, Kuznet's ratio would fall to 4.8 (₹2,074/₹430), the value of the Gini coefficient would fall to 0.34 (from 0.39), and the contribution of *between*-quintile inequality to *overall* inequality would fall to 84 percent (from 87 percent).

3.7. Caste/Religion and Poverty

The previous section was concerned with inequality—the gap between households. But, as we have argued in Section 2, another item of interest is poverty—the shortfall that households experience in terms of an adequate bundle of consumption. This section moves from an analysis of inequality to an examination of poverty.

In two seminal papers, Basu (2001, 2006) proposes a *quintile axiom*, according to which "we should focus attention on the per-capita income of the poorest 20% of the population ('quintile income') and the growth rate of the per-capita income of the poorest 20% ('quintile growth')" (Basu, 2001: 66). Using this axiom, we define a rural/urban household as being "poor" if its MPCE places it in the bottom 20 percent of the distribution of MPCE across rural/urban households. So, according to this definition, a rural household in our sample of rural households is "poor" if its MPCE is less than ₹353 and an urban household is "poor" if its MPCE is less than ₹568.[24] We define the variable POVR *for rural households only* as taking the value 1 for a rural household if it is poor (its MPCE ≤ ₹353), and POVR = 0 if a rural household is not poor (MPCE > ₹353). Similarly, we define the variable POVU *for urban households only* as taking the value 1 for an urban household if it is poor (its MPCE ≤ ₹568), POVU = 0 if an urban household is not poor (MPCE > ₹568).

Following from this, we estimated logit equations with, respectively, POVR and POVU as dependent variables, to answer two questions: (i) what was the relative strength of the different factors, relating to the households, which exercised a significant influence—either positively or negatively—on their probability of being poor? (ii) After taking these factors into account was there still significant correlation between the households' caste/religious group and their probability of being poor? In other words, in terms of (i), we may discover that illiteracy is a cause of poverty and surmise that the reason we observe a greater proportion of SC, relative to HCH, households that are poor is that, compared to HCH households, a greater proportion of SC households are all-illiterate households. So, the fact that a larger proportion of SC households are poor has nothing to do with caste and everything to do with illiteracy: remove illiteracy and the caste basis for poverty will be eliminated. However, in response to point (ii), if we discover, after comparing two sets of all-illiterate households, one from the SC and the other from HCH, that the probability of being poor is significantly higher for SC households than for HCH households, we can say that, even controlling for illiteracy, caste significantly affects the probability of being poor.

A further point connected to point (i) is the following: given that illiteracy positively affects the likelihood of all households being poor, does it affect this probability more for say, SC households than for say, HCH households? If the answer to this is yes, then that, too, provides a caste basis for being poor: illiteracy is bad in terms of consigning households to poverty but it is worse for SC households than for HCH households. In order to uncover points such as these—in which a variable has differential effect on households, from different groups, in their probabilities of being poor—we estimate the logit equations including, as described in equation (3.1), interaction terms.

[24] In this analysis, we exclude households from the "other" groups (OTG). That is, we focus on HCH, HOBC, SC, ST, MOBC, and HCM households.

Table 3.10 shows the proportions of the different social groups who were in the lowest quintile of household MPCE. In a rural context, 8 percent of HCH households, 19 percent of HOBC households, 23 percent of SC households, 45 percent of ST households, 19 percent of MOBC households, and 17 percent of HCM households were in the lowest quintile of MPCE. Table 3.11 shows that, in an urban context, 8 percent of HCH households, 22 percent of HOBC households, 31 percent of SC households, 25 percent of ST households, 41 percent of MOBC households, and 26 percent of HCM households were in the lowest quintile of MPCE. These figures may be interpreted as the *likelihood of being poor* for rural and urban households in the different social groups.

A natural question to ask from the logit model is how the likelihood of being poor (that is, being in the lowest quintile of MPCE) would *change* in response to a change in the value of a "poverty influencing" variable *ceteris paribus*. These changes to the probabilities (or likelihood) of being poor are termed *marginal probabilities*. The marginal probability associated with a variable refers to the *change* in the outcome probability consequent upon a unit change in the value of the variable, and *the values of the other variables remaining unchanged.*[25] For discrete variables (as, indeed, are all the variables reported above), the unit change in the value of a variable refers to a move *from a situation in which the variable takes the value unity* to *a situation in which the variable takes the value zero*, the values of the other variables remaining unchanged.[26] Therefore, the marginal probability of a SC household being poor is:

The probability of being poor when *all* the households are from the SC
less
The probability of being poor when none when all the households are from the *residual* group
   With all the values for the other variables (income, education, etc.) held at their mean values.

---

[25] More formally, $\Pr(\text{POVR}_j = 1) = e^z / (1 + e^z)$ and the marginal probability with respect to variable k is: $\dfrac{\partial \Pr(\text{POVR}_j = 1)}{\partial X_{jk}}$

[26] In the calculations reported here, the values of the other variables were held *at their mean values* in the sample.

These marginal probabilities are reported in Tables 3.13 and 3.14 for, respectively, rural and urban households. These show that—*after*

Table 3.13:

Marginal probabilities of being a poor rural household

	Marginal Probability	Standard Error	Z Value	P Score: Probability > z
OBC Hindu	0.092	0.017	5.34	0.00
Scheduled Castes	0.093	0.021	4.32	0.00
Scheduled Tribes	0.268	0.020	13.38	0.00
OBC Muslim	0.114	0.022	5.11	0.00
High-caste Muslim	0.104	0.021	4.84	0.00
Literate in household	−0.024	0.007	−3.40	0.00
ST × Literate in household	−0.045	0.014	−3.24	0.00
Highest education level of adult in household (medium)	−0.085	0.008	−10.50	0.00
SC × Highest education level of adult in household (medium)	0.052	0.014	3.75	0.00
Highest of adult in household (high)	−0.235	0.011	−21.47	0.00
SC × Highest education level of adult in household (high)	0.074	0.021	3.50	0.00
Household owns land	−0.039	0.019	−2.05	0.04
OBC Hindu × household owns land	0.044	0.021	2.12	0.03
SC × household owns land	0.043	0.021	1.99	0.05
ST × household owns land	0.061	0.023	2.70	0.01
OBC Muslim × household owns land	−0.053	0.032	−1.64	0.10
High-caste Muslim × household owns land	−0.065	0.029	−2.26	0.02
Household owns tube well	−0.072	0.014	−5.33	0.00
Household owns diesel pump	−0.043	0.015	−2.83	0.01
Household owns electric pump	−0.075	0.014	−5.45	0.00
Household owns bullock cart	−0.014	0.011	−1.30	0.19
Household owns thresher	−0.131	0.035	−3.72	0.00
Household owns tractor	−0.180	0.040	−4.45	0.00
Household owns cow	0.004	0.002	1.97	0.05
Household owns draft animal	−0.010	0.002	−5.99	0.00
Household owns buffalo	−0.013	0.002	−6.50	0.00
SC × household owns buffalo	0.010	0.002	4.45	0.00
Number of adults in household	0.043	0.002	17.71	0.00

Source: Author's own calculations from IHDS data.

Table 3.14:
Marginal probabilities of being a poor urban household

	Marginal Probability	Standard Error	Z Value	P Score: Probability > z
OBC Hindu	0.042	0.015	2.83	0.01
Scheduled Castes	0.130	0.020	6.40	0.00
Scheduled Tribes	0.122	0.021	5.82	0.00
OBC Muslim	0.120	0.015	8.07	0.00
High-caste Muslim	0.105	0.023	4.50	0.00
Literate in household	−0.047	0.010	−4.68	0.00
Highest education level of adult in household (medium)	−0.075	0.011	−7.15	0.00
OBC Hindu × Highest education level of adult in household (medium)	0.037	0.016	2.34	0.02
Highest education level of adult in household (high)	−0.351	0.016	−21.41	0.00
OBC Hindu × Highest education of adult in household (high)	0.106	0.022	4.91	0.00
SC × Highest education level of adult in household (high)	0.078	0.025	3.07	0.00
ST × Highest education level of adult in household (high)	−0.131	0.056	−2.35	0.02
OBC Muslim × Highest education level of adult in household (high)	0.126	0.030	4.19	0.00
High-caste Muslim × highest education level of adult in household (high)	0.059	0.034	1.73	0.08
Number of adults in household	0.049	0.003	15.82	0.00
SC × Number of adults in household	−0.012	0.007	−1.85	0.07
High-caste Muslims × Number of adults in household	−0.017	0.007	−2.32	0.02

Source: Author's own calculations from IHDS data.

controlling for other factors[27]—caste and religion significantly *increased* the probability of being poor for *rural and urban* HOBC, SC, ST, MOBC, and HCM households, compared to their HCH counterparts, where households from the HCH comprise the *reference* category. In other words,

[27] These were mother's education, household income, main source of household income, age, region of residence, and rural/urban location.

compared to HCH households, households from all other social groups, whether rural or urban, were more likely to be poor, even after equalizing for non-caste/religious attributes. For example, for a rural SC household, the probability of being poor was increased by nine percentage points over that for a rural HCH household (Table 3.13) and, for an urban SC household, the probability of being poor was increased by 13 percentage points over that for an urban HCH household (Table 3.14). Similarly, for a rural MOBC household, the probability of being poor was increased by 11 percentage points over that for a rural HCH household and, for an urban MOBC household, the probability of being poor was increased by 12 percentage points over that for an urban HCH household.

Furthermore, Tables 3.13 and 3.14 show that several poverty reducing factors impacted differently on the different social groups. For example, in the context of a household having an adult educated up to Matric or higher, urban HCH households benefited by significantly more from this achievement than households from the other groups; similarly, rural HCH households benefited by significantly more from this achievement than their SC counterparts. For example, in a rural context, having a Matric in a household served to reduce the probability of being poor by 24 points for HCH households, but by only 16 points for SC households. In an urban context, having a Matric in a household served to reduce the probability of being poor by 35 points for HCH households, but by 25 points for HOBC households, 27 points for SC households, 22 points for ST households, 23 points for MOBC households, and by 29 points for HCM households. [28]

Table 3.13 also emphasizes a point made earlier relating to the reluctance of upper-caste Hindus to buy food products from persons from the SC: owning a buffalo reduced the likelihood of being poor by 1.3 points for rural HCH households but by only 0.3 points for rural SC households. A final point that Tables 3.13 and 3.14 highlight is that the likelihood of a household being poor falls as the number of adults in it increases. Every additional adult leads to a fall of 4 points in the probability of rural households being poor and to a fall of 5 points in the probability of urban households being poor. However, in an urban context, the additional benefit of another adult, in terms of reducing the probability of being poor, is less for SC and HCM households—by, respectively, 1.2 and 1.7 points—than for HCH households.

[28] Table 3.13: 23.5–7.4. Table 3.14: 35.1—the relevant interaction term coefficient estimate.

3.8. The Decomposition of Inter-caste Differences in the Probability of Being Poor

The preceding section showed that compared to households from other social groups—OBC Hindus, SC, ST, MOBC, and HCM—the likelihood of being poor was lowest for HCH households. Part of the advantage that HCH households have over other households, in terms of a lower probability of being poor, is due to "assets" advantage: HCH households are better endowed with the assets that take households out of poverty. As Table 3.1 shows there are systematic differences in *asset endowments* between households in the different caste groups so that, for example, compared to HCH households, a smaller proportion of SC households contain an adult who is a Matric (or higher). However, another reason for HCH advantage is the fact that they receive a higher return on their assets: education, land, and non-land productive assets. So, for example, a high level of education of adults in a household would result in a lower probability of being poor for *all* households, but this effect would be stronger for HCH households compared to households from other groups.

A natural question that arises from the preceding section is the following. Given that the likelihood of a household being poor is smaller for a HCH household, compared to households from other groups (OBC Hindus, SC, ST, MOBC, and HCM), what proportion of this difference is due to differences in inter-group asset endowments and what proportion is due to inter-group differences in rates of return on assets? The principles underlying the answer of this question are similar to that enunciated in Section 3.5. In order to answer this question, one needs to distinguish between the contribution of inter-group differences *in asset rates of return* and inter-group differences in *asset ownership* to the overall difference between households, belonging to the different groups, in their respective proportions who are poor. The problem is that households from the HCH and households from group X differ in terms of both attributes and coefficients. So the first step is to ask what the HCH/X difference would have been if both sets of attributes were evaluated at a *common* coefficient vector. This difference could then be entirely ascribed to difference in assets since coefficient differences would have been neutralized. Call this difference the *difference due to asset ownership* or the *explained difference.* Then, the *observed* difference less the *explained difference* is the *residual* or *unexplained* difference.

However, the difference between the methodology used here and that employed earlier (in the section "The Decomposition of Inter-caste Differences in Household MPCE") is that in Section 3.5 the equation expressed a *linear* relation between the dependent variable and the explanatory variable while, now, because of the logit formulation, this relation is *non-linear.* So, in operational terms, the decomposition into an *explained difference* and an *unexplained difference* requires a different, and more complex, methodology when the underlying equation is non-linear compared to when it is linear. This is described in the study by Borooah and Iyer (2005a). The results of this decomposition are shown in Table 3.15 (rural households) and Table 3.16 (urban households) for pair-wise comparisons between HCH households and households from, respectively, OBC Hindus, SC, ST, MOBC, and HCM.

Table 3.15 shows that only 23 percent to 29 percent of the difference between HCH and HOBC *rural* households, in their respective proportion of households that were poor, could be explained by differences in asset endowments between households in the two groups. Similarly, only 29 percent to 32 percent of the difference between HCH and SC *rural* households, in their respective proportion of households that were poor, could be ascribed to differences in asset endowments between households in the two groups. The remainder (71 percent–77 percent for HOBC households and 29 percent–32 percent for SC households) could not be so explained and could, plausibly be attributed to differences in rates of return between HCH households and HOBC and SC households. Asset endowment differences, however, played a much bigger part in explaining differences between HCH and MOBC *rural* households (36 percent–61 percent could be so explained) and between HCH and HCM rural households (44 percent–70 percent could be so explained).

Table 3.16 shows that, for urban households, differences in asset endowment played a much bigger role in explaining differences between HCH households and the households from the other groups, in their respective proportion of households that were poor. Now for HOBC households, 43 percent–50 percent of the difference between them and HCH households (in their respective proportion of households that were poor) could be explained by the fact that HOBC households were less well-endowed in terms of "poverty reducing assets" than HCH households. For SC households, the contribution of asset endowments was 41 percent–60 percent, while for HCM households this contribution was as high as 56 percent–73 percent.

Table 3.15:
Attributes versus unexplained effects in explaining differences in the likelihood of being a poor rural household

	HCH versus HOBC	
Raw	*–0.120*	*100%*
	@HCH Coefficients	
Attributes effect	–0.027	23%
Unexplained effect	–0.093	77%
	@HOBC coefficients	
Attributes effect	–0.035	29%
Unexplained effect	–0.085	71%
	HCH versus SC	
Raw	*–0.154*	*100%*
	@HCH coefficients	
Attributes effect	–0.045	29%
Unexplained effect	–0.109	71%
	@SC coefficients	
Attributes effect	–0.049	32%
Unexplained effect	–0.105	68%
	HCH versus ST	
Raw	*–0.385*	*100%*
	@HCH coefficients	
Attributes effect	–0.048	12%
Unexplained effect	–0.337	88%
	@ST coefficients	
Attributes effect	–0.133	35%
Unexplained effect	–0.252	65%
	HCH versus MOBC	
Raw	*–0.111*	*100%*
	@HCH coefficients	
Attributes effect	–0.040	36%
Unexplained effect	–0.070	64%
	@MOBC coefficients	
Attributes effect	–0.068	61%
Unexplained effect	–0.043	39%

Table 3.15 continued

Table 3.15 continued

	HCH versus HCM	
Raw	−0.093	100%
	@HCH coefficients	
Attributes effect	−0.041	44%
Unexplained effect	−0.052	56%
	@HCM coefficients	
Attributes effect	−0.065	70%
Unexplained Effect	−0.028	30%

Source: Author's own calculations from IHDS data.

Table 3.16:
Attributes versus unexplained effects in explaining differences in the likelihood of being a poor urban household

	HCH versus HOBC	
Raw	−0.146	100%
	@HCH coefficients	
Attributes effect	−0.062	43%
Unexplained effect	−0.083	57%
	@HOBC coefficients	
Attributes effect	−0.073	50%
Unexplained effect	−0.073	50%
	HCH versus SC	
Raw	−0.243	100%
	@HCH coefficients	
Attributes effect	−0.100	41%
Unexplained effect	−0.142	59%
	@SC coefficients	
Attributes effect	−0.144	60%
Unexplained effect	−0.098	40%
	HCH versus ST	
Raw	−0.162	100%
	@HCH coefficients	
Attributes effect	−0.057	35%
Unexplained effect	−0.106	65%
	@ST coefficients	
Attributes effect	−0.118	73%
Unexplained effect	−0.044	27%

Table 3.16 continued

Table 3.16 continued

	HCH versus MOBC	
Raw	−0.344	100%
	@HCH coefficients	
Attributes effect	−0.139	40%
Unexplained effect	−0.205	60%
	@MOBC coefficients	
Attributes effect	−0.177	51%
Unexplained effect	−0.167	49%
	HCH versus HCM	
Raw	−0.189	100%
	@HCH coefficients	
Attributes effect	−0.105	56%
Unexplained effect	−0.084	44%
	@HCM coefficients	
Attributes effect	−0.134	71%
Unexplained effect	−0.055	29%

Source: Author's own calculations from IHDS data.

3.8.1. *The Risk of Poverty*

The most usual method of identifying the poor is to establish a cut-off point, ₹z (also termed the "poverty line") and to regard a household as poor if its resources (income or consumption) are less than or equal to ₹z. In the above analysis, we identified a household as being poor if it was placed in the lowest quintile of MPCE, the implied poverty line being ₹353 for rural, and ₹568 for urban, households. Having identified poor households, the next step is to *measure* poverty by means of an aggregate measure that summarizes the amount of poverty in a geographical area (district, region, state, country). The simplest, and most commonly used, measure is the head count ratio (HCR), which is the proportion of households in an area that are "poor."

In the previous section poverty was measured using the HCR. The problem with the HCR is that it does not pay attention to the "depth of poverty" or in other words to the distance between the MPCE of poor households and the poverty line: so, two areas may have the same HCR (that is, the same proportion of households that are poor) but the depth of poverty may be much greater in one region than the other. Another aspect of poverty, pointed out by Sen (1976), was "relative deprivation" as captured by inequality in the MPCE of *poor* households: the greater this inequality among the poor, the greater the level of poverty. Consequently, as Sen (1976) pointed out in his seminal paper, a good measure of poverty should embody all three dimensions. It should contain a measure of the number of poor ("what is the proportion of poor households?"); it should include a measure of the depth of poverty ("how poor are the poor?"); and it should encapsulate "relative deprivation" ("how much inequality is there between the poor?"). A fourth desirable property is that of decomposition: if society can be subdivided into mutually exclusive groups can we express *aggregate* poverty as the sum of the poverty of the groups?

Foster, Greer, and Thorbecke (1984) proposed a measure that embodied all four dimensions. This index, which is derived in the appendix, is referred to here as the FGT index and denoted FGT(α), for a parameter $\alpha \geq 0$: when $\alpha = 0$, FGT(0) is the HCR—it measures the proportion of households that are poor; when $\alpha = 1$, FGT(1) is the aggregate poverty gap; and when $\alpha = 2$, FGT(2) incorporates, in addition to the *head count* and the *aggregate poverty gap*, relative deprivation (as measured by inequality among the poor). The property of the FGT index that concerns this chapter is that of decomposability or, in other words, overall poverty, which can be written as the weighted sum of group poverty.

Box 3.3:
Contribution to poverty and the risk of poverty using the FGT index

Suppose that a population of N households can be subdivided into K subgroups (indexed, $k = 1 \ldots K$) with N_k households in each subgroup. Then by the decomposability property, the aggregate FGT index can be written as the weighted average of the FGT index for each group.

$$\text{FGT}(\alpha) = \sum_{k=1}^{K} \left(\frac{N_k}{N} \right) \text{FGT}^k(\alpha)$$

Where *FGT(α)* is the index calculated over all the households, *FGT^k(α)* is the index calculated over households in group k ($k = 1 \ldots K$), and α is the parameter of the index.

The *percentage contribution* that group k makes to overall poverty is defined as:

$$\frac{\left[\frac{N_k}{N} \times \text{FGT}^k(\alpha) \right]}{\text{FGT}(\alpha)} \times 100$$

Box 3.3 continued

Box 3.3 continued

The *risk of poverty* of group k, denoted ρ_k, is defined as the ratio of the group FGT value to the overall FGT value:

$$\rho_k = \frac{FGT^k(\alpha)}{FGT(\alpha)}$$

$\rho_k > 1$ implies that poverty in group k is greater than poverty in the population; conversely, $\rho_k < 1$ implies that poverty in group k is less than poverty in the population.

Example

Suppose in a population of 104 households, 20 households are from group 1, 36 households are from group 2, and 48 households are from group 3 such that 10 of the 20 households in group 1 are poor; 12 of the 36 households in group 2 are poor; and eight of the 48 households in group 3 are poor.

Suppose $\alpha = 0$. Then FGT(0) = HCR and $FGT^1(0) = 10/20$, which is the HCR for group 1; $FGT^2(0) = 12/36$, which is the HCR for group 2; $FGT^3(0) = 8/48$, which is the HCR for group 3. The aggregate HCR = FGT(0) = 30/104 (30 poor households out of 104) and:

$$\frac{30}{104} = \left(\frac{20}{104} \times \frac{10}{20}\right) + \left(\frac{36}{104} \times \frac{12}{36}\right) + \left(\frac{48}{104} \times \frac{8}{48}\right)$$

which is the decomposability property referred to earlier. Note that this property holds for all α values, not just for $\alpha = 0$. The proportionate contribution of households in group 1 to overall poverty is:

$$\left(\frac{20}{104} \times \frac{10}{20}\right) \div \left(\frac{30}{104}\right) = \frac{10}{30}$$

Similarly, the proportionate contributions of groups 2 and 3 are, respectively, $\frac{12}{30}$ and $\frac{8}{30}$.

So the (percentage) *poverty contributions* by the three groups to overall poverty are, respectively, 33, 40, and 27%.

The *risk* of poverty of households in the different groups is defined as the ratio of the group FGT to the overall FGT: 1.73, 1.16, and 0.58.

Source: Authors.

Table 3.17 shows that the largest contribution to rural and urban poverty—regardless of whether poverty was measured by the HCR ($\alpha = 0$), or by the HCR *and* the depth of poverty ($\alpha = 1$), or by the HCR *and* the depth of poverty *and* "relative deprivation" ($\alpha = 2$)—was made by Hindu households from the HOBC: about one-third to overall poverty was contributed to by this group. The next largest contributor to poverty was SC households: about one-fourth of overall rural and urban poverty was contributed to by this group. An interesting feature of the results in Table 3.17 is that the contribution of ST households to overall rural poverty was 24 percent on the HCR but rose to 32 percent when, in addition to the HCR, the depth of poverty was taken into account and then to 36 percent when in addition to the HCR and the depth of poverty, "relative deprivation" was also taken into account.

Table 3.17:
Percentage contributions by households in different groups to overall poverty

	Rural Households				Urban Households			
	$\alpha = 0$	$\alpha = 1$	$\alpha = 2$	Household Share (%)	$\alpha = 0$	$\alpha = 1$	$\alpha = 2$	Household Share (%)
High-caste Hindus	7.2	5.5	4.9	19	12.6	11.0	10.8	31
OBC Hindus	33.9	32.5	31.3	35	32.4	30.4	29.5	30
Scheduled Castes	25.5	23.3	21.6	22	24.4	26.0	26.4	16
Scheduled Tribes	24.3	31.5	36.2	11	4.2	4.9	5.4	3
OBC Muslims	3.7	3.5	3.3	4	13.5	14.7	15.0	7
High-caste Muslims	4.7	3.1	2.2	6	11.1	11.8	12.2	8
Other groups	0.8	0.6	0.5	4	1.9	1.3	0.8	5

Source: Author's own calculations from IHDS data.
Note: When $\alpha = 0$, poverty is measured by FGT(0), which is the HCR; when $\alpha = 1$, the poverty measure, FGT(1), incorporates the HCR and the "depth of poverty"; when $\alpha = 2$, the poverty measure, FGT(2), incorporates the HCR, the "depth of poverty" and "relative deprivation."

If one compares the contribution of the different groups to poverty, as measured by the HCR, with their respective shares in the total number of households, then ST households made a disproportionately large contribution to rural poverty (24 percent versus 11 percent) and SC, MOBC, and HCM households made a disproportionately large contribution to urban poverty (SC: 24 percent versus 16 percent; MOBC: 14 percent versus 4 percent; HCM: 11 percent versus 6 percent). On the other hand, HCH and OTG households made a disproportionately small contribution to rural and to urban poverty: 7 percent versus 19 percent for HCH rural and 31 percent versus 13 percent for HCH urban. These results are reflected in Table 3.18, which shows that, among rural households, the risk of poverty was highest for ST households (the rural ST poverty rate was 2.2 times the overall rural poverty rate) and that, among urban households, the risk of poverty was highest for MOBC households (the urban MOBC poverty rate was twice the overall urban poverty rate) followed by SC and HCM households.

Table 3.18:
Risk of poverty of the households in different groups

	Rural Households			Urban Households		
	$\alpha = 0$	$\alpha = 1$	$\alpha = 2$	$\alpha = 0$	$\alpha = 1$	$\alpha = 2$
High-caste Hindus	0.39	0.30	0.27	0.41	0.35	0.35
OBC Hindus	0.96	0.92	0.88	1.09	1.02	0.99
Scheduled Castes	1.15	1.05	0.97	1.52	1.63	1.65
Scheduled Tribes	2.23	2.90	3.33	1.24	1.42	1.56
OBC Muslims	0.94	0.89	0.84	2.05	2.23	2.28
High-caste Muslims	0.87	0.57	0.41	1.31	1.40	1.44
Other groups	0.21	0.17	0.14	0.39	0.26	0.18

Source: Author's own calculations from IHDS data.
Note: When $\alpha = 0$, poverty is measured by FGT(0), which is the HCR; when $\alpha = 1$, the poverty measure, FGT(1), incorporates the HCR and the "depth of poverty"; when $\alpha = 2$, the poverty measure, FGT(2), incorporates the HCR, the "depth of poverty" and "relative deprivation."

3.9. Conclusion

The contribution of this chapter was to study the twin issues of inequality and poverty of households in India from the perspective of households' MPCE. The central question that this chapter examined was whether there was a "caste/religion basis" to inequality and poverty in India or whether distributional and deprivation outcomes were "caste/religion blind" so that they were entirely determined by the attributes of the individual households. Our overarching conclusion was that households' outcomes with respect to their position on the distributional ladder, or with respect to their chances of being poor, were dependent in large measure on their caste or religion. So SC, ST, and Muslim households were more likely to be in the lowest quintile of consumption than HCH households.

Within this context, the two significant contributions of the analysis in this chapter were, first, to use data relating to ownership of (non-land) physical assets—tractors, tube wells, electric and diesel pumps, and draft and dairy livestock—to present a more nuanced explanation of inter-household differences in consumption than hitherto attempted for India and second, to allow the effects of consumption-determining factors to vary systematically by the caste of the households. The primary determinants of a household's consumption were its assets where these "productive" assets took four forms: education, land, and physical assets like tube wells and tractors, and labor assets in the form of adult members. In this context, caste/religion disadvantage stemmed from two sources: compared to HCH households, households from other groups (OBC Hindus, SC, ST, MOBC, and HCM) were not as well endowed with assets but, even when they did have comparable assets, these were rewarded at a lower rate than that obtained by HCH households.

A glaring example of this was education, particularly when the educational level attained was Matric or above. A high level of education boosted a household's consumption but, compared to HCH households, SC and HOBC households obtained much less leverage from a good education in terms of higher consumption. Another example was that of households owning buffaloes. The sale of milk from buffaloes served to raise household consumption, but "untouchability" issues relating to the purchase and sale of food items meant that buffaloes did not earn as much for SC households as they did for HCH households.

As Basu (2001) notes, the debate on the goals of development is inching toward a consensus—moving from an unhealthy preoccupation with growth rates in GDP to a more holistic view couched in terms of "inclusive growth" or "comprehensive development." A major part of any strategy for increasing the "inclusivity" part of "inclusive growth" must be to improve the capabilities of persons who populate the lower parts of the income distribution. This involves increasing their endowment of assets, both in terms of human and physical capital, and buttressing these private assets with public goods in the form of good, affordable education, health care, and public utilities. Achieving all this is difficult enough but, in the Indian context, this is made more difficult by the hierarchal and fractured nature of Indian society. This means that many people who are poor suffer a double jeopardy: they are at the bottom of both the income ladder and the social hierarchy. This means that, for many of India's poor, asset acquisition *per se* is not enough to rescue them from poverty. Their way is also blocked by discriminatory attitudes stemming from a feeling of caste and religious superiority. It is these blockages that must also be cleared before India's poor can begin their long march out of poverty.

Appendix

Decomposition in Linear Models

A recent formal exposition of the Blinder–Oaxaca (B–O) decomposition method (named after Blinder, 1973 and Oaxaca, 1973) for *linear* regression models is to be found in Jann (2008). Suppose there are two groups, W and B with Y as an outcome variable such that $E(Y_W)$ and $E(Y_B)$ are the *expected* values of the outcome variable for, respectively, groups W and B. Then,

$$Y_k = X_k'\beta_k + \varepsilon_k, \quad k = W, B \qquad (3.1)$$

where Y_k is the vector of outcomes, X_k is the matrix of observations, and ε_k is the vector of error terms for persons in group k. Since, by assumption $E(\varepsilon_k) = 0$, we have,

$$
\begin{aligned}
R &= E(Y_W) - E(Y_B) = E(X_W')\beta_W - E(X_B')\beta_B \\
&= E(X_W')\beta_W - E(X_B')\beta_B + E(X_B')\beta_W - E(X_B')\beta_W \\
&= E(X_W - X_B)'\beta_W + E(X_B')(\beta_W - \beta_B) \\
&= E(X_W - X_B)'\beta_W + E(X_W - X_B)'\beta_B - E(X_W - X_B)'\beta_B + E(X_B')(\beta_W - \beta_B) \qquad (3.2) \\
&= E(X_W - X_B)'\beta_B + E(X_B')(\beta_W - \beta_B) + E(X_W - X_B)'(\beta_W - \beta_B) \\
&= P + Q + T
\end{aligned}
$$

As Jann (2008) points out, the term $P = E(X_W - X_B)'\beta_B$ in equation (3.2), above, amounts to the difference in mean outcomes that is due to the inter-group differences in the predictors ("the asset endowments effect"); the term $Q = E(X_B')(\beta_W - \beta_B)$ in equation (3), above, amounts to the difference in mean outcomes that is due to the inter-group differences in the coefficients ("the asset returns effect"); and the term, $T = E(X_W - X_B)'(\beta_W - \beta_B)$ amounts to the difference in mean outcomes that is due to an *interaction term* representing the fact that differences in attributes and coefficients exist *simultaneously* between the two groups.

The decomposition represented in equation (3.3) *is formulated from the perspective of group B* because the inter-group difference in predictors is weighted by the coefficients of group *B* to determine the attributes effect, *P*. The *P* component measures the expected change in group *B*'s mean outcome if it had group *W*'s attributes. Similarly, the *Q* component measures the expected change in group *B*'s mean outcome if group *B* had group *W*'s coefficients.

Needless to say, the decomposition in equation (3.3) can also be represented from the perspective of group *W* as:

$$E(X_W - X_B)'\beta_W + E(X_A')(\beta_W - \beta_B)$$
$$+ E(X_W - X_R)'(\beta_W - \beta_R) = P' + Q' + T' \qquad (3.3)$$

Now the endowment effect *P'* measures the expected change in group *A*'s mean outcome if it had group *B*'s attributes and the *Q'* component measures the expected change in group *W*'s mean outcome if group *W* had group *B*'s coefficients and *T'* represents the interaction effect.

As Jann (2008) points out, an alternative decomposition to equations (3.3) and (3.4) is to assume that there is some non-discriminatory coefficient vector, β^*, which should be used to evaluate the contribution of the difference in attributes. Then, the outcome difference can be written as:

$$R = E(Y_W) - E(Y_B) = E(X_W')\beta_W - E(X_B')\beta_B$$
$$= E(X_W')\beta_W - E(X_B')\beta_B + E(X_W')\beta^* - E(X_W')\beta^*$$
$$+ E(X_B')\beta^* - E(X_B')\beta^* \qquad (3.4)$$
$$= E(X_W - X_B)'\beta^* + \left[E(X_W')(\beta_W - \beta^*) + E(X_B')(\beta^* - \beta_B) \right]$$
$$= U + V$$

Equation (3.5) yields a two-fold decomposition in which the term $U = E(X_W - X_B)'\beta^*$ is the part of the outcome difference that can be explained by the difference in attributes, and the term $V = E(X_W')(\beta_W - \beta^*) + E(X_B')(\beta^* - \beta_B)$ is the unexplained part. The latter is usually ascribed to discrimination.

There are two possible variations on equation (3.5). First, suppose $\beta^* = \beta_W$ that is, the non-discriminatory coefficient vector is identified as that associated with group *W*. Then equation (3.4) becomes:

$$R = E(X_W - X_B)'\beta_W + E(X_B')(\beta_W - \beta_B) \tag{3.5}$$

Second, and alternatively, suppose $\beta^* = \beta_B$ that is, the non-discriminatory coefficient vector is identified as that associated with group B. Then equation (3.4) becomes:

$$R = E(X_W - X_B)'\beta_B + E(X_A')(\beta_W - \beta_B) \tag{3.6}$$

In equation (3.6), the difference in attributes between the W and B groups are evaluated at group W's coefficients; in equation (3.7), the difference in attributes between groups W and B are evaluated at group B's coefficients.

In general, the problem of defining $\beta*$, the non-discriminatory coefficient vector, is a big issue in the decomposition literature on discrimination. One possibility (equations 3.6 and 3.7) is to identify $\beta*$ with the coefficients of one of the groups. Another is to regard it as the average of the two group coefficients (Reimers, 1983): $\beta^* = 0.5 \times \beta_W + 0.5 \times \beta_B$. Yet another (Cotton, 1988) is to weight the coefficients by the size of the groups: $\beta^* = n_W \times \beta_W + n_B \times \beta_B$ where n_W and n_B are the proportions in groups W and B.

Inequality Decomposition

Suppose that the total sample of N households is divided into M mutually exclusive and collectively exhaustive groups with N_m ($m = 1 \dots M$) persons in each group. Let $e = \{e_i\}$ and $e_m = \{e_i\}$ represent the vector of expenditures of, respectively, all the households in sample ($i = 1 \dots N$) and the households in group m. Then an inequality index $I(e; N)$ defined over this vector is said to be additively decomposable if:

$$I(e; N) = \sum_{m=1}^{M} I(e_m; N_m)w_m + B = A + B \tag{3.7}$$

where $I(e; N)$ represents the *overall* level of inequality; $I(e_m; N_m)$ represents the level of inequality within group m; A—expressed as the weighted sum of the inequality in each group, w_m being the weights—and B represent, respectively, the *within-group* and the *between-group* contribution to overall inequality.

If, indeed, inequality can be "additively decomposed" along the lines of equation (3.8) above, then, as Cowell and Jenkins (1995) have argued, the proportionate contribution of the between-group component (B) to overall inequality is the income inequality literature's analog of the R^2 statistic used in regression analysis: the size of this contribution is a measure of the amount of inequality that can be "explained" by the factor (or factors) used to subdivide the sample (caste, education, region, etc.).

Only inequality indices that belong to the family of *Generalized Entropy Indices* are additively decomposable (Shorrocks, 1980). These indices are defined by a parameter θ and, when $\theta = 0$, the weights are the population shares of the different groups (that is, $w_j = N_j / N$); since the weights sum to unity, the within-group contribution **A** of equation (3.4) is a weighted average of the inequality levels within the groups. When $\theta = 0$, the inequality index takes the form:

$$I(e; N) = \left(\sum_{i=1}^{N} \log(e_i / \bar{e}) \right) / N \qquad (3.8)$$

$\bar{e} = \sum_{i=1}^{N} e_i / N$ is the mean expenditure over the entire sample. The inequality index defined in equation (3.12) is known as the Theil's (1967) mean logarithmic deviation and, because of its attractive features in terms of the interpretation of the weights, it is the one used in this study to decompose inequality in the MPCE of rural households.

Decomposition in Non-Linear Models (Logit)

There are N households (indexed, $i = 1 \ldots N$) that can be placed in K mutually exclusive and collectively exhaustive groups $k = 1 \ldots K$, each group containing N_k households. Define the variable P_i such that $Y_i = 1$, if the household is poor, $P_i = 0$, if it is not. Then, under a logit model, the likelihood of a household from group k being poor is:

$$\Pr(Y_i = 1) = \frac{\exp(X_i^k \beta^k)}{1 + \exp(X_i^k \beta^k)} = F(X_i^k \hat{\beta}^k) \qquad (3.9)$$

where $X_i^k = \{X_{ij}, j = 1 \ldots J\}$ represents the vector of observations, for household i of group k, on J variables which determine the likelihood it being poor, and $\hat{\beta}^k = \{\beta_j^k, j = 1 \ldots J\}$ is the associated vector of coefficient estimates for households belonging to group k.

The average probability of a household from group k being poor—which is also the mean poverty rate for the group is

$$\bar{P}^k = \bar{P}(X_i^k, \hat{\beta}^k) = N_k^{-1} \sum_{i=1}^{N_k} F(X_i^k \hat{\beta}^k) \qquad (3.10)$$

Now for any two groups, say Hindu ($k = H$) and Muslim ($k = M$):

$$\bar{P}^H - \bar{P}^M = [\bar{P}(X_i^M, \hat{\beta}^H) - \bar{P}(X_i^M, \hat{\beta}^M)]$$
$$+ [\bar{P}(X_i^H, \hat{\beta}^H) - \bar{P}(X_i^M, \hat{\beta}^H)] \qquad (3.11)$$

Alternatively,

$$\bar{P}^H - \bar{P}^M = [\bar{P}(X_i^H, \hat{\beta}^H) - \bar{P}(X_i^H, \hat{\beta}^M)]$$
$$+ [\bar{P}(X_i^H, \hat{\beta}^M) - \bar{P}(X_i^M, \hat{\beta}^M)] \qquad (3.12)$$

The first term in square brackets, in equations (3.12) and (3.13), represents the "rate of return" effect: it is the difference in average poverty rates between Hindu and Muslim households resulting from inter-group differences in returns (as exemplified by differences in the coefficient vectors) to a given vector of asset values. The second term in square brackets in equations (3.12) and (3.13) represents the "assets effect": it is the difference in average poverty rates between Hindu and Muslim households resulting from inter-group differences in asset endowments, when these assets are evaluated using a common coefficient vector. In equation (3.12), the difference in sample means is decomposed by asking what the average poverty rates for Muslim households would have been, *had they been treated as Hindus*; in equation (3.13), it is decomposed by asking what the average poverty rates for Hindu households would have been, *had they been treated as Muslim*. In other words, the common coefficient vector used in computing the asset effect is, for equation (3.12), the Hindu vector and, for equation (3.13), the Muslim vector.

The FGT Index

Suppose that in a population of N households, indexed $i = 1 ... N$, y_i is the MPCE of the ith household and that the households are arranged in ascending order of MPCE: $y_1 < y_2 ... < y_N$. If z is the poverty line, suppose that M of these households are poor where $y = (y_1, y_2, ..., y_M)$ represents the vector of MPCE of the poor households. Then the FGT index is defined with respect to **y**, the parameter α, and the poverty line z as:

$$\text{FGT}(y; z, \alpha) = \frac{\sum_{i=1}^{M}(z - y_i)^{\alpha}}{N \times z^{\alpha}} \tag{3.13}$$

If $\alpha = 0$, $\text{FGT}(\mathbf{y}; z, 0) = M/N$, which is the HCR.

If $\alpha = 1$, $\text{FGT}(y; z, 1) = \dfrac{M}{N} \times R$, where R is the poverty gap ratio

defined as $R = \dfrac{\sum_{i=1}^{M}(z - y_i)}{M \times z}$ which is the mean poverty gap, computed

over poor households,[29] expressed as a ratio of the poverty line, z.[30] Then

$\dfrac{M}{N} R = \dfrac{\sum_{i=1}^{M}(z - y_i)}{N \times z}$ which is the mean poverty gap, computed over *all*

households (poor and non-poor),[31] expressed as a ratio of the poverty

line. If $\alpha = 2$, $\text{FGT}(y; z, 2) = \dfrac{M}{N}\left[R^2 + (1 - R^2)\phi^2\right]$, where ϕ is the

coefficient of variation.[32]

Decomposition Using the FGT Index

Suppose the N households are subdivided into K groups (indexed $k = 1 \ldots K$) with N_k households in each group. Suppose further that there are M_k poor

---

[29] $\dfrac{\sum_{i=1}^{M}(z - y_i)}{M}$

[30] Note that $R = 1 - \dfrac{\mu^P}{z}$, where μ^P is mean MPCE of poor households.

[31] $\dfrac{\sum_{i=1}^{M}(z - y_i)}{N}$

[32] Defined as $\phi = \dfrac{\sigma}{\mu}$, where σ and μ are, respectively, the standard deviation and mean of the distribution.

households in group k, such that $\sum_{k} M_k = M$ with $y^k = (y_{M_1}, y_{M_2}, ... y_{M_k})$ the vector of MPCE of poor households in group k. Then,

$$\text{FGT}(y; z, \alpha) = \sum_{k=1}^{K} (N_k / N) \times \text{FGT}(y^k; z, \alpha) \qquad (3.14)$$

where $\text{FGT}(y^k; z, \alpha) = \dfrac{\sum_{i=1}^{M_k} (z - y_{ik})^{\alpha}}{N_k \times z^{\alpha}}$ is the FGT index computed over

the MPCE of the poor households in group k.

Then the percentage contribution to poverty of households in group k ($k = 1 ... K$) is:

$$\dfrac{(Nk / N)\text{FGT}(y^k; z, \alpha)}{\text{FGT}(y; z, \alpha)} \times 100 \qquad (3.15)$$

And "poverty risk" of group k ($k = 1 ... K$) is:

$$\dfrac{\text{FGT}(y^k; z, \alpha)}{\text{FGT}(y; z, \alpha)} \qquad (3.16)$$

4

Educational Attainment

4.1. Introduction

The previous chapter emphasized the importance of education as—perhaps —*the* most important determinant of a household's position on the economic ladder. In the context of social groups, it is well established that educational attainments vary considerably between India's caste and religious groups. For example, Deolalikar (2010) showed that the completed schooling of the three "deprived" groups—Muslims, SCs, and STs—as a percentage of the completed schooling of upper-caste Hindus was, for those born during 1970–79, 71 percent for Muslims and 66 percent for SC and ST collectively; for the cohort born during 1960–69, the corresponding percentages were 65 percent and 54 percent, respectively. These differences persist notwithstanding the fact that there has been much progress in India in the area of caste disadvantage: Articles 341 and 342 of the Constitution of India allow for special provisions for persons from SC and ST in the form of reserved seats in the national parliament, state legislatures, municipality boards, and village councils (*panchayat*s), job reservations in the public sector, and reserved places in public higher educational institutions. Furthermore, Article 17 forbids the practice of "untouchability," and various amendments to the Prevention of Atrocities Acts provide for severe penalties for crimes against persons from SC and ST.

Other studies that have addressed these questions have focused on the *enrollment* of children at school and, in particular, on differences between social groups in rates of school enrollment (Bhalotra and Zamora, 2010; Borooah and Iyer, 2005b). Since these studies, which were based on data for the late 1980s and early 1990s, the problem of enrollment has become less acute: in 2005, the enrollment rate for every social group was in excess of 90 percent. What is now relevant is not so much whether children are enrolled, but what they learn at school. It is this shift of emphasis from school enrollment to schooling quality—and the related analysis of inter-group disparities in children's educational standards—that is the focus of this chapter.

The data used in this chapter are from the IHDS, which was conducted in 2004–05 by the University of Maryland in collaboration with the National Council of Applied Economic Research, New Delhi, between November 2004 and October 2005.[1] The nationally representative data cover 1,504 villages and 971 urban areas across 33 states and union territories of India. The survey covering 41,554 households was carried out through face-to-face interviews by pairs of male and female enumerators in local languages. The respondents included a person who was knowledgeable about the household economic situation (usually the male head of the household) and an ever-married woman aged 15–49 years. The detailed modules of the survey provide answers to a wide range of questions relating to economic activity, income and consumption expenditure, asset ownership, social capital, education, health, marriage and fertility, etc.

4.2. Testing Children's Abilities in Reading, Writing, and Arithmetic

The IHDS tested (approximately) 12,300 children, aged 8–11 years, in its sample for their ability to read, write, and do arithmetic at different levels.[2] In the assessment of reading, a child was assigned a score of 4 if he/she could read (in English or in any one of a number of Indian languages) a "story"; a score of 3 if he/she could read a "paragraph"; a score of 2 if he/she could read words; a score of 1 if he/she could recognize letters of the alphabet; and a score of 0 if he/she could do none of these. For assessing ability in arithmetic, a child was assigned a score of 3 if he/she could divide; a score of 2 if he/she could subtract; a score of 1 if he/she could recognize numbers; and a score of 0 if he/she could do none

---

[1]   Available from the Inter-University Consortium for Political and Social Research, http://www.icpsr.umich.edu (last accessed on February 17, 2012).

[2]   12,356 children were tested for reading, 12,306 children were tested for arithmetic, and 12,249 children were tested for writing.

of these. In assessing writing ability, a child was assigned a score of 1 if he/she could write a simple sentence (for example, "I like blue color") with two or fewer mistakes; a score of 0 if he/she could not.[3] Sample test sheets for reading and arithmetic are provided in an online appendix to the chapter.[4] The results of these tests are shown in Table 4.1 for boys and in Table 4.2 for girls.

The IHDS distinguished the following eight social groups of which the first three represented Hindus *within* the caste system (that is, brahmins, HCH [kshatriyas and vaisyas], and the OBC [sudras]); the fourth represented Hindus *outside* the caste system (SC); the fifth group was related to tribal groups (ST), and the sixth, seventh, and eighth groups to the other, non-Hindu, religious groups (Muslims, Sikhs, Jains, and Christians). For both boys and girls, the average reading scores were highest for brahmins, "high castes," Sikhs/Jains, and Christians and lowest for OBC, SC, ST, and Muslims. For example, brahmin and SC boys had average reading scores of, respectively, 3.3 and 2.4 (out of a maximum of 4).

This pattern was repeated for arithmetic and for writing: children between the ages of 8–11 years with the highest educational attainments came, on average, from brahmin, "high caste," Sikh/Jain, and Christian households while the lowest achievers were, on average, from OBC, SC, adivasi, and Muslim households. For example, as Figure 4.1 shows, brahmin and SC boys averaged arithmetic scores of, respectively, 2.2 and 1.4 (out of a maximum of 3). Interestingly, there was much less evidence of a gender divide in the scores with the average scores of boys and girls (Figure 4.2) being remarkably close for reading, arithmetic, and writing: 2.7 versus 2.6 for reading, 1.6 versus 1.5 in arithmetic, and 0.71 versus 0.68 in writing.

---

[3] It is important to make clear at the outset that the term "ability" is used in this chapter as meaning "cognitive skills"—that is, to skills acquired and honed through a favorable learning environment—and not to an innate, exogenously given intellectual capacity (Hanushek and Woessmann, 2008). Details of the tests are provided in Desai Adams, and Dubey (2010).

[4] It is our understanding that the IHDS tests were developed by *Pratham*, which is a network of non-governmental organizations dating from 1994, supported by UNICEF, with activities in 14 states in India (http://www.pratham.org, last accessed on April 16, 2012). Further details of the tests can be found in Pratham's Annual Status of Education Reports: http://www.asercentre.org/ngo-education-india.php?p = Tools (last accessed on April 16, 2012).

Figure 4.1:
Reading, arithmetic, and writing scores for boys, by social group

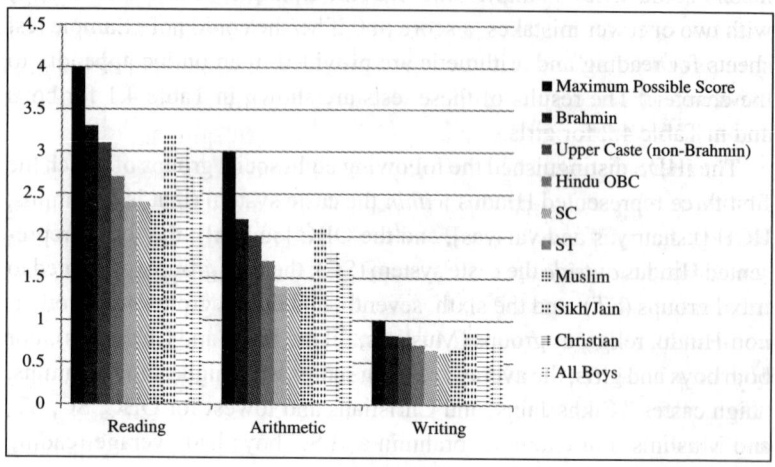

Source: IHDS.

Figure 4.2:
Reading, arithmetic, and writing scores for girls, by social group

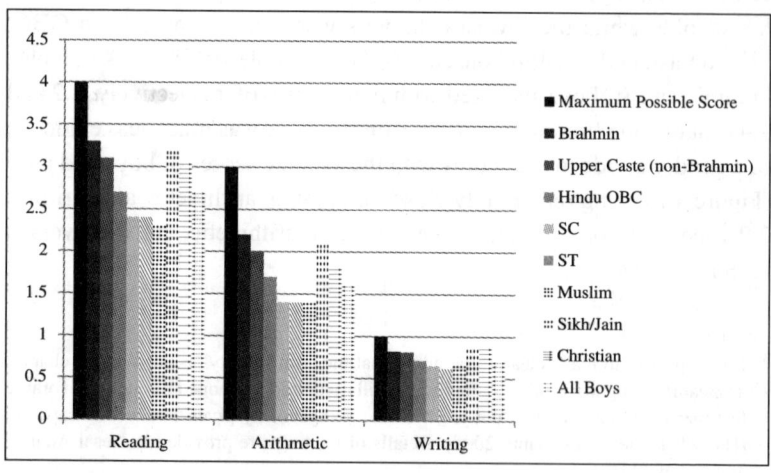

Source: IHDS.

One reason for the inter-group differences, as noted earlier, might be that the school characteristics of children from different caste/religious backgrounds were very different. As Tables 4.1 and 4.2 show, the proportion of children from the "higher" social groups (brahmin, HC Hindus, Sikh/Jain, and Christian households) going to private schools was considerably higher than that for children from the "lower" social groups (OBC, SC, ST, and Muslim households): 47 percent of brahmin boys and 40 percent of brahmin girls were in private schools compared to only 20 percent of SC boys and 16 percent of SC girls.

Another consequence, shown in Tables 4.1 and 4.2, of the greater probability of "upper" group children being in private schools was that the average school fees paid per child by such households was considerably greater than the fees paid by the "lower" groups: brahmin households paid an average school fees of ₹1,515 per year for boys and ₹1,236 for girls, compared to ₹507 for boys and ₹390 for girls, paid by SC households.[5] Higher school fees (for in-school teaching, books, uniforms, etc.) were also correlated with higher expenses on private tuition (that is, engaging a private tutor for out-of-school instruction): on average, brahmin households spent ₹751 per year for boys (and ₹537 for girls) for private tuition compared to expenditure by SC households of ₹249 for boys and ₹192 for girls.

Table 4.1:
Educational characteristics of boys currently in school/college: Higher secondary or below

	Brahmin	High Caste	OBC	SC	Adivasi	Muslim	Sikh/ Jain	Christian	All Boys
School type:									
Government	41	48	61	72	73	57	28	24	59
Private	47	39	29	20	16	30	66	40	29
Other									12
Medium of Instruction:									
Hindi	60	44	49	50	39	39	18	7	46
State language	16	33	38	41	37	31	49	35	36
English	23	21	12	8	19	15	33	41	15
Days absent in last month	3.1	2.1	3.2	3.1	3.3	3.4	1.4	1.0	2.9
Annual school fees (₹)	1,515	1,323	689	507	443	724	2,409	1,684	838

Table 4.1 continued

[5] Compared to Brahmin households, a larger proportion of SC households received school fees from the government (7 percent against 16 percent). However, even when one focused on households that did not receive any government fee support, the average fee per boy (girl) was ₹1,570 (₹1,311) for Brahmins and ₹575 (₹390) for SC.

Table 4.1 continued

School fees	1,570	1,416	788	575	529	742	2,461	1,801	933
without govt. support (₹)									
Annual private tuition (₹)	751	565	280	249	204	266	346	298	342
Average class	5.7	5.5	5.2	5.0	5.0	4.6	5.3	5.8	5.1

Source: IHDS.

The most obvious reason for households in the "higher" social groups favoring private schools and being able to afford higher school fees and private tuition expenditure was that they were better off than "lower" social group households. As Table 4.3 shows, the average annual income of brahmin households (₹91,189) was over twice that of SC and ST households (₹43,020 and ₹43,511, respectively) and considerably more than that of OBC and Muslim households ₹52,472 and ₹55,984, respectively). In terms of household assets (measured by the number of items owned by the household from a given list), households in the "higher" social groups were much better off than those in the "lower" groups: brahmin households owned 17 (out of a total of 30 possible items) compared to 12 by OBC and Muslim households and 10 by ST households. Perhaps as a corollary of their greater likelihood of being in private schools, a larger proportion of children from the "upper" groups were educated in English (Tables 4.1 and 4.2) compared to children from the "lower" groups: 23 percent of brahmin boys and 21 percent of brahmin girls were educated in English compared to only 8 percent of SC boys and 7 percent of SC girls.

The economic strength of the higher social groups was also reflected in their *adult* educational achievements: compared to the literacy rate of 56 percent for persons from SC and 64 percent for persons from OBC, the literacy rate for brahmins was 81 percent. Brahmins had completed, on average, seven years of education (in contrast to the four completed years of SC); 39 percent of brahmins (in contrast to 13 percent of SC) had a "Matric" qualification,[6] and 14 percent of brahmins (in contrast to 2 percent of SC) were graduates.

---

[6] *Matric* is a term commonly used in India to refer to the final year of high school, which ends at 10th standard (10th grade); the qualification received after passing the *matriculation exams"* usually at the age of 15–16 years, is referred to as *Matric (passed).*

Table 4.2:
Educational characteristics of girls currently in school/college: Higher secondary or below

	Brahmin	High Caste	OBC	SC	Adivasi	Muslim	Sikh/ Jain	Christian	All Girls
School type									
Government	48	56	64	75	76	58	33	30	63
Private	40	31	26	16	14	28	61	35	26
Other									11
Medium of instruction:									
Hindi	61	44	46	48	38	37	21	7	44
State language	17	35	41	45	36	32	48	42	38
English	21	18	11	7	21	14	30	40	14
Days absent in last month	3.1	2.1	2.9	3.0	3.4	3.2	1.6	1.3	2.9
Annual school fees (₹)	1,236	1,080	565	390	360	591	2,174	1,510	683
School fees without govt. support (₹)	1,311	1,161	664	450	426	644	2,232	1,541	776
Annual private tuition (₹)	537	498	238	192	165	239	340	258	285
Average class	5.6	5.7	5.0	4.9	4.8	4.5	5.6	5.8	5.1

Source: IHDS.

Although the IHDS did not identify a child's school, it did conduct a survey of nearly 3,800 primary schools in India with a view to ascertaining their characteristics and their resources. Data from this survey showed that 54 percent of primary schools in India were government schools, 32 percent were private schools, and 12 percent were government-aided (private schools). In terms of resources, government primary schools had, on average, the least number of classrooms (4.9), yielding an average class size of 43 students; private schools had an average of 6.5 classrooms for an average class size of 31, while aided schools had an average of 7.8 classrooms for an average class size of 37.

In addition to having larger class sizes, government schools, compared to private and aided schools were handicapped in other ways: 5 percent of government schools compared to 1 percent of aided schools and 2 percent of private schools did not have blackboards in all the classrooms, and 71 percent of government schools compared to 32 percent of aided schools and 40 percent of private schools did not have chairs and desks for all their students; lastly, attendance rates were lowest in government schools

Table 4.3:
Household and person characteristics by social group (215,754 persons)

	Brahmin	High Caste	OBC	SC	Adivasi	Muslim	Sikh/Jain	Christian	All Groups
Percentage of sample	5.6	16.5	33.8	20.1	8.1	12.8	1.7	1.5	100
Annual, household income (₹)	91,189	84,784	52,472	43,020	43,511	55,984	130,681	88,255	59,659
Household assets (items owned out of a total of 30 items)	17	16	12	10	8	12	20	17	12
Literacy rate	81	75	64	56	51	58	78	85	64
Male literacy rate	87	81	73	65	60	64	81	86	72
Female literacy rate	75	68	55	47	43	51	75	83	56
Number of education years completed: all	7	6	5	4	3	4	7	7	5
Number of education years completed: men	8	7	5	4	4	4	7	8	5
Number of education years completed: women	6	5	4	3	3	3	6	7	4
Proportion of persons who are "Matric": all	39	30	18	13	10	13	37	39	19
Proportion of men who are "Matric"	46	35	22	16	13	16	40	41	23
Proportion of women who are "Matric"	32	25	14	9	8	10	34	37	15
Proportion of persons who are graduates	14	9	4	2	2	2	9	11	5
Proportion of men who are graduates	18	11	5	3	3	3	10	11	6
Proportion of women who are graduates	10	7	2	1	1	1	9	10	3
Proportion of men in professional, managerial, technical occupations	9.2	4.4	2.2	1.9	2.2	2.0	4.0	5.0	3.0

Source: IHDS.

with 88 percent of enrolled students attending school on an average day compared to attendance rates of 91 percent for private schools and 94 percent for aided schools.

4.3. Inequality Analysis

Comparing different groups on the basis of their mean test scores (Figures 4.1 and 4.2) ignores inequality in the distribution of scores between the individual children in the groups. Sen (1998) argued that if μ is the mean level of achievement, and I the degree of inequality in its distribution, then the level of social welfare, W, may be represented as $W = \mu (1 - I)$: "this has the intuitive interpretation [that] the size of the pie (μ) [is] corrected downward by the extent of inequality $(1 - I)$" (p. 129).

In this section, we apply this idea to the test scores in the IHDS data. Tables 4.4 and 4.5 show, respectively, for boys and girls, the mean scores (panel 1) by social group and, then, for each group, the degree of inequality in the distribution of scores *within* that group (panel 2). Inequality is measured by the Gini coefficient, which is the most commonly used international summary indicator of inequalities. Following from these observations, the third panel of Tables 4.4 and 4.5 shows, respectively, for boys and girls the "equity adjusted" mean test score, E, for each social group defined as $E = \mu (1 - G)$, where μ is the mean test score of the children in the group (Tables 4.4 and 4.5: panel 1) and G is the Gini coefficient computed over the distribution of test scores across the children in the group (Tables 4.4 and 4.5: panel 2).

The first point to notice about Tables 4.4 and 4.5 is that there was considerably more inequality in the distribution of test scores among children in the "lower" social classes (the OBC, SC, ST, and Muslims) compared to children in the "upper" social classes (brahmins, high castes, Sikh/Jains, and Christians): the Gini coefficient values for SC boys in reading, arithmetic, and writing were, respectively, 0.31, 0.39, and 0.35, while the corresponding values for brahmin boys were 0.16, 0.21, and 0.18.

The second point is that, within the same social group, inequality in scores was similar for girls and boys: the Gini for brahmin girls was 0.18 compared to 0.16 for brahmin boys while the Gini coefficient for SC girls was 0.32 compared to 0.31 for SC boys. Not only were the mean scores of boys and girls in the different competencies very similar, the gender distribution of these scores between the high and low scorers was similar and, for brahmins, highly compressed.

Table 4.4:
Equity-adjusted scores using the Gini coefficient (Boys: 8–11 years)

Group	Mean Scores			Gini of Scores Distribution			Equity-Adjusted Scores		
	Reading	Arithmetic	Writing	Reading	Arithmetic	Writing	Reading	Arithmetic	Writing
Brahmin	3.3	2.2	0.82	0.155	0.214	0.183	2.8	1.7	0.7
High caste	3.1	2.0	0.81	0.191	0.271	0.186	2.5	1.4	0.7
OBC	2.7	1.7	0.71	0.257	0.331	0.288	2.0	1.1	0.5
SC	2.4	1.4	0.65	0.310	0.385	0.352	1.7	0.9	0.4
Adivasi	2.4	1.4	0.62	0.313	0.402	0.382	1.6	0.8	0.4
Muslim	2.3	1.4	0.63	0.326	0.393	0.372	1.6	0.9	0.4
Sikh/Jain	3.2	2.1	0.86	0.166	0.186	0.135	2.6	1.7	0.7
Christian	3.1	1.8	0.87	0.188	0.250	0.131	2.5	1.3	0.8
All boys	2.7	1.6	0.71	0.267	0.342	0.295	2.0	1.1	0.5

Source: Author's own calculations from IHDS data.

Table 4.5:
Equity-adjusted scores using the Gini coefficient (Girls: 8–11 years)

Group	Mean Scores			Gini of Scores Distribution			Equity-Adjusted Scores		
	Reading	Arithmetic	Writing	Reading	Arithmetic	Writing	Reading	Arithmetic	Writing
Brahmin	3.2	2.0	0.80	0.179	0.269	0.190	2.6	1.5	0.7
High caste	3.0	1.9	0.79	0.193	0.284	0.211	2.5	1.3	0.6
OBC	2.5	1.5	0.68	0.301	0.392	0.321	1.8	0.9	0.5
SC	2.4	1.3	0.63	0.321	0.416	0.371	1.6	0.8	0.4
Adivasi	2.2	1.1	0.55	0.335	0.487	0.449	1.5	0.6	0.3
Muslim	2.2	1.3	0.62	0.342	0.408	0.377	1.5	0.8	0.4
Sikh/Jain	3.3	2.1	0.85	0.153	0.221	0.146	2.8	1.6	0.7
Christian	3.2	2.0	0.86	0.155	0.213	0.154	2.7	1.6	0.7
All girls	2.6	1.5	0.68	0.291	0.383	0.321	1.8	0.9	0.5

Source: Author's own calculations from IHDS data.

The equity-adjusted scores show that the gap between children from the "lower" and "upper" classes was considerably greater than that suggested by the unadjusted mean scores: the *unadjusted* reading and arithmetic mean scores for SC boys (2.4 and 1.4, respectively) were 72 percent and 64 percent of the corresponding scores for brahmin boys (3.3 and 2.2); *with equity adjustment*, the SC shortfall, relative to that of brahmins, grew to 61 percent for reading (1.7 against 2.8) and to 51 percent for arithmetic (0.9 versus 1.7).

4.4. Estimating the Relative Strength of Factors Influencing Children's Educational Abilities

Given that the test results in reading, writing, and arithmetic differed markedly between children from different social groups, and given that there were strong inter-group differences in the schooling characteristics of children and in the characteristics of the households to which they belonged, this section seeks to answer two questions: (i) What was the relative strength of the different factors that exercised a significant influence on the children's test outcomes? (ii) After taking these factors into account, was there still significant correlation between the children's membership of specific groups and their test results?

The answers to these questions were provided by estimating econometric equations for reading, writing, and arithmetic with the dependent variable for each equation taking as its values the test scores of the children. Consequently, if N children sat the reading test, then the value of the dependent variable for the ith child ($i = 1, ..., N$) was denoted by $y_i \in [0,1,2,3,4]$. Using these dependent variables, the reading and arithmetic equations were estimated using the *multinomial logit* method and the writing equation, with binary outcomes, was estimated using *logit*.

Since these values were *discrete*, and were also *ordered* (in the sense that a higher value represented a "better" outcome than a lower value), the appropriate method of estimation might have been that of *ordered logit*. However, a critical assumption of the ordered logit model is that of *parallel slopes*. In essence this means that if there is a variable, which affects the likelihood of a person being in one of the ordered categories (for example, mother's literacy on reading score) then it is assumed that the coefficient linking that variable to the different outcomes *is the same across outcomes*. If this assumption is not valid, so that the slope coefficients associated with a variable are different across outcomes, then the method of ordered logit—notwithstanding its advantage of parsimony—is not appropriate and the model should be estimated using the method of *multinomial logit*.

A likelihood ratio test (STATA, 2007: 490) showed that the ordered logit model was not appropriate for estimating the equations employed in this paper and, therefore, multinomial logit was used.

It is possible to compute from the multinomial logit estimates for the reading and arithmetic equations, and the logit estimates for the writing equation, a set of *base probabilities* comprising the probabilities of the different outcomes *when all the variables are set to their mean values.* Following this, a natural question to ask is how the probabilities of the different outcomes (for example, the reading test has four outcomes) would *change* (from these base values) in response to a *change* in the value of any of the variables, if *the values of the other variables remain unchanged.* These probabilities are termed *marginal probabilities.* For continuous variables, the marginal probabilities refer to changes in the probabilities consequent upon a unit change in the value of the variable; for discrete variables, the marginal probabilities refer to changes in the probabilities consequent upon a move from the referenced category for that variable to the category in question.

This chaper presents the multinomial logit estimates—based on data for children between 8 and 11 years of age who were enrolled at school[7]—in terms of their implied marginal probabilities of the *highest* and the *lowest* levels of achievement (hereafter, referred to as "success" or "failure").[8] The estimated (highest/lowest achievement) marginal probabilities for the reading, writing, and arithmetic tests are shown, respectively, in Tables 4.6, 4.7, and 4.8. The base probabilities that anchored these marginal probabilities are shown at the head of each table: so, for example, if all the variables shown in Table 4.6 were assigned their mean values the *predicted* proportions of children obtaining the highest and lowest scores in the reading test were, respectively, 36.5 and 3.4 percent. In the subsequent discussion, the marginal probabilities are presented as percentage point (hereafter, simply point) changes to these base probabilities.[9]

---

[7]   A small proportion of students who took the test were not enrolled at school.

[8]   Namely, being able to read a "story"/cannot even recognize a letter of the alphabet; perform calculations involving division/cannot even recognize a number; write with two or fewer mistakes/write with more than two mistakes.

[9]   So, for example, a marginal probability of 0.02 means the base probability would increase by 2 percentage points and a marginal probability of –0.02 means the base probability would decrease by 2 percentage points.

Table 4.6:
Marginal probabilities from multinomial logit model estimates (Reading)

| | Highest Score: Reading | | | Lowest Score: Reading | | |
| | Base Probability: 0.365 | | | Base Probability: 0.034 | | |
	Marginal Probability	Z Statistic	Prob > z	Marginal Probability	Z Statistic	Prob > z
Parental characteristics						
Literate father	0.034	2.13	0.03	−0.005	−1.39	0.17
Literate mother	0.106	7.49	0.00	−0.015	−3.87	0.00
Father, Matric	0.035	2.22	0.03	−0.012	−2.73	0.01
Mother, Matric	0.069	3.35	0.00	−0.005	−0.56	0.57
Household economic position						
Poor household	−0.056	−3.79	0.00	0.007	2.05	0.04
Household assets	0.007	4.68	0.00	−0.002	−4.85	0.00
School type (Reference: Private school)						
Government school	−0.102	−6.33	0.00	0.025	6.13	0.00
Other schools	−0.047	−1.96	0.05	0.025	2.10	0.04
Medium of instruction (Reference: Other language)						
Hindi	0.234	5.9	0.00	−0.027	−3.18	0.00
State language	0.218	5.41	0.00	−0.020	−2.48	0.01
English	0.187	4.13	0.00	−0.026	−4.50	0.00
Learning time						
School hours/week	0.001	0.75	0.45	−0.001	−3.06	0.00
Homework hours/week	0.005	4.98	0.00	−0.001	−4.29	0.00
Private tuition hours/week	0.007	4.41	0.00	−0.001	−1.97	0.05
Days absent in last month	−0.003	−1.03	0.30	0.002	3.54	0.00
(Days absent)^2	0.000	0.75	0.45	0.000	−2.63	0.01
School grade of child	0.121	22.78	0.00	−0.023	−13.63	0.00
Age of child	0.311	2.79	0.01	−0.072	−2.40	0.02
(Age)^2	−0.015	−2.51	0.01	0.004	2.24	0.03
Girl child	−0.014	−1.21	0.23	0.008	2.75	0.01
Urban area	0.025	1.64	0.10	−0.008	−2.01	0.04
Region of India (Reference: Central)						
North	0.047	2.34	0.02	−0.019	−4.84	0.00
South	−0.133	−6.77	0.00	−0.004	−0.65	0.52
West	−0.053	−2.33	0.02	−0.017	−3.33	0.00
East	−0.081	−3.48	0.00	−0.028	−7.16	0.00
Household social group (Reference: Brahmin)						
High caste	−0.064	−2.41	0.02	0.019	1.12	0.26
OBC (Hindu)	−0.058	−2.23	0.03	0.030	2.05	0.04
SC	−0.102	−3.93	0.00	0.036	2.00	0.05

Table 4.6 continued

Table 4.6 continued

ST	−0.089	−2.83	0.01	0.038	1.70	0.09
Muslim	−0.123	−4.62	0.00	0.047	2.08	0.04
Sikh, Jain, Christian	−0.025	−0.60	0.55	0.002	0.11	0.91
Number of observations for equation			9,190			
Pseudo-R^2			0.147			

Source: Author's own calculations from IHDS data.

The variables associated with these marginal probabilities are grouped under broad headings. Some of these headings have a *referenced category*: for example, under "school type," the referenced category is "private schools"; under "medium of instruction," it is "other languages"; and under "household social group," it is "brahmin." For such variables, the marginal probability refers to the change in the probabilities of success and failure (that is, the highest and lowest levels of achievement) consequent upon a change from the referenced category to the category in question.

Table 4.7:
Marginal probabilities from multinomial logit model estimates (Arithmetic)

	Highest Score: Arithmetic			Lowest Score: Arithmetic		
	Base Probability: 0.192			Base Probability: 0.093		
	Marginal Probability	Z Statistic	Prob > z	Marginal Probability	Z Statistic	Prob > z
Parental characteristics						
Literate father	0.000	−0.01	0.99	−0.005	−0.79	0.43
Literate mother	0.048	4.26	0.00	−0.043	−5.86	0.00
Father, Matric	0.086	6.64	0.00	−0.026	−3.18	0.00
Mother, Matric	0.026	1.72	0.09	−0.027	−2.01	0.05
Household economic position						
Poor household	−0.045	−3.90	0.00	0.032	4.42	0.00
Household assets	0.005	4.41	0.00	−0.004	−4.43	0.00
School type (Reference: Private school)						
Government school	−0.081	−6.33	0.00	0.020	1.65	0.10
Other school	−0.007	−0.42	0.68	−0.032	−2.62	0.01
Medium of instruction (Reference: Other languages)						
Hindi	0.092	2.92	0.00	−0.035	−2.13	0.03
State language	0.071	2.22	0.03	−0.027	−1.67	0.10
English	0.087	2.21	0.03	−0.055	−4.00	0.00

Table 4.7 continued

Table 4.7 continued

Learning time						
School hours/week	0.000	0.08	0.94	−0.001	−3.02	0.00
Homework hours/week	0.003	3.93	0.00	−0.002	−3.09	0.00
Private tuition hours/ week	0.007	6.61	0.00	−0.003	−3.06	0.00
Days absent in last month	−0.008	−3.37	0.00	0.006	5.12	0.00
(Days absent)^2	0.000	2.45	0.01	0.000	−2.72	0.01
School grade of child	0.087	21.70	0.00	−0.041	−15.78	0.00
Age of child	0.338	3.90	0.00	−0.214	−3.88	0.00
(Age)^2	−0.016	−3.51	0.00	0.011	3.68	0.00
Girl child	−0.036	−4.07	0.00	0.040	7.14	0.00
Urban area	0.019	1.61	0.11	−0.016	−2.11	0.04
Region of India (Reference: Central)						
North	0.038	2.43	0.02	−0.060	−8.72	0.00
South	−0.086	−6.52	0.00	−0.059	−6.68	0.00
West	−0.062	−4.09	0.00	−0.010	−0.84	0.40
East	0.089	3.88	0.00	−0.062	−7.76	0.00
Household social group (Reference: Brahmin)						
High caste	−0.035	−1.96	0.05	0.019	0.86	0.39
OBC (Hindu)	−0.058	−3.38	0.00	0.037	1.81	0.07
SC	−0.095	−6.00	0.00	0.057	2.35	0.02
ST	−0.088	−4.83	0.00	0.078	2.45	0.01
Muslim	−0.096	−6.16	0.00	0.056	2.09	0.04
Sikh, Jain, Christian	−0.082	−4.06	0.00	−0.032	−1.18	0.24
Number of observations for equation			9,153			
Pseudo-R^2			0.176			

Source: Author's own calculations from IHDS data.

Table 4.8:
Marginal probabilities from multinomial logit model estimates (Writing)

	Highest Score: Writing		
	Base Probability: 0.753		
	Marginal Probability	*Z Statistic*	*Prob > z*
Parental characteristics			
Literate father	0.022	1.87	0.06
Literate mother	0.077	6.56	0.00
Father, Matric	0.046	3.40	0.00
Mother, Matric	0.055	2.92	0.00

Table 4.8 continued

Table 4.8 continued

Household economic position			
Poor household	−0.055	−4.53	0.00
Household assets	0.002	1.37	0.17
School type (Reference: Private school)			
Government school	−0.094	−7.27	0
Other school	−0.090	−3.35	0.001
Medium of instruction (Reference: State language)			
Hindi	−0.013	−0.43	0.67
Other language	−0.005	−0.16	0.88
English	0.043	1.37	0.17
Learning time			
School hours/week	0.000	0.67	0.50
Homework hours/week	0.004	4.09	0.00
Private tuition hours/week	0.006	3.67	0.00
Days absent in last month	0.001	0.54	0.59
(Days absent)^2	0.000	−1.96	0.05
School grade of child	0.083	19.87	0.00
Age of child	0.317	3.39	0.00
(Age)^2	−0.016	−3.31	0.00
Girl child	−0.025	−2.58	0.01
Urban area	0.035	2.73	0.01
Region of India (Reference: Central)			
North	0.012	0.71	0.48
South	0.066	3.56	0.00
West	0.054	2.81	0.01
East	0.126	7.73	0.00
Household social group (Reference: Brahmin)			
High caste	−0.004	−0.14	0.89
OBC (Hindu)	−0.036	−1.33	0.18
SC	−0.049	−1.73	0.08
ST	−0.090	−2.51	0.01
Muslim	−0.067	−2.13	0.03
Sikh, Jain, Christian	0.015	0.35	0.73
Number of observations for equation		9,116	
Pseudo-R^2		0.179	

Source: Author's own calculations from IHDS data.

4.4.1. *Parental Education and Household's Economic Position*

The first thing to draw attention to in Tables 4.6–4.8 is the importance of parental education and household economic position in influencing the probability of a child succeeding or failing. For example, Tables 4.6–4.8 show that having a literate mother had a significant *positive* effect on the likelihood of *success* in reading (Table 4.6: 10.6 points), in arithmetic (Table 4.7: 4.8 points), and in writing (Table 4.8: 7.7 points); literate mothers also had a significant *negative* effect on the likelihood of *failure* in reading (Table 4.6: 1.5 points) and arithmetic (Table 4.7: 4.3 points); Tables 4.6–4.8 also show that having a father and mother who were Matric (that is, who had successfully completed their school leaving exams) significantly increased the probability of a child's success in reading by, respectively, 3.5 and 6.9 points (Table 4.6); arithmetic by, respectively, 8.6 and 2.6 points (Table 4.7); and writing by, respectively, 4.6 and 5.5 points (Table 4.8).

Belonging to a "poor" household lowered the likelihood of success in all three competencies (by 5.6 points in reading by 4.5 points in arithmetic and by 5.5 points in writing) and raised the likelihood of failure (by 0.7 points in reading, by 3.2 points in arithmetic, and by 4.5 points in writing); conversely, the higher the level of household assets the greater the likelihood of success—and the smaller the likelihood of failure—in reading and arithmetic. However, compared to the effect of poverty on these likelihoods, the effect of wealth was not as marked. This suggests that a lack of wealth (assets) is not as great a barrier to educational achievement as a lack of income (poverty).

4.2.2. *School Type and Medium of Instruction*

The next set of variables affecting the likelihood of success related to the nature of the schools in which the children studied. The overwhelming proportion of children aged 8–11 years went to either government (59 percent boys, 63 percent girls) or private schools (29 percent boys, 23 percent girls); the remainder went to "other schools" comprising: government-aided schools (4 percent), convent schools (2 percent), and *madrassa*s (1 percent).[10] The results in Tables 4.6–4.8 show that, compared to studying in private schools—the referenced school category—studying in a government school significantly lowered the likelihood of success in reading by 10.2 points, in arithmetic by 8.1 points, and in writing by 9.4 points. On the other hand, compared to studying in private schools, studying in "other schools" significantly reduced the likelihood of success in reading by 4.7 points and in writing (by 9 points), without any significant effect on arithmetic scores. At the other end of the scale, compared to private schools, the likelihood of failure in reading was higher in government schools and "other schools" (by 2.5 points) but the likelihood of failure in arithmetic was lower in "other schools" (by 3.2 points).

For a large majority of the children (96 percent), the medium of instruction was Hindi, English or a state language: Assamese, Bangla, Gujarati, Marathi, Oriya, Kannada, Malayalam, Tamil, Telegu, Punjabi; the remainder studied in "other" languages with Urdu being prominent in this category. Using "other" languages as the referenced category, Tables 4.6–4.8 show that in terms of the likelihood of *success*, there was a significant advantage in reading and arithmetic to studying in Hindi, English, or a state language. The advantage of Hindi, English, and state languages over other languages also lay in a smaller likelihood of *failure* in reading and arithmetic. Indeed, writing was the only competency in which, compared to other languages as the medium of instruction, there was no significant advantage to studying in Hindi, English, or a state language. The "language effect," as noted earlier, could possibly be due to the greater isolation from "mainstream" Indian society, of children who did not study in the major languages.

4.4.3. *School, Homework, Private Tuition Hours, and Days Absent*

The results shown in Tables 4.6–4.8 confirmed the importance for learning achievements of classwork, homework, private tuition, and regular school attendance: an increase of 1 hour per week in the number of homework, and private tuition, hours would significantly increase the likelihood of

---

[10] Contrary to popular folklore, only 5 percent of Muslim 8–11-year olds were enrolled in *madrassas*, and only 4 percent of *all* Muslim educational enrollments were with *madrassas*.

success—and significantly lower the likelihood of failure—in reading, arithmetic, and writing; an increase of 1 hour per week in the number of school hours would significantly lower the likelihood of failure (though it would not significantly increase the likelihood of success) in reading and arithmetic; lastly, every additional day missed (per month) of school would significantly increase the likelihood of failure in reading and arithmetic and, also, would significantly decrease the likelihood of success in arithmetic. However, it should be noted that these marginal effects, though significant, were relatively small.

4.4.4. *Grade, Age, Gender, and Urban*

Considering that the children analyzed were aged 8–11 years, every additional year of age had a large positive impact on the likelihood of success—and a large negative impact on the likelihood of failure—in all three competencies.[11] However, the largest effect on children's performance was due to the grade (or class) in which they were studying: a higher grade (or class) improved the likelihood of success in reading, arithmetic, and writing by, respectively, 12.1, 8.7, and 8.3 points, and reduced the likelihood of failure in reading, arithmetic, and writing by, respectively, 2.3, 4.1, and 8.3 points.

In terms of success, the gender effect was significant for arithmetic and writing but not for reading: compared to boys, girls were less likely to succeed in arithmetic and writing by, respectively, 3.7 and 2.5 points. In terms, of failure, the gender effect was significant for all three competencies: compared to boys, girls were more likely to fail in reading, arithmetic and writing by, respectively, 0.8, 4.0, and 2.5 points. In developed countries, the traditional educational disadvantage of females has given way to a situation in which girls outperform boys.[12] For India, however,

[11] The negative marginal probability of success, and the positive marginal probability of failure, associated with the squared value of age shows that these effects diminished with age.

[12] For example, in both Britain and New Zealand, researchers (Eden, 2004; Fergusson and Horwood, 1997) have argued, "girls" educational attainment is higher than that of boys and it is the under achievement of boys that is now currently seen to be the problem" (Eden, 2004: 124), one reason for this being that boys were more prone to disruptive and inattentive classroom behavior that impeded their learning.

the traditional disadvantages of the girl child with regard to nutrition and health care (Borooah, 2004) also extend to education.

Lastly, compared to children in rural areas, the likelihood of success in reading, arithmetic, and writing was significantly higher (though for reading and arithmetic at 10 percent significance) for children living in urban areas and, compared to rural children, the likelihood of failure in all three competencies was significantly lower for urban children.

4.4.5. The Social Group of the Children

Earlier it was observed that there was a considerable gap between the educational attainments of, for example, brahmin and SC children. However, this may have been the consequence of differences between them in their endowments of "attainment-friendly" attributes. If, *after controlling for such attributes*, membership of a social group did not play a significant part in explaining inter-group attainment differences then these could—indeed, would—be eliminated by removing attribute differences. However, if even after controlling for attributes, the social groups to which children belonged were significantly correlated with their educational attainment levels, then this would raise a wider, and more vexed, question of *structural differences* between the groups. Such differences, perhaps due to inter-group differences in the importance attached to learning and, concomitantly, in aspirations and ambition, might impact on children's attainments, over and above inter-group differences in attributes.

Disparities in the educational achievements in the USA among children of different racial backgrounds—with White children doing considerably better than Black and Hispanic children—are well documented (Humpherys, 1988). Stevenson, Chen, and Uttal (1990) in a study of Black, White and Hispanic children in the USA found that ethnic differences in reading scores persisted (but differences in mathematics scores were largely eliminated) even after the effects of mothers' education and family income had been removed.

Table 4.6 shows that after controlling for the "secular" variables—that is, variables unrelated to caste or religion—children from *all* the social groups (except for Sikh, Jain, and Christian children) compared to brahmin children (the representative group) were significantly *less likely* to attain the *highest* reading score. This negative social group effect in reading success was, however, the smallest for high caste and OBC children (respectively, 6.4 and 5.8 points) and largest for Muslim (12.3 points), SC (10.2 points), and ST (8.9 points) children. Conversely, compared to brahmin children, only OBC, SC, ST, and Muslim children were significantly *more likely* to receive the *lowest* reading score; this positive social group effect in reading failure was largest for Muslims (4.7 points) followed by ST (3.8 points) and SC (3.6 points).

Table 4.7 shows that compared to brahmin children, children from *all* the social groups were significantly *less likely* to attain the highest score in arithmetic. This negative social group effect in arithmetic success was the smallest for high caste and OBC children (respectively, 3.5 and 5.8 points) and largest for Muslim (9.6 points), SC (9.5 points), and ST (8.8 points) children. Conversely, compared to brahmin children, only OBC, SC, ST, and Muslim children were significantly *more* likely to receive the *lowest* arithmetic score; this positive social group effect in arithmetic failure was largest for ST (7.8 points), followed by SC (5.7 points), then Muslims (5.6 points), and then the OBC (3.7 points). Lastly, Table 4.8 shows that for writing, SC, ST, and Muslim children, compared to brahmins, were *less likely* to attain the highest score and more likely to receive the lowest score: ST by 9.0 points, Muslims by 6.7 points, and SC by 4.9 points.

Overall, therefore, while children from all the social groups were structurally disadvantaged relative to brahmin children in some or all of the three competencies, this disadvantage was greatest for Muslim, SC, and ST children. Moreover, for these children, structural disadvantage extended over all the competencies, and it included the probability of failure as well as that of success.

4.5. Decomposition by Social Group

In the estimation results reported in Tables 4.6, 4.7, and 4.8, the "social group" effects operated entirely through the intercept term with the slope coefficients being unaffected by the children's social group. The implication was that the marginal probabilities associated with the variables—say, the effect of parental education on reading scores—was the same for brahmins as it was for SC. This assumption can be relaxed by estimating the three equations specified in Tables 4.6–4.8 *separately* for children from the different social groups; this study does so for brahmin and upper caste—"HCH"—children (collectively) and for SC and Muslim children (separately). It should be emphasized that although the HCH coefficients were *numerically* different from the SC (Muslim) coefficients in many cases these differences were not statistically significant. The decompositions reported as follows are based on the *entire* HCH and SC (Muslim) coefficient vectors without regard to whether differences in individual components were statistically significant.

After doing so, the difference between groups, in their respective mean values, were decomposed into an "unexplained" effect, attributable to differences between groups in their coefficients, and an "explained" effect, attributable to differences between groups in their attributes by using the method of Oaxaca (1973) as applied to models of discrete choice (Borooah and Iyer, 2005b).[13] The attributes component was computed by asking what the difference in the proportion of HCH and SC children achieving the maximum score *would have been* if the difference in attributes between them had been evaluated using a *common* coefficient vector.[14] The coefficients component, computed as a residual, was the observed difference *less* the attributes component. This could be ascribed to a "structural advantage" that children from some groups enjoyed over children from other groups. Figures 4.3, 4.4, and 4.5 show the decompositions for the *observed* difference between HCH and SC in the proportions of children attaining the maximum score in, respectively, reading, arithmetic, and writing while Figures 4.6, 4.7, and 4.8 show the results from a similar comparison between HCH and Muslims.

So, Figure 4.3 shows the *observed* difference between HCH and SC in the proportions of children attaining the *maximum* reading score of four points: $0.511–0.304 = 0.207$. The chart on the left shows the amount of the overall gap that is due to the *attributes component* when HCH and SC attributes are both evaluated using HCH coefficients: this is 68 percent; similarly, the chart on the right shows the amount of the overall gap that is due to the *attributes component* when HCH and SC attributes are both evaluated using SC coefficients: this is 76 percent.

---

[13] The details of this non-linear decomposition were contained in an appendix to Chapter 3.

[14] Similarly, for the difference in the observed HCH and Muslim proportions.

Figure 4.3:

The decomposition of the difference between HCH and SC children in the proportion attaining the maximum reading score

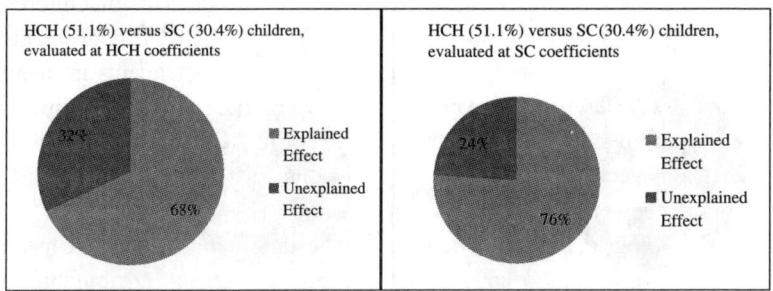

Source: Author's own calculations from IHDS data.

Similarly, Figure 4.4 shows the *observed* difference between HCH and SC in the proportions of children attaining the *maximum* arithmetic score of three points: 0.392–0.174 = 0.218. The chart on the left shows the amount of the overall gap that is due to the *attributes component* when HCH and SC attributes are both evaluated using HCH coefficients: this is 53 percent; similarly, the chart on the right shows the amount of the overall gap that is due to the *attributes component* when HCH and SC attributes are both evaluated using SC coefficients: this is 64 percent.

Figure 4.4:

The decomposition of the difference between HCH and SC children in the proportion attaining the maximum arithmetic score

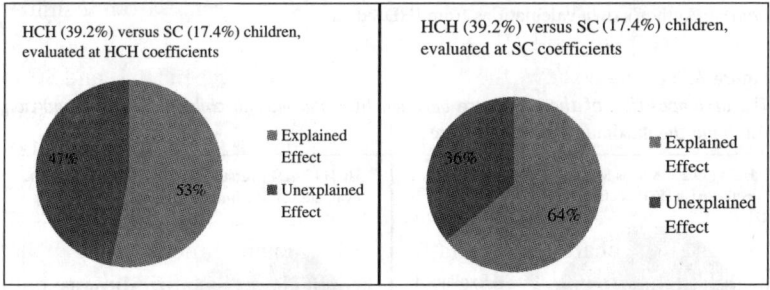

Source: Author's own calculations from IHDS data.

Figure 4.5:
The decomposition of the difference between HCH and SC children in the proportion attaining the maximum writing score

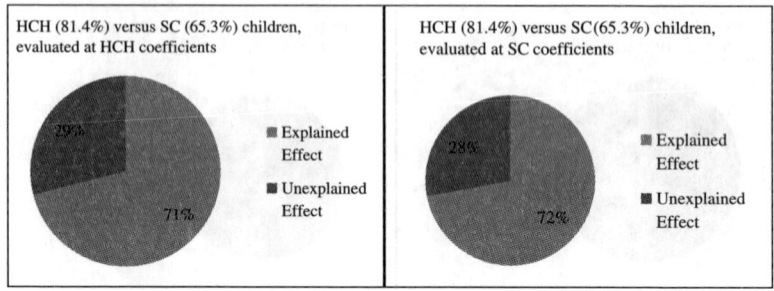

Source: Author's own calculations from IHDS data.

Figure 4.6:
The decomposition of the difference between HCH and Muslim children in the proportion attaining the maximum reading score

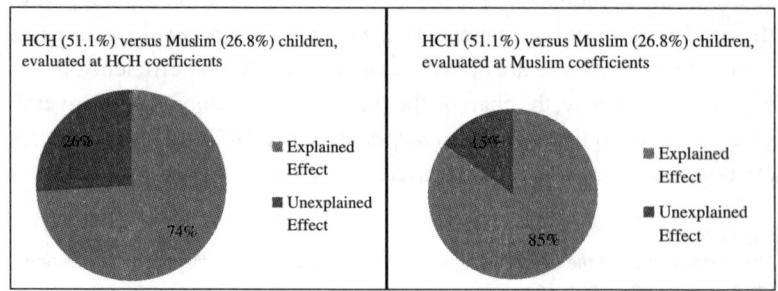

Source: Author's own calculations from IHDS data.

Figure 4.7:
The decomposition of the difference between HCH and Muslim children in the proportion attaining the maximum arithmetic score

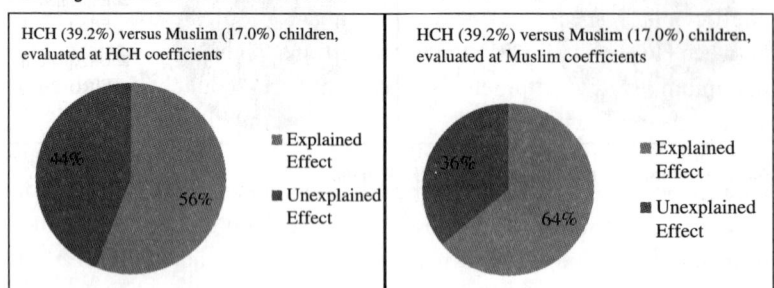

Source: Author's own calculations from IHDS data.

Figure 4.8:
The decomposition of the difference between HCH and Muslim children in the proportion attaining the maximum *writing score*

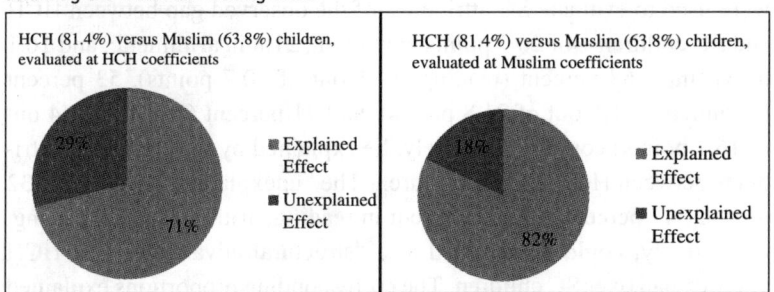

| HCH (81.4%) versus Muslim (63.8%) children, evaluated at HCH coefficients | HCH (81.4%) versus Muslim (63.8%) children, evaluated at Muslim coefficients |

Source: Author's own calculations from IHDS data.

Figure 4.5 shows the *observed* difference between HCH and SC in the proportions of children attaining the *maximum* writing score of one point: 0.814–0.653 = 0.161. The chart on the left shows the amount of the overall gap that is due to the *attributes component* when HCH and SC attributes are both evaluated using HCH coefficients: this is 71 percent; similarly, the chart on the right shows the amount of the overall gap that is due to the *attributes component* when HCH and SC attributes are both evaluated using SC coefficients: this is 72 percent.

Similarly, the left panels of Figures 4.6, 4.7, and 4.8 show that of the observed gaps between HCH and Muslims in the proportions of children obtaining, the maximum reading, arithmetic, and writing scores, respectively, 74%, 56%, and 71% could be explained by differences in attributes between HCH and Muslim children when the attributes were evaluated using HCH coefficients. The right hand panels of Figures 4.6, 4.7, and 4.8 show that when attributes were evaluated using Muslim coefficients, respectively, 85%, 64%, and 82% of the observed gaps between HCH and Muslims in the proportions of children obtaining, the maximum reading, arithmetic, and writing scores, could be explained by a difference in attributes between the two sets of children.

When SC (Muslim) attributes were evaluated at HCH coefficients, the proportion of SC (Muslim) children who obtained the highest score in reading, in arithmetic, and in writing rose from the observed values of 0.304, 0.174, and 0.653 (Muslims: 0.268, 0.170, and 0.638) to 0.370, 0.277, and 0.7 (Muslims: 0.331, 0.267, and 0.699). This is because SC

(Muslim) attributes were now being evaluated using more *favorable* coefficients (that is, those of HCH). Consequently, when HCH coefficients were used to evaluate SC attributes, of the observed gap between HCH and SC children—of 20.7 points in reading, 21.8 in arithmetic, and 16.1 in writing—68 percent (reading: 14.1 out of 20.7 points), 53 percent (arithmetic: 11.5 out of 21.8 points), and 71 percent (writing: 11.4 out of 16.1 points) could, respectively, be explained by differences in attributes between HCH and SC children. The "unexplained" residual of 32 percent, 47 percent, and 29 percent in reading, arithmetic, and writing, respectively, could be ascribed to a "structural advantage" that HCH children had over SC children. The corresponding proportions explained by differences in attributes between HCH and Muslim children were 74 percent in reading, 56 percent in arithmetic, and 65 percent in writing. The "unexplained" residuals (of 26 percent, 44 percent, and 29 percent in, respectively, reading, arithmetic, and writing) could be ascribed to a "structural advantage" that HCH children had over Muslim children.

On the other hand, when HCH attributes were evaluated using SC (Muslim) coefficients, the proportion of HCH children who obtained the highest score in reading, in arithmetic, and in writing *fell* from the *observed* values of 0.511, 0.392, and 0.814 to 0.461 (Muslim: 0.474), 0.313 (Muslim: 0.312), and 0.769 (Muslim: 0.782). These reductions were due to HCH attributes being evaluated using *less favorable* coefficients (that is, those of SC and Muslims). Consequently, of the observed gap between HCH and SC children—of 20.7 points in reading, 21.8 in arithmetic, and 16.1 in writing—76 percent (reading), 64 percent (arithmetic), and 72 percent (writing) could, respectively, be explained by differences in attributes between HCH and SC children. The "unexplained" residual of 24 percent, 36 percent, and 28 percent in reading, arithmetic, and writing, respectively, could be ascribed to a "structural advantage" that HCH children had over SC children. Similarly, of the observed gaps between HCH and Muslim children in the three competencies, 85 percent, 64 percent, and 82 percent in reading, arithmetic, and writing respectively could be explained by differences in attributes. The "unexplained" residuals of 15 percent, 36 percent, and 18 percent in reading, arithmetic, and writing, respectively, could be ascribed to a "structural advantage" that HCH children had over Muslim children.

The fact that Oaxaca-type decompositions (based on evaluating *different* attribute vectors using a *common* coefficient vector) yield different results depending upon the common vector employed has been analyzed by Borooah and Iyer (2005a). Here it may be noted that the structural advantage of HCH children over SC (Muslims) was smallest when the evaluation used the SC (Muslim) coefficients and largest when it was based on the HCH coefficients. Combining the two sets of comparisons provides an estimate range (rather than point estimates) of the values for structural advantage: the structural advantage of HCH over SC children was between 24 percent and 32 percent in reading; 36 percent and 47 percent in arithmetic; and 28 percent and 29 percent in writing. The structural advantage of HCH over Muslim children was between 15 and 26 percent in reading; 36 percent and 44 percent in arithmetic; and 18 percent and 35 percent in writing.

4.6. The Treatment of Children in School

No discussion of the underachievement of children from poor and marginalized groups can be complete without an understanding of how they are treated at school relative to their peers from dominant groups. Thrown in as a minority group with children from the higher social groups, they face discrimination, exclusion, and humiliation. Nambissan (2010) in her study of the experiences of SC children in schools in Jaipur district in the state of Rajasthan concluded that "social relations and the pedagogic processes fail to ensure full participation of SC children and they are subject to discriminatory and unequal treatment in relation to their peers" (p. 282).[15] Sainath (2002) has pointed out that the vast majority of children who drop out at school are girls from the SC and the reason for their high dropout rate is not just poverty but also their treatment at the hands of fellow pupils. As he describes it, girls from the SC sit in the corner where the shoes of the other children are kept, they are not allowed to sit on the *patti*s on which other students sit but, instead, have to sit on the floor, and their entry into the classroom is invariably greeted with chants of *"bhangi ayee hai"* (the toilet cleaner has arrived).

---

[15] STs escape this fate largely because they live in areas where they are the overwhelming majority.

Ramachandran and Naorem (2013), after examining the experiences of SC and ST children in six Indian states—Andhra Pradesh, Assam, Bihar, MP, Orissa, and Rajasthan—concluded that even in states that were highly stratified by caste such as Andhra Pradesh, Bihar, and Rajasthan, there was considerable heterogeneity in the treatment of SC children: caste-based discrimination was explicit in Rajasthan while in Andhra Pradesh and Bihar it was more disguised. They argue that this difference may be due to differences between the states in their political environment—unlike Rajasthan, both Andhra Pradesh and Bihar experienced political and social movements led by the lower castes.

From their study, Ramachandran and Naorem (2013) identified two main instruments of exclusion. The first was language. Often pupils were excluded from a full participation in class room activities because the language of instruction was not their mother tongue. In Assam, for example, children of tea garden laborers, whose mother tongue was Hindi (or some dialect of it), were disadvantaged from being taught in Assamese, which is the official language of the state and the medium of instruction in schools. In Orissa, tribal pupils, who spoke their own dialect, were handicapped by the fact that they were taught in *Odiya*, the state's official language and medium of instruction. Similarly, in the border areas of Andhra Pradesh and in Rajasthan there was disjoint between pupils' mother tongue and the medium of instruction based on, respectively, Telegu and Hindi.

The second area of exclusion—which was underpinned by the gamut of issues associated with pollution and untouchability—was the midday meal scheme, which provided free lunch on school days for children in primary and upper primary classes in government schools.[16] Discrimination in midday meals took several forms: not serving them adequate amounts, making them wait till high caste children have finished their meal, throwing food into their plates so as to avoid any possibility of physical contact, seating them separately from higher-caste children with separately marked plates, and not appointing any persons from the SC as cooks and helpers (Nambissan, 2010; Thorat and Lee, 2010). Another area of contention associated with

---

[16] Also included in this scheme were government-aided, local body, Education Guarantee Scheme and Alternate Innovative Education Centers, Madrassa and Maqtabs supported under Sarva Shiksha Abhiyan and National Child Labor Project Schools run by Ministry of Labor. According to the Indian government, it is the world's largest school feeding program, reaching out to about 120,000,000 children in over 1,265,000 schools.

untouchability was water. In most schools in Rajasthan, children from the higher caste drank water and washed their plates before children from the lower castes and one school had separate water pitchers for SC pupils. The pattern of SC pupils having to wait their turn was repeated in Bihar and MP. Furthermore, in MP, only children from the higher castes were allowed to fetch water for the teachers and guests (Ramachandran and Naorem, 2013).

More recently, Human Rights Watch (2014) has assessed India's *Right of Children to Free and Compulsory Education Act*, which provides for free and compulsory education to all children aged 6–14 years based on principles of equal treatment. They concluded that, notwithstanding the Act's lofty ambitions, even in the second decade of the 21st century, discrimination in Indian schools was flourishing and took multifarious forms. In some of these forms, teachers asked SC pupils to sit separately, made insulting remarks about Muslims and tribal students, addressed SC pupils by their derogatory caste names, never considered them for positions of classroom responsibility, and expected them to perform menial tasks in the school. Such discriminatory behavior contributed to truancy. According to Human Rights Watch (2014), several children from marginalized groups do not attend schools because they are made to feel unwelcome and inferior and, as a corollary, their poor attendance contributes to their low levels of educational achievement.

4.7. Conclusions

This chapter recorded significant inter-group differences in the test scores in reading, arithmetic, and writing of school children in India aged 8–11 years. In particular, children belonging to the "higher" social groups—brahmins, high castes, Sikhs/Jains, and Christians—did significantly better than those from the "lower" groups—the OBC, SC, ST, and Muslims. After controlling for a number of parental, household, and school-related factors, it appeared that children from all the social groups were structurally disadvantaged, in some or all of the three competencies of reading, arithmetic, and writing, relative to brahmin children. However, this disadvantage was greatest for Muslim, SC, and ST children. These children were structurally disadvantaged with respect to all three competencies and their disadvantage included the probabilities of failure as well as success. Using a decomposition analysis, the paper quantified the "structural advantage" that brahmin and high-caste children enjoyed over their SC and Muslim counterparts.

It is possible that a significant part of the underperformance of SC and Muslim children is due to their experience of schools and schooling, as detailed in the previous section. This sense of exclusion is compounded when, on returning from school with homework, many find that their poorly educated, and often illiterate, parents (44 percent of SC, compared to 19 percent of brahmins, in the sample was illiterate) are unable to help them with it. Overlaying this is the fact that most teachers are likely to be non-SC or non-Muslims and, therefore, not understanding of, and perhaps unsympathetic to, the feelings of minority group children.[17]

The role of social identity in shaping outcomes in work and education has been extensively discussed by Akerlof and Kranton (2010). They argued that the traditional economic model in which students, as rational decision makers, weighed the economic costs and benefits of schooling was flawed because it took no account of the constraints imposed by the social identities of the children. Using examples from the USA, they showed that the social burden of being Black or Hispanic led many children from such groups to underperform relative to their White peers even within the same school: consequently, relative to social pressures, the economic return to education in terms of more pleasant and better paid jobs could be a weak determinant of children's efforts at school. The solution for such "identity-based" problems is to view schools not just as imparting skills but also teaching norms of behavior and, by so doing, becoming a sanctuary from the dysfunctional world outside its walls.

If there is force to this argument, then one solution to SC and Muslim educational under-achievement lies in creating a social and cultural environment in schools whereby they cease to be unwelcome and frightening places for children from these groups. This would require teachers to be trained to respect the caste and religious sensitivities of "depressed minorities" in much the same way that teachers in Western countries are trained to be sensitive to racial and religious diversity. This would go a long way in ameliorating the force of the central conclusion of this chapter which is

---

[17] Nambissan (2010) reports that many SC children received only minimal support from non-SC teachers.

that even after controlling for a number of secular factors, children from all the social groups were disadvantaged relative to brahmin children in some or all of the three competencies of reading, arithmetic, and writing. However, this disadvantage was greatest for Muslim, SC, and ST children, and, furthermore, this disadvantage extended over all the competencies, both in the probabilities of success and failure.

Sample Test Sheets

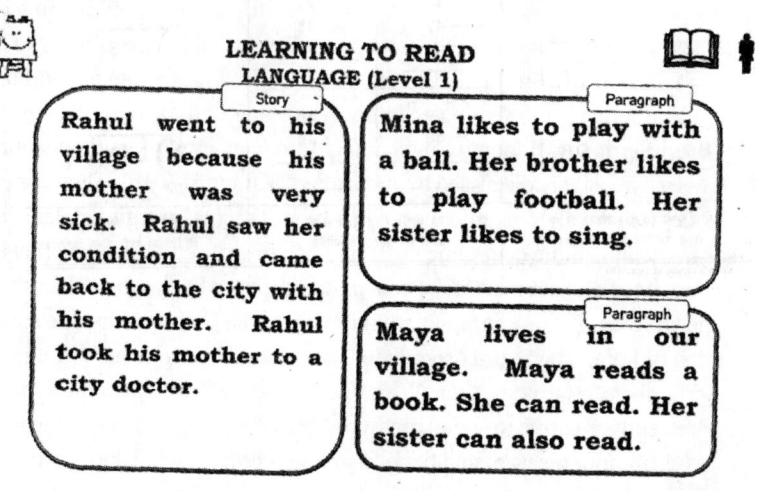

LEARNING TO READ
LANGUAGE (Level 1)

Story

Rahul went to his village because his mother was very sick. Rahul saw her condition and came back to the city with his mother. Rahul took his mother to a city doctor.

Paragraph

Mina likes to play with a ball. Her brother likes to play football. Her sister likes to sing.

Paragraph

Maya lives in our village. Maya reads a book. She can read. Her sister can also read.

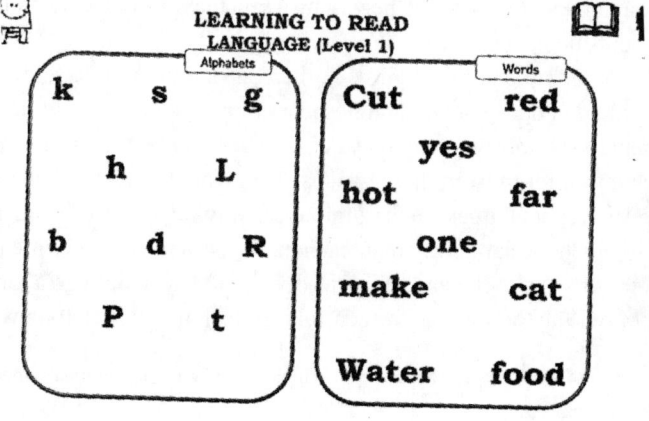

LEARNING TO READ
LANGUAGE (Level 1)

Alphabets

k   s   g
   h   L
b   d   R
   P   t

Words

Cut   red
    yes
hot   far
    one
make   cat
Water   food

गणित

AUGUST 2002 (1)

1		2		3
57	35	56 − 38	74 − 56	7)468(
26	42	46 − 18	75 − 37	5)275(
29	92	63 − 47	94 − 65	8)496(
33	71			
89	98	84 − 68	84 − 46	3)174(

पाँच पूछो (4/5) संख्या 5 में से 4 पहचान होनी चाहिए।

दो करो। (2/2) 2 में से दोनों ही सही होने चाहिये।

एक करो। (1) किया हुआ भाग का सवाल सही होना चाहिए।

5

Child Malnutrition

5.1. Introduction

Even though the incidence of malnutrition in India has improved greatly since independence (see Dreze and Sen, 2013), the prevalence of malnutrition in India is extremely high, relative to other poor countries. In the 1990s, 36 percent of children below the age of five, compared to 21 percent in sub-Saharan Africa were "severely stunted"; 49 percent of women between the ages of 20 and 29 years in India, compared to 21 percent in sub-Saharan Africa had a body mass index (BMI) of less than 18.5 (Svedberg, 2001). On a more recent note, the National Family Health Survey reports that between 1998–99 and 2005–06, there was virtually no improvement in children's weight, and even today India has the highest percentage of undernourished children than almost any other country in the world: the UN report of 2012 states that 43 percent of Indian children were "underweight" and 48 percent were "severely stunted" (terms that are made more precise below) compared to 21 percent and 40 percent for sub-Saharan Africa, and 33 and 39 percent for South Asia, in their entirety.[1] Compounding the suffering that underlies these statistics is the "silence with which it is tolerated, not to mention the smugness with which it is sometimes dismissed" (Sen, 2001a). Chapter 3 pointed to a caste/religious bias to educational attainment with HCH and Sikhs/Jain/Christian children scoring more highly on reading, arithmetic, and writing tests compared to their counterparts who were Muslim or who were from SC and ST. In this chapter, we enquire as to whether there might be a similar caste bias to the likelihood of children who are mal(under)nourished.

---

[1] See UN data, http://data.un.org/Data.aspx?d = SOWC&f = inID%3a220 (for underweight) and http://data.un.org/Data.aspx?d = SOWC&f = inID%3A106 (for stunting).

A child's *height-for-age* is an indicator of "stunting," which is a common manifestation of malnutrition in children in developing countries. Other anthropometric measures employed to assess malnutrition among children are *weight-for-age* for assessing the prevalence of underweight children, and *weight-for-height* for assessing the prevalence of "wasting."[2] We classify the nutritional status of a child as follows: he/she is "not stunted" if his/her height is less than two standard deviations below the World Health Organization (WHO) norm for a child of that age and sex; he/she is "moderately stunted" if his/her height is more than two, but less than three, standard deviations below the WHO norm; and he/she is "severely stunted" if his/her height is more than three standard deviations below the WHO norm (WHO, 2000). An identical definition applies to "not underweight," "underweight," and "severely underweight" children, with the caveat that the word "height" in the definition mentioned earlier is replaced by "weight."

Svedberg (2000) referred to the five *w*'s of malnutrition: What is malnutrition? Who are the malnourished? Where are the malnourished? When are people malnourished? And why are people malnourished? In terms of these questions, this chapter, with its focus on children 0–5 years of age, defines what is malnutrition, it identifies *who* the malnourished children are in terms of their caste/religious group; it locates *where* under-nourished children live in terms of the Indian states; and it studies *when* and *why* children are malnourished by examining the relative strength of the variables that influence malnutrition and, lastly, it adds a sixth question by asking whether there is a caste/religious bias to malnutrition of children in India.

The data used in this chapter are from the IHDS, which was conducted in 2004–05 by the University of Maryland in collaboration with the National Council of Applied Economic Research, New Delhi, between November 2004 and October 2005.[3] The national representative data cover 1,504 villages and 971 urban areas across 33 states and union territories of India. The survey covering 41,554 households was carried out through face-to-face interviews by pairs of male and female enumerators in local languages. The

---

[2] However, unlike these measures, height-for-age is less affected by acute periods of stress at the time of measurement. Sahn and Stifel (2002a) point out that an acute episode of diarrhea or malaria will not affect height-for-age.

[3] Available from the Inter-University Consortium for Political and Social Research (ICPSR), http://www.icpsr.umich.edu (last accessed on August 15, 2012).

respondents included a person who was knowledgeable about the household economic situation (usually the male head of the household) and an ever-married woman aged 15–49 years. The detailed modules of the survey provide answers to a wide range of questions relating to economic activity, income and consumption expenditure, asset ownership, social capital, education, health, marriage, and fertility, etc.

A unique feature of the IHDS is that it included an anthropometric part by which interviewers took the height and weight measurements of *all* children aged 5 years or less. It is these data that form the basis for the results on malnutrition reported in this chapter. However, because these measurements were made as an integral part of the overall survey, the children's anthropometric results could be matched with the circumstances of the households in which they lived. It is the fusion of the anthropometric and the general data, which enables us to answer, for India, the five questions posed by Svedberg (2000).

A genre of studies uses cut-off points to categorize children (for example, as "severely," "moderately," "not" severely stunted") and then employs methods of discrete choice estimation to explain the probabilities of children being in the different categories. We refer to these studies as "category-based" studies: Brennan, McDonald, and Shlomowitz (2004), who studied stunting among children in the Indian states of Karnataka and UP, is a recent example. The use of discrete choice estimation methods—for example, logit, ordered logit, and multinomial logit—is usually justified by arguing that the values of the variable underlying the categories are unobservable: only the categories in which the different individuals find themselves are observed. The dependent variable is treated as taking discrete values, because the variable underpinning these values is a "latent" (or unobserved) variable. A recent innovation in the area of "category-based" nutritional measures is the use of anthropometric measures of nutrition as indicators of living standards. Sahn and Stifel (2002a) applied the methods of poverty analysis to construct "nutritional" poverty measures. In doing so, they extended the measurement of malnutrition beyond a simple enumeration of the proportion of a group that was malnourished to composite measures which, in addition to the proportion malnourished, also paid attention to the severity of malnourishment and to the inequality in nourishment outcomes among those who were malnourished.

However, as Ravallion (1996) has pointed out, in the context of poverty analysis, if the (income) information underlying the categorization (poor/ not-poor) is available for individuals such discrete choice methods needlessly discard the data from which the classifications were obtained (unless the data are measured with error). A similar argument can be made with respect to studies of nutritional status: when the values of anthropometric indicators are available for individual children, one should not ignore these data and focus on a few categories of nutritional status.

The alternative to "category-based" studies is "person-based" studies. In the context of empirical studies of malnutrition, Thomas, Strauss, and Henriques (1991) studied the relation between maternal education and the height of children in Brazil; Sandiford, Cassel, Montenegro, and Sanchez (1995) studied the interaction between maternal literacy and access to health services in affecting the health of children in Nicaragua; Lavy, Strauss, Thomas, and de Vreyer (1996) examined the relation, for Ghana, between the quality and accessibility of health care, and child survival and child health outcomes; Thomas, Lavy, and Strauss (1996) examined, for the Côte d'Ivoire the impact of public policies on child height, child height for weight and adult BMI; Gibson (2001), measured the size of the intra-household externality, arising from the presence of literate members in the household, on height-for-age outcomes for children in Papua New Guinea; and Sahn and Stifel (2002b) tested whether the gender impact on the nutrition of pre-school age children in Africa was different for mother's schooling compared to father's schooling. We refer to these studies, based on an analysis of anthropometric values for individual children, as *person-based* studies.

A common feature of *person-based* studies is that they use ordinary least squares (OLS) regression of some measure of nutritional outcome on a vector of determining variables. However, the fact that OLS regression, with its focus on the mean of the distribution of the dependent variable, does not provide much information on other parts of the distribution is a limitation of the method (Buchinsky, 1998; Koenker and Hallock, 2001). In some cases, particularly with respect to children's health status, this may provide inaccurate information for the design of appropriate policy interventions. For example, in a study of birth weights of babies, it was recognized that OLS methods for studying the efficacy of public policy initiatives for reducing the incidence of low birth weight babies (below 2,500 grams at birth) did not offer a good guide to the appropriate policies required for addressing the problem of low birth weight when it occurred at the lower tail of the birth-weight distribution (Abrevaya, 2001).

The purpose of this paper is to examine the factors that influence height-for-age of children, using both OLS and "quantile regression" (QR). QR allows the regression line to pass through different points (the "quantiles") of the distribution of the dependent variable. It is capable, therefore, of providing a more complete statistical analysis of the relationship between the dependent variable and its covariates.[4] In contrast, OLS allows the regression line to only pass through the mean of the dependent variable.

5.2. Concepts of Stunting and Underweight

As Thomas, Strauss, and Henriques (1991) observed, models of child health outcomes attempt to integrate the biomedical approach, which views health outcomes in terms of a production process into which several factors enter as inputs with a model of the family (Becker, 1981). This results in a "reduced form" of child health functions being estimated. Underlying these reduced forms is the assumption that households maximize a quasi-concave utility function—which depends on consumption, leisure, and the quantity and quality of children—subject to a household budgetary constraint, individual time constraints and the constraint of the child health production function (Behrman and Deolalikar, 1988). The inputs entering into the production function are *inter alia*: the child's diet (including the length of breastfeeding and the age at which the child is introduced to supplementary foods); the quality of health-related infrastructure (including the quality of the water supply and the availability of medical attention and dietary advice); and the level of sanitation in the home. In this model, the demand for child health (Z_i) will depend upon

---

[4] We do not at all mean to imply that *conventional* child health studies deliberately set out to focus on the mean and are uninterested in other parts of the distribution. Instead, we argue that an inevitable concomitant use of OLS in *person-based* studies is that inferences are restricted to variations in the mean in response to changes in variable values. In fact, many scholars have looked at the lower left tail of the distribution by looking at severely stunted children.

the vector of child characteristics (X_i); the vector of household or parental characteristics pertaining to the child (W_i); and the relevant community characteristics vector (V_i). Consequently, $Z_i = Z(X_i, W_i, V_i)$.

The IHDS offers information on two anthropometric measures for the health outcomes of children (between the ages of 0 and 5 years) in the sample: height and weight. If the height, age, and gender of child *i* in the sample were denoted by, respectively, h_i centimeters, a_i months, and g_i (0 if boy, 1 if girl), and if $S_i = \dfrac{[h_i - \mu(a_i, g_i)]}{\sigma(a_i, g_i)} \times 100$ where $\mu(a_i, g_i)$ and $\sigma(a_i, g_i)$ are, respectively, the age- and gender-specific median height, and the standard deviation, in the reference population, then we define the variable, $S_i = \dfrac{[h_i - \mu(a_i, g_i)]}{\sigma(a_i, g_i)} \times 100$. This is the same as the *z*-scores except that the median is used instead of the mean. In other words, S_i is the distance between a child's height and the median height (age- and gender-adjusted) of the reference population, expressed as a percentage of the standard deviation (age- and gender-adjusted) of heights in the reference population. We refer to this as the *standardized height-for-age* (SHfA) *distance*.

Similarly, if w_i kilograms is the weight of the *i*th child, we can define the variable $R_i = \dfrac{[w_i - \lambda(a_i, g_i)]}{\rho(a_i, g_i)} \times 100$ where $\lambda(a_i, g_i)$ and $\rho(a_i, g_i)$ are, respectively, the age- and gender-specific median weight and the standard deviation in the reference population. In other words, S_i is the distance between a child's weight and the median weight (age- and gender-adjusted) of the reference population, expressed as a percentage of the standard deviation (age- and gender-adjusted) of weights in the reference population. We refer to this as the *standardized weight-for-age distance*.

Following from these measures, a child is regarded as "severely stunted" when $S_i < -3$ and "moderately severely stunted" when $-3 \leq S_i^* < -2$; as "severely underweight" when $R_i < -3$ and "moderately underweight" when $-3 \leq R_i < -2$ (WHO, 2000). Information on the reference population was obtained from the Child Growth Standards of the WHO (WHO, 2006) though, internationally, there are also several other survey programs that provide anthropometric data, including the Demographic and Health Surveys funded by USAID, the PAPCHILD surveys funded by the Pan-Arab League and UNFPA, and the LSMS and SDA surveys in sub-Saharan Africa funded by the World Bank.

5.3. Preliminary Results

Figures 5.1 and 5.2 show, respectively, the percentages of girls and boys of age 5 years or less who are "severely stunted," and Figues 5.3 and 5.4 show, respectively, the proprtions of girls and boys of age 5 years or less who are "underweight." Overall, 50 percent of the 9,097 girls and 48 percent of the 9,937 boys in the sample, aged 0–5 years, were "severely stunted" (34 percent of girls "severely" and 16 percent "moderately"; 34 percent of boys "severely" and 14 percent "moderately"), while 29 percent of the girls, and 32 percent of the boys, aged 0–5 years, were "underweight" (13 percent of girls "severely," and 16 percent "moderately"; 14 percent of boys "severely," and 18% "moderately"). The 9,097 girls and the 9,937 boys were disaggregated into seven social groups (discussed in Chapter 3): HCH, OBC Hindus (HOBC), SC, ST, MOBC, HCM. Those households that were in none of these six groups were placed in a residual OTG: these were mostly (non-SC) Christian, Sikhs, and Jains. So, by distinguishing between three caste groups—HCH (brahmins, kshatriyas, and vaisyas); the HOBC (sudras); and the SC (outside the caste system) we employ, as noted in an earlier chapter, a richer caste breakdown of Hindus compared to the usual SC, non-SC distinction adopted by other studies. Similarly, by distinguishing between MOBC and HCM, we depart from the usual stereotype of Muslims as a homogenous community (see The Sachar Committee Report, 2006).

The breakdown by social group shows that the highest rates of stunting for girls and boys, and the highest rates of underweight for girls and boys, were for children from the ST, SC, and MOBC households: for example, 55 percent for ST girls and 54 percent for ST boys for stunting and 35 percent for ST girls and 39 percent for ST boys for underweight. By contrast, the lowest rates of stunting for girls and boys, and the lowest rates of underweight for girls and boys, were for children from HCH and OTG households: for example, 42 percent for HCH girls and 45 percent for HCH boys for stunting and 23 percent for HCH girls and 26 percent for HCH boys for underweight.

The data also showed that there was a rural–urban divide to stunting: 36 percent of rural girls and boys, compared to 29 percent of urban girls and boys, were "severely stunted." The incidence of stunting also fell with a rise in the education level of a household but this fall was appreciable only when the highest level of education of a household adult was Matric or higher. Figure 5.5 shows the incidence of stunting for children between 0 and 5 years of age for three different types of households: when the highest level of education of a household adult was Matric or higher; when the highest level of education of a household adult was less than Matric; when there was no literate person in the household. Only 27 percent of all children in the first household type were severely stunted compared to 36 and 40 percent of all children in, respectively, the second and third household types.

Figure 5.1:
Percentage of girls, 0–5 years old who are severely stunted, by social group (Height-for-age)

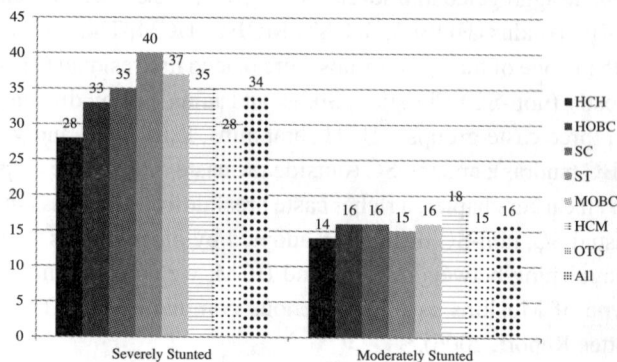

Source: IHDS.
Notes: A child is "severely malnourished" on a height-for-age basis if his/her length/height is more than three standard deviations *below* the median length/height of the reference population.
A child is "malnourished" on a height-for-age basis if his/her length/height is between three and two standard deviations *below* the median length/height of the reference population.
The reference heights and their standard deviations are from WHO (2006).

Figure 5.2:
Percentage of boys, 0–5 years old who are severely stunted, by social group (Height-for-age)

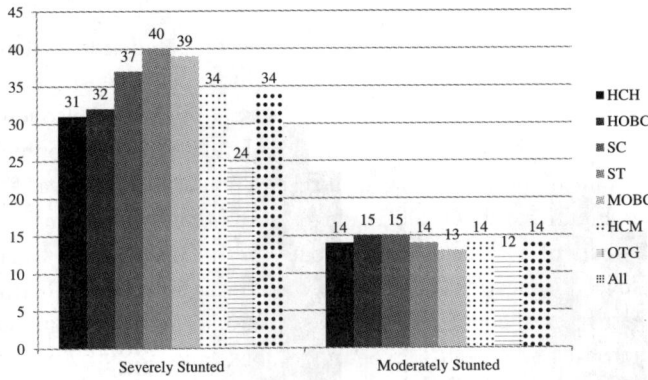

Source: IHDS.

Figure 5.3:
Percentage of girls, 0–5 years old, who are underweight, by social group (Weight-for-age)

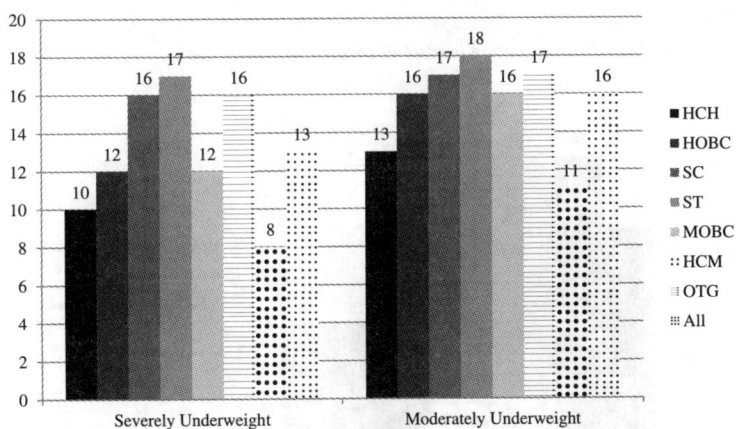

Source: IHDS.
Notes: A child is "severely malnourished" on a weight-for-age basis if his/her weight is more than three standard deviations *below* the median weight of the reference population. A child is "malnourished" on a weight-for-age basis if his/her weight is between three and two standard deviations *below* the median weight of the reference population.
The reference weights and their standard deviations are from WHO (2006).

Figure 5.4:

Percentage of boys, 0–5 years old, who are underweight, by social group (Weight-for-age)

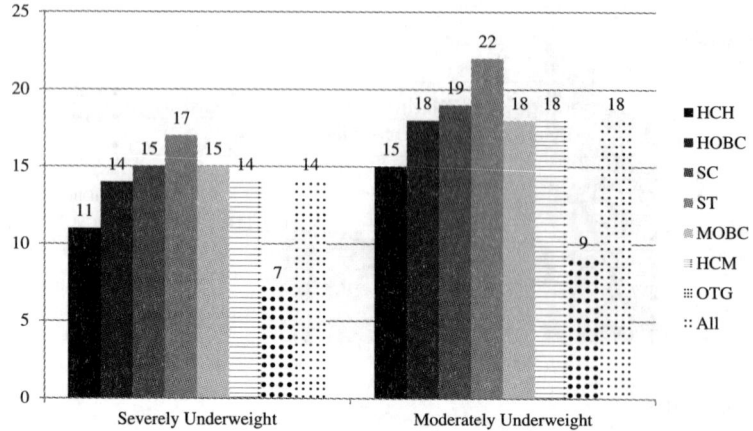

Source: IHDS.

Figure 5.5:

Stunting and household education levels (All children 0–5 years age)

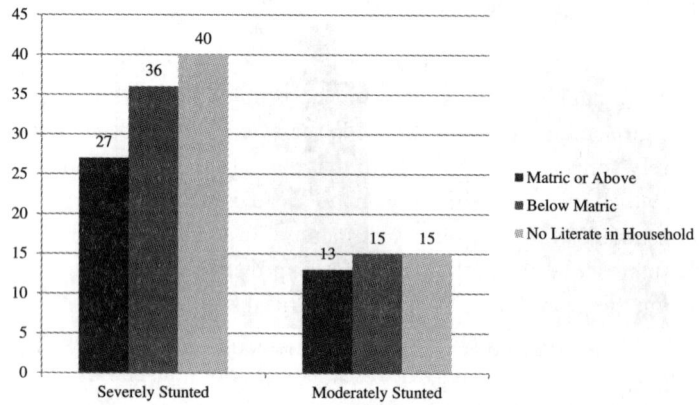

Source: IHDS.

The incidence of stunting also varied by age. It was lowest at birth (only 8 percent were severely stunted) and then rose sharply to assume its highest values for children aged one and two years (43 percent were severly stunted) before falling for older children so that the proportion of five-year olds who were severely stunted was 33 percent.[5] The relationship between age and the incidence of stunting is illustrated in Figure 5.6.

Figure 5.6:
Stunting and age

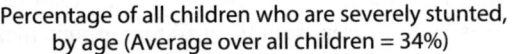

Percentage of all children who are severely stunted,
by age (Average over all children = 34%)

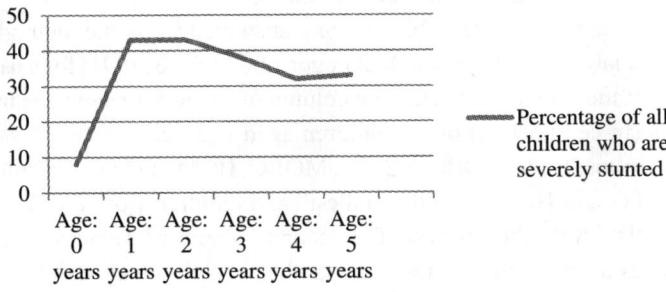

Source: IHDS.

5.4. Nutritional Poverty

The above analysis that focuses on the *proportion* of 19,034 children (9,097 girls and 9,937 boys) between the ages of 0 and 5 years who are "severely stunted," is analogous to that part of the study of poor households, which focuses exclusively on the "head count ratio," the proportion of households whose resources of income or consumption are below a critical threshold. It is well known that, in poverty analysis, the exclusive focus on the proportion of poor persons masks (as discussed in Chapter 3) several important issues relevant to poverty: *inter alia* it does not inform us about the extent to the resources of poor households, which are below the poverty line (the "depth of poverty"); nor does it tell us about the degree of exposure of households from different social groups to be poor (the "risk of poverty"); nor does it tell us about the contribution that households from different social groups make to overall poverty. In a similar way, simply knowing the proportion of children who are (severely)

---

[5] On this evidence, there is little evidence for the "stunting at birth" hypothesis of Osmani and Sen (2003).

stunted or (severely) underweight fails to answer many questions associated with *nutritional poverty*: the degree to which children fall below the "nutritional line" of, say, three standard deviations less than the relevant median (malnourishment depth); the social groups whose children are particularly at risk of being malnourished (malnourishment risk); and the contributions that children from the different groups make to overall malnutrition (malnourishment contribution).

These questions are capable of being answered using the methods of poverty analysis (see Borooah, McGregor, and McKee [1991] for a useful review of these methods). The first column of Table 5.1 shows the mean heights (in centimeters) of the children aged 0–5 years from the seven social groups: HCH, HOBC, SC, ST, MOBC, HCM, and OTG. Children from OTG and HCM were the "tallest" and children from the ST, SC, and MOBC were the shortest. The second column of Table 5.1 shows the shares of each group in the total number of children aged 0–5 years.

The third column of Table 5.1 shows the stunting rate (SR) for each group, defined as the proportion of children in that group, aged 0–5 years, who were *severely* stunted. The highest rate of stunting was for children from the ST (40 percent of ST children were severely stunted), the SC (36 percent of SC children were severe severely stunted), and MOBC (38 percent of MOBC children were severely stunted). Conversely, the lowest rate of stunting was for children from OTG (26 percent of OTG children were severely stunted), HCH (30 percent of HCH children were severely stunted), and HOBC (32 percent of HOBC children were severely stunted).

The fourth column shows the mean height *of severely stunted children* in each group. This shows that the lowest heights of severely stunted children were recorded for HCH and OTG children *even though these groups had the smallest proportion of severely stunted children.*

The fifth column shows the mean stunting gap ratio (MSGR) of severely stunted children.[6] This is the mean distance of the heights of severely stunted children from the "stunting line"—defined as three standard deviations below the median height-for-age—*expressed as a proportion of the stunting line.*

---

[6]   Defined as $\mathrm{MSGR} = \sum_{i=1}^{M}(h_i - z)\Big/ M \times z$, where z_i is the "nutritional line" defined as three standard deviations less than the relevant median height-for-age appropriate for the child.

The sixth column of Table 5.1 computes the *normalized stunting gap ratio* (*NSGR*) of children defined as the mean stunting gap computed over *all* children (setting the stunting gap of non-severely stunted children to zero, that is $z_i = h_i = 0$ if child *i* is not severely stunted).[7] It is easily shown that NSGR = SR × MSGR.

Although the values of *MSGR* are highest for HCH and OTG children, the values of *SR* are also the lowest. This means that in the calculation of the *NSGR*, the two effects (of *SR* and *MSGR*) operate in different directions. Consequently, differences in nutritional poverty between the groups are not as marked when nutritional poverty is measured by *NSGR = SR × MSGR* than when it is measured by just *SR*.

A group's contribution to nutritional poverty depends on the ratio of nutritional poverty within the group to overall nutritional poverty, *weighted by the group's population share*. When nutritional poverty is measured by *SR*, children from the HOBC, by virtue of the fact that they comprise one-third of children aged 0–5 years, make the largest contribution to nutritional poverty.[8] The risk of nutritional poverty is simply the ratio of nutritional poverty within the group to overall nutritional poverty: when this ratio is greater (less) than 1 it implies that children from that group are more (less) likely to be severely stunted than children overall. When nutritional poverty is measured by the SR, children from the ST (20 percent above average), and children from the SC and the MOBC (10 percent above average), face the highest risk of poverty and HCH and OTG children—at, respectively, 10 and 20 percent *below* average—face the lowest risk.

One could also carry out the above analysis for the children who are "stunted"—that is, "moderately" *or* "severely" stunted. In technical terms, this means that all children whose heights are below *two* standard deviations of the median reference height (for their age and gender) fall into this category. These results are shown in Table 5.2. Note that the MSGR is higher in Table 5.1 than in Table 5.2 since the mean nutritional gap is smaller under stunting than under severe stunting; however, the NSGR is lower in Table 5.1 than in Table 5.2 since more values are set to zero under severe stunting compared to stunting.

---

[7] $\text{NSGR} = \sum_{i=1}^{M} (z_i - y_i) \Big/ N \times z_i.$

[8] $32 \cong (33 \times 32)/34.$

Table 5.1:
Nutritional poverty (severe stunting), by social class (Children 0–5 years of age)*

	Mean Height	Population Share	Proportion of Severely Stunted Shildren	Mean Height of Severely Stunted Children	Mean Nutritional Gap Ratio	Normalized Nutrition Gap Ratio	Contribution to Severe Stunting	Risk of Stunting
	(1)	(2)	(3)	(4)	(5)	(6)	(7)	(8)
High-caste Hindu	81.8	18%	30%	69.9	14.6	4.4	16%	0.9
OBC Hindu	81.9	33%	32%	71.4	11.6	3.7	32%	1.0
Scheduled Castes	80.4	22%	36%	71.9	11.8	4.3	24%	1.1
Scheduled Tribes	79.9	9%	40%	71.4	11.9	4.8	11%	1.2
OBC Muslim	79.9	7%	38%	70.8	13.3	5.1	8%	1.1
High-caste Muslim	82.1	8%	34%	71.2	12.1	4.2	8%	1.0
Other Groups	82.9	3%	26%	68.4	14.4	3.7	2%	0.8
All Children	81.3	100%	33%	71.2	12.4	4.2	100%	1.0

Source: Author's own Calculations from IHDS data.
Note: *Nutritional poverty is defined as "severe stunting."

Table 5.2:
Nutritional poverty (moderate or severe stunting), by social class (Children 0–5 years of age)*

	Mean Height (1)	Population Share (2)	Proportion of Severely Stunted Children (3)	Mean Height of Severely Stunted Children (4)	Mean Nutritional Gap Ratio (5)	Normalized Nutrition Gap Ratio (6)	Contribution to Severe Stunting (7)	Risk of Stunting (8)
High-caste Hindu	81.8	18%	30%	75.1	13.0	5.7	17%	0.9
OBC Hindu	81.9	33%	32%	76.0	11.1	5.2	32%	1.0
Scheduled Castes	80.4	22%	36%	75.8	11.5	5.9	24%	1.1
Scheduled Tribes	79.9	9%	40%	75.2	12.0	6.6	10%	1.1
OBC Muslim	79.9	7%	38%	74.5	12.9	6.8	7%	1.1
High-caste Muslim	82.1	8%	34%	75.3	11.4	5.7	8%	1.0
Other Groups	82.9	3%	26%	74.6	12.7	4.9	2%	0.8
All Children	81.3	100%	33%	75.5	11.8	5.7	100%	1.0

Source: Author's own Calculations from IHDS data.
Note: *Nutritional poverty is defined as "stunting," that is "moderate" or "severe" stunting.

5.5. Econometric Results

In the introductory section to this chapter, a distinction was drawn between "person-based" and "category-based" econometric studies of malnutrition: the former type of study used econometric methods on data for individuals to determine the nature and strength of the variables, which significantly influenced malnutrition; the latter type of study used data on individuals to construct nutritional categories ("severely stunted," "moderately severely stunted," "not severely stunted") and then, *in the context of these categories*, used econometric methods to determine the nature and strength of the variables, which significantly influenced malnutrition. Here, we focus on person-based studies.

The dependent variable used was the ratio of the height of a child to the median height, of a child of that sex and age, in the reference population. So, in terms of the notation set out in Section 5.2, the dependent variable took the value Y_i for the ith child, where $Y_i = \dfrac{h_i}{\mu(a_i, g_i)}$, h_i is the height of the ith child, and $\mu(a_i, g_i)$ is the reference median height of the ith child of age a_i and gender g_i. We refer to Y_i as the SHfA of a child in contrast to SHfA distance: $S_i = \dfrac{h_i - \mu(a_i, g_i)}{\sigma(a_i, g_i)}$.

It is easy to transform the definition of nutritional status based on the *SHfA* distance *(S_i)* into one based on *SHfA (Y_i)*. By definition, a child is severely stunted if $S_i > 3$ or equivalently, if

$$h_i - \mu(a_i, g_i) > 3\sigma(a_i, g_i) \Rightarrow Y_i = \frac{h_i}{\mu(a_i, g_i)} > 3\frac{\sigma(a_i, g_i)}{\mu(a_i, g_i)} + 1 \text{ or, in other}$$

words, a child is "severely stunted" if SHfA exceeds 1 plus three times the *coefficient of variation.*

The values $(\mathbf{X}_i)$ of the vector of determining variables that influence the value of y_i may be partitioned into those which relate to the child's characteristics; the child's household and parental characteristics; and the characteristics of the community within which the child lived (Lavy et al., 1996; Shariff, 1999). These characteristics were specified in terms of the following variables:[9]

---

[9]   The theoretical foundations underpinning the model used in this paper are contained in Lavy et al. (1996) and are not repeated here.

1. The social group of the child's household defined in terms of its caste or religion.
2. The *sex* of the child. Sen (2001b) has pointed out that one facet of gender inequality is that there is, in developing countries, a general neglect of girls in respect to factors that contribute to physical well-being: for example, diet and access to, and utilization of, health care facilities (Osmani and Sen, 2003).
3. The *age* of the child in years. Even though the dependent variable controls the age of children, Gibson (2001) and Thomas, Strauss, and Henriques (1991) have pointed to the importance of including age as an explanatory variable. The squared age was entered in order to allow for non-linearities in the effects of age on SHfA.
4. The *literacy* level of the household in terms of whether it contained any persons who were literate. Some of the disadvantages to a person of being illiterate might be mitigated if he/she lived in a household in which other members were literate since, for many activities, having access to the ability of the literate members to read and write may serve as a form of "surrogate" or "proximate" literacy (Basu and Foster, 1998; Basu, Narayan, and Ravallion, 2002; Gibson, 2001).
5. The education level of the household in terms of the highest educational level of an adult in the household. Caldwell (1993) emphasized the importance of educated mothers: they were more likely to demand of their husbands and mothers-in-law that a sick child be treated and they often assumed that it was their responsibility, and not their husbands', to take a child to the health center. Underlying this assumption was the security that education provided of engaging with the non-traditional world of modern health care. Moreover, an educated mother was more able to discuss the welfare of her children, and ways of enhancing their welfare, with health workers.
6. Whether, or not, the child's mother was *anemic*. The inclusion of this variable reflects the view that the under-nourishment of children in India begins in the womb (Osmani and Sen, 2003). Consequently, fetal under-nourishment might be expected to be greater for anemic mothers.
7. The *economic condition* of the household. The IHDS provides details of the income of the households to which the children

belonged. However, for both these variables there could be an endogeneity problem: the same factors that determine poverty could also determine nutritional outcomes in ways other than through poverty.[10]

8. The propensity of children to be in ill-health (and, therefore, in a poor nutritional status) might be expected to depend upon their *housing quality*. This quality was defined in terms of three housing components:

  (i) Whether the kitchen was ventilated.
  (ii) Whether household members, in the absence of access to a toilet, had to defecate in the open.
  (iii) Whether households had access to "safe" (that is, piped) drinking water.

9. Whether children benefited from Anganwadi services.[11]
10. The personal hygiene of the children's mothers, in particular if mothers, after defecating, washed their hands with soap.
11. The Indian state in which the child lived.

The inclusion of these health-determining variables reflects the view that child malnutrition in developing countries is related to poverty and illness and that the incidence of illness depends *inter alia* on whether the child is protected against illness through sanitary housing conditions, the availability of safe water, and access to good health care advice and support (Smith and Haddad, 2000).

Table 5.3 shows the results of estimating, using OLS, an equation with Y_i (the SHfA of the children) as the dependent variable and specified along the lines of 1–11 above. This equation passes through the mean, which is 0.92, implying that, at the mean, the height of a child was 92 percent of its reference median. Table 5.4 shows the estimates from the QR. The first

---

[10] For example, if poorer households are located in areas with inferior social services, the estimated effect of community health facility characteristics may reflect variations in household resources (Lavy et al., 1996).

[11] Anganwadis are village-based early childhood development centers. They were devised in the early 1970s in order to: provide government-funded food supplements to pregnant women and children under five; to work as an immunization outreach agent; to provide information about nutrition and balanced feeding, and to provide vitamin supplements; to run adolescent girls' and women's groups; and to monitor the growth, and promote the educational development, of children in a village.

equation, Q20, passes through the mid-point of the lowest quintile of Y_i; the second equation, Q50, passes through the median value of Y_i; and the third equation, Q80, passes through the mid-point of the highest quintile of Y_i. Since the mean and the median of the distribution of Y_i were virtually identical (0.92), the OLS line and the quantile Q50 line pass through the same point. The first column of Tables 5.3 and 5.4 shows the coefficient estimates; the second column shows the standard error; the third column shows the *t*-value, computed as the ratio of the coefficient estimate and its standard error; and the fourth column shows the *P* value, which is the probability of observing, by chance, a *t*-value greater than the observed t value under the null hypothesis that the coefficient associated with the variable was equal to zero.

The OLS estimates (Table 5.3) show an absence of a *gender effect,* meaning that there was no significant difference between girls and boys in their SHfA. However, the quantile estimates show that, for the lowest quintile equation, the SHfA for girls was significantly lower than that for boys by 0.01 points. However, this difference disappeared at the median and at the 80 percent quintile (Table 5.3: *Q*20, *Q*50, and *Q*80). The null hypothesis that the coefficients of Q20 and the Q50 QR—and the coefficients of Q20 and the Q80 QR were equal—was not accepted with, respectively, $F(19, 4890) = 30.2$ and $F(19, 4890) = 227.9$.

The OLS equation shows a negative *age effect* meaning that the SHfA fell as the age of a child increased but that there was a significant non-linearity (captured by the square of age), so that the "age effect" decayed with age.[12] The QR also suggested a significantly negative age effect and, also, that this effect was greater, the higher the quintile: the "age effect" on SHfA was smallest in the 20 percent quintile, increased at the median, and then increased further at the 80 percent quintile (Table 5.3: *Q*20, *Q*50, and *Q*80). The OLS and QR also pointed to a significant *rural effect* and a *slum effect* whereby *ceteris paribus* the SHfA of rural children was lower than that of urban children and the SHfA of children who lived in slums was lower than that of children who did not. The QR suggested that the "rural effect" and the "slum effect" were both slightly lower at the lowest quintile than at the median or 80 percent quintile.

[12] $Y_i = \alpha \text{AGE}_i + \beta(\text{AGE}_i)^2 \Rightarrow \dfrac{\partial Y_i}{\partial \text{AGE}_i} = \alpha + \beta \text{AGE}_i$. Since $\beta < 0$, the "age effect" declines with age.

Because of co-linearity, all the social groups could not be included in an equation that contained an intercept term. Consequently, the "other group," comprising Sikhs, Jains, and Christians, was taken as the "reference category." The OLS results (Table 5.3) showed that, compared to this reference group, the SHfA for children in all the other groups were significantly lower with MOBC children being the worst affected. However, the QR (Table 5.3) suggested that this *social group effect* diminished through the quintiles until it lost significance (at the 5 percent level) at the 80 percent quintile.

The OLS results show that education played a role in reducing stunting (that is, raising the SHfA) but that the *education effect* was strongest when the household contained an adult who was educated to at least Matric level (Matric +). The Matric + education effect operated most strongly at the lowest quintile of SHfA and less strongly at higher quintiles. At lower levels, education did not play a role in influencing the SHfA. In particular, literacy *per se* was not important in influencing the SHfA nor was maternal or paternal education: it was the highest level of education of an adult in the household, which was the crucial determinant, *provided this level was matric or higher*. There was some evidence of an *economic effect* on SHfA: the SHfA of a child rose with a rise in its household's MPCE (Tables 5.3 and 5.4).

However, four factors relating to, respectively, living conditions, maternal hygiene, breastfeeding, and anganwadis were important determinants of children's SHfA. First, in terms of living conditions, the SHfA was raised when the main source of household drinking water was piped water and the SHfA was reduced when household members had to, for want of toilet facilities, defecate in the open. Second, in terms of breastfeeding, the later the age after which breastfeeding was stopped, and the earlier the age at which food supplements were given to a child, the higher its SHfA. Lastly, the SHfA was higher *ceteris paribus* for children who received food at anganwadis and whose growth was monitored at anganwadis compared to children who did not receive either benefit. In a regional context, compared to children in the Central region (Bihar, MP, Rajasthan, UP, Chhattisgarh, and Jharkhand), which was the reference region, children in the other regions—north (Jammu and Kashmir, Himachal Pradesh, Uttarakhand, Punjab, Haryana, and Delhi); south (Andhra Pradesh, Karnataka, Kerala, and Tamil Nadu), east

Table 5.3:
OLS estimation results from the stunting equation*

	Coefficient	Standard Error	t Value	P Value
Female	0.04	0.44	0.1	0.9
Child's age	−12.06	0.64	−18.9	0.0
(Child's age)^2	1.78	0.11	16.6	0.0
Rural	−2.15	0.60	−3.6	0.0
Metropolitan	−2.37	0.83	−2.9	0.0
High-caste Hindu	−2.49	1.51	−1.7	0.1
OBC Hindu	−2.48	1.47	−1.7	0.1
Scheduled Castes	−3.71	1.53	−2.4	0.0
Scheduled Tribes	−5.23	1.64	−3.2	0.0
OBC Muslim	−4.45	1.65	−2.7	0.0
High-caste Muslim	−2.23	1.66	−1.3	0.2
Monthly per capita consumption expenditure × 100	0.00	0.00	1.7	0.1
Highest education of household adult: Matric or above	1.42	0.53	2.7	0.0
Defecates in open	−0.93	0.55	−1.7	0.1
Piped water supply	1.23	0.54	2.3	0.0
Age breastfed up to	0.08	0.02	3.4	0.0
Age at which diet was supplemented	−0.10	0.04	−2.7	0.0
Vaccinated at anganwadi	3.23	0.79	4.1	0.0
Receives food at anganwadi	2.60	0.74	3.5	0.0
Growth monitored at anganwadi	1.50	0.86	1.8	0.1
North	3.06	0.84	3.6	0.0
South	4.99	0.85	5.9	0.0
East	3.17	0.99	3.2	0.0
West	3.84	0.89	4.3	0.0
Intercept	108.22	2.04	53.1	0.0

Number of observations = 4,446 $\bar{R}^2 = 0.1112$ $\bar{Y} = 91.8$ $\sigma = 14.5$ $F(23,4422) = 25.2$

Source: Author's own Calculations from IHDS data.
Note: *The dependent is the standardized height, $Y_i = $ (Height/Reference median) × 100.

(Orissa, West Bengal, Assam, and the north-east), and west (Gujarat and Maharashtra)—had significantly higher SHfA.

5.5.1. Decomposition by Social Group

In the estimation results reported in Tables 5.3 and 5.4, the "social group" effects operated entirely through the intercept term with the slope coefficients being unaffected by the children's social group. The implication was that the marginal probabilities associated with the variables—say, the effect of household education level on SHfA—was the same for HCH children as it was for ST children. This assumption can be relaxed by estimating the equation specified in Table 5.3 *separately* for children from the different social groups; this study does so for HCH children, on the one hand, and for ST and MOBC children (separately), on the other. It should be emphasized that, although the HCH coefficients were *numerically* different from the ST (MOBC) coefficients in many cases these differences were not statistically significant. The decompositions reported below are based on the *entire* HCH and ST (MOBC) coefficient vectors without regard to whether differences in individual components were statistically significant.

After doing so, the difference between groups, in their respective mean values, were decomposed into an "unexplained" effect, attributable to differences between groups in their coefficients, and an "explained" effect, attributable to differences between groups in their attributes by using the method of Oaxaca (1973). The attributes component was computed by asking what the difference in the proportion of HCH and ST children achieving the maximum score *would have been* if the difference in attributes between them had been evaluated using a *common* coefficient vector.[13] The coefficients component, computed as a residual, was the observed difference *less* the attributes component. This could be ascribed to a "structural advantage" that children from some groups enjoyed over children from other groups. Figure 5.7 shows the decompositions for the *observed* difference between HCH and ST children, and between HCH and MOBC children, in their SHfA values, based on the OLS estimates

---

[13] Similarly, for the difference in the observed HCH and Muslim proportions.

Table 5.4:

Quantile estimation results from the stunting equation: Lowest, median, and highest quintiles

	Bottom 20% of SHfA				Median SHfA				Top 20% of SHfA			
	Co-ef	SE	t	P	Co-ef	SE	t	P	Co-ef	SE	t	P
Female	-1.12	0.57	-2.0	0.0	-0.6	0.45	-1.34	0.2	0.18	0.55	0.3	0.7
Child's age	-5.33	1.77	-3.0	0.0	-8.5	1.16	-7.29	0.0	-13.87	0.84	-16.5	0.0
(Child's age)^2	0.90	0.27	3.4	0.0	1.2	0.17	6.85	0.0	1.85	0.13	14.5	0.0
Rural	-1.97	0.69	-2.8	0.0	-1.9	0.50	-3.86	0.0	-1.71	0.39	-4.4	0.0
Metropolitan	-5.97	1.50	-4.0	0.0	-1.6	0.49	-3.22	0.0	-0.82	0.68	-1.2	0.2
High-caste Hindu	-3.70	1.62	-2.3	0.0	-1.3	1.26	-1.00	0.3	-0.87	1.13	-0.8	0.4
OBC Hindu	-2.14	1.48	-1.4	0.1	-2.1	1.22	-1.71	0.1	-0.88	1.09	-0.8	0.4
Scheduled Castes	-3.82	1.72	-2.2	0.0	-2.5	1.22	-2.07	0.0	-1.02	1.16	-0.9	0.4
Scheduled Tribes	-5.07	1.50	-3.4	0.0	-2.9	1.35	-2.16	0.0	-2.40	0.96	-2.5	0.0
OBC Muslim	-5.51	1.99	-2.8	0.0	-3.7	1.51	-2.47	0.0	-1.54	1.64	-0.9	0.3
High-caste Muslim	-1.14	1.77	-0.6	0.5	-1.2	1.29	-0.90	0.4	-0.12	1.34	-0.1	0.9
Monthly per capita consumption expenditure × 100	0.00	0.00	1.6	0.1	0.0	0.00	2.43	0.0	0.00	0.00	1.4	0.2
Highest education of household adult: Matric or above	2.00	0.79	2.5	0.0	1.6	0.37	4.24	0.0	1.56	0.56	2.8	0.0
Defecates in open	-0.91	0.78	-1.2	0.2	-0.1	0.42	-0.35	0.7	0.17	0.58	0.3	0.8
Piped water supply	1.02	0.82	1.2	0.2	0.7	0.32	2.14	0.0	0.06	0.49	0.1	0.9

Table 5.4 continued

Table 5.4 *continued*

Age breastfed up to	0.07	0.03	2.1	0.0	0.1	0.02	3.55	0.0	-0.03	0.02	-1.2	0.2
Age at which diet was supplemented	-0.18	0.07	-2.6	0.0	0.0	0.03	-1.71	0.1	-0.05	0.05	-1.0	0.3
Vaccinated at anganwadi	-4.39	0.91	-4.8	0.0	-1.9	0.69	-2.72	0.0	-1.03	1.03	-1.0	0.3
Receives food at anganwadi	3.35	0.79	4.2	0.0	1.4	0.75	1.81	0.1	0.81	0.56	1.4	0.2
Growth monitored at anganwadi	0.93	0.92	1.0	0.3	0.1	0.65	0.21	0.8	0.35	0.80	0.4	0.7
North	3.59	1.60	2.3	0.0	2.5	1.04	2.39	0.0	2.16	0.75	2.9	0.0
South	5.90	1.61	3.7	0.0	3.9	0.94	4.14	0.0	4.38	0.94	4.6	0.0
East	3.76	1.81	2.1	0.0	3.7	1.03	3.59	0.0	4.00	0.67	6.0	0.0
West	5.41	1.68	3.2	0.0	4.3	1.12	3.82	0.0	3.51	0.87	4.0	0.0
Intercept	89.61	4.27	21.0	0.0	104.9	2.61	40.19	0.0	122.06	2.17	56.3	0.0

Number of observations = 4,446

Source: Author's own Calculations from IHDS data.
Note: *The dependent is the standardized height-for-age, Y_i = (Height/Reference median)×100.

shown in Table 5.2: 22 percent of the observed difference in SHfA scores
between HCH and ST children and 16 percent of the observed difference
in SHfA scores between HCH and MOBC children could be explained
by differences in attributes.

Figure 5.7:
The decomposition of the difference between HCH and ST children in SHfA values

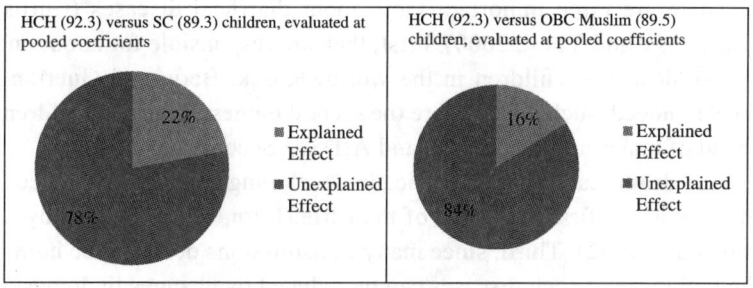

Source: Author's own calculations from IHDS data.

5.6. Conclusions

Behrman, Alderman, and Hoddinott (2004) pointed out that around 800
million people in the world were malnourished in 1999–2001, comprising
about 17 percent of the population of developing countries, and around 12
million children were born each year as low birth weight babies, weighing
less than 2,500 grams. They pointed to the enormous benefits that would
accompany a reduction in the incidence of malnutrition: a reduction in
infant mortality rates, less susceptibility to diseases, higher physical
productivity, and more years of schooling. Our analysis showed, however,
that rather than a child's health and malnutrition being independent the
two phenomena were intimately related. An important conclusion of this
chapter is that good nutrition is not just a matter of feeding a child. It is
equally important to ensure that a child's exposure to illness is minimized
and, if and when the child does fall ill, that prompt and appropriate
treatment is given. In particular, this chapter draws attention to importance
of safe water and good domestic hygiene—*specifically with respect to
toilet facilities*—as determinants of child malnutrition. Both factors act
as barriers to pathogens that cause, among other diseases, diarrhea. The

vast majority of diarrheas are caused by infectious pathogens that reside in feces and which employ a variety of routes to reach new hosts: the pathogen may reach a new host by getting onto fingers and, thereby, into foods and fluids; or the pathogen may enter foods and fluids, without a human intermediary, for example, by flies landing on excreta and carrying the pathogen to foods, or by excreta entering the water supply.[14]

There are three important facts about diarrheal diseases (Curtis, Cairncross, and Yonli, 2000). First, they are responsible for about one in five deaths of children in the world (Kosek, Bern, and Guerrant, 2003). Indeed, such diseases are the second biggest killers of children, ahead of malaria, tuberculosis, and AIDS.[15] Second, most of these 2.5 million deaths each year take place in developing countries, 80 percent of them in the first two years of their life (Bern, Martines, de Zoysa, and Glass, 1992). Third, since many transmissions occur in the home, the incidence of such diseases can be reduced by changes in domestic hygiene. While improvements to infrastructure, such as safe drinking water and effective sanitation facilities, contribute to blocking transmission, they will only be fully effective when they are employed in conjunction with good domestic hygiene practices (Cairncross, 1990). It is true that malnourished children are more susceptible to disease but our results would suggest that children are significantly more likely to be malnourished (more specifically, severely stunted) in the presence of conditions which promote disease, particularly diarrhea.

Indeed, an interesting question that emerges from the regression estimates shown in Table 5.3 is the marked effect that improvements in infrastructure (water supply and sanitation) would have on reducing the incidence of stunting. Currently, 44 percent of the individuals live in households that have piped water and 54 percent of individuals defecate in the open. Under this baseline scenario, 34 percent of children aged 0–5 years of age were severely stunted. Under *universal* provision of piped water (that is, all households in India had piped water) and *universal* provision of sanitation (no person had to defecate in the open), this proportion would fall to 19 percent.

---

[14] Some diarrheas may be caused by metabolic errors, chemical irritation or organic disturbance.

[15] The *Economist*, July 26, 2002, p. 95.

After controlling these two factors, safe water and good domestic hygiene, there was evidence that per-capita monthly consumption expenditure contributed to child malnutrition. There was also evidence that anganwadi services, supplied to mothers and children—through vaccination, the provision of food to children, and monitoring their growth, did much to alleviate child malnutrition. There was, however, a great deal of evidence that the region in which the children resided mattered in terms of their nutritional status with the south— in particular, Tamil Nadu leading the way: for example, the "midday meal" (MDM) menu for school children in Tamil Nadu consists of a variety of food (including eggs provided 2–3 times a week) to the children. This suggests that in order to meet the nutritional challenge, public policy, underpinned by spending, is a powerful tool for fighting malnutrition. van de Walle and Nead (1996) point to the importance of the distributional impact of public spending in developing and transition countries in determining its effectiveness in combating poverty.

The second important finding of this chapter is that, *even after controlling for non-group variables*, the social group to which children belonged played a significant part in determining whether they were malnourished. So, on the basis of both the OLS and the QR estimates, the SHfA (the height of a child as a ratio of the reference height for a child of that age and gender) of SC, ST, and MOBC children was, on average, lower than that for children who were from HCH or "other" group (Sikhs/Jains/Christian) households. A possible explanation for this is inter-group disparity in the amount and quality of nutritional education given to a child's mother.

Nutritional education is important; it provides pregnant mothers with information on prenatal care, institutional delivery, and appropriate feeding practices for children. The latter includes: exclusive breastfeeding for six months; colostrum feeding; and household semi-solid food from seventh month onward. Faulty weaning is a major contributor to child malnutrition (Ghosh, 2006). Here, the role of anganwadi workers (AWWs) is crucial since they are the primary source from which mothers receive nutritional information. In this regard, mothers from marginalized groups are handicapped, relative to mothers from more privileged groups, because AWWs often neglect to visit them to impart information on good nutritional practice.

A study conducted by the IIDS in seven states showed that there were significant differences between mothers in different social groups in the treatment received from AWWs stemming largely from the fact that these workers were not willing to visit SC and Muslim homes. Consequently, SC and Muslim mothers received limited information on prenatal and post-natal services. Even when SC and Muslim were visited, they were not given proper counseling after their children had been weighed and, in some instances, AWWs refused to touch SC children and asked that they be weighed by their mothers. Many SC mothers were not invited for the village health and nutrition day and, even when invited, they were made to sit separately, given food separately, and discouraged from asking questions about their children. Such maltreatment then had the knock-on effect of SC mothers eschewing anganwadi services in order to avoid their attendant humiliations.

At the same time, pilot studies have shown that strategic interventions among marginalized groups can sharply improve their children's nutritional status. For example, the Breastfeeding Promotion Network of India recently conducted an intervention study in 235 villages from three blocks in Bhuj district of Gujarat and provided skill training to AWWs to offer counseling to lactating mothers. As a consequence, exclusive breastfeeding rates increased from 1 percent to 37 percent in the intervened area. This was achieved through the existing ICDS system (Gupta, 2006).[16]

These conclusions are complemented by another important implication of our study, which is that there are important distributional lessons to be learnt from using QR to analyze the nutritional status (as measured by the SHfA) of under-five children in India. Different policy interventions affect children differently, depending on which part of the distribution nutrition they are located in. For example, gender disparity was marked in the lowest quintile of SHfA but not in the higher quintiles. Similarly, a policy of improving access to safe drinking water would benefit children in the lower part of the distribution. The fact that QR was able to not just uncover, but also to emphasize, this distributional aspect of policy means that policy-makers can choose between alternative policies on the basis of their

---

[16] See Garg (2006) and Gopaldas (2006) for details of similar interventions in Chhattisgarh.

average effect and on the basis of which part of the distribution they have the largest impact.

The section on nutritional poverty pursued an alternative to the QR method of investigating the distribution of nutritional outcomes. This alternative is embodied in the work of Sahn and Stifel (2002a), who pointed out that the standard nutritional cut-off points, defining, for example, moderate-or-severe stunting, could be thought of as nutritional "poverty lines." On this interpretation, measures of malnutrition need not be confined to simply computing the proportion of people below the nutrition line (the "headcount ratio"). Instead, we extend the measure of "nutritional poverty" to take account of the mean distance between nutritional outcomes and the nutritional poverty line (the "normalized nutritional gap ratio"). Thus, we extend the methods of modern poverty analysis—pioneered by Sen (1976) and extended by Foster, et al. (1984) to the analysis of nutrition and, thereby provided an alternative to the usual measurement of welfare based on money, income, or expenditure. In particular, the use of decomposable nutritional poverty indices (by means of the poverty index of Foster, et al. 1984, discussed in Chapter 3) allows one to measure the contributions that different subgroups make to overall nutritional poverty and their respective risks of being nutritionally poor. But, in the context of hunger, whatever the analytical perspective, the rewards to a nuanced diagnosis, resulting in more effective policies are considerable.

Appendix on Quantile Regression

An undesirable consequence of the OLS estimates is that the estimated coefficients can be severely affected by outlying observations.[17] In contrast, "robust" estimators, such as the *least absolute deviations* (LAD) estima-tor, are unaffected by extreme observations. In LAD, β^* is chosen so as to minimize the sum of absolute deviations of the errors: $\sum_{i=1}^{N} | y_i - X_i' \beta |$

---

[17] This is likely to be a particular problem in case the distribution of the error tem is "thick-tailed" (Greene, 2003: 448).

The regression line $X_i' \beta^*$ passes through the median, and has the property: $\Pr(y_i \leq X_i' \beta^*) = 0.5$.[18]

A generalization of the LAD estimator, suggested by Koenker and Basset (1978), is to pass the regression line through the cut-off point of any quantile q of the distribution. If $y_1, y_2, ..., y_N$ are a set of ordered observations, then the qth QR estimator, β^q is such that: $\Pr(y_i \leq X_i' \beta^q) = q$. If $q = 0.5$, β^q is the LAD estimator. If $q = 0.1$, the regression line passes through the *lowest decile* so that one-tenth of the observations, $y_1, y_2, ..., y_N$, lie below the regression line, with nine-tenths lying above it. (*N* regressions are run.) Similarly, if $q = 0.25$, the regression line passes through the *lowest quartile* so that one-fourth of the observations, $y_1, y_2, ..., y_N$, lie below the regression line, with three-fourths lying above it. In other words, QR estimates the slope of the y, x line passing through the quantile cut-off points using a generalized version of LAD regression. Consider a specific quantile, say the lowest quintile. There is a point, $\alpha_{0.2}$, which is the cut-off point for the lowest quintile: 20 percent of the distribution lies below $\alpha_{0.2}$ and 80 percent lies above it. QR passes the regression line through this point, $\alpha_{0.2}$, using a variation of the LAD methodology: this involves minimizing a weighted absolute sum of residuals; the weights are such that 20 percent of the observations lie below the line and 80 percent lie above it. The regression is repeated with the other quantiles.

Hence, least squares estimation considers how the conditional mean of y (over the entire distribution) depends upon the covariates X, while QR considers the conditional quantile values, the values at each quantile of the conditional distribution (Buchinsky, 1998; Greene, 2003; Koenker, 2001; Koenker and Hallock, 2001; Wooldridge, 2002). The QR coefficient

---

[18] Because the median, unlike the mean, is insensitive to outlying observations, LAD, unlike OLS, is a robust estimator. If the distribution of *Y* is symmetric, the mean and median coincide. The sample mean is asymptotically efficient under a normal distribution. However, it may still be the case that for certain "thick-tailed" distributions (for example, the Laplace and the Cauchy), the sample median has a lower asymptotic variance than the sample mean. The reason for this is that with "heavy-tailed" data, there are likely to be more extreme observations and the sample median is better than the sample mean at coping with outliers. However, when the distribution is not symmetric, the OLS and LAD estimators differ: the OLS estimates the conditional mean and the LAD estimates the conditional median.

estimate, β_j^q, is interpreted as the change in the qth conditional quantile value of **y** with respect to the jth regressor: $\beta_j^q = \partial \text{quantile}_q(\text{y} \mid \text{X}^j) / \partial x_j$.

QR estimators, β^q, for each value of q enables one to examine how different parts of distribution of y depend on the covariate vector X^j. Thus, for example, the improvement in the quality of the water supply in a village might greatly improve the status of children in the lowest decile of the height-for-age distribution, while having only a small effect on the status of children in the higher deciles. In consequence, the mean improvement in height-for-age might be small but that masks the considerable benefit to the worst-off children. Another advantage of QR is that it is robust, that is, unlike OLS, QR is less sensitive to extreme observations.[19]

The standard errors from QR may be computed analytically (Koenker and Bassett, 1978; Rogers, 1993) for homoscedastic errors, but these understate standard errors in case of heteroscedasticity (Rogers, 1992). Consequently, the standard errors from QR are often calculated using "bootstrapping" methods. In order to calculate bootstrapped standard errors, repeated random samples the number of repetitions being chosen by the analyst—are drawn from the sample data and, for each sample, an estimate of the desired statistic ($\hat{\theta}$) is obtained. This, then, provides a sampling distribution of $\hat{\theta}$ and the standard deviation of this sampling distribution is the "bootstrapped" standard error for that statistic (Guan, 2003). When the sample is large, the bootstrapped standard errors will converge to the true values.[20]

Koenker and Basset (1978) suggested extending the idea of the LAD estimator to other quantiles of the distribution. If $y_1 < y_2 < \ldots < y_N$ are a set of ordered observations of the sample then the cut-off point of the τ *quantile*

---

[19] A common misconception of QR is that, in effect, it fits different curves to different subsamples defined by the values of the dependent variable (if income is the dependent variables then the subsamples might be those in the lowest or in the highest income decile). In fact, QR estimates the regression equation on all the observations but the regression line separates the observations into proportions q and 1-q lying, respectively, below and above q. Estimating an equation over sub-samples, rather than the entire sample, induces the risk of "truncation bias." This would not apply if the sub-samples were structurally different (for example, men and women) but they would apply if the sub-samples were not structurally distinct, that is obtained by dropping observations in an arbitrarily different part of the distribution.

[20] The quantile regressions, reported in this paper, were estimated using the statistical package, STATA.

is a number α_τ such that: $\dfrac{\sum\limits_{i=1}^{N} I(y_i < \alpha_\tau)}{N} = \tau$ and $\dfrac{\sum\limits_{i=1}^{N} I(y_i > \alpha_\tau)}{N} = 1-\tau$,

where $I(y_i \le \alpha_\tau)$ is the *indicator function* taking the value 1 if the statement inside the parentheses (that is, $y_i < \alpha_\tau$ or $y_i > \alpha_\tau$) is true and the value zero if it is false. Thus, τ percent of the observations lie below α_τ and that $(1-\tau)$ percent of observations lie above α_τ.

For example, if $\tau = 0.2$, the quantile is the *lowest quintile* and there is a number $\alpha_{0.2}$ (the cut-off point for the lowest quintile) such that 20 percent of observations take values $< \alpha_{0.2}$ and 80 percent of observations take values $> \alpha_{0.2}$.

The τth QR estimator, β_τ^* solves the minimization problem:

$\min\limits_{\beta} \sum\limits_{i=1}^{N} \rho_\tau(y_i - x_i{'}\beta)$, where ρ_τ is the *check function*: $\rho_\tau(x) = x \cdot (\tau - I$

$[x \le 0])$ for any real number x. This is equivalent to estimating a linear

conditional τth quantile for y, given the vector.

The computation of the weights embodied in the ρ_τ involves the following steps:
(1) Compute the median of the observations (suppose that $\xi = \text{Median}\{y_i\}$) and for *each* observation, $y_i, i = 1, ..., N$, compute its deviation from the median as $x_i = y_i - \xi$. (2) Define $I(x_i) = 1$ if the deviation is non-positive, that is, $x_i \le 0$, $I(x_i) = 0$, otherwise. (3) Choose a value of $\tau =$. (4) With the information in points (1)–(3), for *each* deviation, $x_i, i = 1...N$ compute: $\rho_{\tau i} = \rho_\tau(x_i) = x_i[\tau - I(x_i)]$. So for any quantile, defined by the value of τ, there will be N weights $\rho_{\tau i}, i = 1...N$, defined as above. For a given quantile, the ratio of weights of negative and positive deviations of the same magnitude is $\dfrac{\rho_\tau(-x_i)}{\rho_\tau(x_i)} = \dfrac{-x_i(\tau-1)}{x_i \tau} = -\dfrac{\tau-1}{\tau}$. When $\tau = 0.5$, positive and negative residuals (that is, $x_i = y_i - \xi$) of the same absolute magnitude are weighted equally: $\dfrac{\rho_\tau(-x_i)}{\rho_\tau(x_i)} = 1$. When $\tau < 5$, negative residuals are weighted more heavily than positive residuals of the same absolute magnitude: $\dfrac{\rho_\tau(-x_i)}{\rho_\tau(x_i)} > 1$. When $\tau > 5$, negative residuals are weighted less heavily than positive residuals of the same absolute magnitude:

$\dfrac{\rho_\tau(-x_i)}{\rho_\tau(x_i)} < 1$. For example, when $\tau = 0.2$, $\dfrac{\rho_\tau(-x_i)}{\rho_\tau(x_i)} = 4$; when $\tau = 0.4$,

$\dfrac{\rho_\tau(-x_i)}{\rho_\tau(x_i)} = \dfrac{3}{2}$; when $\tau = 0.6$, $\dfrac{\rho_\tau(-x_i)}{\rho_\tau(x_i)} = \dfrac{2}{3}$; when $\tau = 0.8$, $\dfrac{\rho_\tau(-x_i)}{\rho_\tau(x_i)} = \dfrac{1}{4}$.

6

Health Outcomes

6.1. Introduction

The publication of the Black report (Black, Morris, Smith, and Townsend, 1980) spawned a number of studies in industrialized countries, which examined the social factors underlying health outcomes. The fundamental finding from these studies, particularly with respect to mortality and life expectancy, was the existence of "a social gradient" in mortality: "[W]herever you stand on the social ladder, your chances of an earlier death are higher than it is for your betters" (Epstein, 1998). The social gradient in mortality was observed for most of the major causes of death: for example, Marmot (2000) showed that, for every one of 12 diseases, the ratio of deaths (from the disease) to numbers in a Civil Service grade rose steadily as one moved down the hierarchy.

Therefore, in the end, it is the individual who falls ill, it is tempting for epidemiologists to focus on the risks inherent in individual behavior: for example, smoking, diet, and exercise. However, the most important implication of a social gradient to health outcomes is that people's susceptibility to disease depends on more than just their individual behavior: crucially, it depends on the social environment within which they lead their life (Marmot, 2000, 2004). Consequently, the focus on inter-personal differences in risk might be usefully complemented by examining differences in risk between different social environments.

For example, even after controlling inter-personal differences, mortality risks might differ on occupational class. This might be due to the fact that while low status jobs make fewer mental demands, they cause more psychological distress than high status jobs (Griffin, Fuhrer, Stansfeld, and Marmot, 2002; Karasek and Marmot, 1996; Marmot, 2004) with the result that people in higher-level jobs report significantly less job-related depression than people in lower-level jobs (Birdi, Warr, and Oswald, 1995).

In turn, anxiety and stress are related to disease: the stress hormones that anxiety releases affect the cardiovascular and immune systems with the result that prolonged exposure to stress is likely to inflict multiple costs on health in the form of *inter alia* increased susceptibility to diabetes, high blood pressure, heart attack, and stroke (Brunner and Marmot, 1999; Marmot, 1986; Wilkinson and Marmot, 1998). So, the social gradient in mortality may have a psycho-social basis, relating to the degree of control that individuals have over their lives.[1]

The "social gradient to health" is essentially a western construct and there has been very little investigation into whether in developing countries people's state of health is dependent on their social status. For example, we know from studies of specific geographical areas that health outcomes in India differ systematically by gender and economic class (Sen, Iyer, and George, 2007). In addition, local government spending on public goods, including health-related goods, after controlling a variety of factors, is lower in areas with greater caste fragmentation compared to ethnically more homogenous areas (Sengupta and Sarkar, 2007).

Considering India in its entirety, two of its most socially depressed groups—the *Scheduled Tribes* (ST)[2] and the *Scheduled Castes* (SC)[3]— have some of the worst health outcomes. For example, as Guha (2007) observes, 28.9 percent of persons from the ST and 15.6 percent of persons from the SC have no access to doctors or clinics and only 42.2 percent of ST children and 57.6 percent of SC children have been immunized. Of course, it is possible that the relative poor health outcomes of India's socially backward groups has less to do with their low social status and much more to do with their weak economic position and with their poor living conditions. The purpose of this chapter is precisely to evaluate the relative strengths of economic and social status in determining the health status of people in India. In other words, even after control over

[1] Psychologists distinguish between stress caused by a high demand on one's capacities—for example, tight deadlines—and stress engendered by a low sense of control over one's life.

[2] There are about 85 million Indians classified as belonging to the "Scheduled Tribes"; of these, *adivasi*s (meaning "original inhabitants") refer to the 70 million who live in the heart of India, in a relatively contiguous hill and forest belt extending across the states of Gujarat, Rajasthan, Maharashtra, Madhya Pradesh, Chhattisgarh, Jharkhand, Andhra Pradesh, Orissa, Bihar, and West Bengal (Guha, 2007).

[3] Persons from SC, who number about 18 million, refer to those who belong to India's "Scheduled Castes" and may be broadly identified with the formerly "untouchable" castes, that is, those with whom physical contact—most usually taken to be the acceptance of food or water—is regarded by upper-caste Hindus as ritually polluting or unclean.

non-community factors that Indians belonged to different social groups, encapsulating different degrees of social status, exercise a significant influence on the state of their health!

We answer this question using data from the *Morbidity and Health Care Survey* (M&HC Survey), for the period January–June 2004, conducted over all the states and union territories in India, by the Government of India's National Sample Survey Organisation (NSSO).[4] The M&HC Survey covered 73,868 households, encompassing 383,338 individuals. It examined several aspects of morbidity and health care of the respondents but, from this study's perspective, three of these are of note:

(i) Particulars of household members who died within the past 365 days.

(ii) Particulars of economic independence and ailments on the date of survey of persons aged 60 years or more (hereafter, "elderly" persons).

(iii) Particulars of prenatal and postnatal care for ever married women.

These aspects of morbidity and health care could *inter alia* be correlated with the social background of the households to which the respondents belonged. The M&HC Survey offered information about households in terms of the following social groups:

1. HCH[5]
2. HOBC[6]
3. SC (see footnote)
4. ST, *adivasis*: ST(A) (see footnote 2)
5. ST, Christian: ST(C)[7]

---

[4] For background on the NSSO, see Tendulkar (2007).

[5] Forward caste Hindus were Hindus who were not included in the OBC/Dalit/ST categories. However, since the designation of groups in the OBC category is a state responsibility, a particular (caste) group may be included in the OBC category in one state (that is, be excluded from forward caste Hindus) but be excluded from the OBC category in another state (that is, be included in forward caste Hindus).

[6] These are persons who, while not belonging to ST or SC, nevertheless belong to economic and socially backward groups.

[7] As Guha (2007) notes, ST Christians have been exposed to modern education in English and have a much greater chance of being absorbed in the modern economy. They also live mainly in the hills of north-east India, which are some of the remotest and less accessible parts of the country.

6. MOBC
7. HCM
8. Sikhs/Jains/Christians

The primary aim of this chapter is to examine whether the following health outcomes varied systematically according to the social group to which people belonged:

  (i) The age of death
 (ii) The self-assessed health status of persons 60 years of age or more
(iii) The likelihood of elderly persons, who were in poor health, taking treatment for their ailments
(iv) The likelihood of women receiving prenatal and postnatal treatment

The purpose was to investigate whether, *after controlling for several non-group factors that might impinge on health outcomes*, people's health outcomes were significantly affected by their social group. The existence of a social group effect—whereby groups higher up the social ladder had better health outcomes than groups further down—would suggest that there was a "social gradient" to health outcomes in India. Furthermore, there was the possibility that the "social gradient" existed with respect to some outcomes but not to others. Thereby, this chapter addresses, in the Indian context, an issue that lies at the heart of social epidemiology: estimating the relative strengths of individual and social factors in determining health outcomes.

6.2. Deaths in Households

The M&HC Survey asked households if any of their members had died in the previous year and, if the answer was in the affirmative, collected information about the deceased and some of the circumstances surrounding the deaths. In total, as Table 6.1 shows, 1,716 deaths were reported: 1,634 of these deaths (95 percent) were from households who had experienced a single death in the past year; 70 of these deaths (4 percent) occurred in households who had experienced two deaths; and 12 of these deaths (1 percent) occurred in households who had experienced three deaths.

Of these 1,716 deaths, 9 percent were from ST(A), 18 percent were from SC, 12 percent were Muslim (MOBC + HCM), and 21 percent were HCH (Table 6.1). By contrast, ST, SC, and Hindus comprised 8 percent, 17 percent, and 24 percent, respectively, of the total of the 383,288 persons in the M&HC–NSS sample. Thus, in respect of ST(A) and SC, there was a difference between their proportionate presence in the number of deaths and in their proportionate presence in the sample.[8]

A more marked difference between the groups was in terms of the mean and median ages at death: as Table 6.1 shows, the mean age of death was 43.3 years for ST(A), 41.6 years for SC, 43.4 years for MOBC, and 43.8 years for HCM; by contrast, the mean age at death was 57.5 years for Sikhs and non-ST Christians, 54.2 years for HCH, 49.4 years for ST(C), and 48.4 years for HOBC.

Table 6.1:
Deaths in India, by social group

	NSS Persons by Social Group	NSS Persons by Social Group (%)	Deaths by Social Group (%) Total: 1,716	Mean Age of Death by Social Group	Median Age of Death by Social Group
ST(A)	30,158	7.9	9.2	43.3	45
ST(C)	15,160	4.0	3.8	49.4	55
SC	64,942	16.9	17.6	41.6	45
HOBC	125,508	32.8	33.4	48.4	55
MOBC	18,591	4.9	4.8	43.4	51
HCH	90,371	23.6	21.3	54.2	60
HCM	29,785	7.8	7.2	43.8	50
Christian (non-ST)	3,428	0.9	1.1	57.6	60
Sikh	3,268	0.9	1.2	57.5	65
Other religion	2,077	0.5	0.5	64.6	70
Total	383,288	100	100	47.7	54

Source: NSS 60th Round, Health File.

Table 6.2 shows whether the deceased received medical attention before death. The groups least likely to receive medical attention before death were ST(A) and ST(C): only 59 percent of ST(A) deaths and 53 percent of ST(C) deaths received medical attention in

---

[8] Of the 1,716 deceased, 58 percent were men. For all the groups, the majority of deaths were male except for ST Christians where 55 percent of the 65 deaths in this group were female.

contrast to 76 percent of SC deaths and 73 percent of Muslim deaths. Although, in terms of the overall sample, there was little difference between the proportions of men and women receiving medical attention before death (69 percent men, 71 percent women), there were marked gender differences between some of the social groups: Muslim deaths were more likely to receive medical attention if they were women (80 percent against 70 percent for HCM) while SC deaths were more likely to receive medical attention if they were men (80 percent against 71 percent).[9]

Table 6.2:
Medical attention received before death, by gender and social group

	Total Deaths	Medical Attention Received Before Death as % of Total Deaths	Total Male Deaths	Medical Attention Received Before Death as % of Total Male Deaths	Total Female Deaths	Medical Attention Received Before Death as % of Total Female Deaths
ST(A)	157	59	85	52	72	67
ST(C)	64	53	28	57	36	50
SC	302	76	166	80	136	71
HOBC	573	69	338	66	235	74
MOBC	82	73	46	70	36	78
HCH	366	71	215	72	151	70
HCM	123	74	73	70	50	80
Christian (non-ST)	18	67	13	62	5	80
Sikh	21	81	14	86	7	71
Other religion	8	75	7	71	1	100
Total	1,714	70	985	69	729	71

Source: NSS 60th Round, Health File.

Table 6.3 presents the estimates from regressing the "age at death" on a number of explanatory variables.[10] The first column shows the regression estimates obtained from all deaths in the sample; the second and third columns show the regression estimates obtained from all deaths in, respectively, the "forward" and "backward" states (and union territories)

[9] This could be because SC and Muslims do not seek treatment when they fall sick so that they receive medical treatment only at the terminal stage.
[10] Excluding the 27 deaths that occurred during pregnancy.

of India.[11] The mean ages at death in the forward and backward states were, respectively, 52.4 and 43.7 years—a difference of 8.7 years. After imposing all the controls shown in Table 6.3, the difference between forward and backward states in their averages at death was reduced to 7.4 years (Table 6.3, column 1).

Table 6.3:
Regression estimates of the age at death equation, by "forward" and "backward" states*

	All Deaths	Deaths in Forward States	Deaths in Backward States
Forward state	7.4***	–	–
	(4.80)		
Female	−1.2	−1.9	−0.5
	(0.83)	(0.94)	(0.25)
Laborer	−4.3**	−5.7**	−2.7
	(2.49)	(2.30)	(1.15)
Rural	4.9**	2.2	7.8***
	(2.51)	(0.83)	(2.63)
Structure	−2.9	−0.7	−3.7
	(1.43)	(0.19)	(1.50)
Latrine	1.5	2.5	0.5
	(0.71)	(0.94)	(0.14)
Drain	0.1	−3.2	4.2
	(0.06)	(1.10)	(1.25)
Water source	1.9	−2.5	6.2**
	(1.15)	(1.13)	(2.46)
Water treated	−2.2	−2.9	−2.3
	(1.01)	(1.06)	(0.65)
Water treatment	11.8***	10.9***	12.6***
	(4.25)	(3.12)	(2.79)
Cooking fuel	5.0**	4.6	6.2*
	(2.17)	(1.55)	(1.75)
Total monthly household expenditure	0.0004*	0.0004	0.0005
	(1.67)	(1.00)	(1.31)
*Adivasi*s	−4.9*	−2.9	−6.7*
	(1.71)	(0.59)	(1.78)
Christian ST	−3.9	0.0	−6.5
	(0.94)	(.)	(1.39)
Dalits	− 7.1***	−2.1	−11.5***
	(3.00)	(0.64)	(3.32)
OBC (non-Muslim)	−2.5	−1.8	−3.0
	(1.29)	(0.69)	(1.04)

Table 6.3 continued

[11] "Forward states": Andhra Pradesh, Chandigarh, Dadar and Nagar Haveli, Daman and Diu, Delhi, Goa, Gujarat, Haryana, Himachal Pradesh, Karnataka, Kerala, Maharashtra, Pondicherry, Punjab, Tamil Nadu, and West Bengal. The remaining states and union territories were classed as "backward" states.

Table 6.3 continued

OBC (Muslim)	−8.6**	−5.3	−11.9**
	(2.50)	(1.07)	(2.46)
Muslim (non-OBC)	−6.1**	−6.8*	−6.1
	(2.03)	(1.66)	(1.41)
Constant	43.7***	53.6***	41.3***
	(13.05)	(10.67)	(8.82)
Observations	1624	696	928
R-squared	0.08	0.06	0.07

Source: Author's own calculations from NSS 60th Round, Health File.
Notes: 1. Absolute value of t statistics in parentheses.
2. *Significant at 10%; ** significant at 5%; *** significant at 1%.
3. "Forward states": Andhra, Chandigarh, Dadra and Nagar Haveli, Daman and Diu, Delhi, Goa, Gujarat Haryana, Himachal, Karnataka, Kerala, Maharashtra, Punjab, Tamil Nadu, and West Bengal. The remaining states and union territories were classified as "backward."
4. Structure = 1 if housing type was *pucca*, or semi-*pucca*, or "serviceable" *kutcha* (that is, good); 0 otherwise.
5. Latrine = 1 if the latrines were flushing toilets or emptied into a septic tank; 0 otherwise.
6. Drain = 1 if drains were underground or were covered *pucca*; 0, otherwise.
7. Water source = 1 if the source of drinking water was from a tap; 0 otherwise.
8. Water treated = 1 if drinking water treated; 0 otherwise.
9. Water treated = 1 if the nature of treatment was boiling, filtering, or ultra-violet/resin/reverse osmosis; 0 otherwise.
10. Cooking fuel = 1 if the cooking fuel was gas, *gobar* gas, kerosene, or electricity; 0 otherwise.

The second variable in the regression was gender: Table 6.3 shows that, after controlling for other variables, there was no significant difference between the average ages of the male and female deceased.[12] The next variable was whether the household type in which the deceased lived was a "laborer" household[13]: Table 6.3 shows that, after imposing all controls, the average age at death was 4.3 years lower for laborer, compared to non-laborer, households. Since the sample differences between non-laborer and laborer households in the ages of their deceased was 6.9 years, imposing the controls, reduced this difference but without eliminating it. Table 6.3 also shows that the average age at death was significantly different between laborer and non-laborer households in the forward states but *not* in the backward states. The average age of the deceased was significantly higher,

[12] The sample averages for age at death were 48.4 and 46.2 years for male and female deaths, respectively.
[13] Agricultural or other labor for rural households and casual labor for urban households.

by 4.9 years in rural, compared to urban areas and, in the backward states, the rural–urban difference average age at death was 7.8 years; however, in the forward states, there was no significant difference between rural and urban areas in the average age at death.

After these four controls—state type, gender, household type, and rural–urban sectors—the next set of controls related to the conditions in which the deceased lived.

1. The first component of this was the *type of housing structure* in which the deceased lived: this variable ("structure") was assigned the value 1 if the type was *pucca*, or semi-*pucca*, or "serviceable" *kutcha* (that is, good); and 0 otherwise.

2. The second component of living conditions related to the *quality of the latrines* used by the deceased: the variable "latrine" was assigned the value 1 if the latrines were flushing toilets or emptied into a septic tank; and 0 otherwise.

3. The third component of living conditions related to the *quality of the drains*: the variable "drain" was assigned the value 1 if the drains associated with the deceased's home were underground or were covered *pucca*; and 0 otherwise.

4. The fourth component of living conditions related to the *quality of the source of drinking water* used by the deceased: the variable "water source" was assigned the value 1 if the source of drinking water was from a tap; and 0 otherwise.

5. The fifth component of living conditions related to whether the drinking water used by the deceased was *treated*: the variable "water treated" was assigned the value 1 if the drinking water was treated; and 0 otherwise.

6. If the drinking water in the deceased's household was treated, the sixth component of living conditions related to the *nature of the treatment* of the drinking water: the variable "water treatment" was assigned the value 1 if the nature of treatment was boiling, filtering, or ultra-violet/resin/reverse osmosis; and 0 otherwise.

7. The seventh, and last, component of living conditions related to the *nature of the cooking fuel* used by the deceased's household: the variable "cooking fuel" was assigned the value 1 if the cooking fuel was gas, *gobar* gas, kerosene, or electricity; and 0 otherwise.

Table 6.3 shows that, of these seven living conditions controls, it was only the nature of treatment of drinking water and of the type of cooking fuel used that had a significant effect on the age of the deceased. The average age of deceased persons whose drinking water was boiled or treated through chemical means was, over India in its entirety, 11.8 years higher than that of those whose drinking water was either not treated or treated through "other means"; for "forward" and "backward" states, this difference was, respectively, 10.9 and 12.6 years. Similarly, the average age of deceased persons whose households used gas (including *gobar* gas), kerosene, or electricity as their cooking fuel was 5 years higher than that of those whose households used "other" fuels.[14]

After control of the living conditions of the deceased, the next set of controls related to the economic position of the deceased's household was measured by a household's consumer expenditure in the past 30 days. Table 6.3 shows that an increase of ₹1,000 in monthly household expenditure would raise the average age of death by approximately 0.4 years though, it must be added that, after the other controls had been imposed, the significance of the relation between monthly expenditure and the mean age of death was very weak.

Table 6.3 shows that, *even after imposing all the above controls*, the average age of the deceased was significantly affected by the social group to which they belonged. Compared to the average age at death of Hindus (the control group), the average age at death of ST(A) was 4.9 years lower for India in its entirety and 6.7 years lower for the backward states; SC was 7.1 years lower for India in its entirety and 11.5 years lower for the backward states; MOBC was 8.6 years lower for India in its entirety and 11.9 years lower for the backward states; HCM was 6.1 years lower for India in its entirety and 6.8 years lower for the forward states. By contrast, there was no significant difference in the ages of deceased persons between HCH and the HOBC.

6.3. The Health of Elderly Persons

In the past few decades, improvements in health care in developing countries have increased their citizens' life expectancy with life expectancy in

---

[14] For backward states, this difference was significant only at 10 percent and for forward states it was not even significant at this level.

India increasing from 43 years in 1960 to 64 years in 2011.[15] Table 6.4 shows the perceptions of persons, aged 60 years or more ("elderly persons"), about their state of health: excellent/very good; good/fair; poor. While 25 percent of the entire sample of 33,155 elderly persons described themselves as being in poor health, this description was offered by 28 percent of Dalits and 31 percent of Muslims (OBC and non-OBC). By contrast, only 16 percent of ST Christians and 20 percent of *adivasi*s regarded themselves as being in poor health.

Table 6.4:
Own perception of state of health of persons 60 years and above, by social group

	Excellent/Very Good Health	Good/Fair Health	Poor Health	Total
ST(A)	143	1,525	428	2,096
	6.8	72.8	20.4	100
ST(C)	76	534	115	725
	10.5	73.7	15.9	100
SC	220	3,440	1,423	5,083
	4.3	67.7	28.0	100
HOBC	529	7,848	2,746	11,123
	4.8	70.6	24.7	100
MOBC	73	819	409	1,301
	5.6	63.0	31.4	100
HCH	629	6,867	2,179	9,675
	6.5	71.0	22.5	100
HCM	73	1,315	628	2,016
	3.6	65.2	31.2	100
Christians (non ST)	29	328	143	500
	5.8	65.6	28.6	100
Sikhs	32	295	78	405
	7.9	72.8	19.3	100
Other religions	23	158	50	231
	10.0	68.4	21.6	100
Total	1,827	23,129	8,199	33,155
	5.5	69.8	24.7	100

Source: Author's own calculations from NSS 60th Round, Health File.

Table 6.5 shows the *marginal probabilities* obtained from estimating an ordered logit model in which the dependent variable took the value 1, 2, or 3 depending on whether a person described his/her state of health as excellent/very good, good/fair, or poor. The *marginal probability* associated with a variable is the change in the probability of an outcome, following a change in the value of a variable. For each variable, these probabilities

[15] http://lawmin.nic.in/ncrwc/finalreport/v2b1-2ch5.htm

sum to zero across the three outcomes (that is, the three states of health) and for discrete variables—as are all the explanatory variables used, except *age*—the marginal probabilities refer to changes in the probability of the outcomes, consequent on a move from the default category for that variable to the category in question.[16] For ease of exposition, the subsequent discussion focuses, in the main, on the marginal probability of *regarding oneself* to be in poor health (hereafter, simply, "the probability of poor health").

Table 6.5:
Marginal probabilities from the ordered logit model of own perception of state of health (Persons 60 years and above)

	Poor Health	*Good/Fair Health*	*Excellent/Very Good Health*
Forward state	−0.011**	0.008**	0.003**
	(2.33)	(2.32)	(2.33)
Age	0.052***	−0.039***	−0.013***
	(11.95)	(11.80)	(11.75)
Age squared	−0.0003***	0.0002***	0.0001***
	(8.95)	(8.88)	(8.88)
Female	0.043***	−0.032***	−0.011***
	(9.22)	(9.17)	(9.09)
Low education	−0.016***	0.012***	0.004***
	(2.82)	(2.86)	(2.71)
Medium education	−0.042***	0.030***	0.012***
	(5.76)	(6.11)	(4.98)
High education	−0.074***	0.048***	0.025***
	(8.24)	(10.06)	(6.00)
Rural	−0.009	0.007	0.002
	(1.44)	(1.46)	(1.46)
Structure	−0.032***	0.025***	0.007***
	(4.38)	(4.26)	(4.79)
Latrine	−0.010	0.008	0.003
	(1.59)	(1.59)	(1.57)
Drain	−0.002	0.001	0.0004
	(0.26)	(0.26)	(0.26)
Water source	−0.031***	0.023***	0.008***
	(6.20)	(6.22)	(6.06)
Water treated	−0.043***	0.032***	0.012***
	(5.88)	(6.81)	(6.12)
Water treatment	0.054***	−0.042***	−0.012***
	(5.88)	(5.67)	(6.65)

Table 6.5 continued

[16] In an ordered logit model, the signs of the coefficient estimates associated with a variable do not predict the directions of change in the probabilities of the outcomes and these probabilities have to be separately calculated.

Table 6.5 continued

Cooking fuel	−0.034***	0.025***	0.009***
	(5.12)	(5.20)	(4.85)
Lowest quartile of	0.044***	−0.034***	−0.010***
monthly expenditure	(6.20)	(6.03)	(6.73)
Second quartile of	0.037***	−0.029***	−0.008***
monthly expenditure	(4.77)	(4.63)	(5.25)
Third quartile of	0.022***	−0.017***	−0.005***
monthly expenditure	(3.58)	(3.53)	(3.73)
Adivasis	−0.050***	0.035***	0.015***
	(5.81)	(6.41)	(4.74)
Christian ST	−0.083***	0.052***	0.031***
	(7.07)	(9.79)	(4.75)
Dalits	0.026**	−0.020***	−0.006***
	(3.37)	(3.30)	(3.60)
OBC (non-Muslim)	0.001	−0.001	−0.0004
	(0.29)	(0.29)	(0.29)
OBC (Muslim)	0.055***	−0.043***	−0.011***
	(4.19)	(4.01)	(5.29)
Muslim (non-OBC)	0.081***	−0.065***	−0.016***
	(7.23)	(6.84)	(9.16)
Christian (non-tribal)	0.035*	−0.027*	−0.008**
	(1.79)	(1.74)	(2.05)
Sikh	−0.026	0.018*	0.007
	(1.59)	(1.66)	(1.43)
Other religions	−0.021	0.015	0.006
	(0.82)	(0.85)	(0.75)
Observations	33,130	33,130	33,130

Source: Author's own calculations from NSS 60th Round, Health File.

Notes: 1. Absolute value of t statistics in parentheses.
2. *Significant at 10%; ** significant at 5%; *** significant at 1%.
3. "Forward states": Andhra, Chandigarh, Dadar and Nagar Haveli, Daman and Diu, Delhi, Goa, Gujarat Haryana, Himachal, Karnataka, Kerala, Maharashtra, Punjab, Tamil Nadu, and West Bengal. The remaining states and union territories were classified as "backward."
4. Structure = 1 if housing type was *pucca*, or semi-*pucca*, or "serviceable" *kutcha* (that is, good); 0 otherwise.
5. Latrine = 1 if the latrines were flushing toilets or emptied into a septic tank; 0 otherwise.
6. Drain = 1 if drains were underground or were covered *pucca*; 0, otherwise.
7. Water source = 1 if the source of drinking water was from a tap; 0 otherwise.
8. Water treated = 1 if drinking water treated; 0 otherwise.

9. Water treated = 1 if the nature of treatment was boiling, filtering, or ultra-violet/ resin/reverse osmosis; 0 otherwise.
10. Cooking fuel = 1 if the cooking fuel was gas, *gobar* gas, kerosene, or electricity; 0 otherwise.
11. Low education: literate without schooling, below primary, or primary.
12. Medium education: middle or secondary school.
13. High education: higher secondary or more.

According to Table 6.5: (i) moving from a backward state to a forward state would *reduce* the probability of poor health by 1.1 points; (ii) being female would *increase* the probability of poor health by 4.3 points. The effect of age on the probability of poor health depends not only upon the increase in age but, because of the presence of the non-linear term age^2, also upon the age itself. So, for an additional year in age from N years, age^2 would increase by $(N + 1)^2 - N^2 = 2N + 1$. Therefore, if $N = 60$, the probability of poor health would increase by $5.2 - 121 \times 0.03 = 1.57$ points for an additional year; if $N = 75$, the probability of poor health would increase by $5.2 - 151 \times 0.03 = 0.67$ points for an additional year. In other words, the probability of poor health would increase with age, *but at a diminishing rate*, and, after a certain age ($N = 87$), would not change with increasing years.

Table 6.5 suggests that people's perception of the state of their health was significantly affected by their level of education. Compared to an illiterate person (the default level), the probability of poor health was 1.6 points lower for a person educated up to primary schooling ("low education"); 4.2 points lower for a person educated above primary and up to secondary level; and 7.4 points lower for a person educated up to higher secondary or more.

Living conditions exerted a significant effect on the probability of poor health: good housing conditions ("structure") reduced this probability by 3.2 points; a good source of drinking water ("water source") reduced it by 3.1 points while treating drinking water and, furthermore, treating it "properly" reduced it by, respectively, 4.3 and 5.4 points; lastly, using a "clean" fuel for cooking lowered the probability of poor health by 3.4 points. In total, therefore, good living conditions were capable of reducing the probability of poor health by nearly 20 points.

Over and above, these factors, the economic position of a household also had a significant effect on the probability of poor health: compared to elderly persons from households whose monthly expenditure was in the top quartile (the control group), elderly persons from households whose monthly expenditure was in the lowest, second, and third quartile were more likely to be in poor health by, respectively, 4.4, 3.7, and 2.2 points.

Lastly, even after controlling for all the above factors, Table 6.5 shows that the social groups to which people belonged had a significant effect on their probabilities of poor health: compared to HCH (the control group), ST(A) and ST(C) were *less* likely to be in poor health by, respectively, 5.0 and 8.3 points; on the other hand, the SC, MOBC, and HOBC Muslims were *more* likely to be in poor health by, respectively, 2.6, 5.5, and 8.1 points.

Table 6.6 records the primary ailments of elderly persons who regarded their state of health as "poor." For example, of the 258 such persons who happened to be *adivasis*, 5 percent primarily suffered from gastrointestinal problems, 9 percent from cardiovascular disease, 11 percent from respiratory problems; 12 percent from disorders of the joints; 2 percent from diseases of the kidney or urinary system; 4 percent from neurological disorders; 10 percent from eye disorders; 2 percent from diabetes; 4 percent from fever-related illness; 24 percent from disabilities; 2 percent from accidents/injuries/burns; 1 percent from cancer; and 14 percent from other ailments.

The distribution of the incidence of cardiovascular disease (including hypertension) between the social groups is interesting: 33 percent of non-ST Christians and 19 percent of HCH, Sikhs, and persons from other religions—aged 60 or more and in poor health—suffered from cardiovascular diseases; by contrast, this ailment affected only 4 percent of ST(C), 9 percent of ST(A) and SC, 12 percent of HOBC, and 16 percent of Muslims (MOBC and HCM). Similarly, compared to 6 percent of HCH who were diabetic, only 2 percent of ST(A) and 1 percent of SC had diabetes. On the other hand, 33 percent of ST(C), 24 percent of ST(A), 16 percent of SC, and 18 percent of MOBC—compared to only 12 percent of HCH—suffered from disabilities.[17]

---

[17] Locomotor; visual (including blindness, excluding cataract); speech; and hearing.

Table 6.6:

Ailments of persons 60 years and above who regarded their state of health as "poor," by social group

Soc Grp→ Ailm↓	Adv	ST, CH	Dalits	OBC Non-Muslim	OBC Muslim	Hindu FC	Muslim Non-OBC	CH, Non-ST	Sikh	Oth	TOT
GASTR	13	13	48	96	14	91	55	4	1	0	335
	5.04	16.25	5.13	5.43	4.70	5.77	12.39	3.45	1.85	0.00	6.02
CARD	23	3	85	223	49	298	71	38	10	7	807
	8.91	3.75	9.09	12.62	16.44	18.88	15.99	32.76	18.52	18.92	14.50
RESP	28	10	130	233	46	187	60	7	8	2	711
	10.85	12.50	13.90	13.19	15.44	11.85	13.51	6.03	14.81	5.41	12.77
JOINT	32	8	117	248	25	186	49	22	10	5	702
	12.40	10.00	12.51	14.04	8.39	11.79	11.04	18.97	18.52	13.51	12.61
KIDNY	5	0	20	30	3	44	6	2	3	1	114
	1.94	0.00	2.14	1.70	1.01	2.79	1.35	1.72	5.56	2.70	2.05
NEURO	10	2	43	71	16	86	23	3	1	2	257
	3.88	2.50	4.60	4.02	5.37	5.45	5.18	2.59	1.85	5.41	4.62
EYES	26	3	121	154	22	103	41	11	1	3	485
	10.08	3.75	12.94	8.72	7.38	6.53	9.23	9.48	1.85	8.11	8.71
DIABT	4	2	13	65	13	101	19	9	2	3	231
	1.55	2.50	1.39	3.68	4.36	6.40	4.28	7.76	3.70	8.11	4.15
FEVER	10	6	35	53	6	27	12	1	1	0	151
	3.88	7.50	3.74	3.00	2.01	1.71	2.70	0.86	1.85	0.00	2.71
DISAB	63	26	153	282	53	183	41	6	8	7	822
	24.42	32.50	16.36	15.96	17.79	11.60	9.23	5.17	14.81	18.92	14.77

Table 6.6 continued

Table 6.6 continued

ACC	4	1.55	0	0.00	18	1.93	40	2.26	7	2.35	46	2.92	5	1.13	0	0.00	2	3.70	0	0.00	122	2.19
CANC	3	1.16	1	1.25	17	1.82	33	1.87	4	1.34	31	1.96	4	0.90	3	2.59	0	0.00	1	2.70	97	1.74
OTHER	37	14.34	6	7.50	135	14.44	239	13.53	40	13.42	195	12.36	58	13.06	10	8.62	7	12.96	6	16.22	733	13.17
TOT	258	100	80	100	935	100	1,767	100	298	100	1,578	100	444	100	116	100	54	100	37	100	5,567	100

Source: NSS 60th Round, Health File.

Notes: Definition of ailments—

1. GASTR: Gastrointestinal problems
2. CARD: Cardiovascular disease
3. RESP: Respiratory problems
4. JOINT: Disorders of the joints
5. KIDNY: Diseases of the kidney or urinary system
6. NEURO: Neurological disorders
7. EYES: Eye disorders
8. DIABT: Diabetes
9. FEVER: Fever-related illness
10. DISAB: Disabilities
11. ACC: Accidents/injuries/burns
12. CANC: Cancer
13. Other ailments (OTHER)

Table 6.7 shows the proportion of elderly persons, who were in poor health, from the different social groups who were not taking any treatment for their ailments: 38 percent of ST(A), 44 percent of ST(C), and 33 percent of SC, were not taking any treatment for their ailments in contrast to 15 percent of HCH, 11 percent of non-ST Christians, and 18 percent of Sikhs.

Table 6.7:
Proportion of persons 60 years and above who regarded their state of health as "poor," taking treatment for reported ailment, by social group

	Not Taking Treatment	Taking Treatment	Total
ST(A)	98	157	255
	38.43	61.57	100.00
ST(C)	33	42	75
	44.00	56.00	100.00
SC	302	626	928
	32.54	67.46	100.00
HOBC	470	1,273	1,743
	26.97	73.03	100.00
MOBC	62	233	295
	21.02	78.98	100.00
HCH	239	1,326	1,565
	15.27	84.73	100.00
HCM	118	319	437
	27.00	73.00	100.00
Christians (non-ST)	13	102	115
	11.30	88.70	100.00
Sikhs	10	44	54
	18.52	81.48	100.00
Other religions	4	32	36
	11.11	88.89	100.00
Total	1,349	4,154	5,503
	24.51	75.49	100.00

Source: NSS 60th Round, Health File.

In order to determine the probabilities of different persons taking/not taking treatment for their ailments, we estimated a logit model over the sample of 5,484 elderly persons, who were in poor health, in which the dependent variable took the value 1 if the person was taking treatment and 0 if he/she was not. The marginal probabilities from this model are shown in Table 6.8. Compared to living in a "backward" state, living in a "forward" state significantly increased the probability of taking treatment by 11 points. However, there was no significant difference between women and men, or between persons in the rural and urban sectors, in their probabilities of taking treatment. Having a living daughter had no significant effect on the probability of taking treatment though having a living son raised it by 8.3 points!

The level of education of a person, and the economic position of his/her household, had a significant effect on the probability of taking treatment. Compared to an illiterate person (the default level), the probability of taking treatment was 6.6 points higher for a person educated up to primary schooling ("low education"); 10.8 points higher for a person educated above primary and up to secondary level; and 9.4 points higher for a person educated up to higher secondary or more. Compared to persons from households whose monthly expenditure was in the top quartile (the control group), persons from households whose monthly expenditure was in the lowest, second, and third quartile were less likely to take treatment by, respectively, 16.1, 11.5, and 4.6 points.

Another set of factors affecting the probability of people taking treatment comprised their degree of economic independence, living arrangements, and degree of mobility. Compared to a person who was totally dependent (the default case), the probability of taking treatment was 4.9 points higher for someone who was completely independent and 3.5 points higher someone who was only partially dependent. Compared to living with a spouse, people living without a spouse—whether living alone or with others—were less likely, by 5.1 points, to take treatment. Compared to persons who were totally mobile or else with mobility restricted to the home, people who were confined to bed were more likely, by 5.5 points, to take treatment.

However, even after controlling for all the above factors, Table 6.8 shows that the social groups to which people belonged had a significant effect on their probabilities of taking treatment: compared to HCH (the control group), ST(A), ST(C), and SC were *less* likely to take treatment by, respectively, 10.6, 22.5, and 9.0 points; HCM and the HOBC were less likely to take treatment by, respectively, 7.7 and 5.7 points.

Table 6.8:

Marginal probabilities from the logit model of treatment received for ailments (Persons 60 years and above who regarded their state of health as "poor")

	Marginal Probability of Receiving Treatment
Forward state	0.110***
	(9.28)
Female	0.013
	(1.01)
Low education	0.066***
	(4.67)
Medium education	0.108***
	(5.82)
High education	0.094***
	(3.11)
Living son(s)	0.083***
	(2.85)
Living daughter(s)	−0.21
	(0.98)
Rural	−0.016
	(1.22)
Economically independent	0.049***
	(3.23)
Economically partially dependent	0.035**
	(2.08)
Living alone	0.004
	(0.15)
Living with spouse	0.051***
	(3.93)
Confined to bed	0.055***
	(2.92)
Confined to home	−0.009
	(0.69)
Lowest quartile of monthly expenditure	−0.161***
	(7.84)
Second quartile of monthly expenditure	−0.115***
	(5.19)
Third quartile of monthly expenditure	−0.046***
	(2.64)
ST(A)	−0.106***
	(3.15)
ST(C)	−0.225***
	(3.59)
SC	−0.090***
	(4.20)
HOBC	−0.057***
	(3.34)
MOBC	−0.007
	(0.24)

Table 6.8 continued

Table 6.8 continued

HCM	−0.077**
	(2.82)
Christian (non-tribal)	0.017
	(0.34)
Sikh	−0.059
	(0.97)
Other religions	0.068
Pseudo-R-squared	0.0793
Observations	5,484

Source: Author's own calculations from NSS 60th Round, Health File.
Notes: Dependent variable = 1 if treatment received for reported ailment, = 0, if not received. Absolute value of *z* values in parentheses.
*Significant at 10%; ** significant at 5%; *** significant at 1%.

Table 6.9 assesses the predictive performance of the logit model of taking treatment. A person was predicted as taking (not taking) treatment if the predicted probability from the logit model, of his taking treatment, was greater (less) than half. Table 6.9 shows that of the 5,238 persons predicted to be taking treatment, 4,027 were actually taking treatment—a predictive accuracy of 77 percent; however, only 131 of the 246 predicted to be not taking treatment, were actually not taking treatment—a predictive accuracy of 53 percent. Overall, therefore, 4,158 persons out of 5,484 were correctly classified—as predictive accuracy of 76 percent.

Table 6.9:
The predictive performance of the logit model of the probability of taking treatment for ailment

	Taking Treatment (M)	Not Taking Treatment (~M)	Total
Predicted as taking treatment (+)	4,027	1,211	5,238 $P(M|+) = 76.9\%$
Predicted as not taking treatment (−)	115	131	246 $P(\sim M|-) = 53.3\%$
Total	4,142 $P(+|M) = 90.2\%$	1,342 $P(-|\sim M) = 2.8\%$	5,484 Correctly classified = 75.8%

Source: Author's own calculations from NSS 60th Round, Health File.
Note: Persons, aged 60 years and above, who regarded their state of health as "poor."

6.4. Prenatal and Postnatal Care

The M&HC-NSS provided information, by social group, on the prenatal and postnatal care received by ever-married women below 50 years of age.[18] This care is provided in four stages: (i) pregnancy; (ii) labor, birth and the first two hours after birth; (iii) early neonatal period; and (iv) late neonatal period. It takes the form *inter alia* of skilled care at delivery in hygienic conditions; neonatal resuscitation; prevention of hypothermia; prevention of hypoglycemia; prophylactic eye care; colostrum feeding; counseling on birth spacing; managing low birth weight babies; clean umbilical cord care; pneumonia and sepsis management; immunization and treatment of serious illness.

Table 6.10 shows that compared to 15 percent of HCH women who did not receive prenatal care, such care was not received by 31 percent of ST(A), 38 percent of ST(C), 26 percent of SC, 33 percent of MOBC, and 26 percent of HCM. Similarly, compared to 27 percent of HCH women who did not receive postnatal care, such care was not received by 44 percent of ST(A) and ST(C) women, 37 percent of SC women, 36 percent of MOBC women, and 34 percent of HCM.

Table 6.10:

Proportion of ever-married women who did not receive pre and postnatal care

	Prenatal Care	Postnatal Care
Adivasi	30.5	43.7
Christian ST	37.9	44.1
Dalits	26.2	36.5
OBC (non-Muslim)	22.7	31.3
OBC (Muslim)	32.7	36.4
Hindu (FC)	14.7	26.7
Muslim (non-OBC)	26.1	34.5
Christian (non-ST)	1.5	10.4
Sikh	18.3	31.8
Other religion	14.3	41.0
Total	23.5	33.2

Source: NSS 60th Round, Health File.

[18] The prenatal period is the 22 weeks prior to birth and postnatal period is first six weeks after birth. Both periods are critical for the health and survival of a mother and her baby. For example, almost half of deaths of children under five years of age occur in the post-natal period.

In order to determine the probabilities of women receiving prenatal and postnatal care, we estimated a logit model in which the dependent variable took the value 1 if the woman received the relevant care and 0 if she did not. The marginal probabilities from this model are shown in Table 6.11. Compared to living in a "backward" state, living in a "forward" state significantly increased the probability of prenatal care by 15.3 points, but it did not have a significant effect on the probability of postnatal care. However, compared to urban women, the probability of rural women receiving prenatal and postnatal care was significantly lower respectively by, 2.8 and 4.7 points.

The level of education of women had a significant effect on the probability of their receiving both prenatal and postnatal care. Compared to an illiterate person (the default level), the probabilities of receiving prenatal and postnatal care were, respectively, 9.0 and 4.0 points higher for a person educated up to primary schooling ("low education"); 14.0 and 11.0 points higher for a person educated above primary and up to secondary level; and 15.7 and 14.0 points higher for a person educated up to higher secondary or more.

The economic position of the women's households exercised a significant positive influence on their probability of receiving prenatal care but *not* on their probability of receiving postnatal care: compared to women from households whose monthly expenditure was in the top quartile (the control group), women from households whose monthly expenditure was in the lowest, second, and third quartile were less likely to take treatment by, respectively, 3.3, 4.5, and 2.0 points.

However, even after controlling for all the above factors, Table 6.11 shows that the social groups to which women belonged had a significant effect on their probabilities of receiving prenatal care: compared to HCH woman (the control group), ST(C), MOBC, and HCM were less likely to receive prenatal care by, respectively, 11.5, 8.8, and 4.3 points and non-ST Christians were more likely to receive prenatal care by 16.3 points. By contrast, after controlling for all the above factors, the effects of social group on the probability of receiving postnatal care were much more muted: the only significant social group effects were that, compared to HCH, ST(C) were less likely (by 12.3 points), and non-ST Christians were more likely (by 17.3 points), to receive postnatal care.

Table 6.11:
Marginal probabilities from the logit model of pre and postnatal care

	Prenatal Care	Postnatal Care
Forward state	0.153***	0.019
	(17.8)	(1.53)
Age	−0.002***	−0.001
	(3.56)	(0.59)
Low education	0.090***	0.040**
	(10.5)	(2.73)
Medium education	0.140***	0.110***
	(16.0)	(7.64)
High education	0.157***	0.140***
	(16.9)	(7.81)
Rural	−0.028**	−0.047***
	(2.85)	(3.55)
Laborer	−0.011	−0.020
	(0.64)	(0.85)
Lowest quartile of monthly expenditure	−0.033**	−0.010
	(2.33)	(0.52)
Second quartile of monthly expenditure	−0.045***	−0.013
	(3.33)	(0.73)
Third quartile of monthly expenditure	−0.020*	−0.017
	(1.81)	(1.14)
*Adivasi*s	−0.025	−0.082***
	(1.38)	(3.14)
Christian ST	−0.115***	−0.123***
	(4.19)	(3.09)
Dalits	−0.019	−0.030
	(1.25)	(1.51)
OBC (non-Muslim)	−0.003	0.004
	(0.21)	(0.25)
OBC (Muslim)	−0.088***	−0.041
	(3.62)	(1.40)
Muslim (non-OBC)	−0.043**	−0.029
	(2.16)	(1.15)
Christian (non-tribal)	0.163***	0.173
	(4.46)	(2.78)
Sikh	−0.110*	0.005
	(1.86)	(0.09)
Other religions	0.039	−0.163*
	(0.67)	(1.96)
Pseudo-*R*-squared	0.113	0.028
Observations	9,696	6,874

Source: Author's own calculations from NSS 60th Round, Health File.

6.5. Conclusions

This chapter investigated whether there was a social gradient to health in India with respect to four health outcomes: the age at death; the self-assessed health status of elderly persons; the likelihood of elderly persons, who were in poor health, taking treatment for their ailments; and the likelihood of receiving prenatal and postnatal care. The evidence suggested that living in a forward state (compared to living in a backward state) and belonging to a relatively affluent household significantly improved all four health outcomes. In addition, the age at death and the self-assessed health status of elderly persons was significantly affected by their household living conditions.

The level of education of persons exercised a significant influence on the likelihood of their receiving treatment or care. *Ceteris paribus*, the likelihood of elderly people, who were in poor health, taking treatment increased with their level of education; similarly, compared to poorly educated women, better educated women were more likely to receive prenatal and postnatal care.

However, even after controlling for these "group independent" factors, the social group to which people in India belonged had a significant effect on their health outcomes. Compared to HCH, the average age at death in India—after imposing all the controls—was 4.9 years lower for ST(A), 7.1 years lower for SC, and 6.1 years lower for Muslims (MOBC plus HCM). Similarly, compared to elderly HCH, elderly SC, MOBC, and HOBC were—after imposing all the controls—*more* likely to be in poor health by, respectively, 2.6, 5.5, and 8.1 points. Again, compared to elderly HCH in poor health, SC(A), ST(C), and SC were—after imposing all the controls—*less* likely to take treatment by, respectively, 10.6, 22.5, and 9.0 points and HCM and the HOBC were less likely to take treatment by, respectively, 7.7 and 5.7 points. Lastly, compared to HCH, ST(C), MOBC, and HCM were—after imposing all the controls—less likely to receive prenatal care by, respectively, 11.5, 8.8, and 4.3 points.

There can be little doubt, therefore, that on the basis of data from the M&HC sample, the sample analyzed in this chapter offered *prima facie* evidence of a social group bias to health outcomes in India. However, it is important to note that there are several deficiencies inherent in this study.

First, there are important health-related attributes of individuals (smoking, diet, taking exercise, the nature of work), which are not indeed, given the limitations of the data, cannot be taken account of. All these factors are included in the package of factors termed "unobservable." If these unobservable factors were randomly distributed among the population this, in itself, would not pose a problem. However, there is evidence that there may be a group bias with respect to at least some of these factors. For example, if hard physical work is more inimical to health than more sedentary jobs, then of males aged 25–44 years, 42 percent of ST(A) and 47 percent of SC, compared to only 10 percent of HCH, worked as casual laborers (Borooah, Dubey, and Iyer, 2007).

There is a natural distinction between inequality and inequity in the analysis of health outcomes. Inequality reflects the totality of differences between persons, regardless of the source of these differences and, in particular, regardless of whether or not these sources stem from actions within a person's control. Inequity reflects that part of inequality that is generated by factors outside a person's control. In a fundamental sense, therefore, while inequality may not be seen as "unfair," inequity is properly regarded as being unfair. The point about group membership is that while it may not be the primary factor behind health inequality, it is the main cause of health inequity. This chapter's central message, conditional on the caveats noted earlier, is that belonging to the ST(A) or SC, or being a Muslim in India seriously impaired, using the language of Sen (1992), the capabilities of persons to function in society. This is because, as this study has shown, if you stand at the bottom of the social ladder in India, your risk of suffering premature death, poor health, and a lack of treatment and care is substantially higher than it is for your betters.

7

Employment and Wages

7.1. Introduction

An important concern of public policy in India is to ensure that all individuals, regardless of caste or religion, are treated fairly in the job market. There are two aspects to this concern. The first is whether differences in remuneration between persons fully reflect their difference in productivities or whether these differences might, wholly or in part, be due to "earning discrimination." Oaxaca (1973) developed a methodology for answering this question, and this has subsequently been applied to a variety of labor market situations by *inter alia* Reimers (1983), Neumark (1988), Oaxaca and Ransom (1994), Borooah, McKee, Heaton, and Collins (1995), and Harkness (1996). The second issue is concerns of different likelihoods that persons from different social groups will *ceteris paribus* attain different degrees of occupational success. The issue here is whether these differences in likelihoods are justified by differences in worker distribution or whether they are, wholly or in part, due to "occupational discrimination." Schmidt and Strauss (1975), and Borooah (2001a) are examples of such studies. This paper is concerned with both the issues— "earnings discrimination" and "occupational discrimination"—in the context of the Indian labor market.

In response to the burden of social stigma and economic backwardness borne by people belonging to some of India's castes, the Constitution of India allows for special provisions for members of these castes. Articles 341 and 342 include a list of castes and tribes entitled to such provisions and all those groups included in this list—and subsequent modifications to this list—are referred to as, respectively, "Scheduled Castes" (SC) and "Scheduled Tribes" (ST). Reservation for the SC and ST was designed to assist groups who had known centuries of suppression and who were traditionally isolated from the modern world and from mainstream society.

These special provisions have taken two main forms. The first is action against adverse discrimination toward people from the SC and the ST (discussed in Chapter 1). The second is compensatory discrimination in favor of people from the SC and the ST. Compensatory discrimination has taken the form of guaranteeing seats in national and state legislatures and in village *panchayat*s, places in educational institutions, and the reservation of a certain proportion of government jobs for the SC and the ST.[1]

Reservation policies, or "affirmative action," attempt to increase SC and ST representation in various areas of public life. The reservation of seats in provincial legislatures had its origin in the Madras Presidency when, as early as 1920, 28 out of a total of 65 seats in the Madras Legislative Council were reserved for non-brahmins. This reservation policy allowed a non-brahmin constituency to emerge and enabled the Justice Party (an avowedly non-brahmin party) to win the 1920 elections to the Council. A similar policy in the Bombay Presidency allowed the Marathas to emerge as a powerful political force.

Since independence, there have been, "reserved" constituencies— elections to which may only be contested by SC and ST candidates— for both the national parliament and the state legislatures. The Indian Constitution (Article 330) required SC persons to be given parliamentary representation in proportion to their presence in the population; although Article 331 limited this to 20 years, this period, through successive constitutional amendments has been extended. More recently, Articles 243D and 243T of the 1992 (73rd and 74th) Amendment Acts to the constitution provided for reserved seats for SC persons in every municipality and every *panchayat* in proportion to their presence in the population and, of these reserved seats, not less than one-third were to be held by women.

In terms of a lack of representation in jobs, the basis for public policy in India is job reservation, which had its origins in the western state of Maharashtra when the Maharajah of Kolhapur, in 1902, ordered that half of all government jobs in his state were to be filled by non-brahmins. This was followed by the state of Madras when, in 1920, the Justice Party, having come to (shared) power in Madras, ordered a "caste audit" of government employees and followed this up with measures to increase non-brahmin representation in government jobs. Today, 15 and 7.5 percent of *all* public employment is reserved for persons from the SC and ST, respectively.

---

[1] For the history and evolution of caste-based preferential policies in India, see Osborne (2001).

Articles 15(4) and 16(4) of the Indian Constitution empowers the state to make special provisions for socially and educationally backward classes who were not of SCs or STs. But the definition of the term "backward classes" was deliberately left vague and not defined with the clarity accorded to SCs or STs. More recently, following the recommendations of the Mandal Commission's inquiry into affirmative action policies in India,[2] the 1989–90 government of V.P. Singh took the highly controversial decision to extend reservation of jobs and educational places to members of OBCs defined as those castes or jatis belonging to the sudra varna. Thus, the all-encompassing nature of backward classes under British rule was now given a specific caste-based definition.

In consequence of this decision, a *further* 27 percent of public employment was reserved for the OBC pushing the proportion of *reserved* public employment positions to nearly 50 percent of *all* available places. One possible objective of extending the sweep of reservation policies was to create a historic—and winning—national coalition of "backward class" voters comprising the SC and the OBC, which would mimic Tamil Nadu on a national scale by sweeping away the political hegemony of the "forward" castes.

In common view of the Indian public, job reservation is seen as the most important public concession toward SC and ST and it arouses the strongest of passions.[3] There is, first, the demand to extend reservation to persons who are not from the SC or the ST but who, nevertheless, belong to economic and socially backward groups—the OBC. Second, there is demand from the SC and the ST to extend reservation to private sector jobs (see Bhambri, 2005; Thorat, 2005). Given the fact that issues relating to occupational discrimination and unfair treatment of people belonging

---

[2] B.P. Mandal Commission, 1980.

[3] In arriving at this judgment about who should be eligible for reservation, the criterion has been a person's caste rather than his/her income or wealth. Consequently, groups belonging to what Article 115 of the Indian Constitution calls "socially and education-ally backward classes" have benefited from reservation even though, in practice, many persons belonging to these classes could not be regarded as "socially and educationally backward"; at the same time, many persons belonging to non-backward classes could legitimately be regarded as "socially and educationally backward." Compounding this anomaly is that many of the benefits of reservation have been captured by well-off groups from the depressed classes (for example, *chamars*) while poorer groups (for example, *bhangis*) have failed to benefit. Unfortunately, we are unable to address this issue in this study since the data do not allow a breakdown of the SC by sub-caste.

to certain castes and religions dominate public debate and discourse in India, it is surprising how little academic research there is on this subject (see, however, Borooah, Dubey, and Iyer, 2007; Dhesi and Singh, 1989; Esteve-Bolart, 2004; Ito, 2009; Thorat and Attewell, 2007). Are certain groups treated "unfairly" in the jobs market in India? Unfairly treated with respect to access and/or with respect to wage rates? And, if they are indeed treated unfairly, is it possible to quantify the extent of unfair treatment?

This chapter attempts to answer these questions using unit record data from the latest available round (68th: June 2011–June 2012) of the NSS Employment Unemployment Survey. The NSS employment and unemployment data give the distribution of its respondents who are distinguished by various characteristics, including their caste, religion, and educational levels, between different categories of economic status. Of these categories, the three that are the most important are *self-employed, regular salaried or wage employees,* and *casual wage employees.*

Using these data, we focused on prime-age (22–45 years of age) males and estimated the probabilities of men being in these categories of employment, after controlling for their caste/religion[4] and their employment-related attributes.[5] These estimates were then used, using the methodology detailed below, to decompose the observed difference between the castes in their proportions in the different categories of economic status into an *attributes* and a *discrimination* effect. The NSS data also provided information on the wages earned by the employed respondents in their jobs. Using these data, we estimated wage rate equations with a view to seeing whether *ceteris paribus* the caste (and religion) of the respondents played a role in determining these differences or whether these differences were entirely the product of inter-respondent differences in employment-related attributes.

---

[4] The choice of prime-age males was influenced by the fact that a very large proportion of these men were likely to be active in the labor market, in the sense of being either employed or seeking employment.

[5] Excluded from this analysis were prime-age males who were attending educational institutions; attending domestic duties, and/or producing goods and services for household use (for example, serving, tailoring, weaving); and/or engaged in free collection of goods—for example, vegetables, roots, firewood, cattle feed; rentiers, pensioners, and remittance recipients unable to work owing to a disability; beggars and prostitutes; and *others.*

7.2. Economic Status, Education, and Community

Table 7.1 shows, on the basis of data for the 68th round of the NSS (June 2011–June 2012), the distribution, by their educational standard, of 53,076 prime-age men (22–45 years age) in the 16 major states of India and the Union Territories of Delhi and Chandigarh, between the following categories of economic status:[6]

1. Regular salaried and wage employment (RSWE)
2. Casual wage employment (CWE)

Table 7.1:
Economic status and educational standards of economically active men*

	Illiterate	Literate, But Below Primary	Primary or Middle	Secondary	Graduate	Total
Regular salaried and wage employment	838	603	3,585	5,488	5,246	15,760
	5.3	3.8	22.8	34.8	33.3	100
	11.3	13.9	21.2	35.2	59.4	29.7
Casual wage employment	3,608	1,795	5,590	2,383	223	13,599
	26.5	13.2	41.1	17.5	1.6	100
	48.6	41.4	33.1	15.3	2.5	25.6
Own account workers	2,936	1,906	7,541	7,192	2,695	22,270
	13.2	8.6	33.9	32.3	12.1	100
	39.6	44.0	44.6	46.2	30.5	42.0
Available and searching for work	36	30	194	517	670	1,447
	2.5	2.1	13.4	35.7	46.3	100
	0.5	0.7	1.2	3.3	7.6	2.7
Total	7,418	4,334	16,910	15,580	8,834	53,076
	14.0	8.2	31.9	29.4	16.6	100
	100	100	100	100	100	100

Source: NSS 68th Round.
Notes: *Between 22 and 45 years of age. Numbers refer to June 2011–June 2012.
First figure in a column is the total number in that category; second figure is the row percentage; the third figure is the column percentage.

[6] Excluded from this analysis were prime-age males who were attending educational institutions, attending domestic duties, and/or producing goods and services for household use (for example, serving, tailoring, weaving), and/or engaged in free collection of goods, for example, vegetables, roots, firewood, cattle feed; rentiers, pensioners, and remittance recipients unable to work owing to a disability; beggars and prostitutes; and "others."

3. Own account employment (OAE)
4. Seeking and/or available for work (S&A)

Of these four categories, the first three were the main categories of economic status for prime-age men: 15,760 of the 53,076 men (30 percent) were in RSWE; 13,599 men (26 percent of the total) were in CWE; and 22,270 men (42 percent of the total) were in OAE. Only 1,447 men (3 percent of the total) were S&A.

Being in CWE or in OAE was largely the preserve of poorly educated men while those in RSWE were largely drawn from the ranks of the better educated: of the 13,599 men who were in CWE, 81 percent had an education standard less than secondary school and 27 percent were illiterate; of the 22,270 men in OAE, 56 percent had an education standard less than secondary school and 13 percent were illiterate; on the other hand, of the 15,760 men who were in RSWE, 68 percent were educated to secondary (or above) and 33 percent were graduates (or above).

This study implicitly assumes that becoming a regular salaried or wage worker was the most desirable outcome for prime-age men and, compared to that, self-employment or casual wage worker were inferior outcomes. This assumption is consistent with evidence from the field: for example, Jeffery and Jeffery (1997) in their study of Muslims in Bijnor argued that many Muslims regarded their relative economic weakness as stemming from their being excluded from jobs due to discriminatory practices in hiring. The belief that their sons would not get jobs then led Muslim parents to devalue the importance of education as an instrument of upward economic mobility.[7]

A striking feature of Table 7.1 is how few men were S&A: only 1,447 men (2.7 percent of the total) were unemployed in the conventional meaning of the term. Moreover, job search appeared to be the prerogative of better educated men: of the 1,447 "unemployed" men, 82 percent were educated to secondary level or above and 46 percent were graduates or postgraduates.

Table 7.2 shows the distribution of prime-age men across the categories of economic status by religion and caste. Since nearly 1 in 10 persons from the OBC were Muslim, they are identified, in this study, separately from

---

[7] However, there may be cases where self-employment is the preferred outcome over the available choices. We are unable to take account of such preferences because all we observe is the outcome and not the reasons for the outcome.

the non-Muslim part of the OBC (mostly Hindu, but some Sikhs). These are referred to as MOBC and HOBC, respectively. Table 7.2 clearly shows that OBC prime-age males were different from those belonging to the SC in two important respects. First, both MOBC and HOBC men were *more* likely to be in self-employment (44 and 53 percent, respectively) than men from the SC (30 percent). Second, both MOBC and HOBC men were *less* likely to work as casual laborers (26 and 23 percent, respectively) than men from the SC (42 percent).

Prime-age males from the OBC also differed from their HCH[8] counterparts in two important respects. First, HCH men were more likely to be in RSWE (40 percent) than OBC men (28 percent of HOBC and 22 percent of MOBC men). Second, HCH men were even less likely to work as casual laborers (12 percent) than men from the OBC (23 percent for HOBC and 29 percent for MOBC males).

Table 7.2:
Economic status and caste/religion of economically active men*

	RSWE	CWE	OAW	A&S	Total
High-caste Hindu	5,353	1,536	6,005	495	13,389
	40.0	11.5	44.9	3.7	100
	34.0	11.3	27.0	34.2	25.2
Non-Muslim OBC	5,882	5,477	9,296	494	21,149
	27.8	25.9	44.0	2.3	100
	37.3	40.3	41.7	34.1	39.9
OBC Muslim	851	1,135	1,805	76	3,867
	22.0	29.4	46.7	2.0	100
	5.4	8.4	8.1	5.3	7.3
Non-OBC Muslim (HCM)	775	819	1,903	107	3,604
	21.5	22.72	52.8	3.0	100
	4.9	6.0	8.6	7.4	6.8
Scheduled Castes	2,899	4,632	3,261	275	11,067
	26.2	41.9	29.5	2.5	100
	18.4	34.1	14.6	19.0	20.9
Total	15,760	13,599	22,270	1,447	53,076
	29.7	25.6	42.0	2.7	100
	100	100	100	100	100

Source: NSS 68th Round.
Notes: *Between 22 and 45 years of age. Numbers refer to June 2011–June 2012.
First figure in column is total in the category; the second figure is the row percentage; the third figure is the column percentage.

[8]   That is, Hindus who did not belong to the SC/ST or to the OBC.

Consequently, in terms of a hierarchy of communities with respect to the "desirability" of the economic status of their prime-age men, the SC, 42 percent of whose economically active prime-age men were in CWE and only 26 percent were in RSWE, were at the bottom and the HCH, with 40 percent of their economically active men in RSWE, and only 12 percent of their men working as casual laborers, were at the top; sandwiched between them were the HOBC and the MOBC.

Lastly, Table 7.3 shows the education standards of prime-age men from the different communities. Economically active SC men, and their counterparts from the MOBC, had the lowest level of educational achievement with more than one in five of them being illiterate. The best educated prime-age economically active men were from the HCH, only 5 percent of whom were illiterate and 30 percent of whom were graduates.

Table 7.3:
Education standard and caste/religion of economically active men*

	Illiterate	Literate, But Below Primary	Primary or Middle	Secondary	Graduate	Total
High-caste Hindu	684	587	3,216	4,852	4,050	13,389
	5.1	4.4	24.0	36.2	30	100
	9.2	13.5	19.0	31.1	45.9	25.2
Non-Muslim OBC	2,824	1,769	6,972	6,501	3,083	21,149
	13.4	8.4	33.0	30.7	14.6	100
	38.1	40.8	41.2	41.7	34.9	39.9
OBC Muslim	860	407	1,457	863	280	3,867
	22.2	10.5	37.7	22.3	7.2	100
	11.6	9.4	8.6	5.5	3.2	7.29
Non-OBC Muslim (HCM)	717	402	1,317	791	377	3,604
	19.9	11.2	36.5	22.0	10.5	100
	9.7	9.3	7.8	5.1	4.3	6.8
Scheduled Castes	2,333	1,169	3,948	2,573	1,044	11,067
	21.1	10.6	35.7	23.3	9.4	100.0
	31.5	27.0	23.4	16.5	11.8	20.9
Total	7,418	4,334	16,910	15,580	8,834	53,076
	14.0	8.2	31.9	29.4	16.6	100
	100	100	100	100	100	100

Source: NSS 68th Round.
Notes: *Between 22 and 45 years of age. Numbers refer to June 2011–June 2012.
The first figure in a column is total in category; the second figure is the row percentage; the third figure is the column percentage.

7.3. A Multinomial Logit Model of Economic Status Outcomes

The multinomial logit model (MLM) has been used to analyze occupational outcomes by *inter alia*: Schmidt and Strauss (1975) and Borooah (2001a). The basic question that an MLM seeks to answer is: what is the probability that a person with a particular set of characteristics, will be found in a specific category of economic status (hereafter, simply "status")? These answers were obtained by estimating an MLM where the dependent variable Y_i took the values, 1, 2, or 3 depending upon whether person i was: a regular salaried or wage worker (1); a casual wage worker (2); or was self-employed (own-account worker) (3).[9] In essence, with self-employment ($Y_i = 3$) as the base category, the model consisted of two equations ($Y_i = 1$ and $Y_i = 2$) each of which took the following form:

$$\log\left[\frac{\Pr(Y_i = j)}{\Pr(Y_i = 3)}\right] = f \text{ (landholding social group,}$$

education, state) + error

The MLM was estimated for, respectively, 28,532 prime-age men in the rural sector, and 16,719 prime-age men in the urban sector, who were in *non-family employment*, that is in one of the following (mutually exclusive) categories of economic status: RSWE; CWE; and OAE. Excluded from the analysis were: 1,157 men who were employers, 8,262 men who were unpaid family workers, and the 1,447 men who were available for and seeking work. The detailed estimates are shown in an appendix to this chapter.

---

[8]   With J mutually exclusive and collectively exhaustive outcomes, indexed 1 ... J, the multinomial logit model is defined by a pair of equations. The first, defines *the log odds ratio* of a person i being in status $j > 1$, relative to being in the 'base' status $j = J$, as a linear function of $X_i = \{X_{ik}, k = 1...K\}$, the vector of values of K explanatory variables ($X_{i1} = 1$)

for the person: $\log\left(\dfrac{\Pr(Y_i = j)}{\Pr(Y_i = j)}\right) = \sum\limits_{k=1}^{K} \beta_{jk} X_{ik} = X_i \beta_j$ where Y_i is an integer variable,

which takes the value j if, and only if, outcome j occurs for person i, and β_j is the vector of coefficients associated with outcome j, β_{j1} being the coefficient associated with the intercept term. The second equation defines the probability of outcome j ($j = 1 ... J$) occurring for individual i as: $\Pr(Y_i = j) = \exp(Z_{ij}) / [1 + \sum\limits_{r=1}^{J} Z_{ir}] = F(X_i \beta_j)$

7.3.1. *A Methodology for Measuring Discrimination*

The basic question that the MLM of income distribution sought to answer was: *ceteris paribus* what is the probability that a male, with a particular set of characteristics, will be found in a specific status: RSWE, CWE, or OAE? In order to answer these questions, we evaluated the following *counterfactual* scenarios:

1. We first treated *all* the men in the sample as HCH, with all other non-caste characteristics unchanged. In operational terms, *ceteris paribus* $HCH_i = 1$, $HOBC_i = 0$, $HCM_i = 0$, $SC_i = 0$, and $MOBC_i = 0$, $i = 1, ..., N$. Suppose that, under this scenario, p_j^{HCH} was the average probability of a man belonging to status category j, $j = 0, 1, 2$.

2. Next, we treated *all* the men in the sample as non-MOBC, with all other non-caste characteristics unchanged. In operational terms, *ceteris paribus* $HCH_i = 0$, $HOBC_i = 1$, $HCM_i = 0$, $MOBC_i = 1$, $SC_i = 0$, $i = 1, ..., N$. Suppose that, under this scenario, p_j^{HOBC} was the average probability of a man belonging to status category j, $j = 1 ... 4$.

3. Next, we treated all the men in the sample as non-SC/MOBC, with all other non-caste characteristics unchanged. In operational terms, *ceteris paribus* $HCH_i = 0$, $HOBC_i = 0$, $HCM_i = 1$, $MOBC_i = 1$, $SC_i = 0$, $i = 1, ..., N$. Suppose that, under this scenario, p_j^{HCM} was the average probability of a man belonging to status category j, $j = 1 ... 4$.

4. Next, we treated all the men in the sample as MOBC, with all other non-caste characteristics unchanged. In operational terms, *ceteris paribus* $HCH_i = 0$, $HOBC_i = 0$, $HCM_i = 0$, $MOBC_i = 1$, $SC_i = 0$, $i = 1, ..., N$. Suppose that, under this scenario, p_j^{MOBC} was the average probability of a man belonging to status category j, $j = 1...4$.

5. Lastly, we treated all the men in the sample as from the SC, with all other non-caste characteristics unchanged. In operational terms, *ceteris paribus* $HCH_i = 0$, $HOBC_i = 0$, $HCM_i = 1$, $MOBC_i = 0$, $SC_i = 1$, $i = 1, ..., N$. Suppose that, under this scenario, p_j^{SC} was the average probability of a man belonging to status category j, $j = 1...4$.

The differences between the *adjusted proportions*, p_j^{HCH}, p_j^{HOBC}, p_j^{HCM}, p_j^{MOBC}, and p_j^{SC} are entirely the result of *different* sets of coefficients (HCH, HOBC, HCM, MOBC, and SC) being applied to a *given* set of attributes. These differences may, therefore, be attributed to the "unequal treatment of equals," namely the unequal treatment of men who, *except for their caste/religion,* were identical in every respect. However, the *sample proportions* of men from the different caste groups—denoted, q_j^{HCH}, q_j^{HOBC}, q_j^{HCM}, q_j^{MOBC}, *and* q_j^{SC}—will, in general, be different from the adjusted proportions. This reflects the fact that men from the different social groups differ not just with respect to their caste/religion backgrounds but also with respect to their attributes. Then the overall disparity faced by (say) SC, relative to HCH, men, with respect to a "desirable" status category *j* (for example, RSWE), is measured by the *disparity coefficient,* $1 - \mu_j^{SC}$ where

$$\mu_j^{SC} = \frac{q_j^{SC}}{q_j^{HCH}}, \text{ where: } 0 \le \mu_j^{SC} \le 1$$

If $1 - \mu_j^{SC} = 0$, that is, $q_j^{SC} = q_j^{HCH}$, there is no disparity between males from the SC, relative to their HCH counterparts, with respect to status *j*; at the other extreme, disparity between SC and HCH males, with respect to status *j*, is greatest when $1 - \mu_j^{SC} = 1$ that is , $q_j^{SC} = 0$. However, not all disparity is due to discrimination, defined as the unequal treatment of equals. In order to account for this, the disparity coefficient can, in turn, be decomposed into a "discrimination effect" and an "attributes effect" with the details of this decomposition is provided in Box 7.1.

Box 7.1:
The decomposition of the discrimination coefficient

$$\mu_j^{SC} = \frac{q_j^{SC}}{q_j^{HCH}} = \left[\frac{p_j^{SC}}{p_j^{HCH}}\right] \times \left[\frac{q_j^{SC}}{p_j^{SC}}\right] \times \left[\frac{p_j^{HCH}}{q_j^{HCH}}\right]$$

$$= \lambda_j^{SC} \times \frac{\pi_j^{SC}}{\pi_j^{HCH}} = \lambda_j^{SC} \times \delta_j^{SC}$$

(7.1)

Box 7.1 continued

Box 7.1 continued

Then the discrimination faced by SC, relative to HCH men, is measured by the *discrimination coefficient*, $1 - \lambda_j^{SC}$ where, $\lambda_j^{SC} = \dfrac{p_j^{SC}}{p_j^{HCH}}$ in equation (7.1) above. This represents the ratio of the proportionate representations in status j of SC and HCH males, *where these representations are entirely due to caste/religious factors.* When $1 - \lambda_j^{SC} = 0$, there is no discrimination since $p_j^{SC} = p_j^{HCH}$ and when $1 - \lambda_j^{SC} = 1$ discrimination is at its maximum since $p_j^{SC} = 0$, implying that *ceteris paribus* SC men would be completely excluded from status j. The terms $\pi_j^{SC} = \dfrac{q_j^{SC}}{p_j^{SC}}$ and $\pi_j^{HCH} = \dfrac{q_j^{HCH}}{p_j^{HCH}}$ are the ratios of the sample to the adjusted proportions for SC and HCH households, respectively.

From equation (7.1), the overall disparity coefficient can be written as the sum of the disparity coefficient $(1 - \lambda_j^{SC})$ and a composite term $(\lambda_j^{SC}[1 - \delta_j^{SC}])$:

$$1 - \mu_j^{SC} = 1 - \lambda_j^{SC}\delta_j^{SC} = 1 - \lambda_j^{SC}\delta_j^{SC} + \lambda_j^{SC} - \lambda_j^{SC}$$

$$= (1 - \lambda_j^{SC}) + \lambda_j^{SC}(1 - \delta_j^{SC}) \qquad (7.2)$$

The term $\delta_j^{SC} = \dfrac{\pi_j^{SC}}{\pi_j^{HCH}} = \left(\dfrac{q_j^{SC}}{q_j^{HCH}} \middle/ \dfrac{p_j^{SC}}{p_j^{HCH}} \right)$ in equation (7.2) is a measure of the attributes deficit of men from the SC. The attributes deficit compares the sample ratio of SC and HCH proportions in status j to the corresponding adjusted ratio.

1. If $\delta_j^{SC} = 1$, there is no attributes deficit since the sample and adjusted ratios are equal: $\dfrac{q_j^{SC}}{q_j^{HCH}} = \dfrac{p_j^{SC}}{p_j^{HCH}}$ implying that $\pi_j^{SC} = \pi_j^{HCH}$. In this case, from equation (7.2), $1 - \mu_j^{SC} = 1 - \lambda_j^{SC}$ so that the value of the disparity coefficient equals the value of the discrimination coefficient: *all* of the observed disparity between SC and HCH males in their representation in status j is due to discrimination.

2. If $\delta_j^{SC} < 1$, $(1 - \mu_j^{SC}) > (1 - \lambda_j^{SC})$ since, in equation (7.2), $\lambda_j^{SC}(1 - \delta_j^{SC}) > 0$. The value of the disparity coefficient exceeds the value of the discrimination coefficient: *some* of the observed disparity between SC and HCH

Box 7.1 continued

Box 7.1 continued

males in their representation in status j is due to discrimination and some is due to the fact that, compared to their HCH counterparts, SC men have *inferior* attributes.

3.   If $\delta_j^{SC} > 1$, $(1 - \mu_j^{SC}) > (1 - \lambda_j^{SC})$, since, in equation (7.2), $\lambda_j^{SC}(1 - \delta_j^{SC}) < 0$.

The value of the disparity coefficient is less than the value of the discrimination coefficient: *more than all* the observed disparity between SC and HCH males in their representation in status j is due to discrimination and SC men neutralize some of this discrimination with *superior* attributes compared to their HCH counterparts.

Source: Authors.

7.3.2. Measuring Discrimination

Tables 7.4 and 7.5 show values of the disparity and discrimination coefficients, with respect to RSWE, for men in the rural and urban sectors, respectively, using HCH as the comparator. Tables 7.6 and 7.7 show that the *observed* proportion of HCH men in RSWE was 25.5 percent in the rural sector and 46.3 percent in the urban sector; the *observed* proportion of HOBC men in RSWE was 18.1 percent in the rural sector and 35.9 percent in the urban sector; the *observed* proportion of non-OBC Muslim (HCM) men in RSWE was 13.1 percent in the rural sector and 26 percent in the urban sector; the *observed* proportion of MOBC men in RSWE was 15.1 percent in the rural sector and 24.8 percent in the urban sector; and the *observed* proportion of SC men in RSWE was 17.2 percent in the rural sector and 37.8 percent in the urban sector.

1.   If *everyone* in the sample (the HOBC, HCM, MOBC, and SC men) was treated as HCH (in effect, had their attributes evaluated at HCH coefficients), the proportion of men in RSWE would fall from 26.2 to 21.1 percent in the rural sector and from 48.7 to 43.3 percent in the urban sector. These falls reflect the fact that when the *entire* sample of men was being treated as HCH, it had a *lower* quality of attributes than the HCH sub-sample. Consequently, the adjusted proportions (21.1 and 41.5 percent) were *lower* than the observed proportions of HCH men (25.5 and 43.3 percent) in RSWE.

2. If *everyone* in the sample (the HCH, the HCM, MOBC, and SC men) was treated as HOBC (in effect, had their attributes evaluated at HOBC coefficients), the proportion of men in RSWE would remain unchanged at 18.5 percent in the rural sector and rise from 36.9 to 38.3 percent in the urban sector. These small changes reflect the fact that the attributes of the men in the sample, considered in its entirety, was broadly similar to the attributes of the HOBC sub-sample of men.

3. If *everyone* in the sample (the HCH, HOBC, the MOBC, and the SC men) was treated as HCM (in effect, had their attributes evaluated at HCM coefficients), the proportion of men in RSWE would rise from 13.4 to 16 percent in the rural sector and rise from 26.8 to 31.6 percent in the urban sector. These increases reflect the fact that when the *entire* sample of men was being treated as HCM, it had a *higher* quality of attributes than the HCM sub-sample. Consequently the adjusted proportions (16 and 31.6 percent) were *higher* than the observed proportions of HCM men (13.4 and 26.8 percent) in RSWE.

4. If *everyone* in the sample (the HCH, HOBC, HCM, and SC men) was treated as MOBC (in effect, had their attributes evaluated at MOBC coefficients), the proportion of men in RSWE would rise from 15.4 to 19.3 percent in the rural sector and from 25.2 to 31.6 percent in the urban sector. These increases reflect the fact that when the *entire* sample of men was being treated as MOBC, it had a *higher* quality of attributes than the MOBC sub-sample. Consequently the adjusted proportions (19.3 and 31.6 percent) were *higher* than the observed proportions of MOBC men (15.4 and 25.2 percent) in RSWE.

5. Lastly, if *everyone* in the sample (the HCH, HOBC, HCM, and MOBC men) was treated as SC (in effect, had their attributes evaluated at SC coefficients), the proportion of men in RSWE would rise from 17.6 to 21.3 percent in the rural sector and from 39.1 to 44.1 percent in the urban sector. These increases reflect the fact that when the *entire* sample of men was being treated as SC, it had a *higher* quality of attributes than the SC sub-sample. Consequently the adjusted proportions (21.3 and 44.1 percent) were *higher* than the observed proportions of SC men (17.6 and 39.1 percent) in RSWE.

Box 7.2:
Relation between this chapter's decomposition and an Oaxaca (1973)–type decomposition

It is worth emphasizing the differences between the decomposition method set out above and the standard Oaxaca (1973) type decomposition in a wage regression. The latter decomposes the observed difference in average wage between two groups into an "explained" and an "unexplained" part. The "explained" part has to do with differences in attributes between the two groups and the "unexplained" part is often identified as being due to discrimination. The Oaxaca (1973) decomposition can be extended to binary choice models in which the difference in *average probabilities* of being in a particular category can be similarly decomposed (Nielsen, 1998). However, when applied to models with multiple discrete outcomes, as in the multinomial logit model, the variable to be decomposed becomes the difference in average log odds-ratios,

$\left[\dfrac{\Pr(Y_i = j)}{\Pr(Y_i = 3)} \right]$, which is not so easy to interpret and, in particular, cannot be translated into differences in the underlying probabilities. The method proposed in this section overcomes this.

Source: Authors.

A feature of the results shown in Tables 7.4 and 7.5 is that when the chances of the men in the sample being in RSWE were evaluated using, in turn, the coefficients of each group, the adjusted proportions in RSWE were highest when the HCH coefficients were used. The implication of this is that Hindu coefficients were most favorable for being in RSWE or, in other words, the *same* group of people (that is, *all* the men in the sample) would have had a *higher* chance of being in RSWE had they *all* been HCH compared to *all* being HOBC, or HCM, or MOBC. As argued earlier, 1 minus the ratio of the HCH and the HOBC (or HCM or MOBC) adjusted proportions ($1 - p_j^{HOBC} / p_j^{HCH}$) is the value of the discrimination coefficient against HOBC (or HCM or MOBC), vis-à-vis HCH, men and this, as Tables 7.6 and 7.7 show, was always positive. In terms of RSWE, men from the HOBC, the HCM, and the MOBC were discriminated against vis-à-vis HCH men.

The exception to this general observation arose when all the men in the sample were treated as though they were from the SC. In this case, the adjusted proportions were the same—both for the rural and urban sectors—as those which resulted from treating *all* the men as though they were HCH. In other words, it made no difference to the chances of the men in the sample being in RSWE whether their attributes were evaluated using HCH or SC coefficients; to put it differently, the results shown in Tables 7.4 and 7.5 imply that there was no discrimination against SC, vis-à-vis HCH, men!

The answer to this counter-intuitive result lies in the reservation of jobs for the SC instituted, as noted above, under the aegis of the Indian constitution. A major reason for job reservation was to combat discrimination against persons from the SC who, along with persons from the ST, are arguably the most downtrodden of India's population. Job reservation cannot alter the employment-related attributes of the SC but, *given those attributes*, it can raise the proportion of persons from the SC who secure RSWE by shifting the coefficients of the employment equations in favor of persons from this group. In respect, job reservation for the SC has succeeded in neutralizing the discrimination that they undeniably face from other sections of Indian society. For SC men who, for reasons of discrimination, are turned down for RSWE in favor of an HCH man in the private sector, *where job reservation does not apply*, positive discrimination ensures that there are HCH men who are turned down in favor of SC men in the public sector where job reservation *does* apply. As our results show, the two effects are self-cancelling: positive discrimination in favor of SC men neutralizes its negative counterpart against SC men in the private sector.

So, given their attributes *and the advantage of job reservation* (as reflected in the SC coefficients), SC men achieved an RSWE representation of 17.6 percent in rural areas and 39.1 percent in urban areas. If everyone was treated as an SC male, RSWE representation would rise to 21.3 percent in rural areas and 44.1 percent in urban areas—the superior attributes of the men in the sample in its entirety, relative to men in the SC sub-sample, *would combine with job reservation* (as reflected in the SC coefficients) to yield the higher proportions in RSWE.

These observations then raise the counterfactual question of what the representation of SC men in RSWE would have been had they not been protected by job reservation? In order to see how effective job reservation was in raising the proportions of SC men in RSWE, we consider what these proportions would have been if the attributes of these men had been evaluated using the coefficients of employment-deficit groups who did not benefit from job reservation: OBC and non-OBC Muslims (MOBC and HOBC, respectively). This was implemented by estimating the multinomial logit equations, shown in Tables 7.4 and 7.5, on the Muslim subsample

Table 7.4:
Disparity and discrimination coefficient values for regular salaried and wage employment in the rural sector, by caste and religion

	Observed Proportion	Adjusted Proportion	Disparity Coefficient: $1-\mu_j^c$	Discrimination Coefficient: $1-\lambda_j^c$	Discrimination/ Disparity Ratio (%)
High-caste Hindus	0.262	0.211	$1-(0.262/0.262)=0.0$		
Non-Muslim OBC	0.185	0.185	$1-(0.185/0.262)=0.29$	$1-(0.185/0.211)=0.12$	44.8
Non-SC/OBC Muslims (HCM)	0.134	0.160	$1-(0.134/0.262)=0.49$	$1-(0.160/0.211)=0.24$	49.0
OBC Muslims (MOBC)	0.154	0.193	$1-(0.154/0.262)=0.41$	$1-(0.193/0.211)=0.09$	65.9
Scheduled Castes	0.176	0.213	$1-(0.176/0.262)=0.33$	$1-(0.213/0.211)=0.0$	0

Source : Author's own calculations from NSS 68th Round data.

Table 7.5:
Disparity and discrimination coefficient values for regular salaried and wage employment in the urban sector, by caste and religion

	Observed Proportion	Adjusted Proportion	Disparity Coefficient with Respect to HCH: $1-\mu_j^c$	Discrimination Coefficient with Respect to HCH: $1-\lambda_i^c$	Discrimination/ Disparity Ratio (%)
High-caste Hindus	0.487	0.433	$1-(0.487/0.487)=0.0$		
Non-Muslim OBC (HOBC)	0.369	0.383	$1-(0.369/0.487)=0.24$	$1-(0.383/0.433)=0.12$	45.5
Non-SC/OBC Muslims (HCM)	0.268	0.316	$1-(0.268/0.487)=0.45$	$1-(0.316/0.433)=0.27$	63.6
OBC Muslims	0.252	0.316	$1-(0.252/0.487)=0.48$	$1-(0.316/0.433)=0.23$	56.5
Scheduled Castes	0.391	0.441	$1-(0.391/0.487)=0.11$	$1-(0.441/0.433)=-0.02$	0

Source: Author's own calculations from NSS 68th Round data.

(HCM + MOBC) only and then using these estimates to predict the proportion of SC men in RSWE. Our results show that if SC men had been treated as Muslims, their proportion in RSWE in the *rural* sector would have *fallen* from the observed 17.6 to 16 percent and their proportion in RSWE in the *urban* sector would have *fallen* from the observed 39.1 to 28.3 percent. So, on our estimates, job reservation added 1.6 percentage points to SC male representation in RSWE in the rural sector and added 10.8 percentage points to SC male representation in RSWE in the urban sector.

Job reservation is, of course, one way of raising SC representation in RSWE. Another way is to raise the educational levels of persons from the SC. For example, as Table 7.3 shows, 21 percent of SC, compared to 13 percent of the HOBC and 10 percent of HCM, men were illiterate. At the other end of the educational spectrum, only 9 percent of SC, compared to 13 percent of HOBC and 11 percent of HCM, men were graduates. So, a natural question that rises is by how much would the RSWE representation of SC males improve if their educational levels rose to, say, that of HOBC men?

Our calculations suggest that if men from the SC in the rural sector had the education standards of rural sector HOBC, their proportion in *rural* RSWE would have been 22 percent instead of the observed 17.6 percent and their proportion in *urban* RSWE would have been 42.1 percent instead of the observed 39.1 percent: increase of 4.4 and 3 points, which could be ascribed to the rise in the education standard of men from the SC to the standard of non-MOBC.

Access to RSWE is one aspect of labor market welfare and, as we have argued, job reservation has succeeded in delivering to SC men a share in urban RSWE that is nearly 11 points more than what they might have expected in its absence. However, another aspect of labor market welfare is the *quality* of RSWE. Although this quality has many dimensions, the wage rate obtained in RSWE is arguably, a good encapsulation of these. The next section turns to a discussion of issues relating to wages.

7.4. Wage Rate Determination

The NSS gives the details of a person's current weekly status in terms of whether in the course of a reference week a person was: in RSWE; in CWE; self-employment; or unemployed. The NSS also reports the intensity of work in terms of whether a person, if he was not unemployed, worked a full day (value 1) or a half day (value 0.5). The maximum and minimum number of (full) days an employed person could work was, therefore, 7 and 0.5, respectively.[10] The NSS also reports on the total wages received every person who was employed during that week; dividing wages by the number of days worked then yields the daily wage rate. Hereafter, this is referred to as the wage rate.

Table 7.6 shows that the wage rates for HCH men in rural and urban RSWE were, respectively, 32 and 64 percent above the corresponding SC wage rate: HCH men earned ₹391 and ₹556 per day, while SC men earned ₹296 and ₹339 per day, in, respectively, rural and urban RSWE. The mark-up of the RSWE wage rate over the wage rate for CWE was considerably higher for HCH, compared to SC, men: 2.4 and 2.8 for HCH men in the rural and urban sectors and 1.8 for SC men in both sectors. HCH males also earned 42 percent more in urban, compared to rural, RSWE while MOBC males earned only 2 percent more (₹288 compared to ₹282) and HOBC males actually earned less in the urban, compared to the rural, sector (₹361 versus ₹334).

Table 7.6:
Wage rates (₹) by employment type, rural/urban, and social group

	Rural			Urban			% In RSWE (Rural + Urban)
	RSWE	CWE	RSWE/CWE	RSWE	CWL	RSWE/CWL	
High-caste Hindus	391	165	2.4	556	208	2.7	74
Non-Muslim OBC	327	177	1.8	375	201	1.9	47
Non-OBC Muslims	361	151	2.4	334	164	2.0	43
OBC Muslims	288	196	1.5	282	198	1.4	38
Scheduled Castes	296	166	1.8	339	184	1.8	34
Sample average	341	168	2.0	431	193	2.2	48

Source: NSS 68th Round.

Tables 7.7 and 7.8 show the results of estimating a wage equation, in which the dependent variable was the wage rate (as defined above) for,

---

[9]   By definition, an unemployed person did not work on any day of the week.

respectively, the sample of 15,902 men in rural India and the sample of 10,096 employee men in urban India. The rural and urban equations explained, respectively, 33.5 percent ($\overline{R}^2 = 0.335$) and 26.9 percent ($\overline{R}^2 = 0.269$) of the variation in wage rates among men.

Table 7.7:
Estimates for the wage equation for employees in rural employment

Dependent Variable: Wage Rate Per Day	Coefficient Estimate	Standard Error	t Value	P > t
Regular salaried and wage employment	72.06	3.68	19.59	19.59
High-caste Hindus	5.69	5.26	1.08	1.08
Non-Muslim OBC	−5.84	4.25	−1.37	−1.37
Non-SC/OBC Muslim	2.57	8.11	0.32	0.32
Scheduled Castes	−4.67	4.51	−1.03	−1.03
Land ownership: 2nd quintile	6.40	4.36	1.47	1.47
Land ownership: 3rd quintile	8.68	4.75	1.83	1.83
Land ownership: 4th quintile	13.08	4.63	2.82	2.82
Land ownership: 5th quintile	43.72	5.66	7.73	7.73
Age: 30–35 years	33.51	3.80	8.81	8.81
Age: 35–40 years	59.05	3.83	15.41	15.41
Age: 40–45 years	100.48	4.12	24.40	24.40
Literate but below primary education	9.59	5.51	1.74	1.74
Primary and middle education	11.72	4.23	2.77	2.77
Secondary and higher secondary	60.26	4.88	12.35	12.35
Graduate and above	235.22	6.11	38.52	38.52
NREG card	−36.37	3.26	−11.16	−11.16
Himachal Pradesh	−34.41	9.68	−3.55	−3.55
Punjab	−30.90	8.77	−3.52	−3.52
Uttaranchal	−10.73	12.77	−0.84	−0.84
Haryana	−0.55	9.35	−0.06	−0.06
Rajasthan	−35.81	8.23	−4.35	−4.35
Uttar Pradesh	−89.63	6.73	−13.33	−13.33
Bihar	−65.39	7.61	−8.59	−8.59
Assam	−12.41	9.37	−1.32	−1.32
West Bengal	−59.84	7.54	−7.94	−7.94
Jharkhand	−57.14	9.24	−6.18	−6.18
Orissa	−103.08	7.95	−12.97	−12.97
Chhattisgarh	−138.21	9.85	−14.04	−14.04
Madhya Pradesh	−103.30	8.32	−12.42	−12.42
Gujarat	−84.11	8.83	−9.53	−9.53
Maharashtra	−58.07	7.12	−8.15	−8.15
Andhra Pradesh	−66.12	7.18	−9.21	−9.21
Karnataka	−75.70	8.40	−9.01	−9.01
Kerala	82.50	8.02	10.29	10.29
Intercept	178.36	7.87	22.68	22.68

Source: Author's own calculations from NSS 68th Round data.
Note: NERG, National Rural Employment Guarantee.

Table 7.8:
Estimates for the wage equation for employees in urban employment

Dependent Variable: Wage Rate Per Day	Coefficient Estimate	Standard Error	t Value	P > t
Regular salaried and wage employment	59.28	9.47	6.26	0.00
High-caste Hindus	71.63	12.80	5.60	0.00
Non-Muslim OBC	−34.36	11.91	−2.89	0.00
Non-SC/OBC Muslim	−14.10	18.64	−0.76	0.45
Scheduled Castes	−24.80	13.03	−1.90	0.06
Land ownership: 2nd quintile	35.90	9.08	3.95	0.00
Land ownership: 3rd quintile	90.93	12.58	7.23	0.00
Land ownership: 4th quintile	40.50	16.20	2.50	0.01
Land ownership: 5th quintile	62.95	19.54	3.22	0.00
Age: 30–35 years	62.27	10.02	6.21	0.00
Age: 35–40 years	113.60	9.84	11.55	0.00
Age: 40–45 years	156.54	10.50	14.91	0.00
Literate but below primary education	11.39	18.60	0.61	0.54
Primary and middle education	11.90	13.97	0.85	0.39
Secondary and higher secondary	88.45	14.52	6.09	0.00
Graduate and above	399.78	15.50	25.79	0.00
Himachal Pradesh	−42.87	42.72	−1.00	0.32
Punjab	−20.18	21.01	−0.96	0.34
Chandigarh	84.43	73.53	1.15	0.25
Uttaranchal	−15.32	33.35	−0.46	0.65
Haryana	180.26	22.60	7.98	0.00
Delhi	189.21	26.96	7.02	0.00
Rajasthan	−45.59	20.97	−2.17	0.03
Uttar Pradesh	−38.01	18.14	−2.10	0.04
Bihar	−43.41	23.54	−1.84	0.07
Assam	−18.58	29.95	−0.62	0.54
West Bengal	−64.29	19.55	−3.29	0.00
Jharkhand	11.32	25.47	0.44	0.66
Orissa	−28.52	25.42	−1.12	0.26
Chhattisgarh	−102.40	27.50	−3.72	0.00
Madhya Pradesh	−75.26	20.17	−3.73	0.00
Gujarat	−38.40	20.04	−1.92	0.06
Maharashtra	42.61	16.92	2.52	0.01
Andhra Pradesh	−7.14	19.36	−0.37	0.71
Karnataka	8.64	20.31	0.43	0.67
Kerala	77.60	20.87	3.72	0.00
Intercept	90.43	20.53	4.40	0.00

Source: Author's own calculations from NSS 68th Round data.

The interpretation of the estimates in Tables 7.7 and 7.8 is as follows. A male with all the "reference" characteristics (an MOBC male in CWE, below the age of 30, owning minimal or no land, illiterate, not holding a National Rural Employment Guarantee (NREG) card, and living in Tamil Nadu would earn ₹178 and ₹90 as daily wages in, respectively, the rural and urban sectors. For such a man, working in the *rural* sector in any other state of India (except Kerala, where he would earn ₹83 more) would reduce his wages for example, by ₹58 in Maharashtra and by ₹31 in Punjab. However, working in the *urban* sector, would raise his wage rate in several states: in Delhi by ₹189, in Haryana by ₹180, and in Kerala by ₹78.

The largest contributor to a higher wage rate was being a graduate or higher. Having this educational level would add ₹235 to the wage rate in rural areas and ₹400 to the wage rate in urban areas; in contrast, having a level of education between higher secondary and a diploma would add only ₹60 to the rural wage rate and ₹88 to the urban wage rate. The next biggest contributor was in being in regular employment, as opposed to casual employment, this fact would add ₹72 to the rural wage rate and ₹59 to the urban wage rate. In rural areas, those who had an NREG card would earn ₹36 less in daily wages than those who did not have this card.

Not surprisingly, the wage rate increased with the age of the employee: workers who were aged 40–45 years earned more than workers aged 35–40 years, who earned more than workers aged 30–35 years workers and who, in turn, earned more than the youngest (below 30 years) workers. In a similar fashion, the wage rate was higher for those who owned more assets by way of land: workers who were in the top quintile of land owners earned more than workers in the next quintile and so on.

Caste effects on the wage rate were significant in both rural and urban India, but these were stronger in urban, compared to rural, areas. Compared to the reference group of MOBC, HCH males earned ₹72 more in daily wages in urban areas but only ₹6 more in rural areas; SC males earned ₹25 less in daily wages than MOBC in urban areas but only ₹5 less in rural areas. A slightly surprising feature of the results is that, *compared to OBC men*, men in all the groups—except HCH—had a *lower* wage rate in the urban sector and—except for HCH and non-MOBC—also had a *lower* wage rate in the rural sector. This can largely be explained by the high wage rate for OBC men in CWE—as Table 7.6 shows, MOBC men had the highest CWE wage rate in the rural sector (₹196) and the CWE wage rate of MOBC men in the urban sector (₹198) was only slightly lower than that for non-OBC men (₹201) and considerably higher than that for non-MOBC (₹164) and SC (₹184) males. Excluding HCH males, of the total number of employees in the sample, 59 percent of were in CWE, with 41 percent in RSWE. In terms of the *overall* wage rate, therefore, this put MOBC men at an advantage over men from all groups except HCH males.

7.4.1. *The Decomposition of Wage Rates*

In the previous analysis, a *single* regression was estimated over all the men regardless of the group to which they belonged. The implicit assumption was that the men from the different groups (HCH, HOBC, HCM, MOBC, SC) all faced the *same* regression coefficients in the evaluation of their attributes and that the *only* coefficient that distinguished between them was the caste/religion variable. Under this assumption, as discussed above, caste played a significant role in determining wage rates.

This assumption is relaxed by estimating separate equations between the two groups and allowing the coefficients to be different between them. This raises the following question: when we observe a difference in mean achievement between groups how much of it is due to a difference in attributes and how much is due to a difference in coefficients? So the first step is to ask what the HCH/SC difference (and the HCH/HOBC, the HCH/HCM, and the HCH/MOBC difference) *would have been* if both sets of attributes were evaluated at a *common* coefficient vector. This difference could then be entirely ascribed to a *difference in attributes* since coefficient differences would have been neutralized. Then the *observed* difference less the *difference due to attributes* is the *residual* or *unexplained* difference. It is this residual difference that can, subject to several *caveats*, be interpreted as due to discrimination (see Oaxaca, 1973; Blinder, 1973).

A recent formal exposition of the Blinder–Oaxaca (B–O) decomposition method (named after Blinder, 1973 and Oaxaca, 1973) for *linear* regression models is to be found in Jann (2008) and is set out in detail in the Appendix to chapter 3. Suppose there are two groups, H and S with Y as an outcome variable such that $\overline{Y}_H$ and $\overline{Y}_S$ are the mean values of the outcome variable for, respectively, groups H and S. Then *part of* the outcome difference of $\overline{Y}_H - \overline{Y}_S$ can be explained by the difference in attributes with the remainder representing the unexplained part. The latter is usually ascribed to discrimination.

Box 7.3:
Choosing the common coefficient vector

In general, the problem of defining β^*, the non-discriminatory coefficient vector, is a big issue in the decomposition literature on discrimination. One possibility is to identify β^* with the coefficients of one of the groups. Another is to regard it as the average of the two group coefficients (Reimers, 1983): $\beta^* = 0.5 \times \beta_H + 0.5 \times \beta_S$. Yet another (Cotton, 1988) is to weigh the coefficients by the size of the groups: $\beta^* = n_H \times \beta_H + n_S \times \beta_S$ where n_H and n_S are the proportions in groups H and S. The pair-wise decompositions in this paper were carried out by the pooling the observations for: HCH and SC men; HCH and HOBC men; HCH and HCM men; HCH and MOBC men. Separate pair-wise decompositions were conducted by RSWE and CWE wage rates for the rural and urban sectors: (i) rural RSWE, (ii) rural CWE, (iii) urban RSWE, and (iv) urban CWE.

Source: Authors.

Tables 7.9–7.11 show the results from the decomposition analysis for RSWE in the urban sector. For example, Table 7.12 shows that there was a difference of ₹231 between the HCH and SC male wage rates: ₹573 and ₹341, respectively. Of this difference, ₹144 (62 percent) was due to a difference in attributes between males from the two groups and ₹87 (38 percent) was the "unexplained" difference. Tables 7.10 and 7.11 show that for Muslim males (both HCM and MOBC), the contribution of the attributes difference was much higher, 71 percent for HCM and 77 percent for MOBC males; lastly, Table 7.9 shows that the contribution of the attributes difference was smallest (55 percent) for HOBC males.

Table 7.9:
The decomposition of the difference in daily wage rate between HCH and non-Muslim OBC males (Pooled estimates for urban RWSE wage rates)

	Value	Standard Error	z Value	P > z
HCH: Mean daily wage rate	573	12	47	0
HOBC: Mean daily wage rate	379	7	54	0
Difference between HCH and HOBC persons	193	14	14	0
Decomposition of the difference between HCH and HOBC Males				
Explained	106	9	12	0
Unexplained	88	11	8	0

Source: Author's own calculations from NSS 68th Round data.
Note: Decomposition using 4,461 observations.

Table 7.10:

The decomposition of the difference in daily wage rate between HCH and non-OBC Muslim males (Pooled estimates for urban RWSE wage rates)

	Value	Standard Error	z Value	P > z
HCH: Mean daily wage rate	573	12	47	
Non-OBC Muslim: Mean daily wage rate	353	33	11	
Difference between HCH and HCM persons	220	35	6	
Decomposition of the difference between HCH and HCM males				
Explained	157	14	11	0
Unexplained	63	33	2	0

Source: Author's own calculations from NSS 68th Round data.
Note: Decomposition using 2,746 observations.

Table 7.11:

The decomposition of the difference in daily wage rate between HCH and OBC Muslim males (Pooled estimates for urban RWSE wage rates)

	Value	Standard Error	z Value	P > z
HCH: Mean daily wage rate	573	12	47	0
OBC Muslim: Mean daily wage rate	270	15	19	0
Difference between HCH and MOBC households	303	19	16	0
Decomposition of the difference between HCH and MOBC males				
Explained	232	15	16	0
Unexplained	70	16	4	0

Source: Author's own calculations from NSS 68th Round data.
Note: Decomposition using 2,801 observations.

Table 7.12:

The decomposition of the difference in daily wage rate between HCH and SC Muslim males (Pooled estimates for RWSE wage rates)

	Value	Standard Error	z Value	P > z
HCH: Mean daily wage rate	573	12	47	0
SC: Mean daily wage rate	341	9	37	0
Difference between HCH and SC households	231	15	15	0
Decomposition of the difference between HCH and SC males				
Explained	144	10	15	0
Unexplained	87	12	7	0

Source: Author's own calculations from NSS 68th Round data.
Note: Decomposition using 3,468 observations.

The above observation begs the question of what are the attributes that matter in explaining differences between the social groups in their male wage rates for RSWE in the urban sector? Table 7.13 shows the contributions that differences in the various attributes made to the *overall*

Table 7.13:
Contributions by individual attributes to overall attribute-induced difference in urban RSWE daily wage rates for males

	HCH vs. Non-Muslim OBC			HCH vs. Non-OBC Muslim			HCH vs. OBC Muslim			HCH vs. SC		
	Contribution	z value	p>|z|	Contribution	z value	p>|z|	Contribution	z value	p>|z|	Contribution	z value	p>|z|
Land ownership: 2nd quintile	0	-0.74	0.462	2	1.46	0.15	0	-0.28	0.78	0	-0.45	0.66
Land ownership: 3rd quintile	2	1.69	0.09	7	2.62	0.01	2	0.72	0.47	4	2.12	0.03
Land ownership: 4th quintile	0	-0.75	0.451	2	2.32	0.02	3	2.83	0.01	2	2.55	0.01
Land ownership: 5th quintile	0	-0.7	0.486	3	2.74	0.01	3	2.66	0.01	3	2.78	0.01
Age: 30–35 years	0	0.2	0.845	-2	-0.71	0.48	1	0.26	0.79	1	1.10	0.27
Age: 35–40 years	2	1.11	0.266	1	0.32	0.75	5	1.44	0.15	4	1.40	0.16
Age: 40–45 years	5	1.78	0.075	17	3.66	0.00	20	4.68	0.00	7	2.07	0.04
Literate but below primary education	-1	-1.62	0.106	-1	-1.43	0.15	-2	-1.60	0.11	-1	-1.64	0.10
Primary and middle education	-2	-2.06	0.039	-4	-2.06	0.04	-5	-2.10	0.04	-4	-2.13	0.03
Secondary and higher secondary	-5	-2.44	0.015	2	0.45	0.65	6	1.69	0.09	-5	-1.79	0.07
Graduate and above	75	10.24	0	117	9.25	0.00	162	14.38	0.00	127	14.35	0.00
Himachal Pradesh	1	0.81	0.417	1	0.81	0.42	1	0.81	0.42	0	0.78	0.44

Table 7.13 continued

Table 7.13 continued

Punjab	1	1.89	0.058	3	2.13	0.03	2	2.09	0.04	-1	-1.66	0.10
Chandigarh	1	1.69	0.09	1	1.78	0.08	1	1.78	0.08	0	0.48	0.63
Uttaranchal	1	1.66	0.098	1	1.49	0.14	0	-0.51	0.61	0	1.12	0.26
Haryana	14	4.53	0	20	4.92	0.00	19	4.93	0.00	11	3.64	0.00
Delhi	9	4.59	0	9	3.25	0.00	11	4.76	0.00	-9	-2.86	0.00
Rajasthan	0	-0.13	0.9	0	0.13	0.89	0	-0.14	0.89	0	0.14	0.89
Uttar Pradesh	0	-0.71	0.48	-1	-0.83	0.41	-3	-0.84	0.40	0	0.25	0.80
Bihar	0	0.45	0.65	0	-0.45	0.65	0	0.23	0.82	0	0.37	0.71
Assam	0	0.15	0.882	0	-0.15	0.88	1	1.25	0.21	0	-0.40	0.69
West Bengal	4	1.78	0.075	2	1.59	0.11	5	1.78	0.08	1	1.45	0.15
Jharkhand	0	-0.16	0.871	2	2.24	0.03	0	-0.25	0.80	1	1.88	0.06
Orissa	0	-0.26	0.795	0	-0.49	0.62	0	-0.52	0.60	0	0.50	0.62
Chhattisgarh	1	2.22	0.027	0	0.45	0.66	-1	-2.18	0.03	0	-0.01	0.99
Madhya Pradesh	0	0.58	0.561	-1	-1.11	0.27	0	0.57	0.57	0	0.91	0.37
Gujarat	1	1.87	0.062	0	0.29	0.77	0	0.56	0.58	2	2.09	0.04
Maharashtra	3	1.95	0.051	-21	-4.35	0.00	10	3.86	0.00	0	0.16	0.88
Andhra Pradesh	-2	-1.62	0.106	-2	-1.54	0.12	0	-0.81	0.42	-1	-1.25	0.21
Karnataka	-2	-2.03	0.042	-2	-1.48	0.14	-1	-1.47	0.14	-1	-1.20	0.23
Kerala	-1	-1.37	0.171	2	1.56	0.12	-8	-1.54	0.12	1	1.04	0.30
Total	106	12.24	0	157	10.90	0.00	232	15.99	0.00	144	15.00	0.00

Source: Author's own calculations from NSS 68th Round data.

attributes difference between HCH males and males from the other groups in their urban RSWE wage rate. The largest contribution to the attribute difference between HCH males and males from the other groups was graduate-level education. The difference in this attribute alone accounted for 74 percent of the total attributes difference between HCH and HCM males (₹75 of ₹106); 75 percent of the total attributes difference between HCH and HCM males (₹117 of ₹157); 70 percent of the total attributes difference between HCH and MOBC (₹162 of ₹232); and 88 percent of the total attributes difference between HCH and SC males (₹127 of ₹144).

7.5. Rural Labor Markets: Discrimination in the National Rural Employment Guarantee Act

From a study covering 555 villages in 11 states across India, the IIDS found that the SC casual labor faced discrimination in accessing employment in farm and non-farm activities in various forms and spheres. Discrimination took the form of denial of employment in some types of work. In the farm sector, they tended to face selective exclusion particularly in harvesting of fruits and vegetables. In the non-farm work, exclusion was fairly common in case of various types of household work because of the notion of impurity and pollution associated with the status of untouchables. "Untouchable" women are rarely employed for cooking, cleaning of food grains and other edibles, and milking of animals. The untouchables from the scavenging community face exclusion because of their occupation of manual scavenging, which is considered unclean and polluting.

Even the erstwhile UPA government's showpiece, National Rural Employment Guarantee Act (NREGA) was not immune from discrimination. It emerged that the SC workers faced delays in issuing job cards and other difficulties, which resulted in lower public employment and wage earning. More than 60 percent of SC respondents reported discriminatory behavior of officials and heads of *panchayat* as the reason for only few days of employment under NREGA. Furthermore, 18 percent of SC workers reported that the *Sarpanch* favored workers from his/her own caste and another 18 percent mentioned that the *Sarpanch* failed to tell them about the timing of NREGA work. Furthermore, the average wage earnings of workers from the SC were lower than that of higher caste labor, although the number of days of public employment in some cases was slightly higher for SC workers as compared to higher caste workers.

The discriminatory behavior by the higher caste officials and heads of the *panchayat* takes various indirect and subtle forms, which ultimately result in low earning for SC workers. They also face discriminatory practices at the workplace, which include prohibition to take drinking water from the common water source; higher caste serving drinking water from a distance; separate eating and drinking arrangements for the SC and higher caste workers at the NREGA work site. Table 7.14 from Sabharwal (2011) details some of these forms of discrimination.

Table 7.14:
Caste-based discrimination in wage labor

Spheres of Exclusion Wage Labor—Farm	Nature and Forms of Discrimination (Identifier)	Consequences of Discrimination
1. Hiring: employment	Complete denial in hiring, exclusion of low caste from certain types of jobs, selective inclusion with unequal hiring terms and conditions with respect to hours of works and other terms, hiring for work which is outside the house, denial of work inside the house, compulsive and forced work governed by traditional caste-related obligations, which involve loss of freedom	Less employment days, loss of freedom which leads to bondage, attachment of family and child labor, income loss, high poverty
2. Wages	Complete denial (wages not paid), unfair inclusion: unequal treatment reflected in lower wages (lower than market wages), irregular interval of payment	Low wages, inequality in wages, income loss, high poverty
3. Work conditions (employer–labor/ between laborers)	Discriminatory or differential behavior toward Scheduled Castes in workplace	Loss of dignity, human rights and high poverty

Source: Sabharwal (2011).

7.6. Conclusions

This chapter attempted to quantify the effects of job reservations in India. A major conclusion of the analysis was that it made no difference to the chances of the men in the sample of being in RSWE whether their attributes were evaluated using HCH or SC coefficients; to put it differently, the results showed that there was no discrimination against SC, vis-à-vis HCH, men in terms of their presence among those in RSWE.

The answer to this counter-intuitive result lies in the reservation of jobs for the SC instituted, as noted above, under the aegis of the Indian constitution. The goal of job reservations in India has been to bring about an improvement in the welfare of those who are, and have been for a long time, economically and socially depressed. A major reason for job reservations was to combat discrimination against persons from the SC who, along with persons from the ST, are arguably the most downtrodden of India's population.

Job reservation cannot alter the employment-related attributes of the SC but, *given those attributes*, it can raise the proportion of persons from the SC who secure RSWE by shifting the coefficients of the employment equations in favor of persons from this group. In this respect, job reservations for the SC has succeeded in neutralizing the discrimination that they undeniably face from other sections of Indian society. For SC men who, for reasons of discrimination, are turned down for RSWE in favor of a HCH man in the private sector, where job reservation does not apply, positive discrimination ensures that there are HCH men who are turned down in favor of SC men in the public sector where job reservations do apply. As our results show, the two effects are self-cancelling: positive discrimination in favor of SC men neutralizes its negative counterpart against SC men. However, in comparison to the other groups, Hindu coefficients were most favorable for being in RSWE or, in other words, *ceteris paribus* our sample of men would have had a *higher* chance of being in RSWE had they *all* been HCH compared to *all* being HOBC, or HCM, or MOBC. To put it differently, compared to HCH men, men from the HOBC, the HCM, and the MOBC were discriminated against in respect of RSWE.

Compared to an absence of discrimination, between men from the HCH and the SC, in respect of *access* to RSWE, there was a considerable discrimination between men from these groups in respect of *remuneration* from RSWE. Of the difference of ₹231 between the HCH and SC male wage rates in RSWE (₹573 and ₹341, respectively), 62 percent was due to a difference in *attributes* between males from the two groups and 38 percent was the result of *unexplained* difference. For Muslim males (both non-OBC and OBC), the contribution of the attributes difference was much higher, 71 percent for non-OBC Muslim and 77 percent for MOBC males whereas, at 55 percent, the contribution of the attributes difference was smallest for OBC Hindu males.

In terms of the important attributes that influenced wage rates, the most important was graduate-level education. The contribution of this attribute alone accounted for 70–88 percent of the total attributes contribution to the RSWE wage rate difference between HCH and non-HCH males. If employees from the non-HCH groups could raise their performance in respect of degree-level education to HCH levels, then much of the difference in RSWE wage rates between them and HCH males due to attribute differences would disappear. However, needless to say, differences in RSWE wages due to discrimination would continue.

Appendix: Multinomial Logit Model Estimates From the Employment Equations

Table A7.1:
MLM estimates prime-age men in the rural sector

	Regular Salaried and Wage Workers			Casual Laborers		
	Relative Risk Ratio	z Value	P > |z|	Relative Risk Ratio	z Value	P > |z|
High-caste Hindus (HCH)	1.027	0.30	0.76	0.914	−1.18	0.24
Non-Muslim OBC (HOBC)	0.948	−0.63	0.53	1.271	3.65	0.00
Non-SC/OBC Muslim (HCM)	0.634	−3.84	0.00	0.921	−0.91	0.37
Scheduled Castes	1.437	4.05	0.00	2.191	11.33	0.00
Land ownership: 2nd quintile	1.059	0.83	0.41	0.893	−2.13	0.03
Land ownership: 3rd quintile	0.847	−2.41	0.02	0.727	−6.01	0.00
Land ownership: 4th quintile	0.583	−8.48	0.00	0.322	−22.26	0.00
Land ownership: 5th quintile Quintile	0.353	−15.92	0.00	0.084	−37.06	0.00
Age: 30–35 years	0.669	−8.32	0.00	0.591	−12.38	0.00

Table A7.1 continued

Table A7.1 continued

Age: 35–40 years	0.636	−9.53	0.00	0.462	−18.27	0.00
Age: 40–45 years	0.661	−8.31	0.00	0.398	−20.36	0.00
Literate but below primary education	0.994	−0.06	0.95	0.718	−5.86	0.00
Primary and middle education	1.439	4.99	0.00	0.535	−14.37	0.00
Secondary and higher secondary	2.849	14.51	0.00	0.324	−22.38	0.00
Graduate and above	10.842	30.23	0.00	0.158	−18.05	0.00
NREG card	0.756	−6.38	0.00	2.185	22.36	0.00
Himachal Pradesh	1.075	0.63	0.53	0.999	−0.01	1.00
Punjab	0.732	−2.50	0.01	0.859	−1.32	0.19
Uttaranchal	0.429	−6.00	0.00	0.664	−3.13	0.00
Haryana	0.433	−7.46	0.00	0.733	−2.88	0.00
Rajasthan	0.644	−4.27	0.00	0.758	−2.87	0.00
Uttar Pradesh	0.283	−14.79	0.00	0.607	−6.58	0.00
Bihar	0.190	−16.18	0.00	0.751	−3.45	0.00
Assam	0.351	−9.73	0.00	0.457	−7.72	0.00
West Bengal	0.359	−10.50	0.00	0.473	−8.70	0.00
Jharkhand	0.266	−9.93	0.00	0.756	−2.70	0.01
Orissa	0.450	−7.99	0.00	0.551	−6.39	0.00
Chhattisgarh	0.522	−5.03	0.00	0.714	−2.74	0.01
Madhya Pradesh	0.330	−10.01	0.00	0.438	−8.49	0.00
Gujarat	0.633	−4.15	0.00	0.540	−5.49	0.00
Maharashtra	0.545	−7.04	0.00	0.853	−1.84	0.07
Andhra Pradesh	0.501	−7.77	0.00	0.469	−9.01	0.00
Karnataka	0.532	−6.14	0.00	0.881	−1.28	0.20
Kerala	0.748	−2.55	0.01	2.053	7.20	0.00
	0.768	−2.04	0.04	3.539	12.40	0.00

Note: 27,857 observations on economically active men, 22–45 years of age.
Pseudo $R^2 = 0.1984$.
Reference categories are: OBC Muslims (MOBC); lowest quintile of land ownership; younger than 30 years; illiterate; Tamil Nadu.

Table A7.2:

MLM estimates for prime-age men in the urban sector

	Regular Salaried and Wage Workers			Casual Laborers		
	Relative Risk Ratio	z Value	P > |z|	Relative Risk Ratio	z Value	P > |z|
High-caste Hindus (HCH)	1.648	6.55	0.00	1.060	0.59	0.56
Non-Muslim OBC (HOBC)	1.525	5.75	0.00	1.849	7.54	0.00

Table A7.2 continued

Table A7.2 continued

Non-SC/OBC Muslim (HCM)	0.980	−0.21	0.83	1.106	0.91	0.37
Scheduled Castes (SC)	2.450	10.87	0.00	3.633	14.42	0.00
Land ownership: 2nd quintile	0.860	−3.14	0.00	1.044	0.72	0.47
Land ownership: 3rd quintile	0.793	−4.10	0.00	0.782	−3.29	0.00
Land ownership: 4th quintile	0.841	−2.30	0.02	0.625	−4.36	0.00
Land ownership: 5th quintile	0.475	−8.89	0.00	0.350	−6.91	0.00
Quintile Age: 30–35 years	0.585	−10.39	0.00	0.491	−10.91	0.00
Age: 35–40 years	0.587	−10.76	0.00	0.389	−14.47	0.00
Age: 40–45 years	0.540	−11.88	0.00	0.326	−15.98	0.00
Literate but below primary education	1.075	0.65	0.52	0.746	−3.06	0.00
Primary and middle education	1.303	3.23	0.00	0.459	−10.63	0.00
Secondary and higher secondary	1.640	6.13	0.00	0.188	−20.76	0.00
Graduate and above	3.645	15.43	0.00	0.049	−21.35	0.00
NREG card	0.738	−1.46	0.15	0.544	−2.12	0.03
Himachal Pradesh	1.012	0.10	0.92	0.256	−8.92	0.00
Punjab	1.063	0.17	0.86	0.077	−2.36	0.02
Chandigarh	0.462	−5.11	0.00	0.233	−6.56	0.00
Uttaranchal	0.826	−1.60	0.11	0.425	−5.44	0.00
Haryana	1.253	1.51	0.13	0.145	−7.55	0.00
Delhi	0.765	−2.41	0.02	0.326	−8.13	0.00
Rajasthan	0.491	−7.39	0.00	0.268	−11.90	0.00
Uttar Pradesh	0.375	−8.26	0.00	0.328	−8.39	0.00
Bihar	0.428	−6.15	0.00	0.199	−8.21	0.00
Assam	0.600	−4.89	0.00	0.408	−7.20	0.00
West Bengal	0.550	−4.51	0.00	0.502	−4.41	0.00
Jharkhand	0.643	−3.34	0.00	0.321	−6.59	0.00

Table A7.2 continued

Table A7.2 continued

Orissa	0.936	−0.41	0.68	0.577	−2.77	0.01
Chhattisgarh	0.469	−7.17	0.00	0.288	−10.03	0.00
Madhya Pradesh	0.987	−0.12	0.90	0.239	−9.56	0.00
Gujarat	0.943	−0.62	0.53	0.377	−8.42	0.00
Maharashtra	0.919	−0.80	0.42	0.419	−6.78	0.00
Andhra Pradesh	0.705	−3.11	0.00	0.602	−3.98	0.00
Karnataka	0.949	−0.41	0.68	1.928	5.03	0.00
Kerala	0.774	−2.06	0.04	3.689	10.17	0.00

Notes: 1. 16,125 observations on employed men, 22–45 years of age.
2. Pseudo $R^2 = 0.1416$.
3. Reference categories are: OBC Muslims (MOBC); lowest quintile of land owner-ship; younger than 30 years; illiterate; Tamil Nadu.

The coefficient estimates in Tables A7.1 and A7.2 are to be interpreted as the *change* in the log risk-ratios, $\log\left[\dfrac{\Pr(Y_i = j)}{\Pr(Y_i = 3)}\right]$, consequent upon a unit change in the value of the associated variable. Positive coefficients imply that the ratio increases and negative coefficients imply that it decreases.[11] Because the community, the education standard, the age, and the state categories in addition to being mutually exhaustive, were also collectively exhaustive, one of each category had to be omitted from the equation in order to avoid multi-collinearity in the presence of the inter-cept term. These omitted categories were the *reference categories*: OBC Muslims, "illiteracy," men under the age of 30 years, and Tamil Nadu were the reference categories for, respectively, social group, education, age, and state. The variables shown in Tables 7.4 and 7.5 are binary variables, taking the value 1 if a man belonged to that category and zero if he did not.

[10] However, the direction of change in the probability of an outcome, consequent upon a unit change in X_{ik}, cannot be inferred from the sign of β_{jk}. The reason is that, in a multi-nomial model, a change in the value of a variable for a person changes the probability of *every* outcome for him/her. Since these changes are constrained to sum to zero, whether the probability of a particular outcome goes up or down depends on what happens to the probabilities of the other outcomes.

8

The Position of Women

8.1. Introduction

Unlike women from other social groups in India, women from the SC face three overlapping disadvantages. First, as women, they face all the attendant difficulties of living in a male patriarchal society. Second, they face the opprobrium that higher-caste Hindu society instinctively heaps upon the lower castes. Third, by virtue of being from the SC they are more likely to be poor. In addition, they are also the victims of various social and religious malpractices, such as *devadasi/jogini* which sexually exploit SC women in the name of religion (Pal and Lal, 2010). Given these disadvantages, the problems of SC women are distinct from, and arguably considerably more severe than, that of higher caste women who are not burdened by perceptions of inferiority and are less likely to be poor.

This chapter examines the experiences of SC women vis-à-vis non-SC women and of SC women vis-à-vis SC men in respect to four areas: their educational attainments, their political voice, their experience of discrimination, and their experience of violence both from their partners and from strangers. Dreze and Sen (2013) have drawn attention to the importance of education in empowering women, of offering them choices in life, and of giving them control over their lives and that of their children. In this regard, SC women are woefully behind women from the higher castes. Another area that empowers women is political voice. We show, using original research, that notwithstanding reserved constituencies for the SC and the ST, most of the SC/ST parliamentary representatives are men and very few are women. Women from the SC also have to bear the humiliation that accompanies their low social status. We document the areas in which SC women face exclusion and discrimination. Lastly, it is almost commonplace for SC women to be the victims of violence at the hands of both SC and non-SC men (Narula, 1999).

8.2. Educational Status of Scheduled Caste Women

Figure 8.1 documents the gender divide in terms of educational level by rural and urban sector for SC and non-SC/ST persons. Although high levels of illiteracy and low educational attainment is a general characteristic of women in India, it is particularly low for SC. At the national level, nearly 44 percent of SC women were illiterate, compared to 23 percent of non-SC/ST women. Only 33 percent SC girls had completed primary level of education, only 12 percent had completed middle school, only 9.2 percent had completed secondary/higher secondary education, and only 2 percent were graduates. In contrast, 21 percent of non-SC/ST girls had completed higher secondary and 10 percent were graduates.

Figure 8.1:
Level of educational attainment by sector and gender in 2009–10

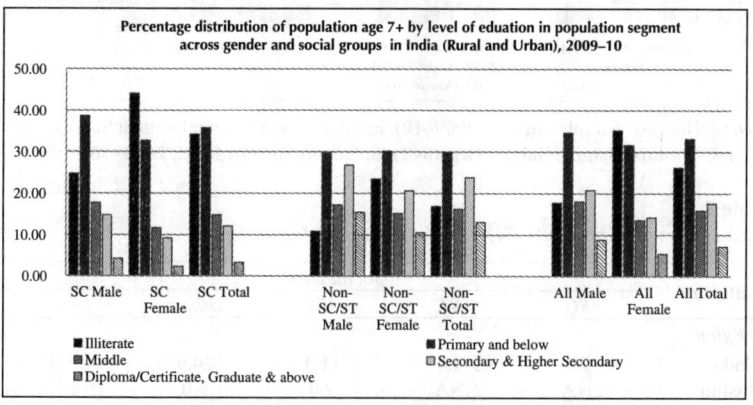

Source: National Sample Survey, (2009–10), Employment & Unemployment Survey: 66th Round, National Sample Survey Organisation, Government of India, 2009–10.

An important aspect of education in an economy that is growing and rapidly modernizing is higher education (HE). The gross enrollment ratio (GER) is a statistical measure for access to education at different levels. Applied to HE, it measures access as a ratio of persons in all age groups enrolled in HE to the total population in age group of 18–23 years. In 2003–04, as per NSS estimates, the GER in HE was about 13.2 percent for India. However, there were significant disparities across social groups. GER was much lower for SC as compared to non-SC/ST, being 7.51 percent and 21.8 percent, respectively. NSS data in Table 8.1 indicate that women belonging to the SC had less access to HE than non-SC/ST women. For instance, in 2003–04, as against the overall average of 11.0 percent for women, GER was 5.6 percent for SC women and 20.0 percent for other women.

Figure 8.2:
Level of educational attainment by social group and gender in 2009–10

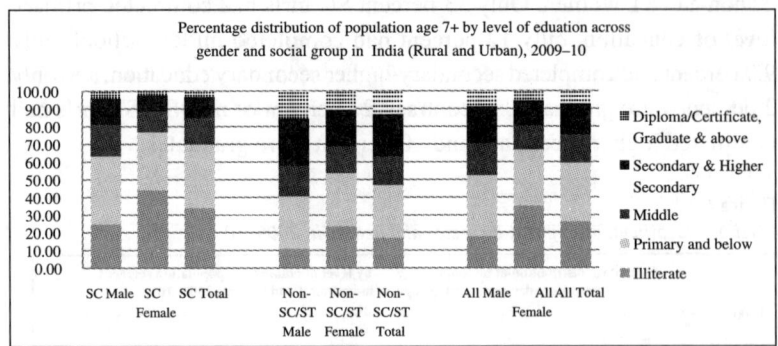

Source: National Sample Survey, (2009–10), Employment & Unemployment Survey: 66th Round, National Sample Survey Organisation, Government of India, 2009–10.

Table 8.1:
Gross enrollment ratio (2003–04) in higher education (percentage)

Category	Social Groups				
	SC	ST	OBC	Others	All
Religion					
Hindu	7.2	4.4	11.3	24.9	13.5
Muslim	NA	NA	7.0	9.0	8.2
Sikh	7.0	NA	NA	20.8	15.6
Females					
Total	5.6	3.2	8.7	20.0	11.0
Rural	2.9	1.8	4.9	9.8	5.4
Hindu	5.3	2.6	8.8	22.6	11.1
Muslim	NA	NA	6.3	7.2	6.8
Sikh	7.1	NA	NA	25.5	18.7
Christian	NA	16.8	NA	42.1	25.3

Source: Thorat (2009a).

8.3. Political Participation by Women: The Status of SC Women in Parliament

The available data on the *Lok Sabha* for the period 1971–2004 reveals the dominance of SC men in politics as compared to SC women. The 15th *Lok Sabha* had a total of 84 SC Members of Parliament (MPs), of whom 72 were men and only 12 were women. However, since 1971, there are more women MPs and, along with that, there has been an improvement in the percentage share of SC/ST women MPs though they continue to be under-represented relative to SC/ST men. For example, the 1971 Lok Sabha had a total of 26 women MPs, of whom six were SC, two were ST, and the remaining 19 were non-SC/ST. Furthermore, the current (15th *Lok Sabha*), which comprises 12 SC/ST women MPs (see Tables 8.2 and 8.3), has the largest number of SC women MPs till date.

Table 8.2:
All-India members of parliament, by caste and gender

Lok Sabha	SC			Others		
	Male	*Female*	*Total*	*Male*	*Female*	*Total*
5th (1971)	86	6	92	400	19	419
6th (1977)	86	0	86	411	19	430
7th (1980)	87	2	89	413	27	430
8th (1984)	80	4	84	403	39	442
9th (1989)	75	4	79	396	22	418
10th (1991)	75	5	80	399	31	440
11th (1996)	77	9	86	398	27	425
12th (1998)	74	10	84	388	32	420
13th (1999)	95	8	103	378	39	417
14th (2004)	67	11	78	395	34	429
15th (2009)	72	12	84	372	40	412

Source: Who's Who Lok Sabha, GoI, 5th to 15th General Elections, www.parlimento-findia.nic.in

Note: The above data show the total number of members elected in the entire tenure of five years. It includes the result of by-elections, re-elections, etc.

Table 8.3:
All-India percentage share of the members of parliament, by caste and gender

Lok Sabha	SC			Others		
	Male	*Female*	*Total*	*Male*	*Female*	*Total*
5th (1971)	93.48	6.52	100.00	95.47	4.53	100.00
6th (1977)	100.00	0.00	100.00	95.58	4.42	100.00
7th (1980)	97.75	2.25	100.00	93.86	6.14	100.00
8th (1984)	95.24	4.76	100.00	91.18	8.82	100.00
9th (1989)	94.94	5.06	100.00	94.74	5.26	100.00
10th (1991)	93.75	6.25	100.00	90.68	7.05	100.00
11th (1996)	89.53	10.47	100.00	93.65	6.35	100.00
12th (1998)	88.10	11.90	100.00	92.38	7.62	100.00
13th (1999)	92.23	7.77	100.00	90.65	9.35	100.00
14th (2004)	85.90	14.10	100.00	92.07	7.93	100.00
15th (2009)	85.71	14.29	100.00	90.29	9.71	100.00

Source: Calculated from Table 8.2.

The number of women MPs was the lowest in the sixth Lok Sabha (the 1977 Janata Party Government), with no SC women MPs, only one from the ST, and 19 non-SC/ST women members. After the 1984 *Lok Sabha*, which had 45 women parliamentarians, women's percentage share declined in the subsequent *Lok Sabha*s till the 13th Lok Sabha of 1999. However, since then, there has been an increase in the number of women parliamentarians. This has also resulted in a slight improvement in the percentage share of SC women parliamentarians, and currently, in the 15th *Lok Sabha*, the representation of women, as noted above, is the highest. However, they continue to be under-represented in the Parliament and constitute only 10 percent of the *Lok Sabha's* members, well below their share in the population and the critical mass of 33 percent.

8.4. Gender- and Caste-based Discrimination Faced by Scheduled Caste Women

In this section, we provide evidence from primary studies on gender- and caste-based discrimination, which SC women face in economic, social, and political spheres. It is this "exclusion-induced deprivation," which differentiates SC women's problems from other women. While there is some systematic evidence of caste and untouchability-based discrimination in social, cultural, and political spheres, there is limited evidence on economic discrimination, which SC women have to face. First, we present evidence on gender discrimination perpetuated by SC men against SC women. Then, we assess the discrimination experienced by SC women economically, socially, and culturally.

8.4.1. Gender-based Discrimination Faced by Scheduled Caste Women

The limited evidence that is available indicates that within the SC community, SC husbands respond to their own oppressed position by violence toward their wives. Not many primary-level studies have been undertaken to examine the issue of patriarchy within the SC community. However, the study sponsored by ADMIM indicates that of the 500 SC women covered in the sample, 43 percent suffered from domestic violence ('Scheduled Caste Women Speak Out', Overview Report: 3). These forms of violence have a strong patriarchal dimension and usually cause physical, sexual, or psychological harm to the victim. SC women recognize the problem of gender exploitation by their men, and therefore, the SC women's movement addresses the issue of patriarchy, which denies these women the opportunity from asserting their choices and participating in decision-making within both the community and the family. The study on violence against SC women, which is supported by the All-India Scheduled Caste Women's Forum, also reveals that SC women face violence in the family.

8.4.2. Caste-based Discrimination in the Economic Sphere

There are very few studies that have been conducted to analyze the nature and form of caste-based discrimination, which SC women face in the economic sphere. Sabharwal and Banerjee (2013) in their pilot study of 216 women with respect to access to the labor market of Delhi found that

SC women were unable to get certain types of employment due to their caste. SC women had difficulties in getting employment for cooking and other household jobs because of the notion of purity and pollution; cooking was mostly done by the upper-caste domestic helpers while sweeping, mopping, and dusting works were performed by lower-caste women (Table 8.4). SC women also had lower average wage earnings as compared to upper-caste women for the same activities of domestic work (Table 8.5).

Table 8.4:
Discrimination in hiring for type of work

Type of Work	Scheduled Caste Women	General Women	Total (N = 216)
Cooking	37.40	62.6	100
Washing utensils	41.0	59.0	100
Washing clothes	57.3	42.7	100
Cleaning (dusting, sweeping, mopping)	62.5	37.5	100

Source: Sabharwal and Banerjee (2013): Data computed from fieldwork, March to May 2013.

A study on midday meal schemes for Rajasthan reported the exclusion of SC as cooks and helpers in almost 60 percent sample villages (Dreze and Goyal, 2003). Similar findings were reported in the studies conducted by Thorat and Lee (2005) (535 villages across MP, Andhra Pradesh, Orissa, Bihar, and UP) and by the IIDS in 2012 in 112 villages across seven states of MP, Jharkhand, Chhattisgarh, Orissa, Bihar, and UP where discrimination in midday meal in schools and anganwadi center (AWC) took the form of not recruiting SC as cook and helper and higher caste refusal to eat if food is cooked by SC cooks.

Table 8.5:
Average wage earnings

Type of Work	Scheduled Castes	General	OBC
Cooking	2,000	3,500	3,000
Washing utensils	500	750	600
Washing clothes	700	1,500	1,000
Dusting, sweeping and mopping	500	1,000	800
Average monthly wages	2,000–3,000	5,000–8,000	3,000–5,000

Source: Sabharwal and Banerjee (2013); data computed from fieldwork, March to May 2013.

Acharya (2010) provides evidence on discriminatory access to SC women and children to primary health services, which in turn leads to lower utilization of health services. She developed an index on one to five scale for the degree of discrimination and found that highest degree of discrimination was reported in the treatment during dispensing medicine followed by diagnostic visit to the doctor (Rajasthan) and conduct of pathological tests (Gujarat). On the other hand, consulting care providers for referral treatment was reported as the area of least discrimination in the scale of one to five. The study indicated that access to information is an area of discrimination as *Scheduled caste*s do not receive any information. This in turn influences their health-seeking behavior and health status. The study reported that health personnel discriminate SC by not visiting their habitations and families. When they do visit, they express discomfort and disrespect for the clients. Further, most health care camps are held in the dominant caste habitations and hence the use by SC communities is restricted. Responses from SC children, in the study, indicate that they would like the health care provider to speak gently using respectful words, consider them equals, spend adequate time, and treat them based on the severity of illness as desirable behaviors (Acharya, 2010).

In another study undertaken by IIDS (2014) on the nature of access and utilization of the *Janani Suraksha Yojana* (JYS) covering 112 villages in seven states (UP, Bihar, West Bengal, Jharkhand, Odisha, Chhattisgarh, and MP) found the following difficulties experienced by SC mothers. The SC mothers reported hurdles in access to government benefits, which included:

1. Health link workers avoid visiting their neighborhood SC localities.
2. They were not informed/ aware of the auxiliary mid-wife timings and village and health nutrition meetings.
3. Often, meetings on health and nutrition in village were conducted in higher-caste neighborhoods, and the lower caste groups were reluctant to attend these meetings.
4. Health care services that required contact between the medical professional and the patient/recipient were impacted negatively, for example, tablets would simply be dropped into the hands of a lower-caste person from a 'contact-safe distance'. SC mothers

indicated that they received less postnatal check-ups and advice, AWWs avoided holding newborn children to weigh them and instead asked mothers to do it, auxiliary nurse midwife avoided holding children's hands for immunization and asked someone from the SC community to dispense polio drops to the SC children.

8.5. Atrocities and Crimes against Scheduled Caste Women

The recorded incidence of atrocities against SC women is much higher than those against non-SC women and may be regarded as a measure of the low status they are accorded in Indian society. SC women are constantly abused and ill treated to remind them of their caste and keep them oppressed. National Crime Record Bureau data showed that the number of registered rape cases increased from 1,000 in 1999 to 1,576 in 2012, amounting to an increase of about 3.5 percent per annum. The official statistics, however, are only the tip of the iceberg. The actual number of cases, many that do not get recorded, is much higher (Pal and Lal, 2010).

The state-wise pattern in Table 8.6 shows that with a national figure of about 6 percent, states like UP, MP, Rajasthan, Kerala, Bihar, and Andhra Pradesh had considerably higher percentage share of rape against SC women as against overall rape cases. Distinctively higher percentage share of rape against SC women in UP indicated the higher vulnerability of SC women to rape in this state.

The form of violence against SC women can be inferred from the primary surveys. A primary-level study conducted by Action Aid in 500 villages across India and an analysis of 1,200 cases (Pal and Lal, 2010) on atrocities against SC women revealed that harassment takes numerous forms: abusive and derogatory language, sexual innuendo, and advances. Pal and Lal (2010) further report that among the total number of cases of atrocities against SC women, rape accounted for the highest percentage, followed by physical assault and molestation. In about one-half of the cases, SC women faced a single form of atrocity (for example, either rape or molestation or physical assault); in about one-third of the cases, they faced double forms of atrocities (for example, kidnapping and rape, physical assault, and murder), and in the remaining cases, more than two forms of atrocities were committed (for example, abduction, rape, and murder; kidnapping, physical assault; and burning to death).

Table 8.6:
State-wise percentage share of rape against scheduled caste women versus all women, 2009

State	All Women	Dalit Women	% Share
Andhra Pradesh	1,188	99	8.3
Bihar	929	90	9.7
Chhattisgarh	976	51	5.2
Gujarat	433	28	6.5
Haryana	603	32	5.3
Karnataka	509	39	7.7
Kerala	568	62	10.9
Madhya Pradesh	2,998	321	10.7
Maharashtra	1,483	105	7.1
Orissa	1,023	63	6.2
Punjab	511	11	2.2
Rajasthan	1,519	163	10.7
Tamil Nadu	596	11	1.8
Uttar Pradesh	1,759	317	18.0
India	21,397	1,346	6.3

Source: National Crime Record Bureau, GOI, 2009.

A primary survey conducted by *Ashraya* Organization about *jogini* estimated the number of *jogini*s in six districts of Andhra Pradesh at around 21,421 (Pal and Lal, 2010: 27). The National Human Rights Commission indicated that Andhra Pradesh had 29,000 *jogini*s (as reported in Hindu; KADAPA, November 23, 2012). A similar practice exists in states like Tamil Nadu, Karnataka, and Maharashtra, where they are designated as *devadasi*s (Pal and Lal, 2010: 27). Following is the story of a girl dedicated as a *jogini*, in her own words:

I was eleven years old when they decided to dedicate me to the goddess. I had no idea what it meant. How could I? The older *jogini*s who had been through this experience, told me to run away. But what could I do? Where could an eleven-year-old girl run to? Where could I hide? So the ceremony took place. I was like a goddess that day. Dressed in wedding-like finery. Flowers and shiny fake jewelry. I felt like a princess. But the old women cried. There were around fifty of them. Old *joginis* who had been used up and thrown out. No one to even give them a meal. Despised and humiliated. Then the men would come and pester me, proposition me. I had no peace. Harassment all day and often at night. It is your duty to come with me, they would insist, after all you are a *jogini*. One day I met the man I loved. He loved me too. We wanted to get married. But the community was furious. 'You can't', they told us. 'The whole village will be cursed. Everyone will die.' ("Human Rights and Dignity of Dalit Women," Report of the Conference at the Hague [2006], P.28; as cited in Pal and Lal [2010]).

8.6. Conclusion

The evidence presented in this chapter indicates that there are similarities as well as differences between the problems faced by SC and non-SC women. Like all women, SC women too suffer from subordination due to the prevalence of a patriarchal system within family, at workplace, and in society at large. Like their poor counterparts from the other women groups, these women also suffer from lack of access to income-earning assets and education, which results in high level of poverty. However, SC women differ from rest of the women insofar as their performance with regard to human development indicators is lower as compared to the rest of the women, and also due to the fact that the causes of a high degree of deprivation suffered by these women lies in their social exclusion. The women who belong to the social grouping of low castes, therefore, suffer from social exclusion and discrimination due to their cultural identity, which other women do not. It is this 'exclusion-induced deprivation' that differentiates the excluded women from rest of the women community. Low-caste women have traditionally faced denial of equal rights in the past which continues in the present, at least in some spheres, if not all. They also tend to become the victims of social and religious practices such as the *devadasi* system, which results in sexual exploitation in the name of religion.

Thus, excluded women are not "just like" the rest of the women. They are also disadvantaged by *who they are*. They suffer from social exclusion, which deprives them of the choices and opportunities to evade poverty and denies them a voice to claim their rights. There is a close interface between patriarchy and social exclusion as they reinforce each other. The women who belong to discriminated groups, therefore, suffer from multiple deprivations associated with gender discrimination, poverty and social exclusion. This chapter has presented selected evidence on the nature and forms of caste-based discrimination suffered by SC women in terms of access to sources of livelihood and social needs. This evidence is, however, very limited, which necessitates study of the nature and forms of discrimination faced by SC women, as women in general, and as SC and poor women in particular.

9

Public Policy: Integrated Child Development (Anganwadi) Services

9.1. Introduction

Launched in October 1975, India's *ICDS* program is its largest national program—and one of the largest such programs in the world—for promoting the health and development of mothers and their children. The scheme is targeted at children below the age of 6 years and their mothers (particularly if they are pregnant and lactating) and the benefits take the form of *inter alia* supplementary nutrition, immunization, regular health checks, referral services, education on nutrition and health, and pre-school learning. In addition, mothers and children are provided with iron, folic acid, vitamin A tablets to combat, respectively, iron deficiency, anemia, and xerophthalmia. The scheme—which is based on the principle that the overall impact of these benefits would be greater if they were provided in an integrated manner, rather than on a piecemeal basis—is administered from a center, called the anganwadi (meaning village courtyard) center—hereafter, AWC—by workers, and their helpers, trained and paid an honorarium under the scheme (Kapil and Pradhan, 1999; Ministry of Women and Child Development, Government of India, http://wcd.nic.in/icds.htm).[1]

Many aspects of the ICDS have been examined by researchers and, in particular, the delivery of specific services (Ghosh, 2006 on feeding practices; Tandon and Gandhi, 1992 on immunization) and the delivery of ICDS services in specific parts of the country (Sundararaman, 2006 on Chhattisgarh; Nayak and Saxena, 2006 on Bihar and Jharkhand; Rajivan, 2006 on Tamil Nadu). However, one aspect of the delivery of ICDS services that has been neglected in the literature is the issue of *who are*

---

[1] These amounted to ₹100 and ₹150 per month for non-matriculate and matriculate workers and ₹35 per month for helpers.

the beneficiaries? Are they mothers (and their children) from deprived groups who, but for the AWCs, might not have received such services and, indeed, might not have been aware of the importance of such services? Or, are they mothers (and children) from more privileged groups who, even in the absence of AWCs, would recognize the importance of such services and have the resources to acquire them from other sources. In both cases, AWCs would add value to the lives of mothers and children but, in the latter situation, they would do so by displacing existing services.

The evidence on social exclusion in relation to the ICDS program is at best mixed and has been summarized by Gill (2012). Three studies of "exclusionary bias" in the delivery of ICDS services (FOCUS, 2009; Mander and Kumaram, 2006; Thorat and Sadana, 2009a) conclude that *locational* factors underpinned, and perpetuated, such bias. First, there was a relative lack of AWCs in SC, ST, and Muslim habitations; second, even in mixed-caste villages, the village AWC was usually not located in the parts in which the deprived groups lived. Although the location of AWCs is an ostensibly neutral factor, Mander and Kumaram (2006) in a study of 14 villages across four states (Andhra Pradesh, Chhattisgarh, Jharkhand, and UP) argued that

> it is not a mere accident that in none of the surveyed mixed-caste villages was the AWC located in the Dalit or adivasi hamlet. The decision to locate not just the AWC, but also other valued institutions and services, in the upper caste so-called "main" village is influenced by the upper caste and class [sic] and politically powerful groups in the village.

However, as FOCUS (2009) showed, ST children in certain sampled districts comprised 27 percent of the total number of children in these districts but as much as 40 percent of the total number of children enrolled in the districts' AWCs. So, even though locational factors might militate against inclusivity, the utilization of ICDS services, as measured by enrollment in AWCs, would suggest that while better location could improve inclusivity, inclusivity itself is not a problem *per se*. On the other hand, Mander and Kumaram (2006) claimed that, in addition to the locational factor (discussed earlier):

> a large number of eligible children from impoverished and food deprived households did not access ICDS services, including supplementary nutrition for infant and small children ... and that the denial of these services is not random or accidental but is frequently the outcome of active social discrimination, based on caste, gender and disability.

Following from this mixed bag of results, some based on data from specific parts of India, the purpose of this chapter is to use all-India data to evaluate the ICDS program from the perspective of inclusivity through: first, econometric estimates regarding the relative strength of the personal and household circumstances of persons in determining the likelihood of utilizing ICDS services; second, estimating the proportion of inter-group differences in utilization rates that is the result of inter-group differences in personal and household characteristics and the residual proportion which is the result of caste/religious identity; and third, suggesting a trade-off between quality and utilization by hypothesizing that the poor quality of ICDS services leads the upper-caste Hindus to exit the ICDS market and seek these services elsewhere.

The evaluation of the ICDS program, as summarized above, is particularly important in the light of the Government of India's view, as articulated in its 11th Five Year Plan, that growth is not perceived as "sufficiently inclusive for many groups, especially Scheduled Castes, Scheduled Tribes, and Minorities" (Planning Commission, 2008). In terms of the Government of India's flagship social welfare programs, of which the ICDS is one (the others being the Total Sanitation Program and the National Rural Health Mission), access to services by people from deprived groups is the key to inclusivity. The observance of inclusion is, of course, exclusion and one of the purposes of this paper is to measure the degree of "exclusionary bias" in the provision of ICDS services or, in other words, to measure the relative access to ICDS services by mothers and children from "deprived" groups, compared to access by those from more "privileged" groups.

The results reported in this chapter are based on data provided by the IHDS for 2005, which asked ever married women between the ages of 15 and 49 (hereafter, "eligible women") about whether they received various types of ICDS services (Desai, Vanneman, and National Council of Applied Economic Research, 2009). There were, in total, 33,482 such women, each woman drawn from a different household, where these (33,482) households were drawn from a variety of social groups and faced different economic circumstances. In addition to information about the women's households, the IHDS also provided information on the circumstances of the women in terms of *inter alia* their age, education level, and number of children. It should be emphasized that this chapter is an analysis of access to ICDS services by women of differing personal and household circumstances. It is not an analysis of their access to health services in general or, about the quality of the health services they accessed or, indeed, about their (and their children's) health outcomes.

9.2. Budgetary Background and Access to ICDS Services

Calculations based on census projections showed that there are 174 million children in the age group of 0–6 years during 2006–07. As Table 9.1 shows, 58.2 million children in the age group of 0–6 years are benefitted from ICDS. Similarly, during 2008–09, there were 177 million children of whom about 72.2 million benefited from ICDS. Though there was an increase in the number of beneficiaries, it still fell short of the children targeted under the ICDS program (Diwakar, 2010).

Table 9.1:
Physical and budgetary performance of ICDS during 11th plan period

Indicators	Unit	End of 10th Plan	11th Plan	
		2006–07	2007–08	2008–09
SNP beneficiaries, children	(in crore)	5.82	6.96	7.22
SNP beneficiaries, mother	(in crore)	1.24	1.47	1.51
Total SNP beneficiaries	(in crore)	7.06	8.43	8.73
Budgetary performance				
Annual outlay	(in ₹100 crore)	40.87	52.93	63.00
Fund released	(in ₹100 crore)	42.11	51.70	62.95
Budgeted cost per beneficiary per day (SNP and general)	(in ₹)	1.59	1.72	1.98
Fund released for SNP	(in ₹100 crore)	1,519	2,062	2,281
Fund released (SNP per beneficiary per day cost for 365 days)	(in ₹)	0.59	0.67	0.72

Source: Calculated using data from Ministry of Women and Child development, Union Budget and MPR March 2009.

According to the 11th plan period, ₹8,480 crore (1 crore = 10 million) was allocated annually for the ICDS services. However, the actual allocation during 2007–08 and 2008–09 was only ₹5,200 crore and

₹6,300 crore, respectively. Thus, there was a shortfall of 39 percent in funding in 2007–08 and 26 percent in 2008–09. Moreover, of the total amount released ₹1,519 crore in 2007–08 (28.7 percent) and ₹2,281 crore in 2008–09 (34.9 percent) was given for the Special Nutrition Program (SNP), while the rest was allocated for non-food components. In case of Supplementary Nutrition Program, 50 percent had to be shared by the state government.

According to its norms, the government had to spend ₹2 per day for children and ₹2.30 per day for pregnant women and nursing mothers for SNP till 2008. Later, it was revised to ₹4 for children and ₹5 for pregnant women and nursing mothers, respectively.[2] The fund released for SNP by the central government shows that only ₹0.59 was provided per beneficiary per day in 2006–07 and it increased to ₹0.72 in 2008–09.[3] There was clearly a huge shortfall in the financial allocation of SNP for the children as per norms, and it was the major reason for the poor quality of food (Diwakar, 2011). Table 9.2 shows that expenditure on ICDS was only 0.8 percent of the total union budget and 0.12 percent of GDP.

Table 9.2:
Share of ICDS allocation in GDP and annual budget

Expenditure Heads (in crores)	2005–06	2006–07	2007–08	2008–09
Expenditure on ICDS	₹3,326	₹4,210	₹5,170	₹6,294
Total union Budget	₹508,705	₹581,637	₹709,373	₹750,884
Expenditure as percentage of annual union budget	0.65	0.72	0.73	0.84
GDP at current price	₹3,586,744	₹4,129,173	₹472,3400	₹5,426,277
Expenditure as percentage of GDP	0.09	0.10	0.11	0.12

Source: Calculated using data from HAQ Center for Child Development (2009), Ministry of Women and Child Development and Economic survey.

[2] F.NO.5-9/2005/ND/Tech (Vol. III). Govt. of India. Ministry of Women and Child Development. Date. February 24, 2009.

[3] The central government provides fund from both SNP and non-SNP components. The total sanction amount per beneficiary (both SNP and non-SNP) of ₹1.59 increased to ₹1.98. Of the total sanction amount for SNP component, the central government's sanction of ₹0.59 increased to ₹0.72. The remaining ₹1 went for non-SNP component. The SNP component is supposed to be shared equally between the state and the central governments.

Against this budgetary background for ICDS, The IHDS distinguished between six different types of ICDS services, which (eligible) women could have received from AWCs:

1. Benefits while pregnant or lactating. These included supplementary feeding, prophylaxis against vitamin A deficiency and control of nutritional anemia. Also included were the immunization of pregnant women against tetanus and nutritional and health education to build the capacity of women to look after themselves and their children.
2. Immunization of child/children against six major diseases: polio, diphtheria, pertussis, tetanus, tuberculosis, and measles.
3. Health checks for children including management of malnutrition, treatment of diarrhea, de-worming, and distribution of medicines. Also included were the antenatal care of expectant, and postnatal care of nursing mothers.
4. Supplementary feeding support for children for 300 days in a year with a view to narrowing the gap between the nationally recommended calorific intake and that received by the children.
5. Monitoring children's growth, with sick or malnourished children and children with disabilities being referred to the primary health center.
6. Providing children with pre-school education. In addition to preparing children for primary school, this service also offers substitute care to young children thus freeing older siblings—particularly girls—to attend school.

The eligible women in the IHDS were asked whether they had received each of the benefits, enumerated above, for (i) their *last* birth and (ii) their *next* to last birth. Since the number of valid responses to these questions was considerably greater in respect to last births, compared to next to last births, it is the answers pertaining to last births that are analyzed in this paper.

Table 9.3 shows that of the 8,755 (eligible) women who gave valid responses to the question "When you were pregnant and lactating did you receive benefits from the AWC such as immunization, supplementary food, etc.?" only 20.5 percent answered in the affirmative. Similarly,

Table 9.3:
Anganwadi benefits received by mother and last born child, by social group

Benefit Type↓	Proportion of Mothers in Group Receiving Benefit (%)								
	Brahmin/High-Caste Hindu	SC	ST (Hindu)	ST (non-Hindu)	Hindu OBC	Muslim (OBC)	Muslim (Upper Class)	Other Groups	Total
While pregnant/lactating	16.5 (2,100)	25.0 (2,368)	37.3 (668)	26.6 (229)	22.0 (3,667)	12.6 (754)	9.7 (880)	6.6 (347)	20.5 (8,755)
Child immunized	20.7 (2,060)	27.8 (2,395)	48.0 (757)	38.6 (254)	29.6 (3,555)	17.9 (726)	9.8 (815)	9.5 (315)	26.2 (10,877)
Child's health checked	17.0 (2,038)	21.5 (2,377)	34.5 (741)	20.6 (253)	21.4 (3,529)	13.2 (722)	10.1 (812)	8.4 (311)	19.7 (10,783)
Child's food received	17.5 (2,035)	26.2 (2,376)	38.0 (739)	31.0 (252)	22.8 (3,516)	12.7 (718)	11.1 (813)	4.5 (311)	21.7 (10,760)
Child's growth monitored	18.2 (2,037)	25.0 (2,368)	37.4 (738)	23.7 (253)	23.9 (3,513)	11.1 (715)	10.0 (812)	6.8 (310)	21.6 (10,746)
Early/pre-school education received	9.4 (2,031)	9.8 (2,355)	12.4 (735)	11.6 (251)	10.3 (3,501)	5.5 (713)	4.9 (810)	2.3 (308)	9.2 (10,704)

Source: IHDS.

Notes: Ever married women between 15 and 49 years of age. Hereafter, "eligible women."
Benefits refer to last birth child.

Figures in parentheses refer to the *total* number of valid responses to the question: "Did you or your child receive this benefit from the anganwadi centre?"

only 26.2 percent of 10,877 women said their (last) child had been immunized at the AWC; only 19.7 percent of 10,783 women said their (last) child's health had been checked at the AWC; only 21.7 percent of 10,760 women said their (last) child had received food from the AWC; only 21.6 percent of 10,746 women said their (last) child's growth had been monitored at the AWC; and only 9.2 percent of 10,704 women said their (last) child had received pre-school education at the AWC. So, approximately one in five mothers said they had received services 1–5 above and less than 1 in 10 said that their child had received pre-school education.[4] These figures are consistent with those from other sources. For example, Sinha (2006) estimated that only 22 percent of India's young children were being served by the ICDS program though she did not provide details by type of benefit.

Table 9.3 also shows that the receipt of benefits varied according to social group. ST Hindu women had the highest rate of utilization (for example, 48 percent of the children of ST Hindu women were immunized at the AWCs) followed by SC and then by ST non-Hindu women (for example, 27.8 percent of the (last born) children of SC women and 38.6 percent of the (last born) children of ST non-Hindu women were immunized at the AWCs). At the other end of the scale, the lowest rates of utilization of AWC benefits were by women who were: Muslim (both from the OBC and from the upper classes), brahmin or HCH and other social groups like Christians, Sikhs, and Jains.[5] So, while it was laudable that the highest rates of utilization of AWC benefits were by SC and ST women, it was worrying that Muslim women from the OBC exhibited such a low rate of utilization compared to, say, HOBC.[6]

A study conducted by the IIDS in four states—UP, MP, Bihar, and West Bengal—covering 895 respondents, corroborates this finding by showing that, compared to upper-caste Hindu mothers, ICDS participation was higher

[4] This last point is particularly worrying since the government describes pre-school education as the "backbone of the ICDS program." See http://wcd.nic.in/icds.htm (last accessed on December 24, 2013).

[5] These figures are also consistent with those from other sources: for example, Thorat and Sadana (2009a), using National Family Health Survey data, showed that 36 percent of SC, and 50 percent of ST children, received at least one service from an AWC, compared to 30 percent of OBC and 28 percent of "other" children.

[6] For example, 29.6 percent of the last born children of Hindu OBC mothers compared to only 17.9 percent of the last born children of Muslim OBC mothers were immunized at the AWCs.

for SC and ST mothers but lower for Muslim mothers. According to this study, 69 percent of Muslim mothers, compared to 78 percent of Hindu mothers, utilized ICDS services provided for children up to 3 years of age and 76 percent of Muslim mothers, compared to 83 percent Hindu mothers, utilized services provided for children in the 3–6 years age group.

Some of the difficulties that Muslim mothers faced in accessing ICDS services also applied to SC and ST mothers. For example, about 38 percent of Muslim mothers complained that AWC workers avoided visiting their locality, which resulted in a lack of information about services available at the AWC. The Human Development Sector (2004), in a report for the World Bank, reported that the community or caste of the AWC worker affected access: in one case cited, a worker was averse to having SC children come to the AWC because her father-in-law objected to the presence of lower-caste children.

In addition, because of the location of the AWC in parts of the village where the upper castes lived (see Mander and Kumaram, 2006), mothers from vulnerable groups had to travel through unfriendly areas to reach the school. It was one thing to brave this journey for the occasional visit to the AWC—to have the child immunized, to have his/her health checked or growth monitored—but it was quite another thing to have to suffer this journey twice daily. Consequently, mothers from vulnerable groups opted out of sending their children to AWCs for pre-school education.

However, overlaying these difficulties faced by mothers from all the vulnerable groups in accessing ICDS services, patriarchal restrictions on the mobility of Muslim women outside the family home, unaccompanied by another household member, were a specific reason for the poor utilization of ICDS services by Muslim mothers. Although SC mothers also had difficulty accessing AWC services—through, for example, the reluctance of AWC workers to visit SC hamlets—they did not, experience any familial restraints on their mobility outside the home. Consequently, by going out of the family home (perhaps, for work), SC mothers were able to acquire information themselves about ICDS services without the intermediation of AWC workers. On the other hand, Muslim mothers, who lacked this mobility, were much more reliant on visits by AWC workers for such information and this restricted their access to ICDS services.

Table 9.4 shows that the lowest rate of utilization of AWC benefits was by well-educated women (Matric or above)[7] with utilization rates by women with zero years, or 1–5 years, or 6–10 years of schooling being roughly similar. Table 9.5 shows that women aged 15–20 years had the highest utilization rate, followed by women aged 21–30 years and with a sharp fall in utilization rates for older women. Table 9.6 shows that poorer women (in the lowest two quintiles of household income) had markedly higher rates of utilization than women from more affluent (quintiles 4 and 5) households. Table 9.7 shows that the women in the southern, western, and northern regions of India had much higher rates of utilization than women living in the central or eastern regions. Lastly, Table 9.8 shows that the utilization rates of AWC benefits was much higher among rural, compared to urban, women.

Table 9.4:
Anganwadi *benefits received by mother and last born child, by education of mother**

| Benefit Type↓ | Proportion of Mothers Receiving Benefit by Years of Schooling (%) | | | | |
	Zero Years	1–5 Years	6–10 Years	> 10 Years	Total
While pregnant/lactating	21.6 (4,543)	24.0 (1,636)	22.0 (3,274)	10.5 (1,560)	20.5 (11,013)
Child immunized	28.6 (4,579)	31.3 (1,644)	26.2 (3,178)	12.7 (1,476)	26.2 (10,877)
Child's health checked	20.4 (4,535)	23.6 (1,639)	20.7 (3,146)	10.9 (1,463)	19.7 (10,783)
Child's food received	24.0 (4,522)	25.5 (1,634)	21.6 (3,141)	10.7 (1,463)	21.7 (10,760)
Child's growth monitored	22.5 (4,515)	25.7 (1,630)	22.8 (3,140)	11.6 (1,461)	21.6 (10,746)
Early/pre-school education received	9.2 (4,494)	11.8 (1,618)	10.0 (3,135)	4.7 (1,457)	9.2 (10,704)

Source: IHDS.
Notes: * Ever married women between 15 and 49 years of age, hereafter, "eligible women." Benefits refer to last birth child.
Figures in parentheses refer to the *total* number of valid responses to the question: "Did you or your child receive this benefit from the AWC?"

[7] "Matric" is a term commonly used in India to refer to the final year of high school, which ends at 10th standard (10th grade); the qualification received after passing the "matriculation exams," usually at the age of 15–16 years, is referred to as "Matric (passed)."

Table 9.5:

Anganwadi *benefits received by mother and last born child, by age of mother**

Benefit Type↓	Proportion of Mothers Receiving Benefit by Age Group (%)				
	15–20	21–30	31–40	41–50	Total
While pregnant/lactating	25.9	23.9	16.4	17.5	20.5
	(911)	(7,407)	(2,460)	(235)	(11,013)
Child immunized	31.9	26.8	22.7	19.0	26.2
	(928)	(7,344)	(2,373)	(232)	(10,877)
Child's health checked	24.5	20.1	17.1	14.0	19.7
	(929)	(7,272)	(2,353)	(229)	(10,783)
Child's food received	24.5	22.3	18.9	19.8	21.7
	(926)	(7,259)	(2,348)	(227)	(10,760)
Child's growth monitored	25.2	22.2	18.8	18.1	21.6
	(925)	(7,249)	(2,345)	(227)	(10,746)
Early/pre-school education received	8.1	9.2	9.9	7.0	9.2
	(913)	(7,223)	(2,340)	(228)	(10,704)

Source: IHDS.

Notes: *Ever married women between 15 and 49 years of age, hereafter, "eligible women." Benefits refer to last birth child.

Figures in parentheses refer to the *total* number of valid responses to the question: "Did you or your child receive this benefit from the AWC?"

Table 9.6:

Anganwadi *benefits received by mother and last born child, by household income**

Benefit Type↓	Proportion of Mothers Receiving Benefit by Quintile of Household Income (%)					
	Q1	Q2	Q3	Q4	Q5	Total
While pregnant/lactating	25.3	24.4	21.8	18.6	13.5	20.5
	(1,790)	(2,189)	(2,298)	(2,247)	(2,301)	(10,825)
Child immunized	32.6	31.6	26.0	23.3	18.5	26.2
	(1,855)	(2,198)	(2,245)	(2,182)	(2,223)	(10,703)
Child's health checked	23.1	23.7	19.4	18.4	14.5	19.7
	(1,838)	(2,181)	(2,230)	(2,167)	(2,194)	(10,610)
Child's food received	27.3	27.6	21.7	19.2	13.9	21.7
	(1,837)	(2,174)	(2,223)	(2,163)	(2,190)	(10,573)
Child's growth monitored	26.6	27.4	21.5	19.1	14.6	21.7
	(1,829)	(2,175)	(2,218)	(2,160)	(2,191)	(10,573)
Early/pre-school education received	10.1	11.7	9.5	8.6	6.2	9.2
	(1,818)	(2,169)	(2,213)	(2,152)	(2,180)	(10,532)

Source: IHDS.

Notes: *Ever married women between 15 and 49 years of age, hereafter, "eligible women." Benefits refer to last birth child.

Figures in parentheses refer to the *total* number of valid responses to the question: "Did you or your child receive this benefit from the AWC?"

Table 9.7:
Anganwadi *benefits received by mother and last born child, by region**

Benefit Type↓	Proportion of Mothers Receiving Benefit by Quintile of Household Income (%)					
	Central	South	West	East	North	Total
While pregnant/ lactating	12.0 (4,125)	33.8 (2,238)	29.6 (1,555)	15.6 (1,392)	25.9 (917)	21.2 (10,227)
Child immunized	20.0 (4,102)	34.5 (2,043)	39.6 (1,436)	24.7 (1,493)	30.1 (1,049)	26.2 (10,123)
Child's health checked	14.6 (4,062)	27.6 (2,026)	34.7 (1,427)	13.8 (1,483)	21.5 (1,048)	20.7 (10,046)
Child's food received	17.0 (4,049)	29.3 (2,022)	25.3 (1,418)	21.4 (1,485)	29.5 (1,048)	22.6 (10,022)
Child's growth monitored	17.7 (4,043)	26.4 (2,017)	32.5 (1,420)	19.9 (1,481)	25.0 (1,047)	22.7 (10,008)
Early/pre-school education received	5.2 (4,034)	16.4 (2,006)	16.2 (1,417)	4.8 (1,476)	10.8 (1,037)	9.5 (9,970)

Source: IHDS.
Notes: *Ever married women between 15 and 49 years of age, hereafter, "eligible women." Benefits refer to last birth child.
Figures in parentheses refer to the *total* number of valid responses to the question: "Did you or your child receive this benefit from the AWC?"

Table 9.8:
Anganwadi *benefits received by mother and last born child, by location**

Benefit Type↓	Proportion of Mothers Receiving Benefit by Location			
	Rural	Urban (Slum)	Urban (Non-Slum)	Total
While pregnant/lactating	26.2 (7,142)	9.5 (222)	9.3 (3,461)	20.5 (10,825)
Child immunized	32.7 (7,314)	19.3 (233)	11.6 (3,156)	26.2 (10,703)
Child's health checked	24.4 (7,255)	15.5 (233)	9.0 (3,122)	19.7 (10,610)
Child's food received	27.9 (7,234)	13.4 (232)	8.1 (3,121)	21.8 (10,587)
Child's growth monitored	27.3 (7,222)	15.1 (232)	9.1 (3,119)	21.8 (10,573)
Early/pre-school education received	11.3 (7,185)	8.2 (232)	4.4 (3,115)	9.2 (10,532)

Source: IHDS.
Notes: *Ever married women between 15 and 49 years of age, hereafter, "eligible women." Benefits refer to last birth child.
Figures in parentheses refer to the *total* number of valid responses to the question: "Did you or your child receive this benefit from the AWC?"

9.3. Estimating the Strength of Factors Influencing the Utilization of ICDS Services

Given that the utilization rates of ICDS services differed between mothers from different caste/religious groups (Table 9.3), and differed also between mothers of different economic/educational/age-related/locational attributes (Tables 9.4–9.8), this section estimates the relative strength of the different factors that exercised a significant influence on the utilization of ICDS services and, in particular, it enquires whether, *after controlling for the non-caste/religion factors*, there was still significant correlation between the mothers' caste/religion and their utilization rates?

The answers to these questions were provided by estimating *logit* equations for each of the six ICDS services provided through the AWCs—namely benefits to lactating mothers, children's immunization, children's health monitoring, children's supplementary, children's growth monitoring, and early education—with the dependent variable for each equation taking the value 1 if the mother utilized that benefit and 0 if she did not.[8] It should be emphasized that in estimating the logit model, it was not possible, for reasons of multicollinearity, to include *all* the categories with respect to the variables: the category that was omitted for a variable is referred to as the *reference category* (for that variable). The explanatory variables for the equations were:

1. *The mother's social group*: Christians, Sikhs, and Jains; SC; ST; OBC Hindu; OBC Muslim; upper-caste Muslim. The reference category was "upper-caste Hindus."
2. The *household income* of the mother, as defined by the quintile of *total* household income, with mothers in households whose income was in the fifth (highest) quintile being the reference category.
3. The *principal source* of the mother's household income: Agriculture, laborer, salary, with mothers in households whose principal source of income was trade comprising the reference category.

---

[8] The logit equation is $\dfrac{\Pr(\text{Utilization}_j = 1)}{\Pr(\text{Utilization}_j = 0)} = \exp\{\sum_{k=1}^{K} X_{jk}\beta_j\} = \exp\{z_j\}$ for M coefficients, $\beta_j, j = 1 \ldots$ M and for observations on K variables.

4. The mother's *age group*: 15–20 years, 21–30 years, 31–40 years, with mothers aged 41–50 comprising the reference category.

5. The number of *years of schooling* of the mother: Zero years, 1–5 years, 6–10 years, with mothers with over 10 years schooling comprising the reference category.

6. The mother's *region of residence*: South (Andhra Pradesh, Karnataka, Kerala, and Tamil Nadu); west (Gujarat and Maharashtra); east (Orissa, West Bengal, Assam, and the North-East), north (Jammu and Kashmir, Himachal Pradesh, Uttarakhand, Punjab, Haryana, and Delhi). The central region (Bihar, MP, Rajasthan, UP, Chhattisgarh, and Jharkhand) was the reference category.

7. Nature of *residential area*: Urban non-slum; urban slum; and rural, with urban non-slum as the reference category.

A natural question to ask from the logit model is how the probability of utilizing a particular service would *change* in response to a change in the value of one of the variables. These probabilities are termed *marginal probabilities*. The marginal probability associated with a variable refers to the *change* in the outcome probability consequent upon a unit change in the value of the variable, *the values of the other variables remaining unchanged.*[9] For discrete variables (as, indeed, are all the variables reported above), the unit change in the value of a variable refers to a move from a situation in which the variable takes the value zero to a situation in which the variable takes the value unity, the values of the other variables remaining unchanged.[10] Therefore, the marginal probability of an SC mother utilizing a particular ICDS service is:

The probability of utilizing the service when *all* the mothers are from the SC
less
The probability of utilizing the service when *all* of the mothers are from the reference category (upper-caste Hindus), with *all* the values for the other variables (income, education, etc.) held constant at their mean values

---

[9] More formally, $\Pr(\text{Utilization}_j = 1) = e^z / (1 + e^z)$ and the marginal probability with respect to variable k is: $\dfrac{\partial \Pr(\text{Utilization}_j = 1)}{\partial X_{jk}}$

[10] In the calculations reported here, the values of the other variables were held *at their mean values* in the sample.

These marginal probabilities are reported in Table 9.9. So, reading across the relevant row of Table 9.9, remembering that the comparator is mothers from the reference group of upper-caste Hindus, the marginal probabilities for SC mothers were + 6 points for lactating mothers, +6 points for immunization, + 4 points for child's health check, + s5 points for child's food, +5 points for growth monitoring, and no change for early education. The corresponding figures for ST were higher: + 14, + 21, + 12, +13, and +11 points for, respectively, lactating mothers, immunization, child's health check, child's food, and child's growth monitoring. Again, the marginal probability associated with early education was zero.

In contrast to the take-up of ICDS services by SC and ST mothers, upper-caste Muslim mothers (compared to mothers from the reference group of upper-caste Hindus) were less likely to avail of *all* ICDS services. The marginal probabilities of upper-caste Muslim mothers were –5 points for lactating mothers, –11 points for immunization, –4 points for child's health checks, –6 points for child's food, –7 points for growth monitoring, and –2 points for early education. Similarly, OBC Muslim mothers (compared to mothers from the reference group of upper-caste Hindus) were also less likely to avail of *some* ICDS services. The (statistically significant) marginal probabilities of OBC Muslim mothers were –3 points for lactating mothers, –4 points for child's food, –6 points for growth monitoring, and –3 points for early education.

In summary, the results detailed in Table 9.9 show—*after controlling for other factors*[11]—the increase in the likelihood of utilizing specific ICDS services was highest for ST mothers, next highest for SC mothers, next highest for Hindu OBC mothers, next highest for upper-caste Hindu mothers, and the lowest for Muslims. So, in terms of reaching mothers from vulnerable groups, the evidence presented here suggests that the ICDS program is tilted in favor of mothers and children from the ST and the SC. However, a worrying feature is that the likelihood of utilizing ICDS services by Muslim mothers was lower than the corresponding likelihood for Hindus. For example, as Table 9.9 shows, the probabilities of Muslim mothers—upper class or OBC—using all or some of the various ICDS services was significantly lower than that for upper-caste Hindu mothers.

---

[11] These were mother's education, household income, main source of household income, age, region of residence, and rural/urban location.

Table 9.9:

Marginal probabilities from logit estimates of AWC benefits (10,573 observations)

	Lactating Mothers' Benefits			Child Immunized			Child's Health Checked			Food Given For Child			Child's Growth Monitored			Early Education		
	dy/dx	Z	P > z %	dy/dx	z	P > z %	dy/dx	z	P > z %	dy/dx	z	P > z %	dy/dx	z	P > z %	dy/dx	z	P > z %
Social group of eligible woman																		
Christians, Sikhs, Jains, and others	-0.09	-5.7	0	-0.09	-3.8	0	-0.07	-3.3	0	-0.13	-8.8	0	-0.10	-5.6	0	-0.05	-7.1	0
Scheduled Castes	0.06	4.5	0	0.06	3.8	0	0.04	3.1	0	0.05	3.4	0	0.05	3.4	0	0.00	-0.5	62
Scheduled Tribes	0.14	6.8	0	0.21	9.3	0	0.12	5.9	0	0.13	6.4	0	0.11	5.6	0	0.01	0.7	50
Hindu OBC	0.03	2.7	1	0.07	5.4	0	0.03	2.6	0	0.03	2.4	2	0.04	3.2	0	0.00	-0.8	45
Muslim OBC	-0.03	-1.7	8	0.00	-0.1	90	-0.02	-1.0	0	-0.04	-2.6	1	-0.06	-3.8	0	-0.03	-3.6	0
Muslim, upper class	-0.05	-3.4	0	-0.11	-6.8	0	-0.04	-2.4	0	-0.06	-3.8	0	-0.07	-4.7	0	-0.02	-2.6	1
Household income of eligible woman																		
Household income quintile 1	0.03	1.9	6	0.02	1.1	26	0.00	0.2	1	0.03	1.8	7	0.03	1.9	6	0.01	0.9	37
Household income quintile 2	0.03	2.1	3	0.03	1.9	6	0.02	1.4	0	0.04	3.0	0	0.05	3.3	0	0.02	2.5	1
Household income quintile 3	0.03	2.2	3	0.01	0.4	70	0.00	-0.1	1	0.02	1.3	20	0.02	1.3	19	0.01	1.3	18
Household income quintile 4	0.02	1.3	21	0.00	0.1	89	0.00	0.4	1	0.02	1.4	17	0.01	1.0	31	0.01	1.1	27
Main income source of household																		
Agriculture	0.04	3.3	0	0.07	4.5	0	0.05	3.6	0	0.06	3.8	0	0.05	3.6	0	0.02	2.3	2
Laborer	0.03	2.2	3	0.01	0.9	36	0.02	1.8	0	0.04	3.3	0	0.04	2.7	1	0.01	1.4	16
Salaried	-0.01	-0.9	35	-0.03	-1.9	6	-0.03	-2.5	0	-0.01	-0.9	37	-0.02	-1.7	9	-0.01	-1.0	34

Table 9.9 continued

Table 9.9 continued

Age group of eligible woman																		
15–20 years	0.01	0.4	69	0.08	2.0	5	0.06	1.6	0	0.00	0.0	99	0.02	0.6	57	-0.01	-0.8	43
21–30 years	0.00	0.2	88	0.06	2.0	5	0.04	1.4	0	0.01	0.4	69	0.02	0.6	55	0.01	0.3	74
31–40 years	-0.02	-0.8	44	0.04	1.2	24	0.03	1.0	0	-0.01	-0.3	78	0.00	0.1	90	0.03	1.2	23
Education of eligible woman																		
No schooling	0.07	4.5	0	0.12	6.9	0	0.06	3.6	0	0.07	4.1	0	0.04	2.6	1	0.03	3.3	0
1–5 years of schooling	0.10	4.8	0	0.17	7.2	0	0.10	4.8	0	0.10	4.7	0	0.08	4.2	0	0.07	4.1	0
6–10 years of schooling	0.07	4.6	0	0.11	5.7	0	0.06	3.9	0	0.07	4.3	0	0.07	4.2	0	0.04	3.3	0
Region of eligible woman																		
South	0.30	20.4	0	0.24	16.3	0	0.20	13.9	0	0.19	13.3	0	0.14	10.2	0	0.15	12.1	0
West	0.24	14.4	0	0.29	16.4	0	0.26	15.5	0	0.13	8.0	0	0.20	11.9	0	0.14	9.8	0
North	0.23	10.6	0	0.21	10.4	0	0.13	7.2	0	0.19	10.1	0	0.13	7.1	0	0.09	5.7	0
East	0.06	3.8	0	0.09	5.4	0	0.00	0.2	1	0.06	4.1	0	0.04	2.7	1	0.00	-0.3	0
Urban/rural																		
Rural	0.13	16.6	0	0.16	16.5	0	0.12	14.2	0	0.15	18.3	0	0.14	15.9	0	0.05	9.4	0
Urban slum	-0.04	-1.5	15	0.06	1.7	8	0.05	1.4	0	0.06	1.7	9	0.06	1.5	13	0.04	1.6	12

Source: Author's own calculations from IHDS data.

Notes: *Reference Categories*. Social Group: High-caste Hindus; Household income: quintile 5. Income by Source: Trade. Education: Over 10 years schooling. Age: 41–50 years. Region: Central. Location: Urban non-slum.

Table 9.9 also shows that mothers whose main source of household income was agriculture or labor work were *more* likely to access all ICDS services compared to mothers whose main source of household income was from other sources; conversely, mothers whose main source of household income was a regular salary were *less* likely to access ICDS services compared to mothers whose main source of household income was from non-salaried sources. Once the source of income had been accounted for, the household income of the mothers (with the richest households as the reference category) did not exert a significant effect on their likelihood of accessing ICDS services except that: (i) the poorest mothers (those whose household incomes were in the bottom two quintiles) were more likely to obtain supplementary nutrition for their children from the AWCs, relative to mothers from better off households and (ii) mothers whose household incomes were in the bottom three quintiles were more likely to access ICDS services while they were lactating.

While the age of the mother was not, in general, a significant factor in affecting the likelihood of her accessing ICDS services, her level of education did play a role. Compared to mothers with more than 10 years of schooling, mothers with fewer years of schooling (6–10, 1–5, none) were more likely to access all the ICDS services. However, in the latter category, there was hardly any difference between mothers with different levels of schooling (6–10, 1–5, none) in their respective likelihoods of accessing ICDS services.

In the context of region, compared to mothers living in the central region (which was the reference region), mothers living in the south of India had the highest likelihood of accessing ICDS services, followed by mothers living in the west and the north of India. In the context of rural/urban location, compared to mothers in urban areas, rural mothers were much more likely to access ICDS services: by 13.1 points for lactating mothers, by 15.8 points for immunization; by 11.8 points for child's health check; by 15.5 points for child's food; by 13.9 points for growth monitoring; and by 5.0 points for early education.

9.3.1. *Caste/Religion-based Probabilities of Accessing ICDS Services*

The basic question that the logit model of income distribution posed was "what is the probability that a mother, with a particular set of characteristics, will *ceteris paribus* access a particular type of ICDS service?" This probability would depend upon the mother's caste/religion and upon her non-caste factors. In this section, we set out a methodology for isolating the probability of accessing an ICDS service, *which depends solely upon caste/religion* and we term these probabilities the *caste/religion-based probabilities* of accessing ICDS services.

In order to derive these structural probabilities to answer these questions, we evaluated the following *counterfactual* scenarios:

1. We first treat *all* the mothers in the sample as HCH. Suppose that, under this scenario, p_j^{UCH} is the average probability of a mother accessing ICDS service j, $j = 1, 2, 3, 4, 5, 6$.

2. Next, we treat *all* the mothers in the sample as upper-caste Muslims. Suppose that, under this scenario, p_j^{UCM} is the average probability of a mother accessing ICDS service j, $j = 1, 2, 3, 4, 5, 6$.

3. Next, we treat *all* the mothers in the sample as OBC Hindus. Suppose that, under this scenario, p_j^{OBCH} is the average probability of a mother accessing ICDS service j, $j = 1, 2, 3, 4, 5, 6$.

4. Next, we treat *all* the mothers in the sample as OBC Muslims. Suppose that, under this scenario, p_j^{OBCM} is the average probability of a mother accessing ICDS service j, $j = 1, 2, 3, 4, 5, 6$.

5. Next, we treat *all* the mothers in the sample as from the SC. Suppose that, under this scenario, p_j^{SC} is the average probability of a mother accessing ICDS service j, $j = 1, 2, 3, 4, 5, 6$.

6. Next, we treat *all* the mothers in the sample as from the ST. Suppose that, under this scenario, p_j^{ST} is the average probability of a mother accessing ICDS service j, $j = 1, 2, 3, 4, 5, 6$.

7. Lastly, we treat *all* the mothers in the sample as Christians, Sikhs, or Jains. Suppose that, under this scenario, p_j^{ST} is the average probability of a mother accessing ICDS service j, $j = 1, 2, 3, 4, 5, 6$.

The differences between the probabilities, p_j^{HCH}, p_j^{HCM}, p_j^{OBCH}, p_j^{OBCM}, p_j^{SC}, p_j^{ST}, and p_j^{CSJ} are entirely the result of *different* sets of coefficients (HCH, HCM, OBCH, OBCM, SC, ST, and CSJ) being applied to a *given* set of attributes. These differences may, therefore, be attributed to the unequal responses of mothers—*who, except for their caste/religion, are identical in every respect*—to various ICDS services. Consequently, these probabilities are referred to as *caste/religion-based probabilities*. They are to be distinguished from the *observed* proportions of mothers from the different caste/religious groups accessing ICDS services: these *observed* proportions depend on the mothers' caste/religion *and* upon their non-caste/religion attributes; the *caste/religion-based probabilities* depend *only* upon the mothers' caste/religion.

Table 9.10 shows the structural probabilities for the seven social groups identified in this study. The third row of Table 9.10 shows that if the entire sample had comprised upper-caste Hindu mothers, the (caste/religion-based) probability of accessing ICDS services would have been: 18 percent for lactating mothers, 21 percent points for immunization; 17 percent for child's health check; 19 percent for child's food; 19 percent for growth monitoring; and 11 percent for early education.

By contrast, as the fourth row of Table 9.10 shows, if the entire sample had comprised upper-caste Muslim mothers, the probability (caste/religion-based) of accessing ICDS services would have been considerably lower: 13 percent for lactating mothers, 12 percent for immunization; 13 percent for child's health check; 14 percent for child's food; 12 percent for growth monitoring; and 18 percent for early education.

At the other end of the spectrum of structural probabilities, as the eighth row of Table 9.10 shows, if the entire sample had comprised ST mothers, the probability (caste/religion-based) of accessing ICDS services would have been considerably higher: 32 percent for lactating mothers, 39 percent for immunization; 28 percent for child's health check; 32 percent for child's food; 29 percent for growth monitoring; and 12 percent for early education.

Section 9.2 showed that, judging on the basis of the raw data, the various components of the ICDS program were tilted in favor of SC and ST mothers. This section delved into the non-caste/religion characteristics of mothers—education, household income (amount and main source), age, region of residence, rural/urban location—which, *in addition to their social group*, determined their likelihood of utilizing ICDS services. The relevant question that it sought to answer was whether mothers from different caste/religious groups, but with *identical* non-group characteristics, have different likelihoods of accessing ICDS services? As the results of Tables 9.9 and 9.10 showed, after controlling for non-group characteristics, SC and ST mothers were more likely to use ICDS services, and Muslim mothers were less likely to use ICDS services, compared to the reference group of upper-caste Hindu mothers.

Table 9.10:

Caste/religion-based probabilities (percentage) of accessing ICDS services, by social group*

Variable	Lactating Mothers			Child Immunized			Child's Health Checked			Food Given For Child			Child's Growth Monitored			Early Education		
	Mean	Min	Max	Mean	Min	Max	Mean	Min	Max	Mean	Min	Max	Mean	Min	Max	Mean	Min	Max
Upper-caste Hindus	18.2	1.1	51.1	21.2	1.8	59.2	17.0	1.9	53.8	19.2	2.1	47.7	18.8	2.8	49.3	11.2	0.7	43.1
Upper-caste Muslims	13.3	0.7	40.8	11.9	0.9	40.6	13.4	1.4	46.1	13.6	1.4	36.9	12.2	1.6	35.9	7.9	0.5	33.1
OBC Hindus	21.3	1.4	56.7	28.0	2.8	68.7	19.9	2.3	59.1	22.1	2.6	52.6	22.7	3.5	55.7	10.5	0.6	41.2
OBC Muslims	15.5	0.9	45.6	21.0	1.8	58.9	15.4	1.6	50.7	15.1	1.6	40.0	13.1	1.8	38.1	7.0	0.4	30.3
Scheduled Castes	24.5	1.7	61.7	26.5	2.5	66.8	21.0	2.5	60.9	23.9	2.9	55.4	23.4	3.7	56.7	10.7	0.7	41.7
Scheduled Tribes	31.8	2.6	71.1	39.4	4.9	79.9	27.8	3.7	70.2	31.6	4.4	65.8	29.2	5.0	64.6	12.1	0.8	45.5
Christians, Sikhs, etc.	8.7	0.4	29.3	13.1	1.0	43.4	10.6	1.0	39.2	6.0	0.5	18.5	8.7	1.1	27.5	3.1	0.2	15.3

Source: Author's own calculations from IHDS data.

Note: *Estimated using IHDS data.*

9.4. Decomposition by Social Group of the Probabilities of Utilizing ICDS Services

From the concluding observations of Section 9.3 follows a more general question: how much of the mean difference in the utilization of an ICDS service between mothers in the different caste/religious groups is due to differences between them in their (non-group) attributes (*attributes contribution*)? And how much is due to the fact that the mothers belonged to different groups (*caste/religion contribution*)? The purpose of this section is to answer this question with respect to the following binary comparisons: (i) upper-caste Hindu versus SC mothers; (ii) upper-caste Hindu versus Muslim mothers; and (iii) upper-caste Hindu versus OBC Hindu mothers.

In the estimation results reported in Table 9.9, the group effects operated entirely through the intercept terms with the slope coefficients being unaffected by the mothers' social groups. The implication was that the marginal probabilities associated with the variables—say, the effect of education on the utilization of ICDS services—was the same for upper-caste Hindu mothers as it was for mothers from the SC. This assumption is now relaxed by estimating the six equations, as specified in Table 9.9, *separately* for mothers who were upper-caste Hindu, Muslim, SC, and OBC Hindu.

After doing so, the difference between the reference group of upper-caste Hindu mothers and mothers from group X (Muslim, SC, or OBC Hindu), in their respective mean utilization rates of a specific ICDS service, was decomposed into an "attributes contribution" and a "caste/religion contribution" using the method of Oaxaca (1973) as applied to models of discrete choice (Sinning, Hahn, and Bauer 2008). The attributes contribution was computed by asking what the difference between upper-caste Hindu mothers and mothers from group X, in their proportions accessing ICDS services, *would have been* if the difference in attributes between them had been evaluated using a *common* coefficient vector? The caste/religion contribution was computed as a residual as the observed difference *less* the attributes contribution: this could be ascribed to the "structural advantage/disadvantage," which mothers from one group enjoyed over those from group X. Note that we do not, and cannot, say where the source of this structural advantage lies. It could result from a tilt by the AWCs toward mothers from certain groups and/or it could be the consequence of upper-caste Hindu mothers opting out of using ICDS services.

The percentage contributions of attributes and caste/religion to the overall difference in utilization rates between upper-caste Hindu mothers and mothers from group X are shown in Table 9.11 for five AWC services.[12] This table shows the decompositions obtained by using the upper-caste Hindu coefficient estimates (that is, the estimates obtained when the equation was estimated over the observations pertaining to upper-caste Hindu mothers) as the common coefficient vector.

Table 9.11:

Decomposition results between upper-caste Hindu mothers and mothers from other groups*

	Upper-caste Hindus versus Muslims				
	Lactating Benefits	*Immunization*	*Health Check*	*Supplementary Food*	*Growth Monitored*
Inter-group difference in *average* utilization rates (pp)	5.4	7.0	5.4	5.6	7.7
Attributes contribution**	13%	48%	40%	32%	29%
Caste/religion contribution***	87%	52%	60%	68%	71%
	Upper-caste Hindus versus SC				
Inter-group difference in *average* utilization rates (pp)	−8.6	−7.2	−4.5	−8.9	−6.7
Attributes contribution**	49%	3%	0%	48%	13%
Caste/religion contribution***	51%	97%	100%	52%	87%
	Upper-caste Hindus versus OBC Hindus				
Inter-group difference in *average* utilization rates (pp)	−5.7	−9.2	−4.5	−5.5	−5.8
Attributes contribution**	35%	18%	23%	26%	11%
Caste/religion contribution***	65%	72%	77%	74%	89%

Source: Author's own calculations from IHDS data.

Notes: * Decompositions were computed using upper-caste Hindu coefficients.

** Difference in average utilization rates due to inter-group *differences in attributes* as a percentage of the overall difference.

*** Difference in average utilization rates *due to differences in caste/religion* as a percentage of the overall difference.

pp: percentage point.

[12] There was hardly any difference between the utilization rates of the two groups for preschool education.

Table 9.11 shows that for lactating mothers, there was a 5.4 percentage point gap between upper-caste Hindu and (all) Muslim mothers in their utilization of ICDS services: of this gap, 13 percent could be explained by the fact that Hindu and Muslim (non-religious) attributes were different and 87 percent was due to difference in religion. However, of the 7-point gap between (upper caste) Hindu and Muslim mothers in their utilization of ICDS services for immunizing their children, 48 percent could be explained by the fact that Hindu and Muslim attributes were different and 52 percent was due to difference in religion. Similarly, of the 7.7-point gap between (upper caste) Hindu and Muslim mothers in their utilization of ICDS services for monitoring the growth of their children, 29 percent could be explained by the fact that Hindu and Muslim attributes were different and 71 percent was due to difference in religion.

In terms of upper-caste Hindus and SC mothers, Table 9.11 shows that, in respect of lactating mothers, there was a –8.6 percentage point gap between upper-caste Hindu and SC mothers in their utilization of ICDS services: of this gap, 49 percent could be explained by the fact that Hindu and SC (non-caste) attributes were different and 51 percent was due to caste difference. Similarly, of the –5.6 percentage point gap between (upper caste) Hindu and SC mothers in their utilization of ICDS services for providing supplementary nutrition for their children, 48 percent could be explained by the fact that upper-caste Hindu and SC attributes were different and 52 percent was due to caste difference.

However, of the –7.2 percentage point gap between (upper caste) Hindu and SC mothers in their utilization of ICDS services for immunizing their children, only 3 percent could be explained by the fact that upper-caste Hindu and SC attributes were different and 97 percent was due to caste difference. Similarly, of the –4.5 percentage point gap between (upper caste) Hindu and SC mothers in their utilization of ICDS services for checking the health of their children, the entire difference was due to caste.

9.5. The Link Between the Quality of ICDS Services and Their Utilization

As the previous sections showed, the evidence is that the utilization rate of ICDS services was higher for mothers and children from "vulnerable" groups (SC and ST) compared to those from relatively "privileged" groups (upper-caste Hindus). If this was purely a supply side effect, such that these services were directed toward vulnerable groups (and away from privileged groups), then the AWCs could be credited for this "socially responsible" orientation of ICDS services. However, if mothers from the privileged group, relative to those from the vulnerable group, spurned ICDS services then the higher utilization of ICDS services by the latter would arise because of demand-side effects. Mothers and children from privileged group would not utilize ICDS services—not because they *could not,* but because they *did not wish* to do so. This effect could arise if it was generally perceived that the quality of ICDS services was poor compared to that of equivalent "market-provided" services. Then, in the face of this general perception of quality difference, it would be persons from the privileged group, with their superior resources, who were more able and willing to buy the higher quality service.

There is a considerable amount of evidence about the poor quality of ICDS services particularly with respect to supplementary feeding and early education. Davey, Davey, and Datta (2008), in interviews with 200 users of ICDS services at 20 AWCs in Delhi reported that a majority (53 percent) of respondents were dissatisfied with the quality of services provided, with the highest levels of dissatisfaction being recorded for: the location of, and space available in, the AWCs (69 percent of respondents), the poor quality of food distributed (67 percent of respondents), and irregular pre-school education (57 percent of respondents). Qadiri and Manhas (2009) in a study of 200 parents in the Kashmir Valley found that 71 percent of parents regarded the AWCs as "ill-equipped to provide pre-school education. The teachers are not properly trained ... and there is no proper schedule or curriculum." Dhingra and Sharma (2011) in a random sample of 60 AWCs in Jammu and Kashmir pointed to the lack of adequate facilities "in terms of space (both indoor and outdoor), quality of accommodation, drinking water and toilet facilities, furniture and fixtures, and teaching/ learning material in AWCs." In a World Bank report, Gragnolati, Shekar, Das Gupta, Bredenkamp, and Lee(2005) also drew attention to the poor facilities at AWCs—most AWCs have no toilet facilities and cooking space is typically inadequate—and to supply-side inadequacies, "especially issues of access, information, and irregularity of food supply." Moreover, they pointed out, in the context of the Supplementary Nutrition component of the ICDS program that "field studies have shown that food is sometimes badly cooked, dry, and salty and should be supplemented by sugar, rice, or vegetables to be more wholesome and palatable to children."

The idea that faced with a drop in product quality, some customers abandon a product for a competing product while other customers remain loyal to it (perhaps, at the same time, voicing their discontent) has been analyzed by Hirschman (1970). On the basis of his "exit-voice" theory of market behavior by consumers, the provision of ICDS services poses a conundrum. If they are to be directed toward vulnerable mothers and their children, then the quality of the services needs to be low for it is the low quality, which keeps away mothers from the privileged groups. On the other hand, any attempt to raise the quality of services will attract mothers from the privileged groups and erode accessibility by vulnerable group mothers.

With fixed resources, ICDS providers have to choose an appropriate mix of quality and quantity of a service: lower service quality means more of the service can be provided; on the other hand, attempts to raise quality means that service quantity has to be reduced. In Figure 9.1, below the curve *TT* represents the trade-off between quality and quantity: the slope of *TT* represents the rate at which, at the margin, quality can be transformed into quantity.[13] The points X and Y represent the minimum acceptable quality levels to mothers from the privileged and vulnerable groups, respectively: mothers from the privileged group will not use the service at or below quality X and mothers from the vulnerable group will not use the service at or below quality Y.

The line *YZV* represents demand for the service by mothers from the vulnerable group. The segment *YZ* of this line also represents market demand since, up to Z, demand by mothers from the privileged group is zero. After Z, when demand by mothers from the privileged group is positive, market demand is represented by *ZW*: for any quality level, market demand (*ZW*) exceeds demand by mothers from the vulnerable group (*ZV*) by the amount of demand by mothers from the privileged group.

So, for a level of quality level between points Y and X, there is excess supply: supply by the government exceeds demand by mothers from the vulnerable group. For the quality level represented by the point X,

---

[13] That is, how much of quality one would have to give up to get an additional unit of quantity.

demand equals supply. Lastly, for quality levels in excess of that at *X*, there is excess demand: demand by mothers from both groups in sum exceeds total supply.

Figure 9.1:

The quality-quantity trade-off by different customer types

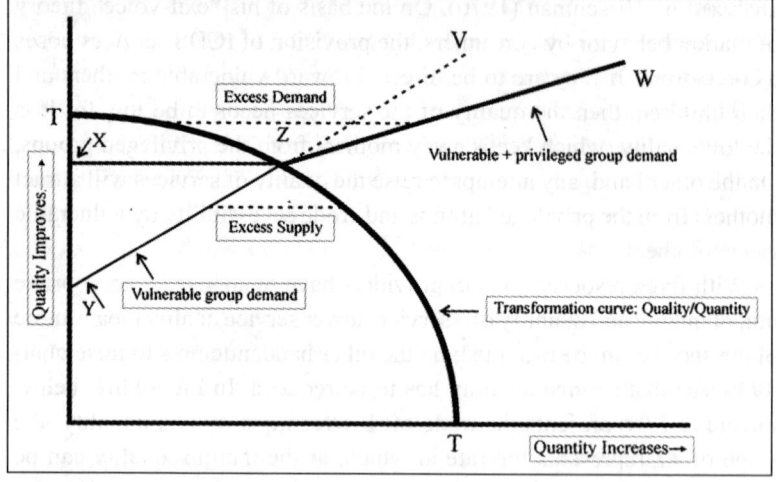

Source: Author.

9.5.1. *Universal Utilization of ICDS*

We have suggested that a good ICDS program would be one in which mothers from privileged groups participate less and mothers from vulnerable and marginalized groups participate more, consistent with a satisfactory quality of ICDS services. While it makes sense to direct limited government resources to needier groups, two questions arise. First, are the resources limited? Or is the bigger problem that most allocated resources don't make it to the village level? Second, it may be that including better-off and more powerful groups in a program would improve the quality of services for everyone. In this section, we address this question.

The Central Vigilance Committee (CVC) on the public distribution system (PDS) appointed by the Supreme Court has said that the criteria for the selection of below poverty line (BPL) households is inappropriate.[14] The finding of the CVC shows that there are large numbers of inclusion and exclusion errors in the provision of BPL and *Antyodaya Anna Yojana* (AAY) cards. The latest (61st) round of the NSSO of the Government of India shows almost a fourth of the poorest families in the country do not have access to any ration card. The other alarming fact is that 16.8 percent of households in the highest INQ have BPL cards while only 49 percent of households in the lowest INQ have BPL or AAY cards (Commissioners 7th report, 2007).

These facts show that government programs targeted toward BPL households have inherent problems in directing the services toward people in need. Access to subsidized food by the poor after the introduction of the targeted public distribution system (TPDS) has worsened at an all-India level. The TPDS performs poorly not only in terms of its objective of providing services for the poor but also in terms of program implementation, which is marked by leakages and corruption. But in states like Tamil Nadu, Andhra Pradesh, Orissa, and Chhattisgarh where PDS is universal or quasi-universal, it covers poor people in need of subsidized grains (Himanshu and Sen, 2013).

Further, the literature on the implementation of "universal" programs shows all poor and needy children are included in the program (Commissioners 7th report, 2007). MDM, which is another universal program covering all the children going to school from classes 1 to 8, provide an opportunity for the children from marginalized section to be included (Harris-White, 1994) and, consequently, poor and the marginalized children are ensured one full meal a day. Universality also means that there is pressure from the public to improve the quality of MDM and governments respond to such pressure. For example, the MDM menu in Tamil Nadu consists of a variety of food (including eggs provided 2–3 times a week) to the children. Even small problems in the program are reported by the media placing the government under pressure to offer immediate redress. In the 1990s, attempts to "target" the PDS in Tamil Nadu met with public resistance and, in consequence, was made "universal" (Harris-White, 2004).

---

[14] Seventh Report of the Commissioners of the Supreme Court in the case: PUCL v. UOI & Others. Writ Petition (Civil) No. 196 of 2001, November 2007.

Before 2006, the ICDS program was intended for only a limited number of beneficiaries. However, a Supreme Court order dated December 13, 2006 declared that the "universalization of the ICDS involves extending all ICDS services to every child under the age of six, all pregnant women and lactating mothers, and all adolescent girls." Dreze's (2006) study found that after the Supreme Court judgment, the number of AWC increased without any commensurate importance being given to the improvement in the quality of services. Consequently, many of the eligible beneficiaries opted out. There is an urgent need to improve the quality of ICDS services along with extending its coverage to make it universal (Dreze, 2006).[15]

9.6. Conclusion

The ICDS program, by addressing the issues of early education, malnutrition, and morbidity, is an imaginative response by the Indian government to the multi-faceted challenge of providing for the health and development of children and their mothers. In its implementation, however, the program embodies several inequalities. Although the ICDS policy stipulates that there should be one AWC per 1,000 persons (and 700 persons in tribal areas), the coverage is much better in the wealthier states. As Gragnolati et al. (2005) show, ICDS coverage by state rises with per capita Net State Domestic Product with five states with the highest prevalence of underweight children—Bihar, MP, Orissa, Rajasthan, and UP—having the lowest coverage, while at the same time, states like Manipur, Mizoram, and Nagaland, which have a low prevalence of under nutrition, have high ICDS coverage.

The second type of inequality is the distribution of AWCs within states: in 1998, while only half the villages from the lowest two deciles of the all-India wealth distribution had AWCs, the ICDS program covered 80 percent of the richest villages in India (Gragnolati et al., 2005). The third

[15] Tamil Nadu leads the way in nutrition program for children with the first nutrition program starting in 1956. The quality of ICDS services in Tamil Nadu is considered better than in most other states (Rajivan, 2006). Similarly, in Andhra Pradesh, forming village-level committees involving different stakeholders in monitoring the program has helped to improve the quality of the ICDS services and caters services to eligible beneficiaries (Sinha, 2006).

type of inequality is locational inequality within a village. Mander and Kumaran (2006) have observed that, in mixed-caste villages, the ICDS center was never located in the SC or ST hamlet.

The fourth type of inequality is based on excluding—or, more accurately, restricting—persons from certain groups from using ICDS services. Mander and Kumaran (2006) provide a comprehensive account about the forms that such exclusion/restriction take. To a large extent, this involved the attitude of the service provider: AWC workers might be reluctant to collect children from lower-caste hamlets; the AWCs might be more reluctant to enroll children from the lower castes, compared to those from the upper castes, if there was an overall ceiling on enrollment; lastly, lower-caste parents might be anxious about how their children would be treated while at an AWC.

However, notwithstanding the validity and, indeed, importance, of these points, the evidence is that, for whatever reasons, mothers from the SC and the ST were more likely—and Muslim mothers less likely—to use ICDS services compared to upper caste and OBC Hindu mothers. This suggests that there is a complexity of factors underlying the observed outcome in terms of group beneficiaries. First, leavening the accounts of exclusion, there might be enlightened and progressive persons involved in the delivery of ICDS services who actively promote the usage of these services by mothers from the SC and the ST. Second, there might be the perception among upper-caste Hindu mothers that the quality of ICDS services is poor—in particular, poor quality food in supplementary nutrition and poor quality pre-school education—and that, recognizing the importance of these services, they would prefer to obtain these elsewhere. So, while the AWC might, as a symbol of caste power, be located in the "main" village where the upper castes reside, it would be used relatively lightly by upper-caste mothers. This is Hirschman's (1970) "exit response" to poor quality products.

Unfortunately, Hirschman's other idea of a "voice response"—namely those that remained in the market expressed their discontent over poor product quality and, thereby, effected improvement—does not carry much credibility when it comes to ICDS services. First, there is the reluctance to even voice discontent. In their survey of 14 villages in four states, Mander and Kumaran (2006) remarked on the reluctance of villagers to criticize the AWCs. Given the nature of the caste hierarchy in rural India, remaining silent in the face of bureaucratic highhandedness is probably a rational strategy for the lower castes since expressions of discontent, rather than resulting in service improvements à la Hirschman (1970), are more likely to result in a denial of service. Second, even if the voice of the deprived was heard, and quality improvements in ICDS services resulted, this would lead to the upper classes entering the market for ICDS services and, thereby, pushing out those for whom these services were intended. That is the catch-22 of the ICDS program.

10

Public Policy: The Rashtriya Swasthya Bima Yojana

10.1. Introduction

The Rashtriya Swasthya Bima Yojana (RSBY, literally "National Health Insurance Program") is a health insurance scheme run by the Indian government for India's poorest households and has won plaudits from the World Bank, the UN, and the ILO as one of the world's best health insurance schemes. Under RSBY, every "BPL" family, holding a yellow ration card,[1] pays ₹30 (less than US$0.7) registration fee for a biometric-enabled smart card containing their fingerprints and photographs. This enables them to receive in-patient medical care of up to ₹30,000 per family, per year, in any of the empanelled hospitals. Pre-existing illnesses are covered from day one, for the household head, spouse, and up to three dependent children or parents. The scheme, which started enrolling on April 1, 2008, has been implemented in 25 states of India with, to date, a total enrollment of 33 million families from whom 4.3 million persons have received treatment under the scheme.

About three-fourths of funding for RSBY is provided by the central government and the remainder by the appropriate state government. The scheme is aimed at BPL workers in the unorganized sector and their families. It also covers all *beedi*[2] workers registered under the *Beedi* Workers Welfare Fund and identity cards are issued by the Welfare Commissioner, Ministry of Labor and Employment/State Government to all domestic workers aged 18 years and above, and all street vendors with a license from Municipal Corporation or Local Bodies.

---

[1] BPL families are entitled to a yellow ration card in contrast to "above poverty line" (APL) families who are only entitled to a white card. The yellow card holders are entitled to a higher ration than the white card holders.

[2] An indigenous "cigarette" made as tobacco wrapped in a leaf.

A crucial requirement for a household to get an RSBY card is that it should be a BPL household. On the basis of a "BPL census" conducted by the Government of India, each household is assigned a poverty score based on its profile.[3] Based on these scores, a government-determined cut-off point (termed the *BPL* cut-off line) is used to separate BPL from above poverty line (APL) households. The last BPL survey was done in 2002 and scores based on this were used for RSBY registration. All the households listed in the BPL category were informal sector workers since any household that had *even one* regular salaried, or formal sector, worker was considered to be an APL household.

The beneficiaries from RSBY belong to different caste and religious groups. In terms of caste, the broad division is between upper-caste Hindus, HOBC, and the SC, the latter comprising the formerly "untouchable" castes. In terms of religion, the broad distinction is between Hindus and Muslims. In this context, this chapter asks two questions. The first is a general question that applies to all RSBY card holders—does the possession of an RSBY card benefit the holder in a *non-health* sphere by, say, improving his/her capacity to function better by virtue of the fact that anxiety with respect to health problems has been alleviated?[4] The second question is a group-specific one. Given that the possession of an RSBY card confers health-related benefits[5]—and may even confer non-health-related benefits—do persons belonging to the dominant groups in Indian society succeed in capturing a disproportionate number of these cards?

We attempt to answer these two questions by using a unique survey of RSBY card holders conducted by the IIDS. This survey of 1,500 BPL households in two Indian states, UP and Maharashtra, with 750 respondents from each state, is described in some detail in Section 10.3. Before that, Section 10.2 informs about how RSBY works.

---

[3] See the appendix for details of BPL calculations.
[4] For example, there might be a greater willingness to make productive investments based on a greater sense of health security.
[5] Compared to a BPL family not holding an RSBY card, a BPL family holding an RSBY card is better off if there happens to be an illness of (comparable gravity) in both families, if only because it is required to spend less on that episode of ill-health.

10.2. How RSBY Works

The implementation of RSBY is based on the public–private partnership model. After a competitive bidding process, a public or private insurance company is given a license to provide health insurance subject to certain conditions. At the time of the bidding, the insurance companies have to provide a list of empanelled hospitals that are prepared to be part of the RSBY scheme for cashless treatment facilities. Both public and private hospitals can be included in the list of empanelled hospitals, which must meet certain basic minimum requirements. Under the scheme, hospitals that specialize in the treatment of various diseases are empanelled so that the beneficiaries can get access to the health care appropriate for their illness.

The insurer must also agree to engage intermediaries with local presence (such as NGOs) in order to provide grassroots outreach and to assist members in utilizing RSBY services after enrollment. The role of these local intermediaries is very important in the success of the RSBY scheme. They have to inform local BPL households about the dates and venues for registration under RSBY and the usefulness of the scheme. The selected insurance companies hire third party administrators (TPA) for enrolling beneficiaries and each state government provides an electronic list of BPL households to the insurance companies.

The TPA plays an important role in the enrollment process. A list of households eligible for RSBY benefits is posted on the village *panchayat* notice board and other important public places a few days before the enrollment date. The TPA also informs villagers about the date and place of enrollment (Rajasekhar et al., 2001). After enrollment, a biometric smart card, carrying a photograph of the head of the household, with biometric information (such as fingerprints) of all five members of a beneficiary's household, is printed and given to the beneficiary against a payment of ₹30. This smart card then allows cashless transactions for in-patient treatment expenses at empanelled hospitals, a list of these hospitals being also provided to the card holder. Only those persons whose biometric information is stored on the smart card can avail of health care facilities under RSBY.

Each empanelled hospital has an RSBY help desk with a card reader machine, which is used to swipe the card so that all health costs related to the card holder's treatment are debited to it. The empanelled hospitals send details of the expenses to the insurance agencies and money is transferred to the account of the empanelled hospitals. It is also mandatory that the persons obtaining treatment through RSBY are given details of the expenses deducted from their smart cards. The entire transaction is cashless and the patients seeking health care through RSBY need not pay any cost for their treatment.

All the transactions under the RSBY are monitored by the central ministry. After enrollment, information about all registered beneficiaries is sent to the Ministry of Labor and Employment and the RSBY desks of all empanelled hospitals in the country are linked to the central server of the Ministry. To help address grievances under the scheme, "redressal committees" have been formed at the central, state, and district levels to manage the complaints of beneficiaries and stakeholders.

10.3. The Survey

The survey that provided the data for the study was located in two states: UP and Maharashtra. The choice of states was based on three criteria: (i) completion of maximum number of years of RSBY; (ii) compared to the all-India average, a greater concentration of SC persons and Muslim in the population; and (iii) compared to the all-India average, a larger enrollment of households in the RSBY scheme. Table 10.1 compares the "RSBY performance" of UP and Maharashtra with that of India in its entirety.

Table 10.1:
Percentage distribution of population by socio-religious groups in study state

State/Sector	SC	ST	Others	Muslim
India (total)	16.2	8.2	75.6	13.4
India (rural)	17.9	10.4	71.7	12.0
Uttar Pradesh (total)	21.1	0.1	78.8	18.5
Uttar Pradesh (rural)	23.4	0.1	76.5	14.9
Maharashtra (total)	10.2	8.9	80.9	10.6
Maharashtra (rural)	10.9	13.4	75.7	5.5

Source: Census of India, 2001, Registrar General of India.

Similar considerations prevailed with the choice of districts to be sampled within each state: Moradabad district in UP and Aurangabad district in Maharashtra. Moradabad was selected for this study because it had a higher proportion of Muslims than its parent state while, in Aurangabad, the proportions of both SC persons and Muslims were higher than the state averages (Table 10.2). The details of the population in the two districts are shown in Table 10.3, while the geographical locations of the two districts, in the context of their parent states, are shown in Figures 10.1 and 10.2.

Table 10.2:
State and district selected on the basis of selection criteria

Study Area	No. of Districts with RSBY	Number of Years	Proportion of Population to the State Average			No. of BPL Families Covered	Hospitals Empanelled	
			SC	ST	Muslim		Govt.	Private
State: Uttar Pradesh	All 70 districts	3	21		19	4,024,719	1,113	679
District: Moradabad		2	17		49	41,643	48	8
State: Maharashtra	All 35 districts	3	10	9	11	2,172,918	1,007	8
District: Aurangabad		2	13	4	20	81,835	38	0

Source: Census of India, 2001, Registrar General of India.

Table 10.3:
Social composition of the populations of Moradabad and Aurangabad districts

Social Composition	Moradabad	Aurangabad
Households	573,100	549,900
Population	3,811,000	2,897,000
SC population	604,300 (15.9)	376,200 (13.0)
Muslim population	1,735,400 (49.5)	1,004,00 (3.5)
Non-SC/non-Muslim population	2,075,600 (54.5)	5,695,00 (19.7)

Source: Census of India, 2001, Registrar General of India.
Note: Figures in bracket is percentage distribution.

Figure 10.1:
Uttar Pradesh

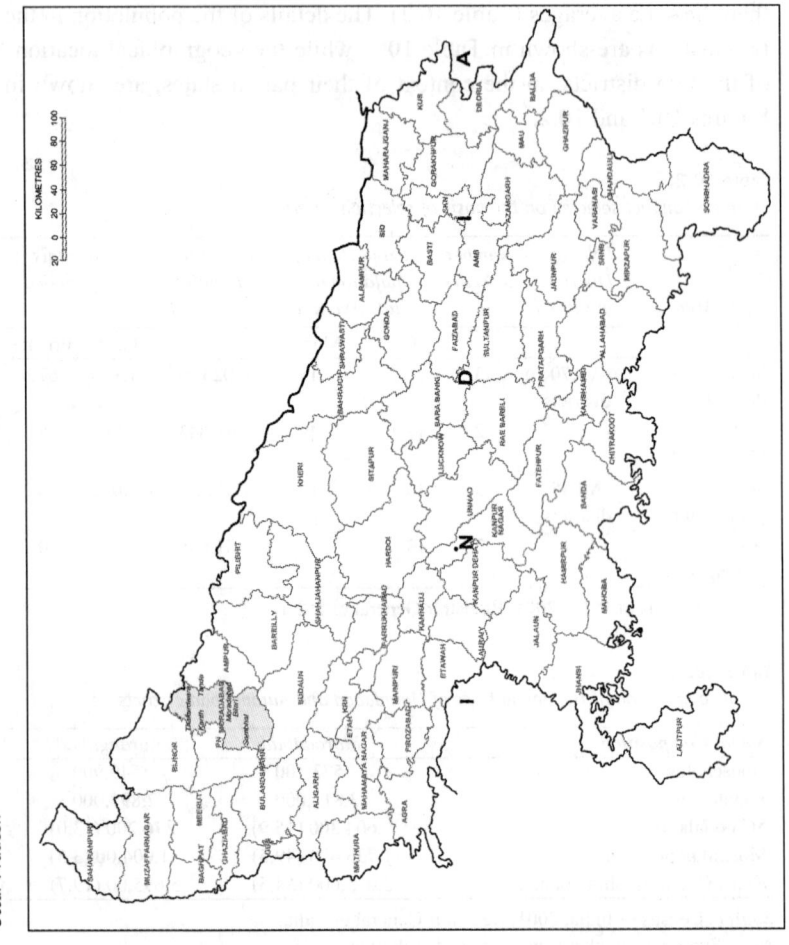

Source: Census of India 2011.

Figure 10.2:
Maharashtra

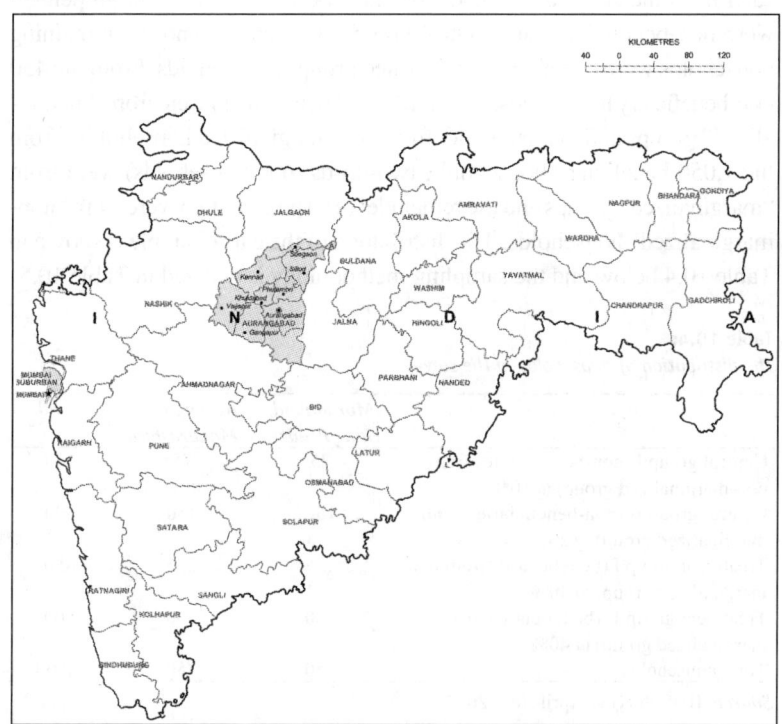

Source: Census of India 2011.

10.3.1. *Sample Selection and Sampling Methodology*

Since the focus of this study is Muslims and persons from the SC (that is, "socially excluded" or "marginalized" groups), we were careful to choose from our respondents an adequate number of such persons from both the "treated" and "control" groups. The "treated" group comprised those that had RSBY cards where some of these card holders were from marginalized groups and the others from non-marginalized groups. The "control" group comprised those that *did not* have RSBY cards where, again, some of these were from marginalized groups and the others from non-marginalized groups

A total of 1,500 sample households were surveyed, with 750 households each from the states of UP and Maharashtra. Out of this total, 30 percent were non-beneficiary (or "control group") households and the remaining households were beneficiary (or "treated group") households. From the 450 non-beneficiary households, two-thirds (300 households) were from "marginalized" groups and the remainder from non-marginalized households. From the 1,050 beneficiary households, two-thirds (600 households) were from "marginalized" groups and the remainder (450 households) were from "non-marginalized" households. The distribution of the entire sample is shown in Table 10.4 below and the sampling methodology is detailed in Table 10.5.

Table 10.4:
The distribution of households in the survey

	Moradabad, Uttar Pradesh	Aurangabad, Maharashtra	Total
Control group I (non-beneficiaries from non-marginalized group) @10%	75	75	150
Control group II (non-beneficiaries from marginalized group) @20%	150	150	300
Treatment group I (beneficiaries from non-marginalized group) @30%	225	225	450
Treatment group II (beneficiaries from marginalized group) @40%	300	300	600
Total households	750	750	1,500

Source: IIDS Survey, April–July 2012.

Table 10.5:
The sampling procedure

Methodology	Details	Respondents
Household survey	A detailed household schedule was canvassed among the sample households. The head or adult member of the household was the key respondent. However, for sections relating to maternity eligible women would be the respondents	Selected 1,500 BPL household (750 from each district)
Focus group discussion	FGDs were conducted to find out the collective information from beneficiary of RSBY	Members of homogeneous socially excluded group
Key informant interviews	Interview with local and central governments helped to contextualize issues that affect the lives of socially excluded beneficiary households, challenges and opportunities for supporting social inclusion, and objective and goals of social interventions such as RSBY	Head of RSBY beneficiary household, local, and central government officials working in social interventions programs

Source: IIDS Survey, April–July 2012.

10.4. The Data

As detailed earlier, the data for the analysis were obtained from a survey of 1,500 BPL individuals in two Indian states, Maharashtra and UP with 750 respondents from each state, conducted between April and July 2012. The respondents were divided into three groups:

1. Those that did not have an RSBY card (hereafter, group 1). There were 450 households in this group comprising 30 percent of the sample of 1,500 households.
2. Those that had an RSBY card but had not used it (hereafter, group 2). There were 789 households in this group comprising 53 percent of the sample of 1,500 households.
3. Those that had an RSBY card and had used it (hereafter, group 3). There were 261 households in this group comprising 17 percent of the sample of 1,500 households.

The survey also provided information on the attributes of the respondents and Table 10.6 shows the average values of some of these characteristics classified according to card status. The main features of the table, in terms of differences between the households of different card status, is that group 3 households had older household heads, a higher income, higher consumption expenditure (both in total and per capita), higher savings, and larger per capita land holding compared to group 1 or group 2 households.

Testing for differences in these variables between the groups, a pairwise comparison suggested that the differences between groups 3 and 1, and between groups 3 and 2, with respect to the age of household head, household income, and monthly household per capita consumption expenditure were significantly differently from zero[6] but differences in monthly household consumption expenditure, household saving, and size of per person land holding were not significantly different from zero.

---

[6] All significance levels quoted in this paper are at the 5 percent level.

300   *Caste, Discrimination, and Exclusion in Modern India*

Table 10.6:
Individual attributes, by RSBY card status

	Household does not have RSBY Card	Household has RSBY Card but has not Used it	Household has RSBY Card and has Used it
Age of household head	45.8	46.2	47.9
Household size	5.5	5.4	5.3
Number of children in household	1.8	1.9	1.8
Number of males in household	2.9	2.9	2.8
Number of females in household	2.6	2.5	2.5
Average household monthly income	5,547	5,569	6,024
Average household monthly consumption expenditure	2,708	2,718	2,891
Average household monthly saving	2,839	2,851	3,133
Average household monthly per capita consumption expenditure	516	522	567
Household land per person	0.39	0.34	0.43

Source: IIDS Survey, April–July 2012.

Using the survey data, we defined three mutually exclusive social groups: (i) SC households (447/1,500 households); (ii) non-SC Hindu households (593/1,500 households), hereafter Hindus; and (iii) non-Hindu and non-SC households (460/1,500 households), hereafter non-Hindus. Table 10.7 shows that of the 447 SC households, 33 percent did not have a card (group 1); 48

Table 10.7:
RSBY card status, by social group

	Household does not have RSBY Card	Household has RSBY Card but has not Used it	Household has RSBY Card and has Used it	Total
Scheduled Castes	149 (33%) [33%]	215 (48%) [27%]	83 (19%) [32%]	447 (100%)
Non-SC Hindus	150 (25%) [33%]	348 (59%) [44%]	95 (16%) [36%]	593 (100%)
Non-Hindus	151 (33%) [33%]	226 (49%) [29%]	83 (18%) [32%]	460 (100%)
Total	450	789	261	1,500

Source: IIDS Survey, April–July 2012.
Note: Figures in ( ) represent row proportions and figures in [ ] represent column proportions.

percent had a card but had not used it (group 2); and 19 percent had a card and had used it (group 3). The proportions for non-Hindu households were comparable. However, compared to SC and non-Hindu households, Hindu households had a lower presence in group 1 (25 percent), a higher presence in group 2 (59 percent), and a lower presence in group 3 (16 percent). In summary, compared to SC and non-Hindu households, Hindu households were more inclined to take out an RSBY card but less inclined to use it.

As Table 10.8 shows, there was no difference in the proportionate presence of illiterate and literate households in group 1: approximately 30 percent from each group did not have a card. Literacy did, however, have an effect on usage: 20 percent of literates, compared to 16 percent of illiterates, were in group 3.

Table 10.8:
RSBY card status, by illiteracy/literacy

	Household does not have RSBY Card	Household has RSBY Card but has not Used it	Household has RSBY Card and has Used it	Total
Illiterate	256	477	138	871
	(29%)	(55%)	(16%)	(100%)
Literate	194	312	123	629
	(31%)	(50%)	(20%)	(100%)
Total	450	789	261	1,500

Source: IIDS Survey, April–July 2012.

Tables 10.9, 10.10, and 10.11 show the proportions in the different status categories by housing and related conditions. Table 10.9 shows that while the proportions not having an RSBY card were roughly similar between households living in *pucca* (made of brick or cement) and *kutcha* (made of mud or wood) houses, households living in *pucca* houses were more likely to use their cards (19 percent) compared to households in *kutcha* houses (12 percent). Similarly, Table 10.10 shows that while the proportions not having an RSBY card were roughly similar between households whose source of water was a tap or a tube well/hand pump, households whose source of water was the tap were more likely to use their cards (20 percent) compared to households whose source of water was tube well/hand pump (15 percent). Lastly, Table 10.11 shows that households whose source of power was electricity were more likely to use their RSBY cards compared to households whose source of power was not electricity.

Table 10.9:
RSBY card status, by housing conditions

	Household does not have RSBY Card	*Household has RSBY Card but has not Used it*	*Household has RSBY Card and has Used it*	*Total*
Pucca	349	600	220	1,169
	(30%)	(51%)	(19%)	(100%)
Kutcha	101	189	41	331
	(31%)	(57%)	(12%)	(100%)
Total	450	789	261	1,500

Source: IIDS Survey, April–July 2012.

Table 10.10:
RSBY card status, by households' source of water

	Household does not have RSBY Card	*Household has RSBY Card but has not Used it*	*Household has RSBY Card and has Used it*	*Total*
Tap	187	319	126	632
	(30%)	(50%)	(20%)	(100%)
Tube well/ hand pump	234	427	114	775
	(30%)	(55%)	(15%)	(100%)
Well	27	40	21	88
	(31%)	(45%)	(24%)	(100%)
Pond/river	2	3	0	5
	(40%)	(60%)	(0%)	(100%)
Total	450	789	261	1,500

Source: IIDS Survey, April–July 2012.

Table 10.11:
RSBY card status, by households' source of power

	Household does not have RSBY Card	*Household has RSBY Card but has not Used it*	*Household has RSBY Card and has Used it*	*Total*
Electricity	234	376	160	770
	(30%)	(49%)	(21%)	(100%)
Kerosene	206	386	96	688
	(30%)	(56%)	(14%)	(100%)
Other	10	27	5	42
	(24%)	(64%)	(12%)	(100%)
Total	450	789	261	1,500

Source: IIDS Survey, April–July 2012.

10.5. Econometric Estimation

A question that requires an answer is why the proportion of households using their RSBY cards—and, by corollary, the proportion of households not using their RSBY cards—varies according to household characteristic. One reason may be that the non-claimants do not need to claim—after all, if no one in the household is ill there is no occasion to claim. The other reason might be difficulty in claiming so that having got a card there is, for some households, a further barrier (perhaps involving bureaucratic form filling) to using the card.

It is hard to believe that the incidence of household illness is different between SC households and Hindu households (Table 10.7); or between illiterate and literate households (Table 10.8); or between households living in *pucca* houses and households living in *kutcha* houses (Table 10.9); or between households whose source of water is the tap and households whose source of water is the tube well/hand pump (Table 10.10); or between households whose source of power is electricity and households whose source of power is kerosene (Table 10.11). Indeed, it is much more plausible to assume that the incidence of household illness would be greater among the second, compared to the first, type of household. An inexorable conclusion would be that the reason that households with less favorable attributes, notwithstanding having an RSBY card, do not claim to the same degree as better off and more privileged households is that they face relatively higher barriers to claiming.

A second question is why certain households did not take out an RSBY card in spite of the fact that all of them were BPL households and, by definition, were eligible for a card. Our hypothesis is that this has to do with area effects rather than with household choice. Households cannot take out RSBY cards if the facilities for doing so do not exist.

In line with the first hypotheses namely that "better off" households might have an advantage in terms of claiming benefits on RSBY, we estimated an equation in which the dependent variable took the value 1 if a household *had a card and claimed*, 0 if it *had a card and did not claim*. Table 10.12 shows the results from estimating such an equation: the results are shown in the form of odds ratios and in terms of marginal probabilities. The latter show how the probability of the event (in this case claiming benefits) would change for a unit change in the determining variable, if the values of the other variables are held constant.[7]

The results shown in Table 10.12 go a long way toward supporting our hypothesis that being better off leads to a higher claim propensity. Higher MPCE by a household, higher household income, and living in a *pucca* house were all significantly associated with a higher probability of claiming RSBY benefits from the set of households holding such cards. Living in Maharashtra, compared to living in UP, significantly raised the proportion of card holders who claimed benefits, from 18 percent in UP to 31 percent in Maharashtra. A surprising feature of the result was that Hindu household card holders were significantly less likely to claim than SC and non-Hindu households. It may be that RSBY restricts the hospitals and doctors from which card holders can receive treatment and this restriction may not accord with Hindu tastes.

Table 10.12:
Logit estimates of the likelihood of card holders claiming on RSBY*

	Odds Ratio	Standard Error	Z	Prob > |z|	Marginal Probability	Standard Error	Z	Prob > |z|
Household monthly per capita consumption expenditure	0.01	0.00	3.0	0.0	0.01	0.00	3.00	0.0
Top income quintile	0.05	0.05	1.1	0.3	0.05	0.05	1.11	0.3
4th income quintile	0.12	0.04	2.7	0.0	0.12	0.04	2.70	0.0
3rd income quintile	0.12	0.04	2.9	0.0	0.12	0.04	2.95	0.0
2nd income quintile***	0.06	0.04	1.5	0.1	0.06	0.04	1.51	0.1
Age of household head	0.01	0.01	1.8	0.1	0.01	0.01	1.75	0.1
Scheduled Caste household	0.01	0.03	0.2	0.9	0.01	0.03	0.19	0.9

Table 10.12 continued

[7]   In this case to the sample mean values of the variables.

Table 10.12 continued

Hindu household**	−0.08	0.03	−2.5	0.0	−0.08	0.03	−2.52	0.0
Pucca house	0.09	0.03	2.7	0.0	0.09	0.03	2.69	0.0
State	0.11	0.03	4.0	0.0	0.11	0.03	3.96	0.0
Tehsil	−0.05	0.03	−1.6	0.0	−0.05	0.03	−1.63	0.1

Source: Author's own calculations from IIDS Survey, April–July 2012.
Notes: * 1,050 observations. **Reference category is other religions. ***Reference category is lowest income quintile.
The dependent variable takes the value 1 if a household has a card and claims, 0 if it has a card and does not claim.

Tables 10.13 and 10.14 show the results for estimating the "card take-up" equation in which the dependent variable takes the value 1 if the household has an RSBY card (regardless of whether it used it or not) and the value 0 if the household does not have an RSBY card. The equation was estimated separately for UP and Maharashtra. The UP results (Table 10.13) showed that the significant effects on the probability of having a card were (i) the location of the household in terms of the village's geography; households in the corner and on the periphery were significantly less likely to have a card compared to households living in the center of the village; and (ii) the *gram panchayat* with which the household was associated.

Table 10.13:

Logit estimates of the likelihood of being an RSBY card holder (Uttar Pradesh) *

	Odds Ratio	Standard Error	Z Value	Prob > |z|	Marginal Probability	Standard Error	Z Value	Prob > |z|
Tehsil	2.32	0.44	4.46	0.00	0.16	0.03	4.67	0.00
Location outside village	0.50	0.14	−2.51	0.01	−0.13	0.05	−2.55	0.01
Location at corner of village**	0.57	0.11	−2.89	0.00	−0.11	0.04	−2.94	0.00
Gram panchayat 1	4.80	1.87	4.02	0.00	0.30	0.07	4.17	0.00
Gram panchayat 2	3.05	1.05	3.24	0.00	0.21	0.06	3.32	0.00
Gram panchayat 3	2.04	0.73	2.00	0.05	0.14	0.07	2.01	0.04
Gram panchayat 4	3.68	1.34	3.57	0.00	0.25	0.07	3.68	0.00
Gram panchayat 5	2.22	0.79	2.26	0.02	0.15	0.07	2.28	0.02

Table 10.13 continued

Table 10.13 continued

Gram panchayat 6	3.36	1.26	3.24	0.00	0.23	0.07	3.31	0.00
Gram panchayat 7***	4.19	2.05	2.94	0.00	0.27	0.09	2.99	0.00

Source: Author's own calculations from IIDS Survey.
Notes:* 742 observations ** Reference category is "inside village." *** The reference category was *Gram Panchayat 8*. The dependent variable takes the value 1 if a household has a card, 0 if it does not have a card.

Table 10.14:
Logit estimates of the likelihood of being an RSBY card holder (Maharashtra) *

	Odds Ratio	Standard Error	Z Value	Prob > |z|	Marginal Probability	Standard Error	Z Value	Prob > |z|
Tehsil	0.70	0.12	–2.13	0.03	–0.07	0.03	–2.15	0.03
Scheduled Caste household	0.98	0.21	–0.09	0.93	0.00	0.04	–0.09	0.93
Hindu household**	1.60	0.31	2.40	0.02	0.10	0.04	2.44	0.02
Age of household head	1.05	0.04	1.34	0.18	0.01	0.01	1.35	0.18
Source of power is electricity	1.47	0.31	1.85	0.07	0.08	0.04	1.86	0.06
Top income quintile	1.23	0.32	0.80	0.43	0.04	0.05	0.80	0.43
4th income quintile	1.77	0.49	2.08	0.04	0.12	0.06	2.10	0.04
3rd income quintile	1.47	0.34	1.66	0.10	0.08	0.05	1.67	0.09
2nd income quintile***	1.59	0.39	1.88	0.06	0.10	0.05	1.89	0.06

Source: Author's own calculations from IIDS Survey, April–July 2012.
Notes: * 750 observations. **Reference category is other religions. ***Reference category is lowest income quintile. The dependent variable takes the value 1 if a household has a card, 0 if it does not have a card.

The results for Maharashtra (Table 10.14) were very different from those for UP (Table 10.13). Now area effects were much less important compared to the ability of better off and more powerful households to obtain RSBY cards. Hindu households were significantly more likely to have an RSBY card than SC or "other religion" households. Households whose source of power was electricity were significantly more likely to have a card than households whose source of power was kerosene. Households in the upper strata of the income distribution were significantly more likely to have a card than households in the lowest INQ. All in all, the allocation of RSBY cards was significantly skewed toward relatively prosperous households.

10.6. Treatment Effects

An important issue in policy analysis is to assess (measure) the outcome or effect of a policy intervention or treatment, which some members of the public receive but others do not. The heart of the analysis lies in constructing two sets of counterfactuals: (i) what the outcome for an individual who received the treatment would *have been if he/she did not get the treatment?* (ii) What the outcome for an individual who did not receive the treatment would *have been if he/she did get the treatment?* The key to quantifying treatment effects lies in answering these two questions.

We consider two forms of treatment: (i) having a card versus not having a card and (ii) having a card *and using it* versus having a card *and not using it*. For reasons of economy, we show the results for only those outcomes for which the ATE was significantly different from zero.

Table 10.15 shows the treatment effects for using a card using the IPW and propensity score matching (PSM) estimators. Using a card (as opposed to having a card *and not using it*) had a significant effect on (i) the ability to generate income from trade and service and (ii) raising the desire to start a new life or expand existing activity. In addition, it had several social effects: it encouraged households to join user groups in the

Box 10.1:

Treatment effects

More formally the treatment is represented by θ, so that $\theta = 1$ represents receiving the treatment and $\theta = 0$ represents not receiving the treatment. Consider an individual i $(i = 1 \dots N)$ and Y_θ represent his outcome. Then if individual i did receive treatment Y_{i1} represents his *observed* outcome and Y_{i0} represents his *counterfactual* outcome; conversely, if individual i did not receive treatment Y_{i0} represents his *observed* outcome and Y_{i1} represents his *counterfactual* outcome. So, for each individual i $(i = 1 \dots N)$, we have two outcomes—Y_{i1} and Y_{i0}—where one is an observed outcome and the other is a counterfactual outcome. Consequently, the *average treatment effect* (ATE) is defined as (dropping the subscript i):

Box 10.1 continued

Box 10.1 continued

$$ATE = E(Y_1 - Y_0)$$

which is the *expected* effect of the treatment on a *randomly drawn person* from the population of persons receiving and not receiving the treatment.

A second quantity of interest that receives attention is the *average treatment effect on the treated* (ATET) defined as:

$$ATET = E(Y_1 - Y_0 | \theta = 1)$$

The concepts of ATE and ATET can be expanded by conditioning on covariates. If **x** is a vector of covariates, then $ATE = E(Y_1 - Y_0 | x)$ and $ATET = E(Y_1 - Y_0 | x, \theta = 1)$. So, the question is: how to estimate ATE and ATET when we have a sample on the Y and θ (in other words, we can observe the outcome for each person and we know whether or not he/she received treatment) and observations on some covariates? The difficulty is that for any individual, we observe $(Y_1 - Y_0)$ *but not both*. The observed outcome, Y is:

$$Y = (1 - \theta)Y_0 + \theta Y_1 = Y_0 + \theta(Y_1 - Y_0)$$

A strong assumption is that θ is independent of Y_1 and Y_0 as would happen with random assignment. However, when assignment is not random, so that there is *self-selection* into treatment, a weaker assumption is required. The *conditional independence* assumption says that *after conditioning on covariates*, the potential outcomes are conditionally independent of the treatment. The *overlap* assumption says that each individual has a positive probability of being included in the treatment. The *independent and identically distributed* assumption says the treatment affects only the concerned household and does not affect other households.

Source: Authors.

village and, from a political perspective, it generated the feeling that the central government understood people's needs.

Box 10.2:
Types of treatment estimators

With this background, the estimators proposed in treatment effects literature fall into the following categories:

1. Estimators based on a model for the outcome variable (regression analysis [RA]).
2. Estimators based on a model for treatment assignment (inverse probability weighted [IPW]).
3. Estimators based on models for both outcome and treatment variables (augmented inverse probability weighted).
4. Estimators that match on covariates (nearest neighbor matching).
5. Estimators that match on predicted probabilities of treatment (propensity score matching [PSM]).

Source: Authors.

Table 10.15:

Treatment effects on outcome variables arising from having an RSBY card, and using it against having an RSBY card and not using it

Outcome	Estimator	
	ATE: IPW	ATE:PSM
Able to generate income from trade and service	0.09	0.10
	(3.09)	(2.53)
Wishes to start a new life or to expand an existing economic activity	0.11	0.10
	(3.11)	(2.37)
Member of a user group in the village	0.11	0.09
	(3.27)	(2.36)
Got support from village/neighborhood	−0.06	−0.06
	(1.60)	(1.52)
Importance of village for local government	−0.1	−0.09
	(1.86)	(1.50)
Central government has reasonable understanding of your situation	0.1	0.11
	(4.23)	(3.44)

Source: Author's own calculations from IIDS Survey, April–July 2012.
Note: PSM, propensity score matching.

Table 10.16 (UP) and Table 10.17 (Maharashtra) show the treatment effects for having a card using the IPW and PSM estimators. Having a card (as opposed to *not* having a card) had a significant effect in UP in generating a greater sense that the central government understood people's needs and that it had attempted to address these needs. The gains in UP among the RSBY card holders were purely political. However, in Maharashtra the gains from having a card extended to ability raise income from trade and service, becoming a member of a user group in the village, and having the confidence to speak up in public.

Table 10.16:

Treatment effects on outcome variables arising from having an RSBY card against not having an RSBY card (Uttar Pradesh)

Outcome	Estimator	
	ATE: IPW	ATE:PSM
Central government has reasonable understanding of your situation	0.06	0.08
	(1.78)	(1.96)
Has the government attempted to address your needs in the past 5 years	0.07	0.07
	(1.70)	(1.81)

Source: Author's own calculations from IIDS Survey, April–July 2012.
Note: PSM, propensity score matching.

Table 10.17:

Treatment effects on outcome variables arising from having an RSBY card against not having an RSBY card (Maharashtra)

Outcome	Estimator	
	ATE: IPW	ATE:PSM
Able to generate income from trade and service	0.04	0.05
	(1.63)	(2.07)
Member of a user group in the village	0.17	0.17
	(4.83)	(3.94)
Did you raise your voice in public events	0.08	0.07
	(2.21)	(1.67)
Central government has reasonable understanding of your situation	0.06	0.11
	(1.78)	(3.44)
Has the government attempted to address your needs in the past 5 years	0.07	
	(1.70)	

Source: Author's own calculations from IIDS Survey, April–July 2012.
Note: PSM, propensity score matching.

10.7. Conclusion

A popular theme in the literature on policy making is the idea of "capture." When industry is regulated, it attempts to "capture" the regulator to make him act in its interest. Lobbyists attempt to capture legislators and pay them to ask questions on their behalf. In a similar vein, desirable policy initiatives are sought to be captured by influential groups. The RSBY card is no exception.

The RSBY poses two barriers: the barriers associated with getting a card even though one might be formally entitled to one and the barriers associated with using a card even though one might be in possession of one. As we have seen, getting a card in UP is essentially barrier free except on grounds of bureaucratic penetration. However, in Maharashtra, those higher up the income ladder, and those in higher social groups were significantly more likely to have a card than those on the lowest rung economically and socially. The same is true of usage. Having got a card, it was the better-off sections of card holders who were more likely to use them.

A possibility that this chapter does not consider is that of "adverse selection." This would suggest that it is precisely the "bad health risk" households—those households which had, or anticipated having, a pre-existing illness in their midst and, therefore, by extension had, or anticipated, a bad non-health-related outcome[8]—that would take out RSBY cards while "healthy" households would not bother. On this "lemons" versus "plums" interpretation (see Akerlof, 1970), we would expect to see card holders to have worse non-health-related outcomes than non-card holders simply because RSBY cards would be relatively more attractive to bad risk, compared to low risk, households. So RSBY cards would be associated with bad outcomes, not because holding an RSBY card *caused* a bad outcome but because households at risk of bad outcomes, through actual or anticipated ill-health, were *attracted* to RSBY cards.

Appendix on BPL Calculations

1. **BPL survey for 9th Plan (1997–2002) (rural):** Annual family income to be less than ₹20,000 and the families should not have more than 2 hectares of land or TV or Fridge. The number of rural BPL families was 6.5 lakh during the 9th Plan. The survey based on these criteria was again carried out in 2002 and the total number of 3.87 lakh families was identified. This figure was in force till September 2006.

2. **BPL survey for 10th Plan (2002–07) (rural):** This survey is based on the degree of deprivation in respect of 13 parameters (with scores from 0 to 4)—land holding, type of house, clothing, food security, sanitation, consumer durables, literacy status, labor force, means of livelihood, status of children, type of indebtedness, reasons for migrations, etc. The Planning Commission fixed an upper limit of 3.26 lakh for rural BPL families on the basis of simple survey. Accordingly families having less than 15 marks out of maximum 52 marks have been classified as BPL and their number works out to 3.18 lakh. The survey was carried out in 2002 and thereafter but could not be finalized due to stay by the SC. The stay was vacated in February 2006 and this survey was finalized and adopted in September, 2006. This survey would form

---

[8]   Like loss of income or output.

the basis for benefits under GoI schemes. The state government is free to adopt any criteria/survey for the state-level schemes.

4. **Kerala government:** Most of the state governments followed the 13 and 7 parameters' definition for identifying the BPL families during the current 10th Plan. Kerala is one of the few state governments that have formulated its own criteria. There are nine parameters and if the family does not have access to four or more parameters, then it is classified as BPL. The nine parameters for urban areas are: no land/Less than 5 cents of land; no house/ dilapidated house; no sanitation latrine; family without color TV; no regular employed person in the family; no access to safe drinking water; women headed household/presence of widow divorcee; socially disadvantaged groups (SC/ST); and mentally retarded/ disabled member in the family. The nine parameters for rural are: no land/less than 5 cents of land; no house/dilapidated house; no sanitation latrine; family with an illiterate adult member; no regular employed person in the family; no access to safe drinking water; women headed household/presence of widow divorcee; socially disadvantaged groups (SC/ST); and mentally retarded/disabled member in the family.

5. **Haryana government:** The BPL survey was carried out as per the GOI guidelines in Haryana and it was based on 13 parameters. The Government has recently discarded it and adopted a new five parameter-based survey. The five points are land, house, household goods, literacy level, and means of livelihood/standard of living. The survey is to be carried out by ex-serviceman who would be paid ₹4 per family.

6. **Maharashtra government:** The Maharashtra government has also decided to conduct fresh BPL survey. About 46 lakh BPL families were identified on the basis of 13-point criteria. There was lot of resentment and a total of 10.56 lakh appeals were filed against the survey. In view of this, they have decided to discard the survey and conduct a fresh one.

11

Conclusion

This book examined 10 areas, namely human development, inequality, poverty, educational attainments, child malnutrition, health, employment, wages, gender, and access to public goods, in which significant inter-group disparities in achievement remained, even after allowing for differences between the groups in their endowment of relevant attributes. In each of these areas, HCH households performed the best and Muslim households and households from the SC and the ST performed the worst, *even after controlling for the (non-group) factors that might have influenced the outcomes.*

However, an analysis of broad areas using large-scale data sets is analogous to describing a terrain using aerial pictures —valuable in terms of identifying the salient features of the landscape, but deficient in terms of capturing its details. Similarly, underlying these 10 broad issues, identified and analyzed in this book, are a myriad areas in which persons and households belonging to marginalized groups are disadvantaged in terms of access and participation, and innumerable ways through which this disadvantage is enforced and policed.

Underpinning all these forms of disadvantage is the practice of "untouchability." This is the greatest taboo of Indian society, the elephant in the room to which none dare draw attention. The Indian Penal Code imposes penalties against the practice of untouchability and against offences committed against Dalits. The earliest of these interventions was the Madras Act of 1938, which made it an offence to discriminate against Dalits in publicly funded facilities such as roads, wells, and public buildings. After Independence, the Indian Constitution abolished "untouchability" and made its practice an offence. This prohibition was strengthened by the Protection of Civil Rights Acts of 1955 and 1976 and the Prevention of Atrocities Acts of 1989 and 1995. Under the Protection of Civil Rights Acts of 1955 and 1976, many anti-Dalit actions became offences. These included *inter alia* prohibiting entry into places of worship;

denial of access to water; denial of access to public places; and denial of goods and/or services. Yet, as Sainath (2002) says:

> I think it is untouchability more than anything else that is responsible for the denial of human rights to this group of people [the SC]. In fact, untouchability is central to caste. It is, and has been for a very long time, an extremely sophisticated economic and political strategy for ensuring a perpetual pool of demoralised, cheap labour that has no sense of its bargaining power.

"Untouchable" casual laborers find it difficult to obtain employment in the farm and non-farm sectors, for example, jobs involving harvesting of fruit and vegetables. Sellers from the SC community of edible products—like milk, fruit, vegetables, and cooked food—find it difficult to find buyers from high castes in rural areas. Because of the notion of impurity and pollution, women from the SC are excluded from household employment and, in particular, they are often not allowed to cook or clean food grains. This notion of purity also affects the implementation of government programs. SC women are not taken as cooks and helpers in the Midday meal program; anganwadi workers are reluctant to visit SC homes under the ICDS program; and doctors and nurses are reluctant to touch SC babies under the *JSY* program, which attempts to reduce natal and neo-natal deaths by promoting institutional delivery of babies. Then, there are outcome disparities associated with schemes relating to food security; reference was made in Chapter 4 to midday meals. Thorat and Lee (2010) pointed out that there were also disparities in treatment with respect to the PDS for food. It transpired that most of the government-approved agents who ran PDS shops were from the higher castes, and they offered preferential service to their own caste members; however, when the owners of PDS shops were from the SC (such as in Andhra Pradesh), these problems disappeared.

In the context of land, sales of land are generally confined to persons of the seller's caste (or higher) and this restricts the entry of SC households into the land-owning class. Furthermore, even when they do get to buy land, lower-caste households do not get good quality land: for example, land that is adjacent to the farms of high-caste cultivators, or near to the village, or adjacent to irrigation project command areas. There are two severities associated with agriculture in India: first, 85 percent of the problem of poor households in India is associated with land issues, either through being landless workers or through being small, marginal cultivators; second, the typical organization of agricultural land in India is such that the higher castes cultivate land at the head of the river, with the tail water being left to the lower castes (Sainath, 2002).

Women from the SC also face caste-based discrimination in access to drinking water. Prasad (2001) in a study of 3,000 SC persons in 50 villages across Andhra Pradesh showed that 74 percent of the SC faced discrimination in access to water facilities. A 1996 survey of 96 villages in Gujarat showed that 46 of these had separate water sources for the SC and in 14 of the remaining 23 villages, SC women could only draw water after the higher caste women had finished (Thorat, 2003; see also Mangubhai and Irudayam, 2003). The problems of access often stem from the fact that housing in villages is organized by caste and that the SC *bastis* (ghettos) are often devoid of infrastructural facilities, which are all located in the higher caste parts of the village.

There are issues with implementation of the legal safeguards through anti-untouchability and Prevention of Atrocities Acts. The problem with the Protection of Civil Rights Acts of 1955 and 1976 was that they treated criminal offences against Dalits often no differently from crimes against non-Dalits. The problem arose because, first, violent crimes against Dalits were more common than similar crimes against non-Dalits, and, secondly, Dalits found it difficult to secure convictions in cases where their person or property was violated: witnesses turning hostile, unsympathetic police, and absconding perpetrators were all part of the *barriers to justice* faced by Dalits. The Prevention of Atrocities Acts of 1989 and 1995 were designed to address this problem. These Acts were grounded on the understanding that Dalits not only faced discriminatory acts but were also victims of violence. The 1995 Act has, for examples, provisions for the establishment of separate courts and special prosecutors to handle cases of anti-Dalit violence. But all these legal remedies are only as effective as the persons who are charged with implementing them. Very often, the dominant castes have a reliable ally in the state's officers who are, mostly, drawn from the same (dominant) castes.

All these observations lead inexorably to the conclusion that groups that live on the margins of Indian society—the SCs, STs, and Muslims—face three kinds of difficulty. First, in the context of the market they face issues of access (for example, not being able to obtain jobs or housing) or disparity (for example, having to accept lower wages or only being offered certain kinds of jobs or housing). This then leads to the general problem of a lack of representation of certain groups in important areas of economic/political activity. Second, in the context of common property resources, they face the problem of dominant groups "privatizing" these resources through violence and converting them into resources over which they exercise "ownership" and control (for example, in terms of access to common property resources like water and forests). Consequently, marginalized groups are bullied and intimidated into having to wait their turn to use common property resources. Third, public policy initiatives that are meant to confer universal benefits are "captured" by dominant groups—often acting in concert with those responsible for delivering these schemes—who then cream off most of the benefits. RSBY, midday meal scheme, and PDS are all cases in point. Often the only way to prevent such capture is to provide, under these initiatives, goods and services of such inferior quality that they are scorned by the dominant groups. The ICDS program illustrates this. Looking into the future, therefore, the social inclusion of marginalized groups depends upon redressing all these three problems.

Like the persons from the SC and ST, Muslims in India are also marginalized but in terms of being seen as "others." However, a major difference between Muslims and the SC is protection under affirmative action: in order to foreshorten the effects of centuries of suppression, the SC are protected under the Indian constitution by reservation policies in public sector jobs and educational institutions and representation on elected bodies. Muslims, on the other hand, do not enjoy any such protection even though, as the Sachar Committee Report (2006) points out, Muslims are grossly underrepresented in public life in India. Only recently, some initiatives are undertaken by government in Muslim-concentrated districts to improve the civic amenities and infrastructural facilities.

So, for Indian society to progress, Hindu social order needs reform. This reformation may not change the caste system much, but it must sweep away the concept and practice of untouchability and with it the attendant notion that certain occupations are so "unclean" that they pollute not only those who work in these but also their progeny. In addition, within the context of the varna system, Hindu society must firmly turn its back on the *Manusmriti*, according to which the gravity of a crime and, therefore the severity of the accompanying punishment, depended on a person's varna. It is these ideas that allow upper-caste Hindus to inflict the most heinous acts of violence on Dalits as punishment for violating some caste-based behavioral norm. Instead, Hindus should embrace the idea that all persons are equal before the law. For, if we are pricked, do we not all bleed? And if we are poisoned, do we not all die?

References

Acharya, S.S. (2010). Caste and patterns of discrimination in rural public health care services. In S. Thorat & K.S. Newman (Eds), *Blocked by caste: Economic discrimination in modern India* (pp. 208–29). New Delhi: Oxford University Press.

Abrevaya, J. (2001). The effects of demographics and maternal behaviour on the distribution of birth outcomes. *Empirical Economics*, *26*(1), 247–57.

Akerlof, G.A. & Kranton, R.E. (2010). *Identity economics: How our identities shape our work, wages, and well-being*. Princeton, NJ: Princeton University Press.

Akerlof, G.A. (1970). The market for 'lemons': Quality uncertainty and the market mechanism. *Quarterly Journal of Economics*, *84*(3), 488–500.

Ambedkar, B.R. (1987). The Hindu social order: Its essential features. In V. Moon (Ed.), *Dr. Babasheb Ambedkar: Writings and speeches*, *3*, 95–115. Mumbai: Higher Education Department, Government of Maharashtra.

Anand, S. & Kanbur, S.M. (1993). The Kuznets process and the inequality-development relationship. *Journal of Development Economics*, *40*(1), 25–52.

Anand, S. & Sen, A.K. (1994). *Human development index: Methodology and measurement*. Human Development Report Office Occasional Paper 12. New York: UNDP.

———. (1997). *Concepts of human development and poverty: A multidimensional perspective*. Human Development Report 1997 Papers. New York: UNDP.

Arrow, Kenneth J. (1972a). Models of job discrimination. In A.H. Pascal (Ed.), *Racial discrimination in economic life* (pp. 83–102). Lexington, MA: D.C. Heath.

———. (1972b). Some mathematical models of race discrimination in the labor market. In A.H. Pascal (Ed.), *Racial discrimination in economic life* (pp. 187–204). Lexington, MA: D.C. Heath.

———. (1973). The theory of discrimination. In O. Ashenfelter & A. Rees (Eds), *Discrimination in labor markets* (pp. 3–33). Princeton, NJ: Princeton University Press.

Atkinson, A.B. (1970), On the Measurement of Inequality, *Journal of Economic Theory*, *2*(3), pp. 244–63.

Basu, K. (2001). On the goals of development. In G.M. Meier & J.E. Stiglitz (Eds.), *Frontiers of development economics: The Future in Perspective* (pp. 61–86). New York: Oxford University Press.

———. (2006). Globalisation, poverty, and inequality: What is the relationship? What can be done? *World Development*, *34*(8), 1361–73.

Basu, K. & Foster, J. (1998). On measuring literacy. *Economic Journal*, *108*(451), 1733–49.

Basu, K., Narayan, A. & Ravallion, M. (2002). Is literacy shared between households? *Labour Economics*, *8*(6), 649–65.

Becker, G.S. (1981), *A treatise on the family*, Harvard: Harvard University Press.

———. (1993). *The economics of discrimination*. Chicago: University of Chicago Press.

Behrman, J. & Deolalikar, A. (1988). Health and nutrition. In H. Chenery & T.N. Srinivasan (Eds), *Handbook of development economics* (Vol.1) (pp. 631–771). Amsterdam: North-Holland.

Behrman, J.R., Alderman, H., & Hoddinott, J. (2004). *Hunger and malnutrition*. Unpublished working paper. Copenhagen: Copenhagen Consensus.

Bern, C., Martines, J., de Zoysa, J., & Glass, R.I. (1992). The magnitude of the global problem of diarrhoeal disease: A ten year update. *Bulletin of the World Health Organization*, *70*(6), 705–14.

Bertrand, M., Chugh, D., & Mullainathan, S. (2005). Implicit discrimination. *American Economic Review*, *95*(2), 94–98.

Bhalotra, S. & Zamora, B. (2010). Social divisions in education in India. In R. Basant & A. Shariff (Eds), *Handbook of Muslims in India: Empirical and policy perspectives* (pp. 165–198). New Delhi: Oxford University Press.

Bhambri, C.P. (2005), Reservations and Casteism, *Economic and Political Weekly*, *XL*(9), 806-08.

Bhaumik, S.K. & Chakrabarty, M. (2010). Earnings inequality: The impact of the rise of caste and religion-based politics. In R. Basant & A.S. Shariff (Eds), *Handbook of Muslims: Empirical and Policy Perspectives* (pp. 235–53). New Delhi: Oxford University Press.

Birdi, K., Warr, P., & Oswald, A. (1995). Age differences in three components of employee well-being. *Applied Psychology*, *44*(4), 345–73.

Black, D., Morris, J., Smith, C., & Townsend, P. (1980). *Inequalities in health: A report of a research working group*. London: Department of Health and Social Security.

Blinder, A.S. (1973). Wage discrimination: Reduced form and structural estimates. *Journal of Human Resources*, *8*(), 436–455.

Borooah, V.K. (2001a). How do employees of ethnic origin fare on Britain's occupational ladder. *Scottish Journal of Political Economy*, *48*, 1–26.

———. (2001b). The measurement of employment inequality between population subgroups: Theory and application. *Labour*, *15*(1), 169–89.

———. (2004). Gender bias among children in India in their diet and immunisation against disease. *Social Science and Medicine*, *58*(9), 1719–31.

Borooah, V.K. & Iyer, S. (2005a). The decomposition of inter-group differences in a logit model: Extending the Oaxaca-Blinder approach with an application to school enrolment in India. *Journal of Social and Economic Measurement*, *30*, 279–93.

———. (2005b). *Vidya, Veda,* and *Varna*: The influence of religion and caste on education in rural India. *Journal of Development Studies*, *41*(8), 1369–1404.

Borooah, V.K., Dubey, A., & Iyer, S. (2007). The effectiveness of jobs reservation: Caste, religion, and economic status in India. *Development and Change*, *38*(3), 423–55.

Borooah, V.K., McGregor, P.P.L., & McKee, P.M. (1991). Regional income inequality and poverty in the United Kingdom. Aldershot: Dartmouth Publishing Company.

Borooah, V.K., McKee, P.M., Heaton, N.E., & Collins, G. (1995). Catholic Protestant income differences in Northern Ireland. *Review of Income and Wealth*, *41*(1), 1–16.

Brennan, L., McDonald, J., & Shlomowitz, R. (March 2004). Infant feeding practices and chronic child malnutrition in the Indian states of Karnataka and Uttar Pradesh. *Economics and Human Biology*, *2*(1), 138–58.

Brunner, E. & Marmot, M. (1999). Social organisation, stress and health. In M. Marmot & R. Wilkinson (Eds), *The social determinants of health* (pp. 17–43). New York: Oxford University Press.

Buchinsky, M. (1998). Recent advances in quantile regression models: A practical guide for empirical research. *Journal of Human Resources*, *33*(1), 88–126.

Cairncross, S. (1990). Health impacts in developing countries: new evidence and new prospects. *Journal of the Institution of Water and Environmental Management*, *4*(6): 571–77.

Caldwell, J.C. (1993). Health transition: The cultural, social and behavioural determinants of health in the third world. *Social Science and Medicine, 36*(2), 125–35.

Cotton, J. (1988). On the decomposition of wage differentials. *Review of Economics and Statistics, 70*(2), 236–43.

Cowell, F. & Jenkins, S. (1995). How much inequality can we explain? A methodology and an application to the United States. *Economic Journal, 105*(429), 421–30.

Curtis, V., Cairncross, S., & Yonli, R. (2000). Domestic hygiene and diarrhoea. *Tropical Medicine and International Health, 5*(1), 22–32.

Davey, A., Davey, S., & Datta, U. (2008). Perception regarding quality of services in urban ICDS blocks in Delhi. *Indian Journal of Public Health, 52*(3), 156–58.

Deolalikar, A.B. (2010). The performance of Muslims on social indicators: A comparative perspective. In R. Basant & A. Shariff (Eds), *Handbook of Muslims in India: Empirical and policy perspectives* (pp. 71–91). New Delhi: Oxford University Press.

Desai, S., Adams, C., & Dubey, A. (2010). Segmented schooling: Inequalities in primary education. In S. Thorat & K.S. Newman (Eds), *Blocked by caste: Economic discrimination in modern India* (pp. 230–252). New Delhi: Oxford University Press.

Desai, S., Vanneman, R., & National Council of Applied Economic Research, New Delhi (2009). India human development survey (IHDS), 2005 [Computer file]. *ICPSR22626-v5*, Ann Arbor, MI: Inter-university Consortium for Political and Social Research [distributor], 2009-06-22. doi:10.3886/ICPSR22626.

DFID. (2005). *Reducing poverty by tackling social exclusion*. DFID Policy Paper. London: Department for International Development.

Dhesi, A.S. & Singh, H. (1989). Education, labour market distortions and relative earnings of different religion-caste categories in India (a case study of Delhi). *Canadian Journal of Development Studies, 10*(1), 75–89.

Dhingra, R. & Sharma, I. (2011). Assessment of preschool component of ICDS scheme in Jammu District. *Global Journal of Human Science, 11*(6), 13–18.

Diwakar, G.D. (2010). Critical appraisal of ICDS programme: Budget and resource analysis. *Journal of the Madras School of Social Work, A Half Yearly Review of Social Work and Social Sciences, Special Edition-II*, 133–146.

———. (2011). Relevance of ICDS programme in post liberalisation period in addressing the malnutrition among 0-6 years children: A case study of Kancheepuram District, Tamil Nadu. In Sigamani and N.U. Khan (Eds), *Reinventing public management & development in emerging economies, advanced research series* (pp. 55–74). New Delhi: Macmillan.

Doniger, W. and Smith, B.K. (1992). *The Laws of Manu*, Penguin Books, London.

Dreze, J. & Sen, A.K. (2013). *An uncertain glory: India and its contradictions*. London: Allen Lane.

Dreze, J. (2006). Universalisation with quality ICDS in a right perspective. *Economic and Political Weekly*, 41 (34), 3706–15.

Dreze, Jean and Goyal Aparajita. (2003). The Future of Mid-Day Meals. Delhi: Centre for Equity Studies.

Eden, C. (2004). Gender and education. In S. Ward (Ed.), *Education studies* (pp. 123–133). London: RoutledgeFalmer.

Elnslie, B. & Sedo, S. (1996). Discrimination, social psychology and hysteresis in labor markets. *Journal of Economic Psychology, 17*, 465–78.

Epstein, H. (1998). Life and death on the social ladder. *The New York Review of Books*, XLV (26–30).

Esteve-Bolart, B. (2004). *Gender discrimination and growth: Theory and evidence from India*. Suntory and Toyota International Centres for Economics and Related Disciplines. London, UK: London School of Economics and Political Science.

Fergusson, D.M. & Horwood, L.J. (1997). Gender differences in educational achievement in a New Zealand Birth Cohort. *New Zealand Journal of Educational Studies, 32*(2), 83–96.

FOCUS. (2009). *Focus on children under six*. New Delhi: Citizens' Initiative for the Rights of Children under Six (CIRCUS).

Foster, J, Greer, J, & Thorbecke, E. (1984). A class of decomposable poverty measures. *Econometrica, 52*(3), 571–766.

Frank, R.H. (1997). The frame of reference as a public good. *Economic Journal, 107*(445), 1832–47.

————. (1999). *Luxury fever: Money and happiness in an era of excess*. Princeton and Oxford: Princeton University Press.

Gang, I.N., Sen, K., & Yun, M.S. (2008). Poverty in rural India: Caste and tribe. *Review of Income and Wealth, 54*(1), 50–62.

Garg, S. (2006). Chhattisgarh: Grassroots mobilisation for children's nutrition rights. *Economic and Political Weekly, 41*(34), 3694–3700.

Ghosh, S. (2006). Food dole or health, nutrition, and development program. *Economic and Political Weekly, 41*(34), 3664–66.

Gibson, J. (2001). Literacy and intra-household externalities. *World Development, 29*, 155–66.

Gill, K. (2012). *Promoting 'inclusiveness': A framework for assessing India's flagship social welfare programs*. Social Policy Working Paper Series – 2. New Delhi: UNICEF.

Gopaldas, T. (2006). Hidden hunger: The problem and possible interventions. *Economic and Political Weekly, 41*(34), 3671–74.

Gragnolati, M., Shekar, M., Das Gupta, M., Bredenkamp, C., & Lee, Y.-K. (2005). *India's undernourished children: A call for reform and action*. Washington, DC: The World Bank.

Granovetter, M. (1995). *Getting a job: A study of contacts and careers* (2nd ed.). Chicago: University of Chicago Press.

Greene, W.H. (2003). *Econometric analysis*. Upper Saddle River, New Jersey: Prentice Hall.

Griffin, J.M., Fuhrer, R., Stansfeld, S.A., & Marmot, M. (2002). The importance of low control at work and home on depression and anxiety: Do these effects vary by gender and social class. *Social Science and Medicine, 54*(5), 783–98.

Guan, W. (2003). From the help desk: Bootstrapped standard errors. *Stata Journal, 3*(1), 71–80.

Guha, R. (2007). Adivasis, naxalities, and Indian Democracy. *Economic and Political Weekly, XLII*(32), 3305–12.

Gupta, D. (2000). *Interrogating caste: Understanding hierarchy and difference in Indian Society*. New Delhi, India: Penguin Books.

Gupta, A. (2006). Infant and young child feeding: An "optimal" approach. *Economic and Political Weekly, 41*(34), 3666–71.

Hanushek, E.A. & Woessmann, L. (2008). The role of cognitive skills in economic development. *Journal of Economic Literature, 46*(3): 607–68.

Haq, M. (1994). *The birth of the human development index*. Human Development Report Office Occasional Paper 1. New York: UNDP.

Harkness, S. (1996). The gender earnings gap: Evidence from the UK. *Fiscal Studies, 17*(2), 1–36.

Harris-White, B. (1994). *Child nutrition and poverty in South India*. New Delhi: Concept Publishers.

———. (2004). Nutrition and its politics in Tamil Nadu. *South Asia Research*, *24*(1), 51–71.

Haughton, J. & Khandker, S.R. (2009). *Handbook of inequality and poverty*. Washington, DC: The World Bank (Retrieved from http://issuu.com/world.bank.publications/docs/9780821376133, last accessed on June 26, 2014).

Heckman, J.J. (1998). Detecting discrimination. *Journal of Economic Perspectives*, *12*(2), 101–16.

Heckman, J.J. & Siegelman, P. (1993). The Urban Institute Audit Studies: Their methods and findings. In M. Fix & R.J. Struyk (Eds), *Clear and Convincing Evidence: Measurement of Discrimination in America* (pp. 187–258). Washington, DC: The Urban Institute Press.

Himanshu and Sen. (2013). "In-Kind Food Transfers - I," *Economic and Political Weekly*, *XLVIII*(45), 46–54.

Hirschman, A.O. (1970). *Exit, voice, and loyalty: Responses to decline in firms, organisations, and states*. Cambridge, MA: Harvard University Press.

Hoff, K. & Pandey, P. (2006). Discrimination, social identity, and durable inequalities. *American Economic Review*, *96*(2), 206–211.

Human Development Sector (2004). *Reaching out to the Child: An integrated approach to child development*. Washington, DC: The World Bank.

Human Rights Watch (2014). *'They Say We Are Dirty': Denying education to India's marginalised*. New York: Human Rights Watch.

Humpherys, L.G. (1988. Trends in levels of academic achievements of blacks and other minorities. *Intelligence*, *12*(3), 231–60.

Ito, T. (2009). Caste discrimination and transaction costs in the labor market: Evidence from rural North India. *Journal of Development Economics*, *88*(2): 292–300.

Jann, B. (2008). The Blinder-Oaxaca decomposition for linear regression models. *Stata Journal*, *8*(4), 453–79.

Jeffery, R. & Jeffery, P. (1997). *Population, gender and politics*. Cambridge: Cambridge University Press.

Kapil, U. & Pradhan, R. (1999). Integrated Child Development Services scheme (ICDS) and its impact on the nutritional status of children. *Indian Journal of Public Health*, *43*(1): 21–25.

Karasek, R. & Marmot, M. (1996). *Refining social class: Psychosocial job factors*. Paper presented at *The Fourth International Congress of Behavioral Medicine*, Washington, D.C., March 13–16.

Kijima, Y. (2006). Caste and tribe inequality: Evidence from India. *Economic Development and Cultural Change*, *54*(4), 369–404.

Koenker, R. (2001). Quantile regression. In S. Fienberg & J. Kadane (Eds.), *International Encyclopaedia of the Social Sciences, Statistics Section* (pp. 8893–8899). Oxford: Elsevier Science Ltd.

Koenker, R. & Bassett, G. (1978). Regression quantiles. *Econometrica*, *46*(1), 33–50.

Koenker, R. & Hallock, K.F. (2001). Quantile regression. *Journal of Economic Perspectives*, *15*(4), 143–56.

Kosek, M., Bern, C., & Guerrant, R.L. (2003). The magnitude of the global burden of diarrhoeal disease from studies published 1991-2000. *Bulletin of the World Health Organization*, *81*(4), 197–204.

Kuznets, S. (1955). Economic growth and income inequality. *American Economic Review*, *45*(1), 1–28.

Lavy V., Strauss, J., Thomas D., & de Vreyer, P. (1996). Quality of health care, survival and health outcomes in Ghana. *Journal of Health Economics, 15*(3), 333–57.

Layard, R. (2006). *Happiness: Lessons from a New Science*. London: Penguin Books.

Lenoir, René. (1974/1989). *Les Exclus: Un Francais sur Dix*. Paris: Editions du Seuil.

Loury, G.C. (2002). *The anatomy of racial inequality*. Cambridge, MA: Harvard University Press.

Lundberg, S. & Startz, R. (2007). Information and racial exclusion. *Journal of Population Economics, 20*(3), 621–42.

Mander, H. & Kumaran, K. (2006). *Social exclusion in ICDS: A sociologist Whodunit*. Retrieved from ftp://ftp.solutionexchange.net.in/public/food/resource/res15071101. pdf (last accessed on October 15, 2014).

Mangubhai, J. & Irudayam, A. (2003). *Water battlegrounds on caste*. Madurai, India: Institute of Development Education, Action, and Ideas.

Marmot, M. (1986). Does stress cause heart attacks. *Postgraduate Medical Journal*, 62(729), 683–86.

————. (2000). Multilevel approaches to understanding social determinants. In L. Berkman & I. Kawachi (Eds.), *Social epidemiology* (pp. 349–67). Oxford University Press: New York.

————. (2004). *Status syndrome: How our position on the social gradient affects longevity and health*. London: Bloomsbury Publishing.

Meyer, B.D. & Sullivan, J.X. (2009). *Five decades of consumption and income poverty*. Working Paper 14827. Cambridge, MA: National Bureau of Economic Research.

————. (2011). Viewpoint: Further results on measuring the well-being of the poor using income and consumption. *Canadian Journal of Economics, 44*(1), 52–87.

Myrdal, G. (1944). *An American Dilemma: the Negro Problem and American Democracy*, New York: Pantheon.

Nambissan, G.B. (2010). Exclusion and discrimination in schools. In S. Throat & K.S. Newman (Eds), *Blocked by caste: Economic discrimination in Modern India* (pp. 253–86). New Delhi: Oxford University Press

Narula, S. (1999). *Broken people: Caste violence against India's untouchables*. New York: Human Rights Watch.

Nayak, N. & Saxena, N.C. (2006). Implementation of ICDS in Bihar and Jharkhand. *Economic and Political Weekly, 41*(34), 3680–84.

Neumark, D. (1988). Employers' discriminatory behavior and the estimation of wage discrimination. *Journal of Human Resources, 23*(3), 279–95.

Nielsen, H.S. (1998). Discrimination and detailed decomposition in a Logit model. *Economics Letters, 61*(1), 115–20.

Oaxaca, R. (1973). Male-female wage differentials in urban labor markets. *International Economic Review, 14*(3), 693–709.

Oaxaca, R. & Ransom, M.R. (1994). On discrimination and the decomposition of wage differentials. *Journal of Econometrics, 61*(1), 5–21.

OECD (2004). *Income disparities in China: An OECD perspective*. Paris: Organisation for Economic Cooperartion and Development.

Osborne, E. (2001). Culture, Development and Government, *Economic Development and Cultural Change, 49*(3), pp. 659–85.

Osmani, S.R. & Sen, A.K. (2003). The hidden penalties of gender inequality: Fetal origins of ill-health. *Economics and Human Biology*, *1*(1), 105–21.

Oyen, E. (1997). The contradictory concepts of social exclusion and social inclusion. In C. Gore & J.B. Figueiredo (Eds), *Social exclusion and anti-poverty policy* (pp. 63–65). Geneva: International Institute of Labour Studies.

Pal, G. & Lal, D. (2010). *Mapping caste based atrocities in India (with special reference to Scheduled caste Women)*. Annual Report 2010-11. New Delhi: Christian Aid and Indian Institute of Scheduled Caste Studies.

Patterson, O. (1982). *Slavery and social death*. Cambridge, MA: Harvard University Press.

Planning Commission (2008). *Eleventh Five Year Plan, 2007–2012: Volume 1 inclusive growth*. New Delhi: Oxford University Press.

Phelps, E.S. (1972). The statistical theory of racism and sexism. *American Economic Review, 62* (4), 659–61.

Prasad, S.D. (2001). *Untouchability practices in Andhra Pradesh*. New Delhi: Actionaid India.

Qadiri, F. and Manhas, S. (2009). Parental perception towards preschool education imparted at early childhood education centres. *Studies on Home and Community Science*, *3*(1), 19–24.

Quigley, D. (1993). *The interpretation of caste*. Oxford: Clarendon Press.

Rajasekhar, D., Berg, E., Ghatak, M., Manjula, B., and Roy, S. (2011). Implementing health insurance: The rollout of *Rashtriya Swasthya Bima Yojana* in Karnataka. *Economic and Political Weekly*, *66*(20), 56–63.

Rajivan, A.K. (2006). ICDS with a difference. *Economic and Political Weekly*, *41*(34), 3685–88.

Ramachandran, V. & Naorem, T. (2013). What it means to be a dalit or tribal child in our schools. *Economic and Political Weekly*, *XLVIII*(44): 43–52.

Ravallion, M. (1996). Issues in measuring and modelling poverty. *Economic Journal*, *106*(438), 1328–43.

———. (2005). A poverty-inequality trade off? *Journal of Economic Inequality*, *3*(2), 169–81.

Ravallion, M. & Chen, S. (2004). *China's (uneven) progress against poverty*. Working Paper 3408. Washington, DC: The World Bank.

Reimers, C.W. (1983). Labour market discrimination against Hispanic and Black men. *Review of Economics and Statistics*, *65*(4), 570–79.

Rogers, W.H. (1992). Quantile regression standard errors. *Stata Technical Bulletin Reprints*, *2*, 133–37.

———. (1993). Calculation of quantile regression standard errors. *Stata Technical Bulletin Reprints, 3*, 77–78.

Rudolph, L.I. and Rudolph, S.E. (1966). The Political Role of India's Caste Associations. In I. Wallerstein (Ed.), *Social Change: The Colonial Situation* (p. 448). New York: John Wiley.

Sabharwal, N.S. (2011). *Dalit women in political space: Status and issues related to their participation, in voices for equity minority and majority in South Asia*. Rindas International Symposium Series 1, The Centre for the Study of Contemporary India, Ryukoku University.

Sabharwal, N.S. & Banerjee, A. (2013). Nature and forms of discrimination experience by scheduled caste women in urban labour market in Delhi. *IIDS Report Series No. 60*.

Sabharwal N.S., Sharma S., Diwakar D., and Naik A.K. (2014). "Caste Discrimination as a factor in poor access to public health service system: A case study of *Janani Suraksha Yojana* scheme,*" Journal of Inclusion Studies*, *1*(1): 148–68.

Sachar Committee Report (2006). *The social and economic status of the Muslim community in India*. New Delhi: Government of India (Cabinet Secretariat).

Sahn, D.E. & Stifel, D.C. (2002a). Robust comparisons of malnutrition in developing countries. *American Journal of Agricultural Economics, 84*(3), 716–35.

———. (2002b). Parental preferences for nutrition of boys and girls: evidence from Africa. *Journal of Development Studies, 39*(1), 21–45.

Sainath, P. (2002). Dalits in India 2000: The scheduled castes more than a half century after independence. *Asia Source*. Retrieved from www.asiasource.org/asip/dalits.cfm (last accessed on September 8, 2014).

Sandiford, P., Cassel, J., Montenegro, M., & Sanchez, G. (1995). The impact of women's literacy on child health and its interaction with health services. *Population Studies, 49*(1), 5–17.

Schmidt, P. and Strauss, R.P. (1975), The Prediction of Occupation Using Multiple Logit Models. *International Economic Review, 16*(2), 471–86.

Sen, A.K. (1976). Poverty: An ordinal approach to measurement. *Econometrica, 44*(2), 219–31.

——— (1992). *Inequality re-examined*. Oxford: Clarendon Press.

———. (1998). *On economic inequality*. Oxford University Press: Delhi.

———. (2000). *Social exclusion: Concept, application, and scrutiny*. Social Development Papers No.1. Manila, Office of Economic and Social Development: Asian Development Bank.

———. (2001a). Hunger: Old torments and new blunders. *The Little Magazine, 2*, 9–13.

———. (2001b). The many faces of gender inequality. *Frontline, 18* (22), 4–14.

Sen, G., Iyer, A., & George, A. (2007). Systematic hierarchies and systemic failures: Gender and health inequalities in Koppal district. *Economic and Political* Weekly, *42*(8), 682–90.

Sengupta, J. & Sarkar, D. (2007). Discrimination in ethnically fragmented localities. *Economic and Political Weekly, 42*(32), 3313–22.

Shariff, A. (1999). *India human development report*. New Delhi: Oxford University Press.

Shorrocks, A.F. (1980). A class of additively decomposable measures. *Econometrica, 48*(3), 613–25.

Silver, H. (1995). Reconceptualizing social disadvantge: Three paradigms of social exclusion. In G. Rodgers, C. Gore, & J. Figueiredo (Eds), *Social exclusion: Rhetoric, reality, responses* (pp. 57–80). Geneva: International Institute for Labour Studies.

Sinha, D. (2006). Rethinking ICDS: A right based perspective. *Economic and Political Weekly, 41*(34), 3689–94.

Sinha, S. (2006). Infant survival: A political challenge. *Economic and Political Weekly, 41*(34), 3657–60.

Sinning, M., Hahn, M., & Bauer, T.K. (2008). The Blinder-Oaxaca decomposition for non-linear regression models. *The Stata Journal, 8*(4), 480–92.

Smith, A. (1776). *An inquiry into the nature and causes of the wealth of nations* (republished, edited by R.H. Campbell and A.S. Skinner. Oxford: Clarendon Press, 1976).

Smith, L.C. & Haddad, L. (2000). *Explaining child malnutrition in developing countries*. Washington, DC: International Food Policy Research Institute.

Smith, J.D. (2009). *The Mahabharata*. London: Penguin Classics.

Srinivas, M. N. (1962), *Caste in Modern India and Other Essays*. Bombay: Popular Prakashan.

———. (1996) (Ed.), *Caste: Its Twentieth Century Avatar*. New Delhi, India: Penguin Books.

STATA (2007). *Stata manual release 10*. College Station, TX: Stata Press.

Stevenson, H.W., Chen, C., & Uttal, D.H. (1990). Beliefs and achievements: A study of Black, White, and Hispanic children. *Child Development*, 61(2), 508–23.

Subramanian, S. (2004). *Indicators of inequality and poverty*. World Institute for Development Economics Research Paper No. 2004/25. Helsinki: WIDER.

Sundararaman, T. (2006). Universalisation of ICDS and community health worker programs: Lessons from Chhattisgarh. *Economic and Political Weekly*, 41(34), 3674–79.

Svedberg, P. (2000). *Poverty and undernutrition: Theory, measurement, and policy*. Oxford: Oxford University Press.

———. (2001). Hunger in India: Facts and Challenge. *The Little Magazine, 2*, 26–34.

Tandon, B.N. & Gandhi, N. (1992). Immunisation coverage in India for areas served by the integrated child development services program. *Bulletin of the World Health Organisation*, 70(4), 461–65.

Tendulkar, S. (2007). National sample surveys. In K. Basu (Ed.), *The Oxford Companion to Economics in India* (pp. 367–70). New Delhi: Oxford University Press.

Theil, H. (1967). *Economics and information theory*. Amsterdam: North-Holland.

Thomas, D., Lavy, V., & Strauss, J. (1996). Public policy and anthropometric outcomes in the Côte d'Ivoire. *Journal of Public Economics, 61*(2), 155–92.

Thomas, D., Strauss, J., & Henriques, M-H. (1991). How does mother's education affect child height. *Journal of Human Resources, 26*(2), 183–211.

Thorat, S. (2003). The Hindu Social System and Human Rights: Enforcement with respect to former untouchables in India, *Combat law,* Issue 4.

Thorat, S.K. (2005), Reservation and Efficiency: Myth and Reality, *Economic and Political Weekly*, XL(9), 808–10.

Thorat, S. (2009a). Dalits in India: Search for a Common Destiny. New Delhi: Sage.

Thorat, Sukhdeo & Attewell, P. (2007). A legacy of social discrimination: A correspondence study of job discrimination in India. *Economic and Political Weekly, 42*(41), 4141–45.

Thorat, S. & Kumar, N. (2008). *B.R. Ambedkar, perspectives on social exclusion and inclusive policies*. New Delhi: Oxford University Press.

Thorat, S. & Sadana, N. (2009a). Discrimination and children's nutritional status in India. *IDS Bulletin, 40*(4), 25–29.

———. (2009b). Caste and ownership of private enterprises. *Economic and Political Weekly, 64*(23), 13–16.

Thorat, S., Mahamallik, M., & Sadana, N. (2010). Caste system and patterns of discrimination in rural markets. In S. Thorat & K.S. Newman (Eds), *Blocked by caste: Economic discrimination in Modern India* (pp. 148–76). New Delhi: Oxford University Press.

Thorat, S. & Lee, J. (2010). Food security schemes and caste discrimination. In S. Thorat & K.S. Newman (Eds), *Blocked by caste: Economic discrimination in Modern India* (pp. 287–307). New Delhi: Oxford University Press.

———. (September 24, 2005), Caste Discrimination and Food Security Programmes. *Economic and Political Weekly, 40*(39): 4198–4201.

UNDP. (1995). *Human development report*. New York: UNDP.

Verma, A.K. (2001). UP: BJP's caste card. *Economic and Political Weekly, 36*, 4452–55.

White, H.C. (1995). Social networks can resolve actor paradoxes in economics and in psychology. *Journal of Institutional and Theoretical Economics, 151*(1), 58–74.

WHO. (2000). *Nutrition in South-East Asia.* New Delhi: World Health Organisation.

———. (2006). *WHO child growth standards: Length/height-for-age, weight-for-age, weight-for-length, weight-for-height and body mass index-for-age—methods and development* (Department of Nutrition for Health and Development). Geneva: World Health Organisation.

Wienk, R.E., Reid, C.E., Simouson, J.C., & Eggers, F.J. (1979). *Measuring discrimination in American housing markets.* Washington, DC: US Department of Housing and Urban Development.

Wilkinson, R.G. & Marmot, M. (1998). *Social determinants of health: The solid facts.* Copenhagen: World Health Organisation.

Wooldridge, J.M. (2002). *Econometric analysis of cross section and panel data.* Cambridge, MA: MIT Press.

Yinger, J. (1998). Evidence of discrimination in consumer markets. *Journal of Economic Perspectives, 12,* 23–40.

Indian History Sourcebook: The Laws of Manu, c. 1500 BCE (translated by G. Buhler). New York: Fordham University. Retrieved from http://www.fordham.edu/halsall/india/manu-full.asp (last accessed on March 15, 2014).

Index

About the Authors

Vani Kant Borooah has held the Chair in Applied Economics at the University of Ulster since 1987. After obtaining his PhD in 1977 from the University of Southampton, he worked for the next 10 years as a Senior Research Officer at the University of Cambridge's Department of Applied Economics, and, concurrently, was a Fellow of Queens College. He is a past President of the European Public Choice Society and of the Irish Economic Association, and is also an Honorary Professor of Economics at the University of Queensland. He was an elected Member of the Royal Irish Academy in 2006, and is currently the Secretary of the Academy. His work has been mainly in the areas of unemployment, inequality, poverty, and economic development.

Nidhi Sadana Sabharwal is an Associate Professor at the Centre for Policy Research, Higher Education, at the National University of Educational Planning and Administration, New Delhi. She has previously served as the Director, Indian Institute of Dalit Studies (IIDS), New Delhi. She has a PhD in Geography from Jawaharlal Nehru University (JNU), and has worked on inter-group inequalities across human development indicators, focusing on the role of caste- and gender-based discrimination in market and non market institutions; diversity and discrimination within higher educational institutions, Mid day Meal and Anganwadi programs; and social protection policies.

Dilip G. Diwakar is Associate Fellow, IIDS, New Delhi. He did his PhD in Public Health from JNU. Before he joined the institute, he had worked with both national and international development organizations for six years. He has published articles in both national and international journals, and contributed to chapters in various books. His main areas of work are marginalization in government programs, rights of urban poor, child nutrition, and health. His research interests include intersection of caste, poverty, and health.

Vinod Kumar Mishra is Associate Fellow, IIDS, New Delhi. He has a PhD from Jawaharlal Nehru University, New Delhi, with specialization in Population Geography. He has published many articles in journals and chapters in books. His main research areas are urbanization, poverty, health, social exclusion, and social protection programs.

Ajaya Kumar Naik is Associate Fellow, IIDS, New Delhi, and has had more than 10 years of research experience in the fields of informal sector, employment, and poverty. As a former full-time consultant at the National Commission for Enterprises in the unorganized sector, he was associated with the task force *Definitional and Statistical Issues related to Informal Economy*. Besides this, he has worked at the Indian Institute of Public Administration and Institute of Applied Manpower Research in different capacities.